# The Third Reich

# Blackwell Essential Readings in History

This series comprises concise collections of key articles on important historical topics. Designed as a complement to standard survey histories, the volumes are intended to help introduce students to the range of scholarly debate in a subject area. Each collection includes a general introduction and brief contextual headnotes to each article, offering a coherent, critical framework for study.

## Published

*The German Reformation: The Essential Readings*
C. Scott Dixon

*The Third Reich: The Essential Readings*
Christian Leitz

*The Counter-Reformation: The Essential Readings*
David M. Luebke

## In Preparation

*The Enlightenment: The Essential Readings*
Martin Fitzpatrick

*The English Civil War: The Essential Readings*
Peter Gaunt

*The Cold War: The Essential Readings*
Klaus Larres and Ann Lane

*The Russian Revolution: The Essential Readings*
Martin Miller

*The French Revolution: The Essential Readings*
Ronald Schechter

# The Third Reich

*The Essential Readings*

Edited by Christian Leitz

*Advisory Editor:*
Harold James, Princeton University

**Blackwell**
Publishing

© 1999 by Blackwell Publishing
Editorial arrangement and introductions © 1999 by Christian Leitz

BLACKWELL PUBLISHING
350 Main Street, Malden, MA 02148-5020, USA
9600 Garsington Road, Oxford OX4 2DQ, UK
550 Swanston Street, Carlton, Victoria 3053, Australia

First published 1999

4   2006

*Library of Congress Cataloging-in-Publication Data*

The Third Reich: the essential readings / edited by Christian Leitz;
     advisory editor, Harold James.
         p. cm. — (Blackwell essential readings in history)
     Includes bibliographical references and index.
     ISBN 0-631-20699-X (alk. paper). — ISBN 0-631-20700-7 (pbk.: alk. paper)
     1. Germany—History—1933–1945—Historiography.  2. National
     socialism—Psychological aspects.  3. Holocaust, Jewish (1939–1945)—
     I. Leitz, Christian.  II. James, Harold.  III. Series.
     DD256.48.T45  1999
         943.086—dc21                                              99–24872
                                                                        CIP

ISBN-13: 978-0-631-20699-6 (alk. paper). — ISBN-13: 978-0-631-20700-9 (pbk.: alk. paper)

A catalogue record for this title is available from the British Library.

Set in 10½ on 12 pt Photina
by Best-set Typesetter Ltd, Hong Kong

For further information on
Blackwell Publishing, visit our website:
www.blackwellpublishing.com

# Contents

# Acknowledgements

The editor and publishers wish to thank the following for permission to use copyright material:

Berg Publishers for Robert Gellately, 'Surveillance and Disobedience: Aspects of the Political Policing of Nazi Germany' in *Germans against Nazism: Nonconformity, Opposition and Resistance in the Third Reich (Essays in Honour of Peter Hoffmann)* (1990) pp. 15–36;

Cambridge University Press for Ian Kershaw, 'Working Towards the Führer: Reflections on the Nature of the Hitler Dictatorship', *Contemporary European History*, 2:2 (1993) pp. 103–18;

Droste Verlag GmbH for Albrecht Tyrell, 'Auf dem Weg zur Diktatur: Deutschland 1930 bis 1934' in *Deutschland 1933–1945: Neue Studien zur nationalsozialistischen Herrschaft*, ed. Karl Dietrich Bracher, Manfred Funke and Hans-Adolf Jacobsen, *Bonner Schriften zur Politik und Zeitgeschichte*, vol. 23 (1992) pp. 15–31; and Hans-Adolf Jacobsen, 'Zur Struktur der NS-Außenpolitik 1933–1945' in *Hitler, Deutschland und die Mächte: Materialien zur Außenpolitik des Dritten Reiches*, ed. Manfred Funke (1978) pp. 137–85;

German Studies Association for Christopher R. Browning, 'Nazi Resettlement Policy and the Search for a Solution to the Jewish Question, 1939–1941', *German Studies Review*, 9:3 (1986) pp. 497–519;

Oxford University Press for Richard J. Overy, 'Germany, "Domestic Crisis" and War in 1939', *Past and Present*, 116 (1987) pp. 138–68;

Routledge for Detlef Mühlberger, 'Conclusion' in *Hitler's Followers: Studies in the Sociology of the Nazi Movement* (1991) pp. 202–9; and

Adelheid von Saldern, 'Victims or Perpetrators? Controversies about the Role of Women in the Nazi State' in *Nazism and German Society, 1933–1945*, ed. David F. Crew (1994) pp. 142–60;

The University of Chicago Press for Omer Bartov, 'Soldiers, Nazis and War in the Third Reich', *Journal of Modern History*, 63:1 (1991) pp. 44–60; and Alf Lüdtke, 'The Appeal of Exterminating "Others": German Workers and the Limits of Resistance', *Journal of Modern History*, 64, Supplement (1992) pp. S46–67;

Verlag Ferdinand Schöningh GmbH for Hans Mommsen, 'Die Opposition gegen Hitler und die deutsche Gesellschaft 1933–1945' in *Der deutsche Widerstand 1933–1945*, 2nd edn, ed. Klaus-Jürgen Müller (Hrsg.) (1990) UTB 1398, pp. 22–39.

Every effort has been made to trace the copyright holders but if any have been inadvertently overlooked the publishers will be pleased to make the necessary arrangement at the first opportunity.

# Glossary

| | |
|---|---|
| AA | Auswärtiges Amt (Foreign Ministry) |
| Abwehr | military intelligence service |
| ADGB | Allgemeiner Deutscher Gewerkschaftsbund (Free Trade Unions) |
| Alltagsgeschichte | history of everyday life |
| AO | Auslandsorganisation der NSDAP (Nazi Foreign Organization) |
| APA | Außenpolitisches Amt der NSDAP (Nazi Foreign Policy Office) |
| Auslandsdeutsche | Germans in foreign countries |
| BdM | Bund deutscher Mädel (League of German Girls) |
| Bekennende Kirche | Confessing Church |
| Betriebsführer | works leader |
| Blitzkrieg | lightning war |
| BVP | Bayerische Volkspartei (Bavarian People's Party) |
| DAF | Deutsche Arbeitsfront (German Labour Front) |
| DAP | Deutsche Arbeiterpartei (German Workers Party) |
| DDP | Deutsche Demokratische Partei (German Democratic Party) |
| DNVP | Deutsch-Nationale Volkspartei (German National People's Party) |
| DVP | Deutsche Volkspartei (German People's Party) |
| Einsatzgruppen | SS extermination units |
| Endlösung | Final Solution |

| | |
|---|---|
| Fremdarbeiter | foreign worker |
| Führerbefehl | personal order by Hitler |
| Gau | Nazi administrative district |
| Gauleiter | head of a Gau |
| Gestapo | Geheime Staatspolizei (Secret State Police) |
| Gleichschaltung | coordination, forcing into line |
| Historikerstreit | historians' conflict or quarrel |
| HJ | Hitlerjugend (Hitler Youth) |
| Innenpolitik | domestic policy |
| judenfrei | free of Jews |
| Jungmädelführerin | young girls' leader |
| KdF | Kraft durch Freude (Strength through Joy) |
| Kolonialpolitisches Amt der NSDAP | Nazi Colonial Policy Office |
| KPD | Kommunistische Partei Deutschlands (Communist Party of Germany) |
| KZ | Konzentrationslager (concentration camp) |
| Länder | German states |
| Landesgruppenleiter | country group leader (AO) |
| Landser | private (soldier) |
| Lebensraum | living space |
| Leistungslohn | performance-based wages |
| Machtergreifung | seizure of power |
| Mitläufer | fellow traveller |
| Mittäter | accomplice |
| Mitteleuropa | Central Europe |
| Mittelstand | middle classes |
| Mittelstandsbewegung | Middle-class movement |
| NSBO | Nationalsozialistische Betriebszellen-Organisation (Nazi 'trade unions') |
| NSDAP | Nationalsozialistische Deutsche Arbeiterpartei (National Socialist German Workers Party, Nazi party) |
| NS-Frauenschaft | Nazi Women's Organization |
| NS-Studentenbund | Nazi Student League |
| Ostheer | German army on the Eastern front |
| ProMi | Reichsministerium für Volksaufklärung und Propaganda (Reich Ministry for People's Enlightenment and Propaganda) |
| Rechtsstaat | state under the rule of law |
| Referat | sub-department, subsection, desk |
| Reichsarbeitsdienst | Reich Labour Service |
| Reichsführer | Reich leader |

| | |
|---|---|
| Reichskommissar | Reich Commissioner |
| Reichsrat | Reich Council (upper chamber of German parliament) |
| Reichsstatthalter | Reich governor |
| Reichstag | Reich Diet (lower chamber of German parliament) |
| Reichswehr | German armed forces (1919 to 1935) |
| RNS | Reichsnährstand (Reich Food Estate) |
| RSHA | SS-Reichssicherheitshauptamt (Reich Security Main Office) |
| SA | Schutzabteilungen (Stormtroopers) |
| Schönheit der Arbeit | Beauty of Labour |
| Schwarzes Korps | Black Corps (predecessor of SS) |
| SD | SS-Sicherheitsdienst (SS Security Service) |
| Soldat | soldier |
| Sopade | Sozialdemokratische Partei Deutschlands im Exil (Social Democratic Party of Germany in Exile) |
| SPD | Sozialdemokratische Partei Deutschlands (Social Democratic Party of Germany) |
| SS | Schutzstaffel |
| Stahlhelm | right-wing paramilitary organization |
| Treuhänder der Arbeit | Trustees of Labour |
| Untermensch | sub-human |
| Vaterland | fatherland |
| VDA | Volksbund für das Deutschtum im Ausland (League for Germandom Abroad) |
| Vernichtungskrieg | war of annihilation |
| Vierjahresplan | Four-Year Plan |
| Volksbewegung | people's movement |
| Volksdeutsche | ethnic Germans |
| Volksempfänger | people's radio |
| Volksgemeinschaft | National Community (also Racial or People's Community) |
| Volksgenosse | national comrade |
| Volksgerichtshof | People's Court of Law |
| Volkspartei | people's party, party representing all classes |
| Volkstumsführung | leadership of ethnic Germans |
| VoMi | Volksdeutsche Mittelstelle (SS-Office for Ethnic Germans) |
| VR | Volksdeutscher Rat (Council of Ethnic Germans) |
| Wehrmacht | German armed forces (1935 to 1945) |

| | |
|---|---|
| Weltanschauung | world view, ideology |
| Werksgemeinschaft | works community |
| Zentrumspartei | Centre Party (Party of political Catholicism) |

# General Introduction

## Christian Leitz

In 1945, the most destructive war the world has ever seen ended, yet interest in the regime that bore sole responsibility for its outbreak remains unabated. This interest is not confined to academic circles. As the most notable recent controversy, on 'ordinary Germans and the Holocaust', clearly demonstrates, sections of the public, particularly in Germany, continue to show an active interest in the history of the Third Reich. Certain other members of the public also entertain an ongoing interest in the events of the 1930s and 1940s, though in a much more worrying way. So-called 'revisionist' authors and publishers provide a partisan minority with a rather different version of the history of Nazi Germany in general and the Holocaust in particular.[1] For some time now, support for extreme right-wing parties and organizations has been on a disquieting upward trend. This is true for a number of countries, but, not surprisingly, is of most concern in the two countries, Austria and Germany, which, both physically and politically, acted as the birthplaces of Hitler and his National Socialist party.[2]

Hitler and the Third Reich thus continue to exercise a fascination upon people – and not purely for historical reasons. According to one count 120,000 publications on Adolf Hitler have been produced,[3] and there is still no end in sight to interesting new evidence as well as

[1] For a 'representative' view of a 'revisionist' writer, see the interview with Ernst Zündel, in Marie Ueda, *Testimony of the Twentieth Century; Before and After the Berlin Wall*, San Francisco, 1996, 46–63.
[2] For the rise of extreme right-wing parties in the 1990s, see section V: 'The Rebirth of Fascism' in Roger Griffin (ed.), *International Fascism; Theories, Causes and the New Consensus*, London, 1998, 286–324.
[3] Guido Knopp, *Hitler. Eine Bilanz*, Munich, 1997, 8.

sensationalist new 'revelations'. Guido Knopp, himself a contributor to the ongoing dissection of Hitler and his regime makes a telling point about the continued fascination:

> We [Germans] would love to detach ourselves from him, would love to be a 'normal' country. Yet, we are constantly and mercilessly led back to him. We continue to be Hitler's heirs whether we like it or not. We cannot rid ourselves of him . . . To be able to cope with Germany's trauma, Hitler, we need to confront ourselves with him.[4]

These constant reminders are not confined to Germany alone. Other nations also continue to be confronted with the events and effects of the period 1933 to 1945. The war and the Holocaust, appeasement and collaboration have left an indelible imprint upon many countries. As Sebastian Haffner reminded us in the late 1970s:

> Today's world, whether we like it or not, is the work of Hitler. Without Hitler there would have been no partition of Germany and Europe; . . . without Hitler, there would be no Israel; without Hitler there would be no de-colonization, at least not such a rapid one; there would be no Asian, Arab, or Black African emancipation, and no diminution of European preeminence.[5]

One may haggle with individual elements of Haffner's conclusion (in particular with its latter part), but it cannot be denied that Hitler's rule had a dramatic and lasting effect. Around the world, the public's memory is regularly refreshed by evocations of the image of Hitler, his regime, and the crimes committed during his Third Reich.

Before, during, and after the Gulf War, for example, parallels were frequently established between Saddam Hussein and Adolf Hitler. We were reminded about the mistakes of the 1930s, i.e. appeasement, while Saddam Hussein's murderous campaigns against the Kurds were compared to Nazi genocide. Current discussions about the establishment of a permanent International Criminal Court to prosecute 'evil leaders', including Saddam Hussein, have immediately invited references to the Nuremberg tribunal. Another example is the murderous civil war in the former Yugoslavia. War criminals have already been indicted. Again, as in the case of the Iraqi leadership, reports of Nazi-style genocide have featured regularly in the world media.

---

[4] Ibid., 8–9.
[5] Sebastian Haffner, *Anmerkungen zu Hitler*, Munich, 1978, cited by Gordon A. Craig, 'Man of the People?', *The New York Review*, 20 Nov. 1997, 20.

Hitler is also invoked in comparison to anatomies of various Communist regimes. An increased knowledge of these regimes has led a growing number of scholars, politicians and journalists to draw parallels between the Nazis and Communists. Some insist that no distinction should be drawn between the murderous conduct of the Nazi dictatorship and that of Communist regimes,[6] or that in fact Nazi atrocities were both quantitatively and qualitatively of a lower order than the crimes of Stalin (or more broadly of Communist dictatorships).[7] The most notable example of this trend is the recent *Le Livre noir du communisme*, in particular the views of Stéphane Courtois who took responsibility for editing and introducing the volume.[8]

It can be cynically argued that Courtois has followed a similar sequence of events to the Daniel Goldhagen path – make a shocking statement, market the book well, sell the book, stir up a heated debate, sell even more and see the book become a publishing sensation. In Courtois's case, the particular statement is his estimate of the total number of victims (between 85 and 100 million) of the various Communist regimes between 1917 and 1989 and, even more controversially, Courtois's deliberate comparison of his estimate to that of the victims of Nazism (which he puts at 25 million). As in the case of Goldhagen's *Hitler's Willing Executioners*,[9] the debate surrounding *Le Livre noir* and in particular Courtois's introduction, has partly centred on

---

[6] One such view, expressed by the German historian Ernst Nolte in the mid-1980s, set off a major 'quarrel' among scholars, the so-called *Historikerstreit*. See in particular Richard J. Evans, *In Hitler's Shadow: West German Historians and the Attempt to Escape from the Nazi Past*, New York, 1989; Charles S. Maier, *The Unmasterable Past: History, Holocaust, and German National Identity*, Cambridge, MA, 1988; Geoff Eley, 'Nazism, Politics, and the Image of the Past: Thoughts on the West German *Historikerstreit*, 1986–1987', *Past and Present* 121, 1988, 171–208; B. Heuser, The Historikerstreit: Uniqueness and Comparability of the Holocaust', *German History* 6, 1988, 69–78.

[7] According to the director of the Institute for Contemporary History in Munich, as cited by Michael Burleigh, 'the Nazi period will gradually lose its salience in the collective memory of contemporary Europeans, being supplanted by the "much longer lasting experience of suffering" under the Communists': quoted in Burleigh (ed.), *Confronting the Nazi Past: New Debates on Modern German History*, London, 1996, 1.

[8] Stéphane Courtois et al., *Le Livre noir due communisme: crimes, terreur, répression*, Paris, 1997. Two contributors, Jean-Louis Margolin and Nicholas Werth, subsequently criticized Courtois for some of his conclusions.

[9] Daniel J. Goldhagen, *Hitler's Willing Executioners: Ordinary Germans and the Holocaust*, London, 1996. On the public and academic debate of Goldhdgen's book, see Johannes Heil and Rainer Erb (eds), *Geschichtswissenschaft und Öffentlichkeit. Der Streit um Daniel J. Goldhagen*, Frankfurt/Main, 1998 and Robert R. Shandley (ed.), *Unwilling Germans: The Goldhagen Debate*, Minneapolis and London, 1998.

scholarly rigour. In contrast to the responses to Goldhagen's thesis, however, reactions to *Le Livre noir* are more easily separable along political and ideological lines: scathing criticism from the Left and strong support from the Right.[10]

At its present stage, the dispute is as inconclusive as the still lingering 'Goldhagen debate'. Only one point is certain. By highlighting the criminal nature of communist regimes, Courtois et al. have undoubtedly attracted public interest. It is, however, very unlikely that the 'special status' of Hitler and the Third Reich will be affected. Though very supportive of the conclusions drawn in *Le Livre noir*, Martin Malia has pinpointed the precise reasons for this:

> Communism's fall . . . brought with it no Nuremberg trial, and hence no de-Communization to solemnly put Leninism beyond the pale of civilization; and, of course, there still exist Communist regimes in international good standing. Another reason for our dual perception is that defeat cut Nazism down in the prime of its iniquity, thereby eternally fixing its memory in full horror. By contrast, Communism, at the peak of *its* iniquity, was rewarded with an epic victory – thereby gaining a half-century to lose its dynamism, to half-repent of Stalin and even, for some unsuccessful leaders, to attempt giving the system a 'human face'. . . . The final factor in establishing Nazism's distinctiveness, of course, is the Holocaust, considered as the historically unique crime of seeking the extermination of an entire people.[11]

As Malia concludes with cynical resignation, 'all comrade-questers after historical truth should gird their loins for a very Long March indeed before Communism is accorded its fair share of absolute evil.'[12] Even while some scholars are trying to establish a new (or rather old) paradigm of the more horrendous crimes of the communists compared to those of the Nazis, their efforts are constantly hampered by additional evidence about and new debates on Nazi Germany. Such developments help to constantly rekindle the interest in the latter. The most obvious example of recent years is undoubtedly the aforementioned 'Goldhagen debate'.

---

[10] For a critique of various media reports on Courtois and the book, see Serge Halemi, 'Tapis rouge', *Le Monde Diplomatique*, Dec. 1997, 23 (http://www.monde-diplomatique.fr/MD/1997/12/HALIMI/9664.html). The same issue also contains an example of a very damning review of *Le Livre noir*: Gilles Perrault, 'Communisme, les falsifications d'un "livre noir"' (http://www.monde-diplomatique.fr/MD/1997/12/Perrault/9660.html). The weekly *Die Zeit* has played an important role in instigating debate in Germany; see the series of articles in issues 24 to 31, 1998.
[11] Martin Malia, 'The lesser evil?', *Times Literary Supplement*, 27 Mar. 1998, 3.
[12] Ibid., 4.

If sales figures are the central determinant of quality, Daniel Goldhagen's *Hitler's Willing Executioners* has achieved a powerful position among writings on the Third Reich. Yet, the book contains a number of flaws, most notably the lack of convincing evidence to support Goldhagen's claim that ordinary Germans willingly participated in the Holocaust because of a unique eliminationist anti-Semitic disposition. It is therefore very difficult to commend it as a new basis for our understanding of the Holocaust. The commercial success of the book has, in fact, been both a blessing and a burden to other scholars – a blessing because of the attention it has again drawn to the terrible crimes committed against the Jews (and other groups) between 1939 and 1945, a burden because of the need to make the public understand the obvious defects in Goldhagen's work. In his review of the book, István Deák succinctly summarized this problematic combination:

> Goldhagen should be criticized neither for his choice of topic nor for his vivid description of mass murder. And although the thesis that anti-Semitism was an important factor in the Holocaust is hardly new, it should be emphasized. But the end should not justify the means. What stands out is the book's preconceived notions and unsubstantiated claims; its intended shock value instead of its historical value.[13]

As Goldhagen's astounding reaction to another review of his book has demonstrated, he does not take criticism lightly.[14] Yet, as his book reveals, he is not adverse to criticizing other historians for the apparent shortcomings of their work. One of the historians who has been singled out by Goldhagen is Christopher Browning. Most of Goldhagen's criticism of Browning's work is directed at a book, *Ordinary Men*, whose subject matter, the role of the German Reserve Police Battalion 101 in the Holocaust, is also central to Goldhagen's study.[15]

[13] István Deák, 'Holocaust Views: The Goldhagen Controversy in Retrospect', *Central European History* 30, 1997, 295–307. On the flaws of the book, see also, *inter alia*, Hans-Ulrich Wehler, 'The Goldhagen Controversy: Agonizing Problems, Scholarly Failure and the Political Dimension', *German History* 15, 1997, 80–91.
[14] The review in question is Ruth Bettina Birn (in collaboration with Volker Riess), 'Revising the Holocaust', *Historical Journal* 40, 1997, 196–215. In autumn 1997, Goldhagen apparently had his British solicitor send a letter to Birn threatening her with a defamation lawsuit; see *Frankfurter Allgemeine Zeitung*, 4 Nov. 1997, and *Der Spiegel*, 10 Nov. 1997.
[15] Christopher Browning, *Ordinary Men: Reserve Police Battalion 101 and the Final Solution*, Cambridge, 1992; see part III (Police Battalions: Ordinary Germans, Willing Killers) of Daniel J. Goldhagen, *Hitler's Willing Executioners; Ordinary Germans and the Holocaust*, London, 1996. Goldhagen's critical comments about *Ordinary Men* are all relegated to various, often lengthy footnotes; see, in particular, p. 534, n. 1.

Even before Goldhagen's book burst onto the scene, Browning had emphasized how serious a mistake it would be to confine the responsibility for the mass killings of Jews simply to the Nazi regime and its fanatical servants, most notably in the SS. Browning instead highlighted the role ordinary Germans played in the mass destruction of life without using, however, the same simplistic explanation as adopted by Goldhagen. In fact, before *Ordinary Men* appeared in print, Browning had already assumed a very influential position in the historical debate on the evolution of the 'Final Solution' by his cogent rejection of the 'intentionalist-functionalist divide'[16] (see Reading 11: Holocaust/'Final Solution').

Irrespective of their differences, both Browning's and Goldhagen's work exemplify the direction of recent publications on the Third Reich. The experiences, attitudes and involvement of the German people in the Third Reich have been drawing very detailed attention from researchers. As a result, a much more diverse picture of German society during the Nazi period has emerged. Instead of a simple division into active perpetrators – the Nazi regime – at the top and passive victims – the German population – at the bottom, we are now faced with a variety of levels and degrees of responsibility among the latter group. While the ideology and policies of the regime must continue to be the centrepiece of any examination of the Third Reich, one can no longer simply reduce its history to the regime and its direct servants.

Both traditional approaches and more recent trends are reflected in the readings in this collection. Readers may, of course, quibble with the selection of 'essential readings' – what is essential to one historian is not necessarily of the same relevance to another. Selecting articles and excerpts is an exercise determined by such diverse criteria as length, copyright permissions and, most importantly, personal choice. Even if one strives for impartiality, editing is a subjective activity.

Preferences are naturally influenced by the specific impact of the publications of certain scholars on any budding historian and by the wider impact individuals have had on our understanding of the Nazi period. To historians of the Third Reich, the authors included in this Reader are instantly recognizable. Each has made a vital contribution to our understanding of the history of Nazi Germany; some, most notably Ian Kershaw and Hans Mommsen, in more than one area.

---

16 Apart from the article in this reader, see also Christopher Browning, 'Beyond "Intentionalism" and "Functionalism": A Reassessment of Nazi Jewish Policy from 1939 to 1941', in Thomas Childers and Jane Caplan (eds), *Reevaluating the Third Reich*, New York, 1993, 211–33.

This is not to deny, of course, that others have made significant contributions. Most aspects of the history of the Third Reich are highly disputed fields with substantial numbers of combative scholars. None of the views espoused by the authors in this Reader have escaped critical comment from other historians, and the readings themselves often refer critically to previous publications or to earlier and ongoing historical debates. The Reader therefore should not be used in isolation, but rather as a basis for further reading and discussion.

Few issues have been as widely discussed as the question of how Hitler managed to gain power in the first place. In this context, Reading 1 (Rise of the NSDAP) examines the question of who the Nazis were, both in terms of the party's membership and of its electoral support. Although the breadth of the social basis of the Nazi movements is now being highlighted by other historians,[17] Detlef Mühlberger's pioneering work prepared the way for the conclusive debunking of traditional perceptions of the (lower) middle-class background of National Socialism.

As a corollary to the content of Reading 1, Albrecht Tyrell briefly summarizes in Reading 2 (Seizure and Consolidation of Power) the reasons for Hitler's rise to power. Tyrell moves on to provide a more detailed overview of the consolidation of the regime's power in 1933 and 1934, including the process of political and social *Gleichschaltung*.[18] Conjointly, both readings form an essential basis for later sections of the Reader.

Readings 3 (Foreign Policy) and 4 (Economy) also stress aspects of the Third Reich which have long been considered vitally important. The catastrophic events of the period 1939 to 1945 made it a pressing need to explain how the world ended up at war in the first place, and scholarly interest in Hitler's foreign policy led to some of the earliest historical debates about the Third Reich[19] In the late 1960s, Hans-Adolf Jacobsen published a landmark interpretation of the evolution and machinery of the foreign policy of the Third Reich. Its main aspects and conclusions are summarized in Reading 3.

[17] See, most recently, the contributions (including one by Detlef Mühlberger) to Conan Fischer (ed.), *The Rise of National Socialism and the Working Classes in Weimar Germany*, Providence RI, Oxford, 1996; see also Peter D. Stachura, 'National Socialism and the German Proletariat, 1925–1933: Old Myths and New Perspectives', *Historical Journal* 36, 1993, 701–18.

[18] Also still useful is Karl Dietrich Bracher, 'Stages of Totalitarian "Integration" (Gleichschaltung): The Consolidation of National Socialist Rule in 1933 and 1934', in Hajo Holborn (ed.), *Republic to Reich: The Making of the Nazi Revolution*, New York, 1973, 109–28.

[19] The outstanding early example is, of course, the lengthy debate caused by A. J. P. Taylor's *The Origins of the Second World War*, London, 1961.

An important part of the history of 'Hitler's road to war' is the regime's economic preparations for the forthcoming conflict. Richard Overy's contribution answers a central question: How did the Nazi regime manage to pull Germany out of the economic depression and, at the same time, create a massive war machinery? While Overy concedes that such an undertaking created various problems, he strongly opposes the thesis that the problems amounted to a crisis which ultimately forced Hitler to go to war in 1939.[20]

The war machine in action is the subject of Reading 5 (Army). The *Wehrmacht* has been of long-standing interest to scholars, most obviously, of course, to military historians. Bartov's work constitutes a clear break with most traditional portrayals of the army.[21] The central concern of the article is not combat, strategy or technology. Instead, its focal point is the involvement of the German army in atrocities in the East, a topic which, for many decades after the Nuremberg Trials, had been deliberately sidestepped.

While Reading 6 (*Volksgemeinschaft*) is also concerned with the *Wehrmacht*, it is specifically interested in the relationship between the German workers and the Nazi regime.[22] As in the case of Bartov, Alf Lüdtke's conclusions depart strongly from the traditional orthodoxy.[23] In place of a simplistic portrayal of the members of the *Wehrmacht* and the German working-class as either victims, innocent bystanders or even heroes, both authors present a much more complex picture of German society in the Third Reich. In a wider context, Lüdtke's article

[20]  On the 'crisis thesis' see the translation of Tim Mason's original exposition ('Innere Krise und Angriffskrieg 1938/1939') 'Internal Crisis and War of Aggression, 1938–1939', in Tim Mason [Jane Caplan, ed.], *Nazism, Fascism and the Working Class*, Cambridge, 1995, 104–30.

[21]  For a detailed account of Bartov's research and conclusions see his *Hitler's Army; Soldiers, Nazis, and War in the Third Reich*, Oxford, 1991; see also O. Bartov, *The Eastern Front, 1941–45: German Troops and the Barbarisation of Warfare*, London, 1985; and, more recently, O. Bartov, 'Savage War', in Burleigh (ed.), *Confronting the Nazi Past*, 125–39.

[22]  See also A. Lüdtke, 'The "Honor of Labor": Industrial Workers and the Power of Symbols under National Socialism', in David F. Crew (ed.), *Nazism and German Society 1933–1945*, London, New York, 1994; and Ulrich Herbert, ' "The Real Mystery in Germany": The German Working Class during the Nazi dictatorship', in Burleigh (ed.), *Confronting the Nazi Past*, 23–36.

[23]  A critical analysis of the state of the debate on workers' attitudes towards the Third Reich can be found in Tilla Siegel, 'Whatever was the attitude of German Workers? Reflections on Recent Interpretations', in I. Kershaw, M. Lewin (eds), *Stalinism and Nazism: dictatorships in comparison*, Cambridge, 1997, 61–77. On workers in Austria, see Tim Kirk, *Nazism and the Working Class in Austria; Industrial Unrest and Political Dissent in the 'National Community'*, Cambridge, 1996. On the experience of foreign workers, see Ulrich Herbert, *Hitler's Foreign Workers; Enforced Foreign Labour in Germany under the Third Reich*, Cambridge, 1996.

also contributes to the debate about the extent to which the Nazi regime's attempted transformation of German society into a *Volksgemeinschaft* (National Community) succeeded.[24]

Reading 7 (Police State) also accentuates the importance of a more nuanced interpretation of aspects of the Third Reich.[25] As in the two preceding readings, an easy black-and-white division of German society is rejected. In contrast to Bartov's and Lüdtke's subjects of inquiry, however, the focus of Robert Gellately's article is an organization that has always been firmly located at the 'black' end of the spectrum. Gellately, of course, has no intention of exonerating the Gestapo, but he does want to contextualize it. He shows convincingly that the traditional image of an all-powerful secret police keeping control of a passive population does not stand up to close historical investigation.[26]

The division of German women into perpetrators and victims is the central subject of enquiry of Reading 8 (Women). In contrast to readings 1 to 7, however, the subject matter of Adelheid von Saldern's article does not boast the same long-standing tradition of historical research.[27] Nevertheless, as Saldern's analysis of the contrasting views of two influential scholars, Gisela Bock and Claudia Koonz, reveals, the comparatively recent cultivation of this particular field of history has already produced acrimonious debate. Again, as in previous readings, simple answers as eschewed by Saldern in favour of an analysis which explores the complexity of the role of women in the Third Reich.

While Bartov, Lüdtke, Gellately, and Saldern firmly reject a blanket condemnation of ordinary Germans, they do confront the reader with the complex nature of their actions. In Reading 9 (Hitler as Dictator) Ian Kershaw considers a vital explanatory factor for the attitudes of many Germans. It is impossible to understand German society under the Nazi regime without examining closely the leader of this regime. It is undisputable that 'Working Towards the *Führer*' was not simply a cliché phrase to many Germans who, both directly and indirectly, drew

---

[24] On success or failure of Nazi *Volksgemeinschaft* policies see Detlev J. K. Peukert, *Inside Nazi Germany: Conformity, Opposition and Racism in Everyday Life*, London, 1987; David Welch, *The Third Reich: Politics and Propaganda*, London, 1993. For a summary of the wider debate on whether or not the Nazi regime can be seen as a force of modernization, see Mark Roseman, 'National Socialism and Modernisation', in Richard Bessel (ed.), *Fascist Italy and Nazi Germany: Comparisons and Contrasts*, Cambridge, 1996, 197–229.

[25] For a detailed account of Robert Gellately's research and conclusions, see his *The Gestapo and German Society: Enforcing Racial Policy, 1933–1945*, Oxford, 1990.

[26] For a traditional portrayal of the Gestapo, see, *inter alia*, J. Delarue, *The Gestapo: A History of Horror*, New York, 1987.

[27] One of the first important examinations of the position of women in the Third Reich was provided by Jill Stephenson, *Women in Nazi Society*, London, 1975.

justification for their actions from Hitler. What is disputable, however, is whether Hitler conformed to the 'strong leader' image the public had of him.[28]

A minority of Germans recognized Hitler and his henchmen for what they really were: not Germany's saviours, but its destroyers; not *Führer* (leaders) who deserved total support, but *Verführer* (seducers) who deserved to be eliminated. As Hans Mommsen shows in Reading 10 (Resistance), Germans from various social and political backgrounds risked, and lost, their lives for their beliefs. For some, this realization came only after they had already held positions among the ranks of the perpetrators. Therefore, despite continued efforts to prove the contrary, even the history of the resistance against Hitler does not allow an all-encompassing and simple division into 'good and bad' Germans.[29] As previously indicated, Reading 11, the final article in this collection, contains Christopher Browning's important contribution to the historical debate on the evolution of the 'Final Solution'.

Teaching and learning about the Third Reich have become considerably more complex tasks than they were thirty or even twenty years ago. As most of the readings in this collection demonstrate, some 'certainties' have been either replaced by new and more complex theses or are the subject of unresolved debates. Simple answers, particularly on the role of ordinary Germans, no longer suffice. I hope that this Reader will inform students about major aspects of the darkest period in German history, and even more importantly, will challenge the preconceived ideas that all students bring to the study of this particular subject.

---

[28]   For a critical comparison of various historical perceptions of Hitler, see John Lukacs, *The Hitler of History*, New York, 1997. For a summary of the debate on Hitler's position in the Third Reich by an advocate of the 'strong leader' thesis, see the introduction to Martin Moll (ed.), *'Führer-Erlasse' 1939–1945*, Stuttgart, 1997. The 'weak dictator' thesis was first advanced by Hans Mommsen; see his 'National-sozialismus', in *Sowjetsystem und demokratische Gesellschaft: Eine vergleichende Enzyklopädie*, vol. 4, Freiburg, 1971.

[29]   The most recent attempt at 'sanitizing' the history of the resistance has been Joachim Fest's *Plotting Hitler's Death: The Story of the German Resistance*, New York, 1997. For more information on the 'varieties' of German resistance, see David C. Large (ed.), *Contending with Hitler: Varieties of German Resistance in the Third Reich*, Washington D.C., 1991; F. Nicosia and L. D. Stokes (eds), *Germans against Nazism: Nonconformity, Opposition and Resistance in the Third Reich (Essays in Honour of Peter Hoffmann)*, New York, Oxford, 1990; see also the various contributions to the Supplement issue of *Journal of Modern History* 64, 1992.

# Rise of the NSDAP

# 1

# Conclusion to *Hitler's Followers*

## Detlef Mühlberger

Originally appeared as Detlef Mühlberger, 'Conclusion' in *Hitler's Followers: Studies in the Sociology of the Nazi Movement* (Routledge, 1991) pp. 202–9.

### Editor's Introduction

In the Reichstag elections of July 1932 the NSDAP received 37.3 per cent of the vote, making the party by far the largest party in the German parliament. Millions of Germans voted for the Nazis. Who were these people? Of what social background were the 850,000 members who had joined the party by 30 January 1933? What was the social composition of the SA and SS? These questions have occupied scholars and other observers ever since the Nazi party started on its rise in the 1920s. As Detlef Mühlberger reminds us in the following excerpt, the conclusion to his study *Hitler's Followers*, the reason for this continued interest is simple. 'It is only by identifying as precisely as is possible those *who* were Nazis that one can give a meaningful and convincing answer to the question of *why* they were Nazis.'

Mühlberger gives precisely such 'a meaningful and convincing answer', and it is one that clashes with traditional perceptions of party support. Instead of subscribing to the view that the Nazis constituted a movement of the *Mittelstand*, Mühlberger makes a strong case for the Nazi party to be viewed as a *Volkspartei*. It was a mass movement, Mühlberger argues, joined by members from all classes (though with a strong bias towards young males) and supported at elections by voters from all classes. Even though the lower middle class was undoubtedly over-represented in the party, the millions of workers who gave their support to the Nazis must not be overlooked. Not only had the Nazi party 'taken its name from the working class', it also 'attained national prominence as a mass formation supported by the lower middle class' and, in a modification of Michael Kater's conclusion,[1] substantial sections of the working class. Workers

[1] Michael H. Kater, *The Nazi Party*, Oxford, 1983, 71.

were not immune to the attraction of Hitler and his movement before 1933 nor, as Omer Bartov and Alf Lüdtke remind us in their contributions to this reader, did they remain entirely detached from the regime after 1933.

# Conclusion to *Hitler's Followers*

## Detlef Mühlberger

The analyses of the social contours of the Nazi Party membership at the regional level presented in *Hitler's Followers* demonstrate the ability of the Nazis to mobilize support from various occupational groups and from all social strata from the mid-1920s onwards. The degree of support derived from the various classes represented in the Nazi Party in the regions evaluated was not constant, while the diversity of the occupational and class configuration of the numerous Nazi branches is often quite striking even within the same region. The ability of the Nazi Movement to reflect in broad terms the social geometry of the population of the regions in which it was recruiting is a feature of its development in the late 1920s and early 1930s. This is not to ignore the fact that the NSDAP in the Western Ruhr in 1925 and 1926, or in Württemberg or Hesse-Nassau in the late 1920s and early 1930s, or in South-Hanover-Brunswick in the period 1925 to 1933, mirrored the social structure of the (male) working populations of these regions imperfectly.

Obviously the Nazi Party was not, as a section of its party title proclaimed, a 'socialist . . . workers' party in any of these regions, not even in the Ruhr region, where the number of party members mobilized from the lower class was comparatively high in the mid-1920s among the admittedly low degree of overall support mobilized by the NSDAP at that time, and where it probably sustained a high level of lower-class support throughout the period before 1933. To suggest, however, that the high incidence of lower-class support for Nazism in the Ruhr may simply be explained as the consequence of the social structure of the region in which 'fascism's normal social constituency (was) greatly underrepresented',[1] is not a tenable argument. Such an approach assumes that the 'normal constituency' of the NSDAP was middle-class, and if this was indeed so, it raises the question of why the Nazis secured significant support in areas predominantly lower-class in their social composition. It does not help either in explaining why many Nazi Party branches in various other regions of Germany were overwhelmingly based on lower-class recruits. Arguing on the basis of the empirical evidence advanced here that the Nazis were able to secure a considerable number of

---

[1] This is the line of argument advanced by Richard J. Overy in his review article 'Fascist Societies', *Social History Society Newsletter*, 13 (1988), p. 13.

members drawn from the lower class does not ignore the fact that the NSDAP was differently constituted in sociological terms in comparison with the KPD, the only true working-class party active in the Weimar era, or the SPD, still strongly anchored in the lower class, even though it was in the process of losing its mono-class structure.[2] It is highly improbable that any KPD branches, or even any SPD branches, would have had a rank and file membership in which the lower class did not provide the absolute majority of support, with *Mittelstand* elements generally representing a marginal factor. In the case of the Nazi Party the social structure of its branches, as demonstrated in all regions examined here, does not conform to any class pattern. Although many Nazi branches, especially the larger branches, were based on a strong core of support drawn from the lower- and middle-middle class, a considerable number were overwhelmingly lower-class in their social structure. The Nazi Party recruited from the lower class to a considerable extent, though nowhere near as exclusively from this social stratum as the KPD or SPD.

That a section of the lower class supported Nazism should not be surprising, even if it is an idea which is anathema to socialist or marxist historians who, understandably, do not wish to see the lower class tainted by any association with such a nauseating creed as National Socialism. One is not talking about the odd token lower-class supporter, the equivalent of the relatively few *Mittelstand* and upper-class types, and even the odd 'aristocrat', to be found in the SPD or perhaps also the KPD, but a sizeable section of the working class. It must be borne in mind that only about 1.3 million workers were members of socialist and marxist parties for much of the 1920s and early 1930s,[3] and that at most only approximately half of the 22 to 25 million workers and their adult dependants gave their electoral support to socialist and marxist parties in the late 1920s and early 1930s,[4] with the combined vote for

[2]   According to statistics produced by the KPD in 1927, unskilled and skilled workers made up 80 per cent of its membership; see H. Weber, *Die Wandlung des deutschen Kommunismus. Die Stalinisierung der KPD in der Weimarer Republik* (Frankfurt a. M., 1969), p. 282. In the occupational breakdown of its membership provided by the SPD in 1930 (based on a sample of 100,000 members), 'workers' accounted for 59.5 per cent, the 'petty bourgeoisie' for 17.3 per cent, 'intellectuals' for 1.5 per cent, and 'others' for 21.7 per cent; figures cited in R. N. Hunt, *German Social Democracy 1918–1933* (New Haven/London, 1964), p. 103.

[3]   On 1 January 1931 the SPD's membership was 1,037,384 (including approximately 100,000 members drawn from the middle class); see Hunt, *German Social Democracy*, p. 100. The KPD had a paid-up membership of 259,155 (and a registered membership of 381,000) in December 1931; see Weber, *Wandlung des deutschen Kommunismus*, p. 364.

[4]   Cf. Tim Mason, *Sozialpolitik im Dritten Reich. Arbeiterklasse und Volksgemeinschaft* (Opladen, 1978), pp. 56 and 62.

the SPD and KPD rising from 12,417,772, secured in the May *Reichstag* election of 1928, to the highpoint of 13,329,420 obtained in that of July 1932.[5] Bearing in mind the not insignificant support also given by Catholic workers to the Centre Party, and the sprinkling of membership support given by the lower class to what were basically bourgeois parties, such as the DDP, DVP and DNVP, there existed a considerable pool of workers who were not politically engaged elsewhere. It is from this reservoir that the Nazis attracted its sizeable lower-class membership and electoral following, as well as from workers formerly mobilized by non-socialist parties. It is highly unlikely that the Nazis secured much support from those lower-class individuals who were active in the various parties and trades unions constituting the working-class movement in the Weimar era, though some marginal cross-over cannot be ruled out.[6] It would be foolish to suggest, of course, that the bulk of the lower class was ever attracted to Nazism to the point of joining the Nazi Party, either before or after the collapse of the Weimar Republic, but what is clear is that along with the KPD, SPD, and the Centre Party, the Nazi Party was increasingly important in politicizing and organizing the lower class in the latter part of the 1920s and early 1930s.[7] All these parties recruited from the lower class, but with variable success. In all of these parties such diverse representatives of the lower class as agricultural workers, unskilled and semi-skilled workers in industry and crafts, and trade and transport, were represented, though factory workers or the unskilled proletariat employed in large units of production were more likely to find their way into the KPD or SPD than the NSDAP. Unskilled and semi-skilled agricultural and forestry workers, miners, unskilled factory workers, lorry drivers, mechanics, textile workers, dock workers, skilled craft workers of various description, and domestic workers – to name but a few 'categories' of workers which constituted the lower class in the 1920s and 1930s – were all likely to rub shoulders with members of their own class in the branches of the KPD, SPD, Centre Party of Nazi Party, though they were undoubtedly less likely to come into contact with various *Mittelstand* and 'elite' types in the KPD or SPD than the Nazi Party or Centre Party. Like the KPD, but unlike the SPD and probably also the Centre Party, it was primarily the

[5]  Figures taken from Jürgen Falter, Thomas Lindenberger and Siegfried Schumann, *Wahlen und Abstimmungen in der Weimarer Republik. Materialien zum Wahlverhalten 1919–1933* (Munich, 1986), p. 41.

[6]  For example, 7 per cent of the 'old fighters' analysed by Theodore Abel had been members of left-wing movements; cited by Mason, *Sozialpolitik*, p. 54, n. 21.

[7]  Gerhard Schulz has argued that the Nazi Party may well have ranked second behind the SPD in its ability to mobilize working-class support in the early 1930s; see Gerhard Schulz, *Aufstieg des Nationalsozialismus. Krise und Revolution in Deutschland* (Frankfurt a. M./Berlin/Vienna, 1975), p. 551.

younger age-groups of the lower class which were pulled into the Nazi orbit, a feature in evidence in the case of the Western Ruhr Nazi Party membership in 1925 to 1926 and in the overall age profile of the SS and the strongly lower-class SA, and suggested by the age-structure of the Nazi Party membership as a whole.[8] One other aspect of the lower-class support secured by the Nazis is that the propensity of workers to join the movement was much greater among those who lived in rural or small-town communities. Although in absolute numeric terms workers resident in cities and larger towns constituted the largest part of lower-class support within the Nazi Party and the SA, the response rate in percentage terms of those workers living in smaller communities was noticeably higher. Community size does not appear, however, to have affected the response rate of the lower class in the case of the SS, in which the lower class represented roughly half of the membership, irrespective of whether these units were based in predominantly rural or small-town communities, or larger towns and cities.

In three of the four regional case studies on the NSDAP evaluated, the lower- and middle-middle class constituted the relative majority of the membership. In the sizeable party branches situated in the cities of Stuttgart, Frankfurt and Brunswick, this social stratum formed the absolute majority of members, and in the case of Wiesbaden almost half of the membership. The invariable dominance of the *Mittelstand* element in city branches is not, however, a feature of branches situated in medium-sized or smaller towns, nor in the branches established in rural areas. Although the age profile of the Nazi Party membership in *Gaue* Württemberg-Hohenzollern and Hesse-Nassau-South could not be established, the evidence available on the Ruhr NSDAP and on *Gau* South-Hanover-Brunswick, suggests that the bulk of the lower- and middle-middle-class elements active in the party came from dependent white-collar employees rather than from the independent *Mittelstand*. The often high percentage of those classified as 'merchants' in individual branches evaluated in this study, especially in such large city branches as Frankfurt, Wiesbaden and Stuttgart, involved primarily dependent commercial employees rather than independent merchants or shopkeepers (the latter almost invariable made their independent position clear). The bulk of NSDAP, SA and SS members masquerading as 'merchants' were much too young to have secured an independent economic position. The age factor also ruled out any significant support

[8]  Some 42.2 per cent of the members who joined the Nazi Party before 31 January 1933 (and were still in the party by 1 January 1935) were aged between 18 and 30; a further 27.8 per cent were in the 31 to 40 age group. Figures taken from *Partei-Statistik. Stand 1. Januar 1935. Band 1: Mitglieder*. Herausgeber: Der Reichsorganisationsleiter der NSDAP (Munich, n.d.), p. 204.

for the NSDAP from among the independent (master) craftsmen resident in either urban or rural communities. Under-represented within the Nazi Movement in these regions, as well as within the membership of the SA and the SS, were independent farmers, the core of the rural *Mittelstand*. It is probable that the great majority of those described as 'farmers' who were active in the Nazi Movement before 1933 were in their twenties and early thirties, which suggests that one is dealing with sons of farmers, rather than with farmers as such. This would explain the under-representation of farmers reflected in the *Partei-Statistik*, and the decision to encourage farmers to join the party, which conditioned the recruitment policy of the NSDAP from 1935.[9]

Although calculations and estimates of the size of the German elite (upper-middle class and upper class) during the Weimar era vary,[10] empirical evidence on the social structure of the Nazi Party at the macro level[11] points to a significant over-representation of this social stratum within the Nazi Party before 1933, an over-representation less marked in the case of the SA and the SS. Academic professionals, and to a lesser extent university students, formed the core of the elite supporting Nazism, particularly in Nazi branches situated in larger towns and cities. The enrolment pattern of the elite joining the Nazi Party in *Gaue* Hesse-Nassau-South and Sough-Hanover-Brunswick, as well as the recruitment pattern of the SS, suggests that a correlation exists between the rate of response by the elite and the community size factor, with strong

[9]   Cf. *Partei-Statistik*, p. 56.

[10]   The size of the 'elite' in Weimar society ranges from the 0.84 per cent suggested by Theodor Geiger to 3.3 per cent noted by Carl Dreyfuss. Michael Kater's calculations based on the 1933 census returns result in an elite component of 2.78 per cent (Kater includes managers, higher civil servants, academic professionals, students and entrepreneurs in the 'elite' category); see Michael Kater, *The Nazi Party. A Social Profile of Members and Leaders, 1919–1945* (Oxford, 1983), pp. 12–13 and p. 241, table 1. Paul Madden, who bases his calculations of the size of the elite on the 1925 census returns, suggests a figure of 1.1 per cent (Madden includes only capitalists, industrialists, large landowners, and persons with private incomes in the 'elite' category); see Paul Madden, 'The Social Class Origins of Nazi Party Members as Determined by Occupations, 1919–1933', *Social Science Quarterly*, 68 (1987), pp. 272–3, table 2.

[11]   According to Michael Kater the elite made up 9.2 per cent of Nazi recruits (*N*: 2,186) in the period 1925–32, and 12.2 per cent of Nazi recruits (*N*: 3,316) in 1933; see Michael Kater, 'Quantifizierung und NS-Geschichte. Methodologische Überlegungen über Grenzen und Möglichkeiten einer EDV-Analyse der NSDAP-Sozialstruktur von 1925 bis 1945', *Geschichte und Gesellschaft*, 3 (1977), p. 477, table 10. Cf. Kater's re-working of material provided by Werner Studentkowski and Paul Madden for the period 1925 to 1930 shows that the 'elite' component among Nazi recruits ranged between 6.3 and 8.8 per cent according to Studentkowski's data, and between 4.8 and 8.4 per cent according to Madden's data; see Kater, *Nazi Party*, pp. 244–5, table 3.

support mobilized in cities and large towns, and negligible enrolment in rural and small-town environments. This relationship was not, however, a universal one, given the different pattern of elite recruitment in the Nazi Party in *Gau* Württemberg-Hohenzollern and that of the SA units previously analysed.[12]

The presence of a sizeable working-class following in the NSDAP and SS, and especially the dominance of this social stratum -within the SA and the HJ, as well as the strong contingent of support drawn from the elite element of German society by the Nazi Party, and to a lesser degree the SS, argues against the validity of the middle-class thesis of Nazism, and suggests that it would be unwise to continue to adhere to this interpretational hypothesis. To describe the Nazi Movement as a 'pre-eminently lower-middle-class phenomenon'[13] or to characterize the NSDAP as 'a predominantly lower-middle-class affair'[14] is misleading. The perpetuation of the middle-class thesis of Nazism in the light of the empirical evidence now available on the rank and file membership of the party, the SA and the SS, as well as the more limited data on the HJ,[15] both at the macro and micro level, is untenable. It is clear that in the period following the re-formation of the Nazi Party in 1925 and its

[12]   See Mühlberger, *Hitler's Followers*, ch. 6.
[13]   Kater, *Nazi Party*, p. 236.
[14]   Peter Stachura, 'The Nazis, the Bourgeoisie and the Workers during the *Kampfzeit*', in Peter D. Stachura (ed.), *The Nazi Machtergreifung* (London, 1983), p. 28.
[15]   Peter Stachura characterizes the membership of the HJ as 'predominantly working class', with 65 to 70 per cent of its membership being drawn from the working class before 1933. Stachura does not analyse any raw material on the social structure of the HJ's membership as such, but uses summaries of the social background of HJ members contained in Nazi reports on *Gaue* Munich-Upper Bavaria, Hamburg, South Bavaria, and the Rhineland. See Peter Stachura, *Nazi Youth in the Weimar Republic* (Santa Barbara/Oxford, 1975), pp. 58–62. My own breakdown of the HJ in the Palatinate, based on a complete membership record of 2,053 members who joined the organization between 1928 and April 1932, also points to the strong lower-class base (57.4 per cent were recruited from the lower class) of the HJ in this region; see Detlef Mühlberger, 'Germany', in Detlef Mühlberger (ed.), *The Social Basis of European Fascist Movements* (London, 1987), p. 110, table 2.11. It seems that this high incidence of lower-class support was not universal, however. A report on the HJ membership in *Gau* South-Hanover-Brunswick (*N*: 1,200) as in February 1931 listed the following groupings:

| | |
|---|---|
| Young workers | 37% |
| Commercial apprentices | 14% |
| Farmers | 11% |
| Free occupations | 15% |
| School children, students | 23% |

Taken from *Führer zum Gautag der Nationalsozialistischen Deutschen Arbeiter-Partei am 21. und 22. Februar 1931 in der Stadt Braunschweig.* Herausgeber: Propaganda-Abteilung der Gauleitung Südhannover-Braunschweig, p. 31; copy in NHStAH, Hann. 310 I/G No. 17/1.

*Machtergreifung* eight years later the Nazi Movement as a whole, that is the NSDAP along with a number of its more important auxiliary organizations, mobilized a following which was remarkably heterogeneous in social terms. Moreover, the polymorphic nature of the Nazi Movement is reinforced by the considerable research which has been undertaken on the electoral basis of Nazism[16] in the last decade, which also undermines the validity of the middle-class thesis of the Nazi electorate first suggested in the 1930s, a view popularized by many scholars in the post-1945 period.[17]

The Nazi Party was, as the Nazis themselves asserted in the 1920s and 1930s, a *Volkspartei*, a mass movement in which all classes were represented. This is not to ignore the fact that the sociological structure of the NSDAP, the SA and the SS mirrored the social composition of German society imperfectly, either at the macro or micro level. The lower- and middle-middle class and elite were over-represented and the lower class under-represented within the NSDAP and the SS before

[16] Among the extensive literature dealing with the social background of the Nazi electorate see especially Thomas Childers, *The Nazi Voter. The Social Foundations of Fascism in Germany, 1919–1933* (Chapel Hill/London. 1983); Dirk Hänisch, *Sozialstrukturelle Bestimmungsgründe des Wahlverhaltens in der Weimarer Republik. Eine Aggregatdatenanalyse der Ergebnisse der Reichstagswahlen 1924–1933* (Duisburg, 1983); and Richard Hamilton, *Who voted for Hitler?* (New York, 1982). Especially important among the enormous output on this question by Jürgen W. Falter in the last decade are the following: 'Wer verhalf der NSDAP zum Sieg? Neuere Forschungsergebnisse zum parteipolitischen und sozialen Hintergrund der NSDAP-Wähler 1924–1933', *Aus Politik und Zeitgeschichte*, B 28/29 (1979), pp. 3–21; 'Wählerbewegung zur NSDAP 1924–1933. Methodologische Probleme – Empirisch abgesicherte Erkenntnisse – Offene Fragen', in Otto Büsch (ed.), *Wählerbewegung in der europäischen Geschichte* (Berlin, 1980), pp. 159–202; 'Die Wähler der NSDAP 1928–1933: Sozialstruktur und parteipolitische Herkunft', in Wolfgang Michalka (ed.), *Die nationalsozialistische Machtergreifung* (Paderborn/Munich/Vienna/Zürich, 1984); (with Dirk Hänisch) 'Die Anfälligkeit von Arbeitern gegenüber der NSDAP bei den Reichstagswahlen 1928–1933', *Archiv für Sozialgeschichte*, 26 (1986), pp. 179–216; 'Der Aufstieg der NSDAP in Franken bei den Reichstagswahlen 1924–1933. Ein Vergleich mit dem Reich unter besonderer Berücksichtigung landwirtschaftlicher Einflußfaktoren', *German Studies Review*, 9 (1986), pp. 319–59; (with Reinhard Zintl) 'The Economic Crisis of the 1930s and the Nazi Vote', *Journal of Interdisciplinary History*, 18 (1988), pp. 55–85. All these studies demonstrate the broad social base on which the electoral support of the NSDAP rested. For a review of the debate on the sociology of the Nazi electoral constituency see Peter Manstein, *Die Mitglieder und Wähler der NSDAP 1919–1933. Untersuchungen zu ihrer schichtmäßigen Zusammensetzung* (Frankfurt a. M./Bern/New York/Paris, 1988), pp. 165–93.

[17] See, for example, Seymour Martin Lipset's characterization of 'the ideal-typical Nazi voter in 1932' as being 'a middle-class self-employed Protestant who lived either on a farm or in a small community'; Seymour Martin Lipset, *Political Man* (New York, 1960), p. 149.

1933. In the case of the SA the lower class was over-represented within its ranks, though the match between its social composition and that of the adult male population on which it was exclusively based was much closer. The characterization of the Nazi Movement as a *Volkspartei* does need to be qualified, however. It was a predominantly male affair on the one hand,[18] and primarily a movement of the younger age groups of German society on the other.[19] In these aspects of its membership structure the Nazi Movement did not represent the totality of German society before 1933.

Establishing an accurate picture of the social basis of the Nazi Movement is obviously not an esoteric exercise but of fundamental importance in any attempt to understand the Nazi phenomenon. It is only by identifying as precisely as is possible those *who* were Nazis that one can give a meaningful and convincing answer to the question of *why* they were Nazis. It is this latter question which has exercised the imagination of numerous scholars since the appearance of Nazism in the 1920s, based on answers to the former question which were basically informed – at least until the 1970s – by a mixture of observation, educated conjecture, intuition, assumption, assertion and guesswork, and little, if any, concrete data. The entrenchment of the middle-class thesis of Nazism early on in the debate on Nazism which evolved from the late 1920s, and its acceptance by Marxist and non-Marxist scholars alike as *the* diagnosis to subscribe to, has conditioned much of what has been written about the phenomenon in the pre- and post-war periods. Much intellectual capital is now invested in very sophisticated explanatory models of Nazism which are, ultimately, predicated on the erroneous notion that one is dealing in essence with a middle-class, or lower-middle-class, affair. Even scholars who have done so much to provide new *empirical* evidence on the sociology of Nazism which undermines the *Mittelstandsbewegung* approach, and here Michael Kater's important pioneering work springs especially to mind, continue to advocate the old orthodoxy.

Obviously not all of the questions surrounding the sociology of Nazism are answered in the present work. There is need for further detailed analysis of the social base of the NSDAP at the regional and local level to provide a more comprehensive geographic coverage than that which is provided here. Access to material on the social structure

---

[18]    According to the *Partei-Statistik*, females accounted for 5.9 per cent of the Nazi membership before 14.9.1930, 7.8 per cent of those who joined between 15.9.1930 and 30.1.1933, and 4.4 per cent of those who rushed to join the party after the 30.1.1933. Percentages calculated on the basis of data in *Partei-Statistik*, pp. 26 and 30.

[19]    See n. 8.

of the Nazi Party in Thuringia or Saxony, for example, which may be deposited in the archives of the German Democratic Republic, would be particularly useful, given that we know virtually nothing specific about the social contours of the Nazi Party in the central-eastern parts of Weimar Germany, except the information contained in the *Partei-Statistik*.[20] The question of the social types who entered and left the Nazi Party before 1933 needs much more work,[21] while further evidence on the social background of those who entered the SS before 1933 is also required.

The Nazi Movement was indeed, as the Nazis themselves claimed, a *Volksbewegung* in social terms. It was the unfortunate ability of the Nazi Party, despite its contradictory and cretinous ideology, to secure mass support drawn from *all* social groupings in the late 1920s and early 1930s, both in membership and electoral terms, which gave it its strength. The reasons behind the turn to Nazism by wide sections of German society, by people from all walks of life, by Catholics and Protestants, by those resident in rural and urban areas, will undoubtedly continue to be an important object of analysis, but must be based on as accurate an evaluation of the class base of the phenomenon investigated as is possible. Acceptance of the fact that irrational political behaviour is not the prerogative of any particular class, but of sections of all class groupings, is an essential step to the ultimate understanding of the very complex social response on which Nazism was based.

[20]  Regional studies on the Nazi Party produced by East German scholars, such as Gerhard Neuber's study on Berlin entitled 'Entwicklung und Wirken der NSDAP und ihrer Organisationen in der Reichshauptstadt 1920–1934' (Dr. phil. thesis, Humboldt Universität Berlin, 1976), are not very illuminating on the class basis of the Nazi Party.

[21]  I am at present working on this aspect, dealing with the membership fluctuations of the Nazi Party in *Gaue* Württemberg and Hesse-Nassau-South.

# Seizure and Consolidation of Power

# 2

# Towards Dictatorship: Germany 1930 to 1934

## Albrecht Tyrell

Translation by Christian Leitz of Albrecht Tyrell, 'Auf dem Weg zur Diktatur: Deutschland 1930 bis 1934', in Karl Dietrich Bracher, Manfred Funke and Hans-Adolf Jacobsen (eds), *Deutschland 1933–1945. Neue Studien zur nationalsozialistischen Herrschaft*, Düsseldorf, 1992, 15–31.

*Editor's Introduction*

On 30 January 1933, Adolf Hitler, leader of the largest party in the Reichstag, was made Reich Chancellor of the Weimar Republic. Hitler's appointment, a constitutional act, has frequently been mislabelled as *Machtergreifung*. Hitler, clearly, did not seize power. However, the rapid progress of events which began with Hitler's appointment and ended on 2 August 1934 with the union of the offices of president and chancellor in the person of 'the *Führer* and Reich Chancellor Adolf Hitler' did amount to a seizure of complete power. In quick succession, Hitler and his fellow Nazi leaders implemented radical policies in order to make Germany's government their own, thus turning democracy into dictatorship.

The second contribution to this Reader establishes a chronological and thematic basis for the remaining articles. Albrecht Tyrell provides both a sketch of the last phase of the rise of the Nazis up to 30 January 1933, and a more detailed account of the establishment of the Nazi dictatorship in the subsequent period preceding Hindenburg's death. In addition, Tyrell's treatment of the period of *Gleichschaltung* introduces issues that are discussed in many of the articles in this reader. Such origins, or early indications, of later developments include the willingness of the army leadership to accommodate itself with the new regime (see the reading by Bartov), the ambivalent attitude of the working class towards the new regime (see the reading by Lüdtke), the establishment and activities of the Nazi police apparatus (see Gellately), the beginnings, and first setbacks, of resistance activities against the new regime (see Mommsen), the nature of the dictatorship and the role of Hitler (see Kershaw), and the instigation of criminal acts against, among other groups, the Jews (see Browning).

# Towards Dictatorship: Germany 1930 to 1934

*Albrecht Tyrell*

By celebrating 30 January 1933 as the day of their 'seizure of power', the Nazis fabricated a double contraction of the term. Hitler neither seized nor conquered the chancellorship; it was handed to him in a process which could have been prevented even in the last days of January. When the comprehensive conquest of power finally commenced on 30 January, it was to last for about eighteen months. An outline of history and effects leading up to the stabilization of Nazi rule of this infamous day will be offered in this reading.

I

At the heart of the political programme of Adolf Hitler and his National Socialist German Workers Party (NSDAP), renamed in 1920 from the original German Workers Party (DAP) of 1919, was the inner unification and the mental, physical and material preparation for war of the German *Volk*. In order to achieve this, 'Marxists' and all those defending the democratic system had to be eliminated. The whole process would see the establishment of an authoritarian Greater German state led by a superior race which would be able to usurp hegemonic leadership in Europe.

For ten years the NSDAP made little headway towards its objective. It only attracted a mass following and thus a weighty role in German politics owing to a combination of factors which had evolved beyond Nazi control. The opportunity to grow into something more than a radical outsider arrived with the world economic crisis of the late 1920s.[1]

As an immediate effect the crisis completely undermined the fragile consensus among parties and organizations of the Weimar democracy. Pressured by their supporters in trade unions and employers'

[1] On the development of the NSDAP see Wolfgang Horn, *Führerideologie und Parteiorganisation in der NSDAP (1919–1933)*, Düsseldorf, 1972; Peter Manstein, *Die Mitglieder und Wähler der NSDAP (1919–1933)*, Frankfurt/Main, 3rd edn, 1990; Gerhard Schulz, *Aufstieg des Nationalsozialismus. Krise und Revolution in Deutschland*, Frankfurt/Main, 1975; Albrecht Tyrell, *Führer befiehl . . . Selbstzeugnisse aus der 'Kampfzeit' der NSDAP*, Bindlach, 2nd edn, 1991.

associations, the SPD and DVP, left and right wing of the Grand Coalition of 1928, decided against further compromises which may have prevented the fall of the Müller government in March 1930. The attitude of SPD and DVP was tantamount to a self-elimination of the representatives of the parliamentarian democracy. It facilitated the transition towards an authoritarian presidential system also catered for by the Weimar constitution.[2]

Originally intended for periods of crisis, the dualism of the constitution juxtaposed parliament with a strong Reich presidency. 'Dictatorship article' 48 of the constitution gave the president the right to pass emergency decrees whenever the Reichstag proved to be unable to act. If the Reichstag decided to annul an emergency decree, the president had the power to dissolve parliament and appoint or dismiss chancellor and government ministers without the Reichstag's consent. *De facto*, the president was thus able to govern almost without parliamentary control. During those critical first years of the Republic, the first President, Friedrich Ebert, repeatedly used his powers for the protection of the democratic system. Yet, these rights also enabled parties to withdraw from parliamentary responsibility. Moreover, it offered opponents of the parliamentary system a legal lever – if the parties failed to stop them.

And that is precisely what happened in 1930. Paul von Hindenburg, already over 80 years of age, had long desired an authoritarian 'government above the parties', in particular without the Social Democrats. Influential advisers (especially from among the *Reichswehr* leadership) who were not subject to any controls made him even more determined to act accordingly. In view of the functional weakness of the Reichstag, and despite being backed by the Centre Party, the new Chancellor, Heinrich Brüning, decided against governing in a parliamentary manner. As a result, the Reichstag's function was limited to toleration of government. Although the Reichstag had only been elected two years prior, Brüning decided to have it dissolved shortly after he had been appointed. Democracy moved one step closer towards disintegration when the elections of 1930 gave the NSDAP 18.3 per cent of the vote, compared to the May 1928 results of 2.6 per cent, making it the second strongest party. The democratic formation of a majority government had become impossible. Influenced by his irresponsible advisers, among

---

[2]  On the collapse of the Weimar Republic see Karl Dietrich Bracher, *Die Auflösung der Weimarer Republik*, Düsseldorf, 5th edn, 1984; Martin Broszat, *Die Machtergreifung. Der Aufstieg der NSDAP und die Zerstörung der Weimarer Republik*, Munich, 2nd edn, 1987; Eberhard Kolb, *Die Weimarer Republik*, Munich, Vienna, 1984; Hans Mommsen, *Die verspielte Freiheit. Der Weg der Republik von Weimar in den Untergang 1918 bis 1933*, Berlin, 1989; Hagen Schulze, *Weimar. Deutschland 1917–1933*, Berlin, 1982.

them a growing number of representatives of the East Elbian landed elites, Hindenburg relinquished his trust in Brüning in May 1932. The new Chanellor Franz von Papen worked towards a complete dissolution of parliamentarism, replacing it through an authoritarian reorganization of state and economy.

As shown by the party's election result, the political landscape had changed dramatically in favour of the NSDAP. The unspectacular results of the party's internal stabilization during the years of waiting now proved their worth. With the crisis of state and economy taking effect, the NSDAP was able to win over large sections of the nationalistic and anti-democratic electorate and increasing numbers of disenchanted former supporters of the moderate parities. In addition, the party mobilized many first-time voters and former non-voters. Although party membership fluctuated strongly, a substantial number of party supporters remained tied to it permanently.

Yet, the anti-democratic force which was building up with the NSDAP only achieved a decisive effect in semi-official or indirect cooperation with influential forces within the established power structure of the Republic. While working with the DNVP and the *Stahlhelm*[3] against the Young Plan of 1929, Hitler pulled his trump card: those anti-parliamentarian forces represented by the DNVP chairman Alfred Hugenberg needed a mass basis because an authoritarian government could not survive for long without support from the population. This support was not only offered by Hitler, but he seemed able to expand it. Despite some scepticism towards style and tone of the Nazis, the change in circumstances in 1930 made Hitler also a potential partner for other political camps. Even Brüning and the Centre attempted to have the government tolerated by the NSDAP. They hoped that the party's radicalism would be worn off by giving it political responsibility.

Hitler was under no pressure to accept such offers while Nazi voting figures were going up and it appeared possible to kill off the Republic in democratic elections.[4] In 1932, however, the NSDAP clearly reached the limits of its electoral potential and thus the limits of its prospects of gaining power on its own. To gain such a decisive lever of power as the

---

[3]   On the policies of the DNVP and other parties in the last years of the Weimar Republic see Erich Matthias and Rudolf Morsey (eds), *Das Ende der Parteien 1933*, Düsseldorf, 1960; on the political role of the *Stahlhelm* see Volker R. Berghahn, *Der Stahlhelm, Bund der Frontsoldaten 1918–1935*, Düsseldorf, 1966.
[4]   On the discussions among NSDAP leaders about the various ways to political power see Albrecht Tyrell, 'Der Aufstieg der NSDAP zur Macht', in Karl Dietrich Bracher, Manfred Funke and Hans-Adolf Jacobsen (eds), *Die Weimarer Republik 1918–1933, Politik, Wirtschaft, Gesellschaft* (Schriftenreihe der Bundeszentrale für politische Bildung, vol. 251), Bonn, 1987, 477ff.

Reich chancellery, Hitler needed patronage. His own powers were insufficient to overcome the final hurdle. Under the given circumstances, the Reich President held the key to Hitler's ambitions. That Hitler managed to gain access to Hindenburg was made possible by the conservative-authoritarian circles of Brüning's successors Franz von Papen and Kurt von Schleicher. They intended to use the NSDAP as a tool against the parties of the left and the trade unions and to overcome the parliamentary system. With the help of the mass support of the Nazis they hoped to legitimize their ideas of an authoritarian, employer-friendly new order without having to hand over power to Hitler. Social revolutionary elements in the NSDAP and above all in the SA would be tamed. Threatened by the economic crisis the East Elbian agrarian elites played a significant role among those speaking out in favour of Hitler. Most business leaders were closer to von Papen than to Hitler and only came to an arrangement with the NSDAP after Hitler's appointment as Chancellor – then, however, quite rapidly. Although the party received donations from industrial and banking circles before January 1933, it was certainly not dependent on big business.[5] Yet, the latter contributed none the less to the failure of the Republic by adopting an attitude which helped to undermine democracy.

Hitler remained distrustful towards attempts to tame him. His fear of becoming dependent made him insist on taking over the chancellorship after he had lost the elections for the Reich presidency in April 1932. In August Hindenburg brusquely opposed Hitler's appointment. Yet, Hitler continued to insist on his demand even though this seemed to endanger the very foundation (his seemingly unstoppable success) of his position inside and outside the party.

Among members and voters who had hoped for constructive measures to help the needy population such stubbornness caused disappointment and resentment. With the *Machtergreifung* (seizure of power) expected in 1931/32 the SA was looking forward to unrestricted actions against political enemies and rewards and benefits for such actions. In the Reichstag elections of November 1932, three months after the party's electoral triumph of 31 July (37.3 per cent), the NSDAP lost two million votes (33.1 per cent). In view of this development Reich Organization Leader Gregor Strasser, the second most important man in the party, and other party officials were prepared to enter a government led by Schleicher. They were confident that the party's dynamism would prove to be too powerful for its coalition partners. Yet, they did not manage to have it their way. By resigning from all party offices Strasser unwittingly increased the confusion which had gripped the NSDAP.[6] Hitler had come to a dead end.

At this critical juncture at the end of 1932 Papen's intrigues manoeuvred Hitler back onto the main road. After Schleicher had convinced Hindenburg to make him Chancellor at the beginning of December, Papen felt kicked out. Assisted by agreements with Hugenberg and the leaders of the *Stahlhelm* (and supported by some of the president's advisers) Papen managed to convince Hindenburg to make Hitler chancellor and himself Vice-chancellor of a 'Government of National Concentration'. It was the firm belief of Hitler's 'sponsors' that the government's three Nazi ministers were reliably surrounded by eight DNVP or non-party conservative-national ministers some of whom had previously belonged to Papen's own cabinet.

That Hitler and the unscrupulous dynamism of the Nazis were underestimated reveals the level of personal responsibility of the key protagonists which, alongside Weimar's birth defects, deficiencies in its constitutional structure and foreign, economic and psychological pressures, had a significant, indeed in the final phase decisive, impact on setting the course towards 30 January 1933.

## II

30 January 1933 may be used as a symbol for the Nazi *Machtergreifung*, yet, as has already been stated, it represents only the beginning of the comprehensive conquest of power.[7] What was the starting position from which the Nazi rule evolved? The Nazi contingent in the cabinet consisted of Reich chancellor Hitler, Reich interior minister Wilhelm Frick and Reich minister without portfolio Hermann Göring. The latter also acted as interior minister of the most important federal state, Prussia, which made up two-thirds of the territory of the German Reich. The

---

[6]   On the crisis of the NSDAP see Udo Kissenkoetter, *Gregor Strasser und die NSDAP*, Stuttgart, 1978; Axel Schildt, *Militärdiktatur mit Massenbasis? Die Querfrontkonzeption der Reichswehrführung um General von Schleicher am Ende der Weimarer Republik*, Frankfurt/Main, New York, 1981.

[7]   For a synopsis see Martin Broszat and Norbert Frei (eds), *Das Dritte Reich im Überblick. Chronik, Ereignisse, Zusammenhänge*, Munich, Zurich, 2nd edn, 1989; Norbert Frei, *Der Führerstaat. Nationalsozialistische Herrschaft 1933 bis 1945*, Munich, 1987; Klaus Hildebrand, *Das Dritte Reich*, Munich, Vienna, 3rd edn, 1987; Gotthard Jasper, *Die gescheiterte Zähmung. Wege zur Machtergreifung Hitlers 1930–1934*, Frankfurt/Main, 1986; Hans-Ulrich Thamer, *Verführung und Gewalt. Deutschland 1933–1945*, Berlin, 1986; see also Karl-Heinz Minuth (ed.), *Akten der Reichskanzlei, Regierung Hitler 1933–1938. Die Regierung Hitler, Teil 1: 1933/34*, Boppard, 1983.

Nazis also headed governments in various smaller states. Not only was the NSDAP clearly in a minority position in the Reich government, it also failed to control a majority in the Reichstag – even together with its coalition partner, the DNVP (8.9 per cent of the vote in the elections of November 1932). The NSDAP and DNVP were thus unable to demand the rescinding of presidential emergency decrees. While the NSDAP and SA had been preparing themselves for such a situation, they were still faced with a number of independent forces which adopted either an oppositional of a wait-and-see attitude towards the Nazis. In fact, future conflicts over objectives appeared very likely with those agencies which supported the new government or at least viewed it with interest.

The Nazi leadership therefore needed to tackle four tasks simultaneously: To secure permanently their newly-gained position of power, the Nazis had to eliminate all known opponents and get rid of or paralyse all organizations and institutions which might cause a threat. At the same time the Nazis needed to expand their power against their coalition partners by replacing opponents in key positions in state and society with reliable individuals or by creating new purpose-made institutions. The relationship to two power blocs, big business and *Reichswehr*, proved to be particularly complex. When they had helped, indeed partly prepared Hitler's appointment, both had been pursuing their own agenda. While Hitler attached great significance to both institutions, he was initially unable to influence them directly – hence his efforts to make his and their partially identical objectives a basis for cooperation. The future development of the relationship depended heavily on whether business and military leaders were to demand a say in the political goals of the regime (either via Hitler's coalition partners or directly) or whether the implementation of policies favouring business and military would prevent a potential anti-National Socialist pact and restrict their objectives to the economic and military sector. Whether business and military leaders could be gradually pushed to the margins of the political arena depended on the success of the regime and whether the population were to recognize National Socialism as the source of the regime's accomplishments. The fourth important task faced by the Nazis was therefore to achieve a change in the political-psychological climate. In order to replace the hitherto dominant feeling of despair with a mood of optimistic belief in the Nazi-inspired 'national rising' the party had to achieve not only an impression of activism and determination but also visible progress. For this purpose, the party had already learnt to master suitable methods such as mass propaganda and the oppression of political and ideological opponents.

The Nazis approached the tasks with an unscrupulous though not necessarily systematic determination. Nazi superiority over their coalition partners became particularly apparent in the manner in which the quest for power was extended to all areas of state and society and that both party and SA[8] proved to be suitable instruments to force through this 'totalitarian' agenda. Nazi pressure from below not only supported the demands and policies of the chancellor and party leader, but party and SA also developed their own strongly expansionist dynamism during the takeover of power.

Even before he was sworn into office, Hitler outplayed for the first time the two potentially most powerful cabinet members, Vice-chancellor von Papen and the 'economic dictator', Minister of Economics and Agriculture, Hugenberg. He convinced them to agree to the dissolution of the Reichstag followed by new elections, a process which could only benefit the NSDAP. During the period of election campaigning which ended on 5 March the government parties received substantial financial support from big business even though (with the exception of a pro-Hitler wing already active in 1932) a majority had previously given preference to a government led by Papen to one led by Hitler.[9]

Virtually all restrictions upon the Nazi propaganda and street terror apparatus were removed while new emergency decrees were introduced with the deliberate intention of impeding oppositional activities, above all meetings and publications of the left-wing parties. By handing the office of the Prussian Ministry of the Interior over to the Nazis, Hitler's coalition partners had given him control of the largest police force in the Reich. In addition, most of the 50,000 auxiliary police signed up by Göring in February came from the ranks of the SA and SS. On a local level, SA and party acted against opposition politicians and party officials. During the first half of 1933 tens of thousands were put into concentration camps (KZ) which were run by the police, SA or SS (since autumn 1933 by the political police only, that is *de facto* by the SS). In the KZ political opponents of National Socialism were to be 're-educated', instead prisoners were arbitrarily maltreated and their labour rigorously exploited without any right to appeal.[10]

Just before the elections Hitler was able to use the presidential emergency decree ('for the protection of the people and the state') of 28 February 1933 to create perhaps the most important, certainly the most characteristic basis of National Socialist rule. Whether the Nazis were

[8]    On the role of the *Sturmabteilungen* in 1933/34 see Peter Longerich, *Die braunen Bataillone. Geschichte der SA*, Munich, 1989, 165ff.

[9]    See the overview in Hans-Erich Volkmann, *Wirtschaft im Dritten Reich*, vol. 1: 1933–1939, Munich, 1980, 42ff and Reinhard Nebe, *Großindustrie, Staat und NSDAP 1930–1933*, Göttingen, 1981.

[10]    Falk Pingel, *Häftlinge unter SS-Herrschaft. Widerstand, Selbstbehauptung und Vernichtung im Konzentrationslager*, Hamburg, 1978.

behind the Reichstag fire of the evening of 27 February or whether, as appears most likely, an act of protest by a lone perpetrator, Marinus van der Lubbe, unintentionally played into their hands, is less significant than the fact that (and the manner in which) the new rulers took advantage of this alleged signal for a communist revolution. The government employed the so-called Reichstag Fire Decree (*Reichstagsbrandverordnung*) to repeal the fundamental political rights of the Weimar constitution 'temporarily' – *de facto* forever.[11] Introduced in a seemingly legal manner the state of emergency opened up the opportunity for future arbitrary application. The public at large accepted the new situation as its effects were initially directed mainly against the widely perceived revolutionary danger of the Communists. Their party was smashed and thousands of officials were arrested or had to go underground.

Despite such massive interference the result of the only semi-free March elections did not live up to Hitler's expectations. Only together with its coalition partners from the *Kampffront Schwarz-Weiß-Rot*[12] (8 per cent) did the NSDAP (43.9 per cent) achieve a small majority in the Reichstag. Hitler immediately focused on the complete elimination of parliament. At the same time, he aimed to make himself independent of the emergency decree powers of the Reich President which had hitherto been the basis of measures implemented by the government. A combination of pressure and verbal promises, effectively supported by the cleverly arranged symbolic reconciliation of the 'movement of the new Germany' and old Prussia (the photo of the Hitler-Hindenburg handshake of 21 March at the official opening of the Reichstag in the garrison church of Potsdam was printed in all newspapers) ensured a two-thirds majority in the Reichstag for Hitler's Enabling Law (*Ermächtigungsgesetz*) to change the constitution. With the KPD (12.3 per cent) forcibly kept away from parliament, only the SPD (18.3 per cent) voted against the euphemistically entitled 'Law for the Relief of Hardship of the People and the Reich' (*Gesetz zur Behebung der Not von Volk und Reich*). It enabled the government to pass laws without having to consult Reichstag and Reichsrat.[13]

Hitler's coalition partners welcomed the concentration of power in the executive and the removal of the separation of powers. The Catholic Centre Party (11.2 per cent), the most important of the middle-class parties of the centre, voted for the law because it hoped to prevent Hitler

[11]    Uwe Broderson (ed.), *Gesetze des NS-Staates*, Bad Homburg v.d.H., 1968, 69.

[12]    Until 1918, black–white–red had been the colours of the German Reich.

[13]    Rudolf Morsey (ed.), *Das 'Ermächtigungsgesetz' vom 24. März 1933*, Düsseldorf, 1992. The Reichstag renewed the Enabling Law in 1937 and 1939, and Hitler himself renewed it in 1943.

from ruling in a totally despotic fashion and to preserve some influence in the interest of its members and the 'Catholic cause'. Not only was such hope not shared by all Centre Party members, it also proved to be deceptive. Other expressions of loyalty did not help either – by voting in favour of the Enabling Law the centre and right-wing parties had deprived themselves of their own basis of existence. The SPD was banned on 22 June, all other parties dissolved themselves over the following two weeks. The *Stahlhelm* was subordinated to the SA. Hugenberg resigned from his ministerial posts on 27 June, the day which also marked the end of his party, the DNVP. He was replaced by two National Socialists. With the 'Law against the Formation of Political Parties' (*Gesetz gegen die Neubildung von Parteien*) of 14 July all parties other than the NSDAP were banned. Germany had officially become a one-party state.[14]

The Reichstag Fire Decree and the Enabling Law provided the Nazis with the mean to break through the constitutional system of the Weimar Republic at any point which seemed expedient to them. After his emigration from Berlin to the United States in 1938, Ernst Fraenkel, lawyer and later political scientist, used his personal observations to describe the Nazi system of power fittingly as a 'dual state' (*Doppelstaat*). This meant that the Nazis condoned the existence of a 'normative state' (*Normenstaat*) which, as a rule, respected established or new laws alongside a 'prerogative state' (*Maßnahmenstaat*) which, if necessary, ignored the very same laws.[15] In principle, the rule of law was not guaranteed any longer as the 'prerogative state' repressed it further and further. The continued existence of a legal framework – even the Weimar constitution of 1919 was never formally annulled – proved to be advantageous beyond the period of *Machtergreifung*. Not only did it allow the superficial pacification of everyday life, but it also gave the 'national revolution' a semblance of legality when it eliminated the *Rechtsstaat* in a seemingly constitutional manner.

When the Nazis intervened in the administrative and legal apparatus, their priority was to combat opponents of the regime and any individuals who refused to oblige Nazi demands for inclusion and subordination. Special decrees and courts ensured that public law and political criminal justice were increasingly removed from normal legal procedures. In April 1934 the *Volksgerichtshof* (People's Court of Law) with its members appointed by Hitler replaced the *Reichsgericht* (Reich Court) as the highest authority in cases of political crime. As a 'political tool fulfilling

[14]   Broderson (ed.), *Gesetze*, 74ff.
[15]   Ernst Fraenkel, *Der Doppelstaat*, Frankfurt/Main, Cologne, 1974, 13.

a political function in quasi-legal procedures' the *Volksgerichtshof* passed around 5,000 death sentences until 1945.[16]

Initially a kind of party police bound directly to Hitler, the SS evolved into a particularly important instrument of the extra-normative powers of the *Führer*. Within one year, Heinrich Himmler, qualified farmer and since 1929 *Reichsführer-SS*, managed to take control of the political police in all federal states. From April 1934, assisted by Reinhard Heydrich, head of the SS-*Sicherheitsdienst* (SD), Himmler directed the gradual centralization of the political police and its simultaneous removal from state control from the offices of the Prussian Secret State Police (Gestapo).[17]

Among the methods which the Nazis employed to remove the pluralistic democratic system, *Gleichschaltung* played a special role. By either using or threatening to use force the Nazis took over leading positions in public offices and in important institutions and associations. Thus, politically disempowered, their members were pulled together in unified organizations.

Under the pretence of having to unify the Reich the *Länder* (states) were coordinated in March and April 1933. Simultaneously, pressure was applied from above (Berlin) and below (SA and NSDAP rank-and-file) to force the establishment of National Socialist governments. On 11 April Göring took over the Prussian Minister Presidency from von Papen while in all other states Hitler installed Reich governors (*Reichsstatthalter*) who, with one exception, were also NSDAP *Gauleiter*. These newly-created authorities neither had clearly defined areas of responsibility nor were they clearly tied into the administrative hierarchy. In January 1934 the *Länder* lost their sovereign rights to the Reich and the state parliaments were dissolved. This *de-facto* centralization was, however, not brought to an official conclusion by the heralded Reich reform. The *Länder* continued to exist and the dual power structure, minister president versus Reich governor, was never abolished and was to cause a multitude of administrative problems.[18]

From February 1933 civil servants at community, state and Reich level were exposed to National Socialist pressure. In response, they either cooperated eagerly or conformed obediently. The first wave of arbitary

---

[16] Wolfgang Wagner, *Der Volksgerichtshof im nationalsozialistischen Staat*, Stuttgart, 1974, 861ff; see also Lothar Gruchmann, *Justiz im Dritten Reich 1933–1940. Anpassung und Unterwerfung in der Ära Gürtner*, Munich, Vienna, 2nd edn, 1990.

[17] Hans Buchheim, *SS und Polizei im NS-Staat*, Bonn, 1964, 33ff, 41; Shlomo Aronson, *Reinhard Heydrich und die Frühgeschichte von Gestapo und SD*, Stuttgart, 1971.

[18] Peter Diehl-Thiele, *Partei und Staat im Dritten Reich*, Munich, 1969, 37ff.

purges of politically unreliable individuals ended in April when the 'Law for the Restoration of the Professional Civil Service' (*Gesetz zur Wiederherstellung des Berufsbeamtentums*), its title again misleadingly glossing over its actual purpose, was introduced. It officially sanctioned the dismissal of civil servants for being 'nationally unreliable', Jewish, or having been appointed due to their membership of a political party. In addition, the law was aimed towards intimidating and disciplining others.[19]

While suppressing the KPD and getting rid of the influence of the SPD had been applauded by large sections of the bourgeoisie and in particular by business and *Reichswehr* leaders, the Nazis received a similar response from the same groups for their elimination of the three main trade unions with their millions of members. Yet, the Nazis pursued an additional objective with such measures: not only did they aim to destroy power bases of their political enemies, they also hoped to prepare the workers for Nazi objectives and, if possible, even win them over to the National Socialist cause. The dual strategy of wooing workers with notions of reconciliation and social harmony and using force was consequently more than simply a tactical trick. On 10 April 1933, the Reich government made 1 May, traditionally the day of labour movement demonstrations, a paid 'Holiday of National Labour'. On the very day, the trade unions were unable to oppose joint mass rallies as their membership, already demoralized by the lengthy crisis, had been further weakened by fear, opportunism and the swing in the nation's mood. On 2 May, SA and NSDAP officials and their supporters were able to occupy trade-union offices unopposed.[20]

Labour relations and company structures were subsequently reorganized in an authoritarian manner. All trade-union members were 'transferred' to the newly-founded DAF (German Labour Front), an organization affiliated to the NSDAP though legally independent. DAF took over the substantial trade-union assets, and its membership, though officially voluntary, grew to 20 million workers, employees and employers by 1938. DAF largely focused on the ideological-political training and the social welfare of its members, the latter task with the aim of increasing labour productivity. Large sections of the population did indeed regard improved social services and institutions such as

---

[19]   Hans Mommsen, *Beamtentum im Dritten Reich*, Stuttgart, 1966; Jane Caplan, 'Civil Service Support for National Socialism. An Evaluation', in Gerhard Hirschfeld and Lothar Kettenacker (eds), *Der 'Führerstaat': Mythos und Realität. Studien zur Struktur und Politik des Dritten Reiches*, Stuttgart, 1981, 167ff.
[20]   On the above and following see Tim W. Mason, *Arbeiterklasse und Volksgemeinschaft. Dokumente und Materialien zur deutschen Arbeiterpolitik 1936–1939*, Opladen, 1975.

the KdF (NS-Community Strength through Joy) with its leisure activities and holiday trips as promoting social progress and the concept of *Volksgemeinschaft*.

Instead of elected workers' representatives the authoritarian regime used *Betriebsführer* to look after the needs of both workers and employers. Yet, the elimination of trade unions and works committees did not automatically make employers absolute masters of their companies. After their introduction in May 1933 the so-called *Treuhänder der Arbeit* (Trustees of Labour) determined all wage-related issues. These 'middle-men' between employers and employees were civil servants from the Reich Labour Ministry and were thus bound by governmental orders. Nazi wage policies were, however, decidedly biased towards property and business owners. Despite the growing cost of living the Nazis froze the hourly wage rate at the crisis level of 1932 in order to boost rearmament by reducing the demand for consumer goods.

Unlike the working class, big business arranged itself with the new regime in a much more cooperative manner. Regime and business leaders shared a number of important objectives, most notably the elimination of socio-political sources of friction and an increase in production, the latter to be largely achieved by an enormous expansion of state expenditure on rearmament.[21] Anti-capitalist aspirations among wide sections of the party's middle-class membership were usually pushed aside with the regime glossing over its lack of interest propagandistically and with a few social 'sweeteners'. The financial pressures created by rearmament left little room for the demands of craftsmen and small retailers.[22] The industrial sector, and in particular the 'engines' of rearmament, heavy and chemical industry, managed to retain a high degree of autonomy during the first three years of the regime. Such autonomy was, however, limited to private and governmental economic policy. Business leaders were unable to manipulate Hitler's foreign policy and his preparations for war.

In 1933, the Nazi leadership took control of all agrarian associations and organizations including those involved in the processing and

---

[21]  Rearmament expenditure in 1933 amounted to 0.7 billion Reichsmark (RM), other expenditure to RM5.6 billion. In 1934 the figures were 3.3 and 5.9, and in 1936 9 and 7.9 respectively; Karl Dietrich Erdmann, *Die Zeit der Weltkriege*, Stuttgart, 1976, 404. See also Hans-Erich Volkmann, 'Die NS-Wirtschaft in Vorbereitung des Krieges', in Wilhelm Deist, Manfred Messerschmidt, Hans-Erich Volkmann and Wolfram Wette, *Ursachen und Voraussetzungen der deutschen Kriegspolitik (Das Deutsche Reich und der Zweite Weltkrieg*, Vol. 1), Stuttgart, 1979, 239ff.
[22]  Adelheid von Saldern, *Mittelstand im 'Dritten Reich'. Handwerker-Einzelhändler-Bauern*, Frankfurt/Main, New York, 1979.

trading of agricultural products.[23] Under the leadership of Reich Peasants Leader and Minister of Agriculture Richard Walther Darré, the RNS (Reich Food Estate) reached a membership of nearly 17 million in the second half of the 1930s. Since the regime anticipated a high degree of self-sufficiency in foodstuffs, it responded positively to demands made by the crisis-wracked farming community, in particular demands for stable prices and stable property conditions.

The process of *Gleichschaltung* was also extended to professional associations, youth organizations – on 1 December 1936 the HJ (Hitler Youth) was officially put in charge of educating Germany's youth when outside parental and school supervision[24] – the education sector, culture and, of course, the media. On 13 March 1933, Joseph Goebbels, hitherto the party's Reich Propaganda Leader, was promoted to the position of Reich Minister for People's Enlightenment and Propaganda. Goebbels put all his energy into the expansion of his apparatus 'for the influencing of people's minds, and the promotion of state, culture and economy', for propaganda abroad and the supervision of Germany's cultural life.[25] In summer 1933, Goebbels' ministry took control of the supervision and direction of Germany's press, a control which was subsequently tightened by forced changes to staff and by economic pressure. Since Goebbels recognized that radio would be a particularly valuable means to influence the masses, he instigated the large-scale production of a cheap receiver, the *Volksempfänger*, and communal listening in factories and other locations.[26]

Nazi propaganda largely managed to convince an essentially receptive population and foreign observers that the policies of the new regime were unified and purposeful (which they were certainly not all the time) and that there was sufficient reason for optimism. Germany's economic recovery, strongly assisted by the positive development of the world economy, public work-creation schemes and eventually by rearmament, certainly helped.

Goebbels also took an active interest in Germany's cultural life by creating and supervising the Reich Chamber of Culture. As one of its main tasks the Chamber organized the removal of 'undesirables' by

---

[23]  Horst Gies, 'Die Rolle des Reichsnährstandes im nationalsozialistischen Herrschaftssystem', in Hirschfeld and Kettenacker, *Der 'Führerstaat'*, 270ff; Volkmann, 'Die NS-Wirtschaft', in his *Wirtschaft im Dritten Reich*, 213ff; Saldern, *Mittelstand*, 67ff, 113ff.
[24]  Broderson (ed.), *Gesetze*, 81f.
[25]  Decree on the Responsibilities of the Reich Ministry for People's Enlightenment and Propaganda, 30 June 1933; ibid., 159ff.
[26]  Ansgar Diller, *Rundfunkpolitik im Dritten Reich*, Munich, 1980.

applying the arbitrary criterion of 'the *Volk*'s healthy emotions' – which usually amounted to dull anti-modern mass taste. Membership of the chamber was compulsory. *Kulturschaffende* (creative artists) who were refused access, in particular Jews, were faced with a total ban on their work and in many cases they were forced to emigrate.

By demanding total control the Nazi regime created particular problems in the education and training sector and in its relationship with the churches. At the centre of Nazi ideology and their perception of people were *Volk* and race. These concepts were neither clearly defined nor clearly definable, yet such vagueness only helped to heighten their attraction, especially during the *Kampfzeit* ('years of struggle'). Precise steps for the re-formation of state and society which became possible after the *Machtergreifung* had only been vaguely alluded to. Those measures which were introduced proved to be largely of a negative nature. The process of pushing Germany's 500,000 Jews (less than one per cent of the Reich population) out of public life was immediately put into motion by depriving them of their rights and by arbitrary attacks by party and SA members.[27] Forced sterilization was legalized 'in order to prevent hereditarily ill offspring'.[28]

Since National Socialism as an ideology lacked clear-cut demarcations, it was possible to derive differing programmatical demands for individual sectors of state and society. In a number of cases this led to internal party competition which was only heightened by the particular circumstances which evolved during the *Machtergreifung*. The Nazi regime had not always ensured that the elimination of opponents and the securing of power were clearly coordinated. Various party agencies were therefore able to create their own power bases. By insisting on earlier demands or by branching out into new areas of activity they then proceeded to realize their own interpretation of Nazi ideology.[29]

Despite the vagueness of their ideology the Nazis were in no doubt that by emphasizing *Volk* and race (*Recht ist was dem Volke nützt*) they

[27]   Uwe Dietrich Adam, *Judenpolitik im Dritten Reich*, Düsseldorf, 1972, 46ff; Helmut Genschel, *Die Verdrängung der Juden aus der Wirtschaft im Dritten Reich*, Göttingen, 1966; Avraham Barkai, *Vom Boykott zur 'Entjudung'. Der wirtschaftliche Existenzkampf der Juden im Dritten Reich 1933–1943*, Frankfurt/Main, 1988.

[28]   Broderson (ed.), *Gesetze*, 116ff; Kurt Nowak, *'Euthanasie' und Sterilisierung im 'Dritten Reich'. Die Konfrontation der evangelischen und der katholischen Kirche mit dem Gesetz zur Verhütung erbkranken Nachwuchses und der 'Euthanasie'-Aktion*, Göttingen, 2nd edn, 1980, 64ff.

[29]   On the effects on the education sector of the internal party rivalries see, for instance, Horst Scholz, *Nationalsozialistische Ausleseschulen. Internatsschulen als Herrschaftsmittel des Führerstaates*, Göttingen, 1973; Manfred Heinemann (ed.), *Erziehung und Schulung im Dritten Reich*, 2 vols, Stuttgart, 1980.

made a claim on the entire person. Unavoidably, this led to conflicts with the churches which would not allow the subordination of God's authority to state decrees. An immediate break was, however, not opportune to Hitler as he tried to prevent tense relations with the large church following. His efforts in 1933/34 to use the churches for his own ends received considerable support among the church hierarchy and their followers.[30] In an atmosphere of national recovery the new regime pronounced order, social harmony, and the fight against Marxism, Liberalism, materialism and moral decline – objectives which all corresponded to Christian principles. By signing the Concordat with the Vatican in July 1933, Hitler allowed the Catholic Church to retain its area of influence. Not long after, however, deliberate anti-Church measures were introduced with the intention of pushing the Church out of the public sphere, in particular out of the education and youth sector.

Initially, the Protestant Churches, organizationally and doctrinally less unified than their Catholic counterpart, showed some interest in the creation of a united Reich church. The state, however, proceeded to give massive support to the Nazistic 'German Christians' who worked towards a 'dejewification' of church and Christian doctrine. This was immediately resisted by a minority, most notably by the so-called *Bekennende Kirche* (Confessing Church) which, from 1934, tried to work against the *Gleichschaltung* and restriction of church activities. Like their Catholic counterparts this opposition was based above all on the recognition that the basic religious truths of Christianity were incompatible with National Socialist ideology. Only rarely, however, were protests voiced against the obvious crimes, later mass murders, committed by the regime.

During the process of safeguarding and expanding its power the NSDAP did not simply take over leading political and administrative offices in the manner of a normal change of government. Instead, the Nazis frequently adopted an uncoordinated and arbitrary approach which, as previously explained, included taking control of associations and organizations beyond state control. In doing so lower party echelons were rarely guided by purely political motives. Nazi *alte Kämpfer*[31] expected both to be rewarded for their actions and to be included in the running of the country: hence the wide-spread autocratic distribution of offices on a local and municipal level. Frequently, conflicts erupted between various party agencies and officials. Arbitrary interventions

---

[30]   Klaus Scholder, *Die Kirchen und das Dritte Reich*, vol. 1 *Vorgeschichte und Zeit der Illusionen 1918–1934*, vol. 2 *Das Jahr der Ernüchterung 1934*, Frankfurt/Main, 1977, 1985.
[31]   Those actively involved in the 'years of struggle'.

and attacks removed the political power which the civil service had derived from its relative unity and influence. Its ability to function properly was also affected even though the Nazis, lacking qualified personnel and detailed expertise, depended on the cooperation of civil servants. Added concerns about the attitude of business and military leaders made it increasingly necessary in summer 1933 to restrict the dynamism of the party and SA.

On 6 July 1933, after the dissolution of the parties, Hitler declared an end to the 'National Socialist Revolution'.[32] Yet the demands of the party and SA were not at all satisfied. Adding to that dissatisfaction was the increasing reduction of their main tasks, aggressive propaganda and the conquest of the streets. The 'Law to Secure the Unity of the Party and the State' (*Gesetz zur Sicherung der Einheit von Partei und Staat*) of 1 December 1933 was to make the NSDAP a body of public law. As 'bearer of the German idea of the state and insolubly coupled to the state' the party's position vis-à-vis the state apparatus had been visibly boosted[33] though this step did not constitute a clear-cut institutionalization of the party's role. Hitler's slogan 'The party commands the state'[34] sounded unambiguous, but proved to be realizable only in a largely indirect way as the NSDAP had not been able to take over, or at least infiltrate, most of the existing bureaucratic structures immediately. That most Nazis who took over public offices in 1933 shared a desire for orderly administrative procedures only created more conflict between party agencies with their numerous special demands and civil authorities from the ministerial bureaucracy down to the local communities.[35]

As a mass organization the power of the NSDAP decreased.[36] Until 1933 the various organizational sections of the party had been kept together by their common struggle. After the *Machtergreifung*, however, a process of differentiation began within the party which led to the loss of important functions and created competition from within the party's own ranks. Nazi Reich propaganda leader Goebbels transferred the central direction of propaganda activities to his own ministry. DAF and SS became almost totally autonomous, the former due to its financial

---

[32] Max Domarus, *Hitler. Reden und Proklamationen 1932–1945*, vol. 1, Munich, 1966, 286ff.
[33] Broderson (ed.), *Gesetze*, 78ff.
[34] Diehl-Thele, *Partei und Staat*, 18ff.
[35] Horst Matzerath, *Nationalsozialismus und kommunale Selbstverwaltung*, Stuttgart, 1970.
[36] See Jeremy Noakes, 'The Nazi Party and the Third Reich: The Myth and Reality of the One Party State', in J. Noakes (ed.), *Government, Party, and People in Nazi Germany*, Exeter, 2nd edn, 1981, 11ff.

independence from the party (and because its leader, Robert Ley, did not use his other role as the party's Reich Organization Leader to take command of the party Gauleiter). Both organizations increasingly appropriated tasks in the education and control of the population. Competing agencies also weakened the party's role in the training of future leaders. In the main, the NSDAP retained the propagandistic indoctrination and political-ideological control of the population both communally and privately at district and local branch level. The party also used its block and cell system together with affiliated professional organizations for the training of its members and for social welfare activities.

A few functionaries, however, held a significant share of power. Through Rudolf Heß, previously Hitler's secretary and from April 1933 the Führer's deputy in party matters, the party was able to influence Reich policies. Although Heß lacked assertiveness (but had the power-conscious Martin Bormann, his chief-of-staff, at his side), he was made a Reich minister on 1 December 1933 after he had already attended cabinet meetings since June. After 1934 all ministries had to involve him in their legislation and decree procedures. In addition, they were obliged to include Heß in the appointment and promotion of higher civil servants.

The SA failed to find a new role for itself. It proved to be largely unsuccessful in gaining favourable positions against its competitors in state and party. Moreover, during 1933/34 its activities made it increasingly a doubly disruptive factor. On the one hand, SA members, among them many unemployed, felt insufficiently rewarded for their sacrifices in the struggle for power – hence their vociferous call for a 'Second Revolution' to satisfy their social demands. On the other hand, a challenge was posed to the Reichswehr by plans for the future role of the SA. These had been developed by, above all, the SA's chief of staff, the retired army captain Ernst Röhm. Röhm intended to unite SA and Reichswehr into a 'People's Army' in which the former would use its quantitative superiority to become the dominant force.

Despite the vagueness of Röhm's notions the Reichswehr, still limited in size by the Treaty of Versailles (100,000 men), had reason to feel alarmed. Yet, the demands made by the SA also ran counter to Hitler's intentions. Under the given circumstances a qualitatively superior attack force, as planned by Hitler, could only be created by expanding the existing cadres of the Reichswehr, not, however, by the time-consuming process of reshaping the street-fighting troops of the party.[37]

[37]   Klaus-Jürgen Müller, *Das Heer und Hitler. Armee und nationalsozialistisches Regime 1933–1940*, Stuttgart, 1969, 89ff.

Since entering office Hitler had made a conscious effort to convince the *Reichswehr* to keep still, indeed support the Nazis, while they stabilized their hold on power. The *Reichswehr* (and big business) could have seriously disrupted this process, yet Hitler again benefited from an initial concurrence of aims. Both he and the military leadership aimed to revise the political and military restrictions imposed by the Treaty of Versailles, to attain military parity, to rearm and to increase the military preparedness of the German population. It was of no consequence that views on the future employment of the military instrument might have differed. As early as December 1933 it was decided to expand the strength of the *Reichswehr* in peacetime to 300,000 men.

Attempts to achieve some understanding between SA and *Reichswehr* remained unsuccessful. On 30 June 1934, Hitler finally used rumours that Röhm was planning a putsch as a pretext to have him and other SA leaders killed by the SS with the assistance of the *Reichswehr*. The SA emerged as a politically insignificant mass organization which was largely concerned with the military training of men before and after their military service.[38] The SS, however, was rewarded by having its official subordination to the SA removed. Instead the organization was made directly answerable to Hitler.

Even though the *Reichswehr* managed to maintain its role as the nation's sole 'bearer of arms', its independence had suffered from its involvement in the murders. Morally already corrupted by the regime the *Reichswehr* leadership's position was weakened further immediately after Hindenburg's death on 2 August 1934. Not only was Hitler permitted to combine the offices of Reich chancellor and Reich president, the *Reichswehr* also agreed to swear an oath of total obedience to the *Führer*. Increasingly thereafter the *Wehrmacht* (the official title of the armed forces from 1935) came to be preoccupied with its growing military tasks. Political activities, so strongly pursued before 1933, were reduced to a point where the military leadership ceased to be an independent political factor.[39] Little resistance was shown when, in February 1938, Hitler pushed aside certain concerns about the methods and ultimate objective of his foreign policy. In making himself supreme commander of the *Wehrmacht* Hitler demonstrated very clearly that the armed forces had become a complete tool of his regime.

---

[38] Longerich, *Die braunen Bataillone*, 220ff.
[39] For an overview see Wilhelm Deist, 'Die Aufrüstung der Wehrmacht', in Deist et al. *Ursachen und Voraussetzungen*, 400ff.

III

Developments since 1933 show that the most significant, initially independent protagonists, Hitler and his party, big business and Reichswehr as well as the only briefly independent administrative apparatus, shared a sufficient number of objectives to allow close cooperation – even if business and military leaders did not necessarily share Hitler's ultimate goal, the domination of Europe based on racial principles. That Hitler largely satisfied the particular aims of these groups enabled him to incorporate them more strongly into his overall system. The rapid consolidation of the Nazi regime was achieved with the conquest of positions of power in both politics and society, the implementation of *Gleichschaltung*, and the use of propaganda and terror. By the second half of the 1930s, business and *Wehrmacht* leaders had forfeited their political power to the Nazi leadership. Their *Gleichschaltung* followed suit and with it their subordination to the primacy of politics embodied by Hitler. A reversal of this process was, however, not attempted as both groups continued to benefit from the policies of the Nazi regime.

Until Hindenburg's death the complex process commonly known as *Machtergreifung* had neither evolved systematically nor been completed. As a preliminary result the cooperation between the national conservative enemies of democracy and the National Socialists laid, however, the foundation for the subsequent evolution of the Nazi system of rule. The 2nd August 1934 saw the establishment of National Socialism as the leading political power in Germany, even if its embodiment the 'Führer and Reich chancellor' Adolf Hitler tolerated only limited independent developments within the framework of the system. In practice this meant that Hitler was able to delegate and legitimize authority on any level he judged it advisable to do so, a practice quite similar to that within the NSDAP before 1933. Both the control and separation of powers were removed. Not only did constitutional law experts not speak out against the Reichstag's acclamation of Hitler as 'the people's supreme judge', they even eagerly supported the move which had been instigated in light of the events of 30 June 1934.[40] When using the political, bureaucratic, military and economic apparatus Hitler was not bound to legal norms. Once a decision had been taken, it could result in a law or decree or even, as a *Führerbefehl*, in a personal order.

Below Hitler, however, the seizure of power did not lead to an orderly and systematic allocation of responsibilities between state agencies and

[40]  Domarus, *Hitler*, vol. 1, 421 (13 July 1934).

various party officials. A multi-layered jumble of responsibilities emerged and expanded.[41] Under such circumstances, it was usually much more important to possess personal connections, especially with Hitler, than to have specialist knowledge. This conclusion strongly contradicts the regime's claim that it accomplished the 'monolithic unity' of political power over the divisions which had previously existed in the pluralistic parliamentary democracy. This was already recognized by shrewd contemporary observers.

This conflict between the various structural features of the Nazi system of rule remained its fundamental characteristic. Throughout its history the Third Reich never advanced beyond the provisional arrangement which had emerged during the period of *Machtergreifung*.

---

[41]   See, for instance, Reinhard Bollmus, *Das Amt Rosenberg und seine Gegner. Zum Machtkampf im nationalsozialistischen Herrschaftssystem*, Stuttgart, 1970; Hans Mommsen, 'Hitlers Stellung im nationalsozialistischen Herrschaftssystem', in Hirschfeld and Kettenacker (eds), *Der 'Führerstaat'*, particularly 57ff; Jeremy Noakes, 'Oberbürgermeister and Gauleiter: City Government between Party and State', in ibid., 149ff; see also Manfred Funke, *Starker oder schwacher Diktator? Hitlers Herrschaft und die Deutschen*, Düsseldorf, 1989.

# Foreign Policy

# 3

# The Structure of Nazi Foreign Policy 1933–1945

## *Hans-Adolf Jacobsen*

Translation by Christian Leitz of Hans-Adolf Jacobsen, 'Zur Struktur der NS-Außenpolitik 1933–1945', in Manfred Funke (ed.), *Hitler, Deutschland und die Mächte; Materialien zur Außenpolitik des Dritten Reiches*, Athenäum/Droste Taschenbücher Geschichte, Düsseldorf, 1978.

### *Editor's Introduction*

The study of Nazi Germany's foreign policy and international relations may have become rather marginalized, but its centrality to our under-standing of the Third Reich has not diminished. To Hitler, it was distinctly clear that the achievement of his objectives hinged upon the successful conduct of foreign policy, including, of course, the preparation and waging of war. It is an undeniable fact that all other goals of the Third Reich, including its economic plans, its anti-Semitic policies, and its pursuit of a 'classless' society or *Volksgemeinschaft*, depended in one way or another upon the regime's foreign policy.

Yet, as Hans-Adolf Jacobsen shows, Hitler's central goals were pursued within a chaotic structure. A multitude of agencies, of which the Foreign Ministry, the official organ of foreign policy, was just one, competed for control of Nazi foreign policy. But Hitler, Jacobsen writes, was not a 'weak dictator'. Instead, the Führer presided over polycratic chaos without losing sight of his objectives.

Although we need to see Jacobsen's article in the context of what other historians have published more recently on foreign policy-making in the Third Reich,[1] it continues to provide a useful basis for the discussion of

[1] See in particular Stefan Kley, *Hitler, Ribbentrop und die Entfesselung des Zweiten Weltkriegs*, Paderborn, 1996; Klaus Hildebrand, *Deutsche Außenpolitik 1933–1945, Kalkül oder Dogma?*, Stuttgart, 5th edn, 1990; Marie-Luise Recker, *Die Außenpolitik des Dritten*

a multitude of issues related not only to Nazi foreign policy, but also more generally to the structure and operation of the regime.

Reiches, Munich, 1990; Charles Bloch, *Le IIIe Reich et le monde*, Paris, 1986; Gerhard L. Weinberg, *The Foreign Policy of Hitler's Germany: Diplomatic Revolution in Europe, 1933–36*, Chicago, 1970; Gerhard L. Weinberg, *The Foreign Policy of Hitler's Germany; Starting World War II 1937–1939*, Chicago, 1980.

# The Structure of Nazi Foreign Policy 1933–1945

*Hans-Adolf Jacobsen*

After Hitler had been appointed Reich Chancellor in 1933 – the first step towards the realization of his political plans – he and his closest confidants were faced with the question of which state and party institutions they had at their disposal and which ones they needed to create in order to undertake the tasks they had in mind. Under the Weimar Republic the instruments of foreign policy were derived from constitutional theory, international obligations, and the practice of domestic policy-making. Although Reich president, Reich chancellor and foreign minister were usually the key figures in the political power play, they frequently had to take heed of the views of Reichstag, Foreign Policy Committee, parties, experts, the public and individuals or coordinate their intentions with them even when it seemed unnecessary owing to the minor significance of a matter in hand.[1] During the process of totalitarian *Gleichschaltung* Hitler reduced a large portion of those offices essential to the process of forming democratic opinion, yet it would be a mistake to assume that the Third Reich saw less competition and mutual control among groups than before 1933.

After the event, and for the purpose of justification, appearances and sham legitimacy, Hitler had certain foreign policy decisions 'sanctioned' by popular plebiscite. In doing so he also intended to send a strong signal to the world that the German people were firmly united. He 'proved' to the western democracies that the Nazi state practised 'better democracy' when it 'ensured the confidence of the people' in every one of its steps.

Initially advised by those ministers connected with foreign policy, later also by Göring, the outsider Ribbentrop, and finally Bormann, Hitler personally determined from the beginning the major foreign policy objectives. In doing so he demonstrated Germany's national interests to other states. Over the years, his growing expertise and successes led him to take decisions in an increasingly high-handed manner. Nonetheless, in the wider area of foreign policy he allowed state and party offices extensive scope for activities of the most diverse nature.

[1]  For a comprehensive analysis of the foreign policy of the Weimar Republic see Peter Krüger, *Die Außenpolitik der Republik von Weimar*, Darmstadt, 1985.

Although Hitler, as Führer and Reich Chancellor, determined policy guidelines which even the party had to observe unconditionally, these did not always correspond to the aims espoused by the NSDAP in the 1920s. Initially, a number of compromises had to be arrived at, tactical retreats had to be mounted and partial renunciations had to be announced while Germany needed to rearm and was going through the 'danger zone' of the period to 1938. This apparent contradiction between theory and practice bewildered some *alte Kämpfer* ('old fighters') who did not really understand that this departure from the central demands was solely necessitated for dialectical reasons. On occasion, they, in fact, interpreted it as 'treason against the idea'. This 'cover-up' was taken to a point where in 1936, for instance, the press was ordered not to cite indiscriminately sections in *Mein Kampf* pertaining to foreign policy. The book, the press was told, had been written in 1924 and was based on the 'political situation then'; today its importance was purely that of 'a historical source'.

*Reichsführer* Rosenberg advised a French journalist in 1935 that *Mein Kampf* contained many points about Germany's policies towards Eastern Europe which were not worth discussing today. Germany wanted to get its house in order and avoid war. Proof of its good intentions were the treaty with Poland (1934) and the trade relations with Russia even though anything that might serve Soviet-Communist propaganda was of course stopped. Such comments were very much along the lines of those made by Hitler. Repeatedly, he emphatically told the public that his 'active peace policy', which corrected his writings, would reserve him a place in the annals of history. In a similar vein, German diplomats reassured foreign representatives that Hitler's expositions in *Mein Kampf*, which had often led to erroneous conclusions about the foreign policy direction of the Reich, had evolved as a domestic broadsheet under the 'impact of a lost war and the events in the Ruhr which preoccupied Germany at the time'. Not the 'printed word' of the past was of relevance, but the present-day peace and reconciliation policy of the Führer and Reich Chancellor.[2]

Today we know that many statesmen at home and abroad came to believe in these appeasing remarks because only with difficulty could they imagine a radicalization of Germany's foreign policy in accordance with Nazi demands. Vociferous pronouncements of slogans such as, to name only two, that of the 'volkish state' or the 'Germanic community of faith' were regarded as pure propaganda which no rational person should take at face value.

---

[2]   All above quotes in Hans-Adolf Jacobsen, *Nationalsozialistische Außenpolitik 1933–1938*, Frankfurt/Main, 1968, 16ff.

The instruments of Nazi foreign policy evolved in two ways. On the one side the old state offices, which were only gradually subjected to *Gleichschaltung*, initially continued to work relatively undisturbed by outside influences. These offices included the Foreign Ministry, the Reich Interior Ministry, the Reich Economics and Finance Ministries and the Reich Defense (from 1935 War) Ministry, the latter of particular importance in the area of secret intelligence gathering. On the other side a series of new and non-governmental offices of the party and the economy emerged which competed with the traditional institutions and among themselves. Their struggle for positions of power and the occasionally rather confusing frontlines which arose from it formed an essential characteristic of the National Socialist Führer state. None of these offices was given a distinct and clearly delimited area of responsibility. This can be attributed largely to the fact that the totalitarian state suspended the separation of powers and replaced it with the Führer principle which meant being answerable to those above and critical of those below. It can also be explained however by the fact that, due to their totally insufficient expertise, the Nazi leaders never really managed to move beyond a stage of experimentation and improvisation. In all likelihood, Hitler often consciously failed to take clear-cut decisions in order to play individuals off against each other, to strengthen his position as the person holding the most important reins and to maintain his absolute position of power. In addition, he repeatedly avoided taking decisions in acknowledgement of certain tactical requirements or out of consideration for the sensibilities of high-ranking party officials.

From 1933, it was typical of the style of Nazi foreign policy that Hitler increasingly put leading state and party personalities in charge of special missions or instructed them to interpret his 'peaceful' approach, that is a policy aimed only towards 'equal status' and 'the restoration of honour'. In the Reich and abroad it was up to, among others, Goebbels, Ley, Rosenberg, Heß, Göring, Schacht, Keppler and Oberlindober to do the sounding out and make the pronouncements. Apart from taking over delicate and secret missions, they were to take care of the manipulation of public opinion and to calm those outside Germany who had been outraged and incensed by the first excesses of the Nazi revolution. For such purposes Hitler also sometimes used other even more credible groups, including initially representatives of the churches. At the same time, it also happened that individual Gauleiter were ordered into the Reich Chancellery where Hitler gave them special assignments of a foreign political nature.

There can be no doubt that even more serious consequences resulted from the activities of the *Reichsministerium für Volksaufklärung und Propaganda* (ProMi) and numerous non-governmental agencies, most notably the *Außenpolitisches Amt* (APA) under Rosenberg, the *Auslandsorganisation* (AO) under Bohle, the leadership committees for *Volkstum* policies of the *Dienststelle Ribbentrop*, and the SS under Himmler. In fact, other groups or organizations of the party and certain associations also tried to gain some influence, among those the HJ, the RNS, the *Reichsarbeitsdienst*, the *NS-Frauenschaft*, the *Kolonialpolitisches Amt der NSDAP*, several Gauleiter and the *NS-Studentenbund*. In their own fields, each of them regarded it as their mission to realize the Führer's will at home and abroad. As a whole, however, the bounds of their activities were quite limited.

Before examining the functions of the most important offices within the framework of Nazi foreign policy, it will be necessary to describe the traditional instrument of foreign policy – the *Auswärtiges Amt*.

### Auswärtiges Amt (AA)

An important step in the development of Germany's Foreign Ministry was the Law on Provisional Reich Power of 10 February 1919 which turned the AA (like other Reich agencies) into a Reich ministry headed by a minister who was answerable to the Reichstag. Simultaneously all previous undersecretaries of state were replaced by permanent state secretaries. Shortly afterwards Privy Councillor Schüler's reform brought about the merging of the previously separate diplomatic and consular career tracks and the dissolution of the specialist departments. Instead, six *Länderabteilungen* were created largely along regional lines (Depts. II–VII: so-called 'regional system'). In practice, however, this turned out to be too large a fragmentation and too personnel-intensive to be financially viable. Towards the end of 1921 the number of regional departments was therefore reduced by half. This organizational system was largely continued until 1936. During this fifteen-year period the AA was structured as follows:

I. Department for Personnel and Administrative Questions.
II. Department Europe (apart from Britain, Russia, and the countries bordering the Baltic and Scandinavia).
III. Department Britain, America, Africa, Orient (Turkey).
IV. Department Scandinavia, Poland, Russia, the countries bordering the Baltic (including Memel), Upper Silesia, and the Far East.

In addition, specialist departments (V. Department for Legal Affairs, and VI. Department for Cultural Affairs) were formed as it was obviously not possible to deal with all tasks within the regional structure. Further components of the structure were the Foreign Trade Office, the Protocol (created from Special Department E, i.e. etiquette) and the two *Referate* Germany and the League of Nations.

On 15 May 1936 the AA was restructured in a way that amounted basically to a reintroduction of the *Realsystem* which had been dominant until 1918. The regional departments were united into the *Politische Abteilung* (Political Department) while all tasks of an economic nature were taken over by the *Handelspolitische Abteilung* (Department for Trade Affairs). From 1936 the AA consisted of five specialist departments of equal standing (Administration/Personnel, Politics, Trade, Law, Culture), Press-Protocol and *Referat D* (Sub-department Germany). This structure remained the basis of the ministry until 1945.[3]

The responsibilities of the AA resulted from the guidelines issued by each Reich chancellor, from traditional practices and general obligations in the fields of politics, economics and culture. The AA represented the official interests abroad of the German Reich, its people and state. In doing so the ministry was always conscious of the instrumental character of its activities. To master the manifold tasks and problems in Europe and around the world, diplomats and senior civil servants, who had been chosen by a particular method and trained according to uniform principles, needed to observe carefully foreign and domestic policy developments – if relevant to Germany's foreign policy – in all countries. To achieve this they had to collect all news material, sift through it and assess it on the basis of their own requirements. Their most important task consisted therefore in putting together a reliable picture of the outside world in the light of Germany's interests – thus providing a secure basis on which foreign policy decisions could be arrived at or any possible alternatives considered. The primary part of this process consisted in the constant exchange of experiences and impressions between delegations abroad and the headquarters in Berlin. The AA received a daily stream of a great variety of open or secret telegrams and reports – with a corresponding amount of dispatches going out. This kind of work demanded of each civil servant a high degree of expertise and a strong sense of responsibility.

Closely connected was the second task which required the AA, after collating and considering the information available to it, to offer Germany's political leaders proposals and recommendations in the field

[3]   Cf. the brief overview by H-G. Sasse in *100 Jahre Auswärtiges Amt 1870–1970*, Bonn, 1970, 23ff, and P. Seabury, *Die Wilhelmstraße. Die Geschichte der deutschen Diplomatie 1930–1945*, Frankfurt/Main, 1956.

of foreign policy. This process took place through the official channels (via permanent state secretary and foreign minister to the Reich chancellor) with the AA conducting all resulting matters of a diplomatic and foreign political nature according to the instructions of the minister. As it had to implement decisions taken at the highest level, outstanding professional ability was required. The AA certainly played an important role in the revisionist policy pursued between 1933 and 1938 and as an active representative of German interests abroad.

A further area of responsibility consisted in representing Germany to the outside world. If possible, the AA had to eliminate opposition against the Reich and to defend it against any damaging exertion of influence by foreign states. It had to direct Germany's numerous legations abroad (from consulate to embassy level) in a uniform manner, to lay down the 'language' to be used towards each host country, to promote trade and to intensify cultural exchange. Above all, however, the AA was entrusted with the protection and care of Reich Germans abroad, a task which, during the Third Reich, frequently led to sharp controversies between the representatives of Reich and party.

*Referat D*, reintroduced in 1933, was instructed to observe political developments at home as far as these were relevant to foreign policy. At the same time, the department also acted as liaison office to the organizations of the NSDAP and supported the permanent state secretary in the coordination of the political work of the AA towards various domestic agencies. Finally, it kept a check on attempts by foreign countries to influence domestic policy making.

After a reduction at the end of the First World War staffing levels of the AA slowly increased to reach 2,232 officials at the beginning of the 1930s and 2,665 in 1938. Under Ribbentrop the increase accelerated rapidly to 6,458 in 1943, an expansion of 143 per cent.

After the outbreak of war in 1939 the AA experienced a number of important changes. In order to cope with the demands created by the conduct of war, a considerable number of new departments and offices were established (among others for economic warfare, prisoners of war, civilian internees, military legislation, front propaganda and the fight against enemy propaganda). Of even greater importance was the fact that Ribbentrop and his staff of close collaborators followed the Führer around on his journeys (later in his mobile headquarters) instead of staying in Berlin. In 1940 *Referat D* was expanded to become *Abteilung Deutschland* (Department Germany) (under Ribbentrop's confidant Martin Luther) which was to cooperate, among others, with Himmler's *Reichssicherheitshauptamt* (journeys of diplomats abroad, combating political enemies, etc.), to control the information department of the AA and to supervise ministry publications. After Luther's fall in spring

1943[4] the department was broken up and divided among groups *Inland I* and *II*, both directly subordinated to Ribbentrop. At the same time, various top-ranking positions were newly filled.[5]

In examining the work of the AA during the period 1933 to 1945 it becomes apparent that it lacked one of the most important preconditions for a successful operation: the trust of the country's leadership in the organization. Under the influence of Heß, Ribbentrop, Göring, Rosenberg, Goebbels, Bormann, Himmler and various party offices Hitler's distrust of civil servants and diplomats grew. In spring 1934, referring to them as a 'society of conspirators', Hitler lamented that he was bound by the pledge made at the time of the formation of his cabinet that the Reich President had control of the army and the AA. Later, his verdict was to be even more biting. With hindsight, he explained that, 'before Ribbentrop's time [the AA] had been a proper dumping ground for the intellegentsia'. Yet Hitler did not carry out his intention to 'sweep out' the worst *Kamarilla*[6] after Hindenburg's death, in particular as the behaviour of his diplomatic representatives abroad gave him few grounds for attacking them. Until 1938, Hitler intervened only sporadically in personnel decisions of the AA. He apparently hoped to have this problem resolved in a different manner. He largely left it to his deputy and the Reichleiter and Gauleiter to fight this running battle. Only in the context of the events of late 1937 and early 1938 (the Blomberg-Fritsch Crisis) did Hitler feel the need to undertake a fundamental reshuffle. He replaced Neurath, who had headed the AA since 1932, with his favourite, Joachim von Ribbentrop. Initially, the latter introduced few changes to the diplomatic apparatus. Ribbentrop's most significant moves were the replacement of the ambassador in Rome, Ulrich von Hassell, with Hans-Georg von Mackensen, the recall of Herbert von Dirksen from Tokyo (he was made ambassador in London) and the appointment of General Ott as new ambassador to Japan. Ribbentrop also placed his embassy secretary Ernst Woermann (from London) and a third of his closest collaborators from his *Dienststelle* (among them Luther) in influential positions. At the same time he followed the advice of Albrecht Haushofer and made Ernst von Weizsäcker his new permanent state secretary and put Erich Kordt in charge of his ministerial office.

Hitler and other leading Nazis criticized AA officials because they were convinced that the latter neither truly believed in National Socialist principles nor truly acted accordingly. The Nazi leadership presumed

---

[4]    Luther had tried to have his boss Ribbentrop removed from office.
[5]    See Seabury, *Die Wilhelmstraße*, 195ff; M. Broszat, *Der Staat Hitlers*, Munich, 1969, 365ff.
[6]    Clique.

that only very few diplomats were true 'proponents of the will of the New Reich'. Such comments by diplomats as 'youthful impetuousness had to be given a chance to peter out' (Haushofer), only provided Hitler and his collaborators with additional ammunition for their occasionally biting criticism. Gradually, however, they had to acknowledge that, because of their lack of expertise and personnel, none of the other state and party agencies involved in foreign policy was able to replace the AA. Moreover, the latter had lost little of its prestige and authority at home and abroad.

Much of this had to do with the social structure of the civil servants in the AA. Although with personnel files still closed no precise statements can be made about the background of diplomats,[7] it can be assumed that a majority of members came from aristocratic, senior civil servant and officer families. In general, it can be argued that the members of the senior diplomatic service formed a largely homogeneous, to a certain extent quite exclusive group which Neurath skilfully managed to shelter from irksome attempts at intervention by the party. Most AA officials held strongly conservative views shaped by daily routine and a belief that the conscientious civil servant should stand above the parties. Their attitude was well summed up by Sir Harold Nicholson's comment: 'Loyalty is one of the fundamental pillars of the foreign service.' It can certainly be argued that only a small minority fully identified itself with the National Socialist creed. Many simply retained the cool distance of the superior expert while their behaviour was marked by the morally subjectivist view of always having had the better interests at heart. According to Gauleiter Bohle's view, as expressed to *Reichsführer*-SS Himmler in 1944, of 690 members of the AA about 600 were still opposed to National Socialism due to their denominational ties. Yet, over the years diplomats had shown an increasing adeptness at accommodating themselves to the regime and at representing its views abroad, even against their own convictions. The director of the legal department of the AA, Friedrich Gaus, admitted after the war that it pained him to remember that diplomats, even if they had continued to oppose National Socialism, produced a 'show of devotion and obedience' which became particularly apparant during the Second World War in many parts of Europe and the wider world. Significantly, most top diplomats remained in their posts both in the ministry and abroad.

At 52 years, the average age of German diplomats was about 12 to 15 years above that of the new Nazi elite. If we compare, for instance,

---

[7]   See, however, now Hans-Jürgen Döscher, *Das Auswärtige Amt im Dritten Reich. Diplomatie im Schatten der 'Endlösung'*, Berlin, 1987.

the age of members of APA, AO and *Dienststelle Ribbentrop* with that of the AA, we are faced with an even more glaring gap of about an additional four to five years. The diplomats of the AA had gained their most crucial impressions and experiences in Imperial Germany and during the First World War. The attitudes and minds of the young Nazi members of the competing agencies, however, had been shaped by the lost war, the Weimar period and the period of transition, so radical in form. The age, or more precisely generation, gap was an important factor in the many conflicts both at home and abroad.

Until Neurath's departure, the AA contained very few total outsiders. First among these was the German ambassador in Washington, Hans Luther, whom Hitler had sacked as Reich Bank President in 1933 because he had refused to make available the means to finance rearmament. A second example was Franz von Papen, Vice Chancellor in Hitler's cabinet, who was sent on a special mission to Vienna after the putsch of 25 July 1934 had so miserably failed and a conservative-Catholic politician was required to calm down the heated atmosphere. Appointed as the Reich's Representative for Disarmament Questions in 1934 and ambassador to London in 1935 Ribbentrop was a further example. Fourth was Dr. Sahm, former Mayor of Berlin, who after having clashed with Goebbels' supporters, was put in charge of the legation in Oslo. From 1936 to 1937 General Faupel represented the Reich in General Franco's Spain. Eventually, he was recalled early after German and Spanish officials had sharply criticized his high-handed approach.

In the headquarters in Berlin outsiders constituted only a small minority. If we ignore Josias von Waldeck-Pyrmont's brief 'visit' to the personnel department in 1933–4, Gauleiter Bohle and his collaborators can be regarded as the first 'intruders' after Bohle had been appointed *Chef AO im Auswärtigen Amt* in 1937. He was the first of a number of party members to enter the AA with the next addition provided by Ribbentrop in 1938. Yet, the Nazis never succeeded in undermining the homogeneity of the service to a significant degree.

It is likely that, in 1933, two envoys were newly appointed due to their membership of the NSDAP. Among these 'concessions' was Viktor zu Wied who had joined the party in January 1932. After having gone into retirement in March 1933 he was unexpectedly sent as envoy to Stockholm in October of the same year. At the same time, Baron von Thermann, Consul General First Class in Danzig, was promoted to Envoy First Class and dispatched to Buenos Aires. Apart from being a member of the party he had also joined the SS. A further example was Hermann Kriebel who had participated in Hitler's putsch attempt of 1923. In 1934, the latter personally appointed Kriebel to the position of Consul

General in Shanghai. A former lieutnant colonel, Kriebel had worked as military adviser to Chiang Kai-shek from 1929 to 1933. In 1939 he advanced to head the personnel department of the AA. Another active Nazi, Kriebel's deputy Hans Schröder, formerly *Landesgruppenleiter* of the AO in Cairo, eventually took over the personnel department in 1941.

During the war, Ribbentrop's hitherto good relationship with Himmler cooled markedly particularly after the Foreign Minister had come to realize that he was to play only a minor role in the reorganization of Europe. Seeking support from old SA activists, Ribbentrop made a succession of SA leaders ministers, or quasi-'Reich governors', first Manfred von Killinger in 1940 (Bucharest), followed by Dietrich von Jagow (Budapest), Ludin (Pressburg), Siegfried Kasche (Agram) and Beckerle (Sofia) in 1941. Even these appointments however did not strengthen Ribbentrop's position. In spring 1943, after a major crisis of trust in the AA, Ribbentrop dealt a decisive blow against the old civil service. He recalled Weizsäcker, Woermann and Gaus, made his confidant Gustav Adolf Steengracht von Moyland Permanent State Secretary, and filled other leading posts in the AA with his protégés. Consequently, all new departments of the AA were headed by his own, younger people while only the three core departments (politics, law and trade) continued to be run by professional diplomats of the Weimar period (Hencke, Albrecht and Wiehl).[8]

It is difficult to judge the level of party membership among senior diplomats and civil servants. Even though some overviews exist, they tell us very little about the true political stance of the civil service. Seven of 92 senior civil servants in the headquarters in Berlin had joined the NSDAP before 30 January 1933, a further 26 until 1937 while no documentation on membership exists for 21 others. Accordingly, approximately one third of the civil servants were party members, though the proportion was to increase subsequently. In 1940, again in Berlin only, 71 of 120 senior civil servants were members of the NSDAP. Considering the reality of the period 1933 to 1945 it can, however, be assumed that many of these members were either fellow travellers, opportunists or pressured into joining. Very few exhaustive conclusions can also drawn about membership of the SS. In 1938, the list of SS ranks included von Neurath as SS-*Gruppenführer*, Permanent State Secretary von Weizsäcker as SS-*Oberführer*, Ambassador von Mackensen and Dr Woermann as SS-*Standartenführer*, yet these positions constituted so-called honorary ranks without practical implications or leadership duties. With the possible exception of Mackensen these diplomats

---

[8] Cf. N. Rich, *Hitler's War Aims*, vol. II *The Establishment of the New Order*, New York, 1974.

were anything but typical representatives of the Nazi leadership elite. Some diplomats, among them G. von Nostitz, Albrecht von Kessel, H. Blankenhorn and Theodor Kordt, fought against the Nazi system in their own way. Together with his closest colleagues, Permanent State Secretary von Weizsäcker attempted 'foreign policy obstruction' to prevent the outbreak of war in 1938/39, and its expansion in the East in 1940/41. Above all, by taking part in the plot against Hitler, Adam von Trott zu Solz, Eduard Brücklmeier, Hans-Bernd von Haeften, Richard Kuenzer, Ulrich von Hassell and Friedrich Werner von der Schulenburg demonstrated extraordinary strength of character. After the failure of the assassination attempt of 20 July 1944, the regime's retaliatory measures struck the AA in all their cruelty.[9]

## Auslandsorganisation der NSDAP (AO)

Based on the Foreign Department of the NSDAP, which Gregor Strasser had founded in 1931, the *Auslandsorganisation der NSDAP*[10] was launched under its own name in 1934. The AO's principal driving force was its ambitious young leader Ernst Wilhelm Bohle. Within a few years, backed by the trust and powerful position of the Führer's deputy Rudolf Heß, Bohle was able to expand a small insignificant department into an apparatus of 800 employees, experts and officials. While the heterogeneous nature of its personnel and its structure prevented the AO from becoming a true competitor of the AA, it did usurp a special role in Nazi foreign policy. By 1939 AO membership reached 65,000 (including 30,000 seamen).

The structure of the AO was determined by the *Führer* principle with controlling powers extending from the headquarters down to the country groups and eventually to all outposts abroad. The organization was undoubtedly not as dangerous as many countries assumed when they interpreted AO activities as fifth-column work. On the other hand, the services rendered by the AO to Germans abroad were not quite as harmless and selfless as its representatives and the Nazi propaganda apparatus tried to make out. Essentially, the AO constituted a strange mixture. Foremost among its tasks was the ideological indoctrination of Reich Germans abroad although it was not able to resort to the same rigourous means which were available to state and party at home. The AO also failed to live up to its objective of turning Germans abroad, in

[9]   On the resistance against Hitler, including on the role of members of the AA, see the chapter by Hans Mommsen in this collection.
[10]   Cf. Jacobsen, *Nationalsozialistische Außenpolitik*, 90ff; Donald M. McKale, *The Swastika outside Germany*, Kent State University, 1977.

particular in European border territories, into the tools of an active foreign policy. Overseas, apart from being active in the economic field, its efforts were largely concerned with combating both anti-German propaganda and assimilation policies of other countries. It would be going too far to see its American activities as preparations for the future conquest of the American hemisphere (as one recent study has put it).

Bohle's intervention among German ethnic groups was not due solely to his belief in the totality of National Socialist indoctrination, but also due to his desire for more political power. During the years leading up to the outbreak of the war, however, he had to bow to the tactical demands of the regime's foreign policy. Ground gained by the AO was soon lost again in favour of either Ribbentrop or the SS.

Bohle and his closest collaborators regarded the AO not solely as an instrument of power. Both the AO's demands and its operations were seen as a logical outcome of the victory of the Nazi movement in Germany. Spurred on by the desire not to take second place to their Gauleiter 'comrades' in the Reich, the AO leadership fought for the new *Volksgemeinschaft* to be applied also to Germans abroad. Even though most of these *Auslandsdeutsche* lived in a different social and political environment, they too were to be indoctrinated and carried away by the spirit of the 'New Time'. While, essentially, the process of *Gleichschaltung* was successfully applied to German colonies abroad – not least due the active involvement of Germany's diplomatic representatives – the results were modest. By 1937 no more than six per cent of all Reich Germans abroad had become party members. While many more sympathized with the Third Reich, at no point did this amount to a potential instrument of power. Viewed critically, the AO's operations abroad amounted to a spectacular failure.

The AO also fulfilled a considerable number of other functions which can either be put down to initiatives by local party leaders or to special objectives. Such functions varied, of course, from country to country and depended very much on the ambition, energy and authority of each party leader. Within the general framework of AO activities few limits existed for the imaginativeness of each of the organization's representatives – as long as an appearance of non-intervention in the domestic affairs of the host country was kept up. This guide-line was strongly emphasized in particular during the period of Germany's so-called shielding from abroad.

As espionage was not part of the official responsibilities of local or country group leaders, such activities proved to be the exception. It is not surprising that the *Abwehr* and the Gestapo wanted to make use of Nazi sympathizers among the Germans abroad. Rarely, however, did they provide advance information to the AO.

The AO did not control Germany's foreign policy. It was not legitimized to do so; nor did it possess the necessary expertise. Apart from its intervention in the Spanish Civil War, the AO did not influence foreign policy decision-making. Instead, it was supposed to supervise the ideological manner in which Germany's representatives implemented Hitler's guidelines and decisions and how these were presented to both the host country and the Germans living there. As such the AO unavoidably gained some influence over personnel decisions within the AA. It could do little, however, against senior diplomats. These were located outside the AO's sphere of influence by virtue of the fact that they had frequently been appointed by Hitler himself whose trust they enjoyed.

When it came to decisions about appointments, the AO did not really prove to be an effective force. In view of the total number of Reich representatives abroad and civil servants in the headquarters, the AO brought about only a negligible amount of changes. Cautious estimates reveal that until 1939 only about twenty to thirty AA officials were removed from their posts while nearly the same amount of AO members entered the diplomatic service. In 1937, after a long struggle, Bohle was appointed Permanent State Secretary in the AA. The homogeneity and character of the AA were certainly not significantly affected by this 'exchange'.

With regard to the disputed international cooperation of fascists only the occasional cautious contact can be detected between the AO and other fascist parties. The organization did, however, play down its operations, stressing only its national objectives, and denying officially all contacts with other right-wing groups abroad. The AO certainly did not shy away from sympathizing with like-minded organizations and establishing contacts without official instructions.

During the period 1933 to 1939, Germany's bilateral relations with numerous countries around the world, among them Holland, Hungary, Sweden, the United States, South America, South Africa, and Switzerland, suffered due to the organization's activities or its attempts at agitation. Worries about 'Pan-Germanism', about the establishment of a 'state within a state', and about a fascist conspiracy caused disquiet abroad. Insufficient understanding of the problems of the 'host country' and a lack of tact, both so characteristic of young, mostly inexperienced representatives, only heightened the concerns. In some cases the situation worsened to such an extent that both sides temporarily recalled their ambassadors (as in the case of Brazil). Although semiofficial and official departments and offices issued appeasing statements, a mistrust of a global organization prevailed abroad, particularly as it was assumed that the AO blindly obeyed orders from Berlin. It was left to the imagination of the individual, or to a rational assessment of Nazi doctrine, to work out the kind of directives Reich Germans would eventually receive from the regime.

As early as 1936 the Nazis adopted a more militant tone when they announced that not only would they look after Germans abroad, but also, if necessary, provide them with armed protection. In some countries, such ambitions were, of course, doomed to failure from the outset. In recognition of the special conditions in the United States, for instance, the AO leadership emphatically prohibited all organized activities in that country.

As a whole, the 'performance' of the AO abroad bears no relation to the tensions and disagreements which it created between other states and Germany – even if we take into consideration the fact that many Reich Germans abroad regarded the work of the AO as an instance of 'progress' compared to the cliquishness of the 1920s, and as an expression of closer bonds with the Reich. Bohle and his men did not realize, however, that despite the relative unity among Germans outside the Reich's boundaries, the political leadership would not be able to use party comrades abroad as a true instrument of power. In fact, Bohle's organization, intended as it was as an authentic copy of the movement inside the Reich, was doomed to become a source of constant unrest and growing instability, in particular once the direction of Nazi foreign policy had become more radical, indeed, eventually, openly expansionist. Repeated assurances by diplomats and party leaders that the AO would always respect a country's legal rights, were disproved by the reality of the policies of the Nazi regime. Even though other countries also provided cultural support to their countrymen and women, Nazi Germany was the only state (with the exception of the Soviet Union) which attempted to discipline and organize its people abroad, aiming towards uniformity, indoctrination, loyalty to the Führer, and obedience to his orders. As long as the world remained at peace, foreign countries might have had reason to believe Germany's reassurances that it would not intervene in their affairs. Yet, as soon as tensions arose, suspicions grew corresponding to Hitler's more bellicose behaviour. The belief spread that, one day, the Reich Germans abroad would become a Trojan Horse. Such views stimulated the imagination of journalists and publishers, most notably in states which either found themselves in the immediate vicinity of Germany's sphere of power or feared a violent revision of the Treaty of Versailles. In practice, however, the activities of the AO did not constitute a real threat as they were intended more for the Reich Germans than the 'host country'. Seen as a whole, the AO did little 'which might have shaken the world!' It was in the nature of things that, for propagandistic and other reasons, the AO was blamed for much, even if it was either not true, or exaggerated or based on unreliable generalizations. Repeatedly, the organization was compared to the Comintern and its underground activities.

Bohle's aim to make Nazis abroad 'favoured guests' in their countries was evidence for either a frivolous cynicism or an almost unbelievable naïvety. The latter assumption may well be more accurate if we consider Bohle's (young) age and his, subjectively, sincere idealism for the 'good cause'. This was simply further proof of the inability of many party leaders involved in Nazi foreign policy to assess correctly foreign countries in all their diversity. Some Germans abroad either formed majorities in certain areas or lived as a minority among other minorities (as was the case in Poland and Czechoslovakia). Others were of German origin, but refused resolutely to be incorporated into the Reich or to be 'looked after' by it, because they were either patriots or masters of their own country. Many simply wanted to express their cultural individuality in order to be able to make demands of a regional nature (e.g. in the Alsace). Above all, however, the great majority had already been assimilated into the society of their country. Despite attachments to their old home country they had ceased to see themselves as part of the German people (e.g. Germans in the United States[11]). The AO, however, refused to accept such distinctions and judged Germans abroad purely by its own one-sided ideological standards.

After the outbreak of war the AO had to scale down part of its functions and to take over new tasks, such as, for instance, assisting in the evacuation of Reich Germans and their return home; taking reprisals for the 'maltreatment' of German internees abroad; undertaking propaganda work, etc. Yet, until Heß's flight in May 1941, the AO was able to maintain its position in the party apparatus and within the AA. Subsequently, however, Ribbentrop tried to eliminate his opponents. He suggested to Hitler that he should transfer to the AA the responsibilities of the AO. Under the influence of Bormann, Hitler refused though he agreed to have Bohle removed from his post as Permanent State Secretary in the AA. Accordingly, Bohle was given secret orders in November 1941. Until the end of the war his role remained confined to that of his original area of responsibilities within the party. As demanded by Bormann in no uncertain terms, Bohle continued his attempts to influence Germans abroad to support the spirit and aims of National Socialism.

---

[11]    Most recently, Nazi *Volkstum* policies in the United States have been examined by Cornelia Wilhelm, *Bewegung oder Verein? Nationalsozialistische Volkstumspolitik in den USA*, Stuttgart, 1998.

*Volkstumsführung* (The Ordering of Ethnic Germans)

In some ways, the change of direction in Germany's foreign policy during the period 1933 to 1939 finds an instructive reflection in the organization and centralization of *Volkstumführung* in the Third Reich.[12] Both the changing structural conditions and the various methods used by *Volkstum* politicians provide evidence for the process of radicalization which, determined by the level of domestic stabilization and the international position of the Reich, moved inexorably ahead. As long as it was necessary to play down or deny the foreign policy objectives of the party after its takeover of power, *volksdeutsch* activities had to be conducted without any official direction by party and state. In 1933 the Führer's deputy therefore put together the *Volksdeutscher Rat* (Council of Ethnic Germans) and installed it as an advisory and executive organ. As proof that the NSDAP was opposed to any intervention in the affairs of foreign countries, Heß made a written commitment to the autonomy of the VR. The Council's authority depended on Heß's position in state and party and the great experience of its eight members. With one exception, none of this circle of experts, homogeneous in origins, education and opinions, belonged to the party. During the period of shielding Germany from abroad the VR seemed to be the ideal mediator between state and ethnic Germans abroad, particularly as the NSDAP did not possess any experienced *Volkstum* experts. Yet, the VR never managed to get beyond a mediatory position between rival groups, and between older and younger ethnic Germans (the latter usually organized in so-called regenerationist movements).

The members of the VR were 'in the prime of their lives' (aged between 40 and 50), lives that had been shaped by the experience of world war, by border struggles and by university studies. They had gained their expertise in southeastern Europe, the Baltic region, the Sudetenland and Alsace-Lorraine. They also owed their position of power to the close personal relationship between Heß and its chairman, Karl Haushofer. Moreover, they benefited from the predicament faced by the Nazi leaders; in his first few years in power, Hitler was neither able nor willing to do without the cooperation of well-known and able men of national-conservative conviction. Similar to the civil servants of the AA, such men helped him to make the regime appear less threatening. The available evidence makes, however, more than just questionable Hermann Rauschning's claim that, as early as

---

[12]   Jacobsen, *Nationalsozialistische Außenpolitik*, 160ff; H-A. Jacobsen (ed.), *Steinacher, H., Bundesleiter des VDA 1933–1937. Erinnerungen und Dokumente*, Boppard, 1970.

1934, Hitler secretly initiated the VR members into the revolutionary methods of Nazi *Volkstum* policies.

From its beginnings, the VR's work ran into difficulties. Its members did not get any backing from the party and its organizations. While they saw the Council's so-called independence as a sign of strength, it soon revealed itself as a sign of weakness and presented a large target to any opponents. Some members came under heavy fire because their behaviour did not correspond to the ideas of the 'old guard'. There was also the fact that, due to his wife's origins, Haushofer was only able to work in the 'twilight'. Even though he had a great influence on Heß, he shunned the limelight and did not firmly defend his cause. Hampered by bouts of illness, Hitler's indecisive deputy (Heß) did not live up to his position in the party hierarchy and became increasingly dependent on Bormann, his chief of staff. Brooding and full of doubts, Heß was only kept going by his faith in Adolf Hitler. As a member of the discontented generation he felt that the sacrifices made during the First World War had been in vain. Full of blinded idealism this generation believed that under the Swastika Germany would regain a position of power.

Yet, it proved to be even more damaging to the VR that its views on *Volkstum* did not concur with National Socialist ideology – even though this fact was only to emerge over time. *Volkstum* for the sake of *Volkstum*, even in a spirit of regeneration, did not reflect the demands the party made on the leaders of the ethnic Germans. In the struggle for the souls of the Germans outside the Reich the party called for unambiguous orientation towards and dogmatic ties with its ideology. The party opposed the artifical separation made between Reich and ethnic Germans though it accepted that, for tactical reasons, such a separation had to be temporarily accepted. Even this recognition did not stop it, however, from combating the VDA-spirit, its 'liberalistic' concepts and its charitable activities.

While the VR's membership and activities represented a moderate direction in Germany's foreign policy, the establishment of the *Büro von Kursell* (von Kursell's Office) in 1935 saw a change towards a more extreme course. This agency was not autonomous. Indeed, though operating in secrecy, it was an official party office which was subordinated to Ribbentrop as the Deputy Führer's representative for foreign political questions. It was headed by an *alter Kämpfer* who had been awarded the party badge in gold and was therefore protected from attacks from within the party. His collaborators, mostly younger (i.e. 30 to 40 years old) party, and in some cases SS, members, were a much more heterogeneous group than the VR. They had little experience in the area of *Volkstum* policy even though they showed much interest in it. The authority of the office was based on Heß's position and the party membership of its employees. Despite Kursell's conciliatory manner he eventually clashed with Himmler, a conflict which led to his downfall.

Both the VR and the *Büro von Kursell* strove for a unified authoritative leadership in all questions concerning ethnic Germans. Heß explicitly declared their exclusive responsibility for some countries. Yet, from the beginning, their political power bases in these countries proved to be too weak. Apart from the fact that they had to camouflage their work and avoid any agitation, they did not have any executive powers to give strength to their demands. If their recommendations and instructions were not heeded, they could not react with effective 'sanctioning measures'.

In order to bring quarrelling parties to their senses it did not suffice to deny entry permits, to ban contacts, to end diplomatic relations, and to pronounce moral verdicts. Like Germany's state offices, both organizations opposed the cessation of financial aid because they feared that it would not always hit the guilty party, but instead threaten the existence of the whole of Germandom abroad. They were therefore not able to assert themselves against ethnic German groups feuding with each other. They coordinated, arbitrated (especially when they had been asked by others), acted as mediators, urged unity, and they even repeatedly took unpleasant decisions in the interest of regenerationist movements. Yet, they nevertheless rarely managed to stop the incessant battle about direction and leadership abroad. Apart from some standardization of those Reich German organizations active in the *Volkstum* sector, and support for Konrad Henlein in the Sudetenland, the VR failed to achieve any visible successes. As early as 1934/35 the VR fell victim to party intrigues. Subsequent developments showed very distinctly that an authoritative headquarters, able to take clear-cut decisions in this sector, did not emerge until 1937.

The intended *Gleichschaltung* of the ethnic German groups in Europe was not, as argued in various publications, a true copy of the events in Germany, but was rather an expression of the individual attitude of Germans abroad as well as a consequence of the position of power and freedom of action in foreign policy which Germany had gradually acquired. Many of the forces in the regenerationist movements, both moderate and radical, demanded much more resolutely than was desirable to the rulers in Berlin to be voluntarily subordinated to the Reich (partly for financial reasons). Repeatedly, the latter warned about rash steps and advised calm, concerned as they were during the building-up phase about the reputation of the Third Reich and about any undesirable disputes with neighbouring countries. Initially, the Nazi regime only reluctantly and very cautiously intervened in the largely politically motivated struggle for the sole leadership of the ethnic German groups. Until 1938, the ethnic Germans were certainly not a disciplined part of an all-German political structure. Despite its pre-1933 foreign-policy principles the Nazi leadership largely tried to match *Volkstum* policies with present tactical requirements.

Confusing conflicts thus determined the struggle among Germans abroad, a struggle supported in their own way by the diverging forces in the Reich. Jealousy, ambition and problems between old and young frequently played a greater role than particular conditions for unification dictated by German state and party offices. In addition, the ethnic groups did not have any distinctive leadership personalities, apart from Henlein in the Sudetenland.

Only in particularly crisis-ridden instances did the AA abandon its passivity towards the question of the leadership of ethnic groups. Even then all it did was ask Heß to restrain the party organizations. Hitler, on the hand, cleverly remained in the background. For obvious reasons he initially refrained from demarcating areas of responsibility more precisely. Hitler carefully avoided having his name dragged into the discussions about the conflicts among the ethnic groups in Europe. In most cases, he only intervened (even among other state and party offices) when his subordinates seriously endangered the prevailing course of his foreign policy by taking measures of too high-handed a nature. His interest in the activities of the ethnic groups increased, however, during 1937 when he personally introduced SS-*Obergruppenführer* Werner Lorenz[13] into his new post as leader of the *Volksdeutsche Mittelstelle* (VoMi), granting him the relevant written powers in summer 1938.

The establishment of VoMi[14] constituted a decisive political restructuring of the *Volkstumführung*. VoMi's authority was based less on the experience of its staff than on their black uniforms and the instructions issued by Hitler. Aged between thirty and forty and largely jurists, VoMi's members were all SS officers. The organization was headed by two close confidants of the *Reichsführer*-SS and *Reichsführer*-SD. During the domestic tensions of the period 1933 to 1937, when the frontlines were not clearly demarcated, Himmler and Heydrich had kept in the background waiting for the right moment to expand their positions of power. After having brought down von Kursell they stepped in. With VoMi they held for the first time an instrument of foreign policy which they were later to use ruthlessly to further their own interests. Germany's *Volkstum* policy

---

[13]    Lorenz had been suggested to Hitler by Himmler.
[14]    Still useful as an overview is R. L. Koehl, *RKFDV: German Resettlement and Population Policy 1939–1945*, Cambridge, 1957.

thus underwent a radicalization at a time when, as symbolized by the removal of Reich Economics Minister Hjalmar Schacht, the economic objective of Germany's long-term reintegration into the world economy had to be viewed as a failure, while the new economic course was characterized by autarchic objectives to be pursued until the Reich had gained additional *Lebensraum*. In the meantime, Germany's foreign policy turned towards open expansion.

With VoMi a command centre for ethnic German affairs was established, and its authority was neither altered nor affected by other party offices. Once a clear dividing line had been drawn between Reich and ethnic Germans, VoMi moved on to more urgent decisions. It did not shy away from threatening reprisals. By clearly favouring certain wings among the ethnic groups abroad it laid the foundations for tighter leadership and thus for the process of *Gleichschaltung*. Subsequently, ethnic groups could be exploited, if required, as a means of indirect aggression though Hitler only twice made use of this option. All available evidence indicates that he viewed with scepticism the effectiveness of this revolutionary tool. Instead, Hitler relied on the traditional instrument of power politics, the *Wehrmacht*; and, full of determination, he prepared it for the eventual conquest of foreign territories. As is well known, from 1937/38 military planning in the Third Reich was aimed towards taking the strategic offensive.

### Außenpolitisches Amt der NSDAP (APA)

Since Rosenberg's APA[15] did not have a visible impact on diplomatic decisions prior to 1938, historians have previously underestimated how important the organization was for the realization of the ideological foreign-policy objectives of the NSDAP. Yet, diplomacy was only one aspect of Nazi foreign policy, indeed not even the most important one. With its origins going back to the years 1931/32, APA only started to become active after the takeover of power. From twenty-four staff in 1933 it increased in size to about 80 in 1938. All were party members aged mostly between 30 and 40. The organization was structured along thematic and geographical lines and functioned in the figurative sense of an iceberg; only a minor part of its activities was known to the public, the essential part, however, happened under cover. To a certain extent, APA used a cell structure. Staff members did not always know of each other's plans and tasks.

---

[15]   Cf. Jacobsen, *Nationalsozialistische Außenpolitik*, 45ff; see also R. Cecil, *The Myth of the Master Race: Alfred Rosenberg and Nazi Ideology*, London, 1972.

Its research, activities of a foreign political nature, and agitation were concentrated in four areas. In the first of these, the secret preparations for the partition of the USSR, Germans formerly resident in Russia were registered, anti-Soviet national movements were given cautious support, albeit without any promises for the future, efforts were directed towards the expansion of a chain of economically dependent states around the Soviet Union (particularly in southeastern Europe) and future plans for partition were discussed with Italy, most notably with Enrico Insabato, Mussolini's eastern expert. As the driving force in this area, Georg Leibbrandt would later play an important role in the Reich Ministry for the Occupied Eastern Territories.

As a foundation of foreign policy Rosenberg tried to establish the 'Nordic Community of Fate' as the common heritage for the future of Europe. Nazi cultural policy propagated the ideas of common racial roots and heroic ideology in an effort to accelerate and 'spiritually' deepen the process of *Aufnordung* ('re-nordicization').

In APA's Foreign Policy Instruction Centre, the new ideal of a total transformation of all social forces of the twentieth century and the need for Germany's leadership of the continent was conveyed to young Nazis, the new foreign policy elite, while state officials received the same training from the party leadership.

Central to APA's agitation was, however, the determined ideological struggle against 'World Jewry' and 'World Bolshevism', a struggle which, from 1935/36, was again conducted quite openly. In speeches, articles and pamphlets Rosenberg's ideologues emphasized the 'aggressive military potential' of the Soviet Union and the massive boost world communism had received from the Franco-Soviet Pact of 1935. Czechoslovakia was referred to as the 'main aircraft carrier' of the Bolshevists. It was proclaimed that, with the Soviet Union gaining in strength, a new age of Genghis Khan was setting in. Others also incessantly repeated such slogans, drumming them into the German population. Moreover, it soon became clear that Rosenberg put forward a specific equation: Russia meant Bolshevism, and Bolshevism was identical with Judaism. Only by partitioning Russia could the world enemy be eliminated. During the Reich party congress of September 1935 Rosenberg labelled Bolshevism as the 'work of a foreign race'. Bolshevism, he argued, was not an economic theory, but political action which misled and stirred up the people. Ninety per cent of its leadership were Jews, the true representatives of this ideology. Lenin himself was 'infected by the Jewish virus' and a 'child of the steppe', not therefore a European. Inverting the Bolshevist belief that Fascism or National Socialism constituted the 'most rapacious and aggressive form of capitalism', Rosenberg declared that Bolshevism was the highest form of Judaism. With such 'parasites' no compromise was possible. The victory of National Socialism had been the heaviest blow to Zionists and Bolsheviks. Rosenberg therefore concluded sharply that anyone fighting against Germany today made himself an ally of Bolshevism.

### Reichsministerium für Volksaufklärung und Propaganda (ProMi)

Established in March 1933, the Propaganda Ministry[16] held a special position in Germany's foreign policy. Although it was anchored in the state sector, its methods and objectives made it much more part of the new Nazi institutions. Its global conduct of propaganda for Nazi Germany, its use of the mass media, and its many special operations revealed the talent and fanaticism of Joseph Goebbels who frequently applied his passionate aspirations to intervene in the domestic disputes about authority and influence, albeit with varying degrees of success.

Among his most important tasks was the anti-Bolshevist propaganda, a logical consequence of the pre-1933 revolutionary foreign policy programme of the Nazis. During the first few months of 1933, this propaganda was largely directed against the so-called planned 'armed rising' of the Communists at home, but, with the systematic elimination of all major 'enemies of the state' by the totalitarian regime, it was soon redirected towards the external 'enemy', World Bolshevism and its practices. The men surrounding Goebbels, above all Haegert (Head of Dept. II: Propaganda), Hasenöhrl (Head of Dept. III: Foreign Countries), and Taubert (Section Chief) made it their aim to fight Bolshevism on all levels, and to 'brand' it as the true threat to human culture, to the stability of Europe, and thus to peace and prosperity. Their imaginativeness knew no bounds and they were not at all choosy about their methods which were aimed at diverting world public attention from the events in Germany onto the situation in the Soviet Union, and subsequently prepare the German people for the struggle against any 'world order alien to the regime'.

Reducing everything to black and white they contrasted the conditions in the Soviet Union with the 'constructive determination of the National Socialists', i.e. their reconstruction achievements and 'cultural creativity'. Such a cliché had a certain effect upon some groups in Germany. Abroad, however, it failed to do the same. Goebbels' propa-

---

[16]    Cf. Jacobsen, *Nationalsozialistische Außenpolitik*, 452; E. K. Bramstedt, *Goebbels und die nationalsozialistische Propaganda 1925–1945*, Frankfurt, 1971; H. Heiber (ed.), *Goebbels-Reden* vol. 1: 1932–1939, Düsseldorf, 1971; W. A. Boelcke (ed.), *Wollt Ihr den totalen Krieg? Die geheimen Goebbels-Konferenzen 1939–1943*, Munich, 1969.

gandists certainly faced a particular difficulty. Officially, the new Reich government pursued friendly, mutually advantageous relations with the Soviet Union. Fighting communism was regarded as a domestic political matter in which no interference from outside was tolerated. Consequently, the ProMi was forced to build up a cover organization which was not supported by either state or party, but which could be used for a purposeful propaganda campaign primarily against the Comintern (the Third Communist International). By adopting the Soviet model, i.e. the fictitious and propagandistic separation between Soviet government and Comintern headquarters in Moscow, the ProMi hoped to be able to beat the fiercest opponent with its own weapons. This cover office was initially named *Gesamtverband deutscher antikommunistischer Vereinigungen e.V.* (Association of German anti-Communist Organizations), but became known from 1934 as *Antikomintern.* It was to concentrate and unify the fight against communism in such a way as would preserve the independent work of associated organizations and personalities. Leading figures, among them its head Adolf Ehrt as well as Greife and von Deringer, had been born in Russia and had made decisive experiences during the Bolshevik revolution. The broad area of responsibility of the *Antikomintern* was well defined; central to its so-called education and information work was the activities of the Comintern around the world. The Comintern's 'subversive activities and dangerousness' for Europe and the other continents was to be mercilessly uncovered or rather ruthlessly exposed. It was seen as essential to open people's eyes towards the revolutionary and subversive intentions of the communists, and to destroy their horror stories about the Third Reich. It is easy to understand that the world-wide fighting and victory slogans of the Comintern offered an excellent target for such determined activities.

The political ideas of the ProMi differed to some degree from those of Rosenberg and other party leaders. Goebbels and Taubert, the ministry's central protagonists, regarded the battle to be fought as a total counter-attack against Bolshevism, the mortal enemy and Judeo-Bolshevik 'world destroyer'. They were also convinced that Bolshevism was both created and headed by the Jewish race, but that it was not to be interpreted as a 'Mongolian attack'. Their fanatical and determined enmity was directed above all against Moscow as the 'clique of international professional revolutionaries', against the 'Judeo-Bolshevik oppressors' and thus against the 'actual wire-pullers' of attempts at world revolution. It certainly reflected their concept, at least in propagandistic terms, when the Führer's deputy declared in April 1937 that Germany's struggle was not directed 'against those Slavic people ruled and oppressed by Bolshevism', but against 'the world revolution conducted by the Comintern'. Germany was not an enemy of the Slav, but the 'bitter and irreconcilable enemy of the Jews, and of the Communism which they had spawned'.

From 1933 to 1937, the *Antikomintern* showed a considerable level of activity. Yet, it failed to score major foreign political successes. Compared with the international achievements of its enemy, the Comintern, which worked together with legal and illegal Communist parties in over seventy countries of the world and made use of such rousing slogans as 'Workers of the World Unite', its work remained piecemeal, its frontal attack against Bolshevism without decisive punch outside the Reich. ProMi's propaganda work did, however, yield some successes, particularly in the western democracies which, until the end of 1937, regarded Germany as a kind of bulwark against Bolshevism. How effective Goebbels proved to be in the field of propaganda abroad during the period 1933 to 1945 has not yet been thoroughly examined. A few interesting measures and plans can, however, be highlighted.

In 1933, the starting point for the propaganda campaign was the perception of the socialist society in the Soviet Union. Food shortages and physical deprivation in many parts of the Soviet Union convinced the ProMi to castigate the hunger conditions with garish headlines in newspapers, magazines, and on placards. 'Hunger letters' from the Soviet Union were published in order to make Germany and the public worldwide aware of the untenable conditions in the East. At the same time, Germany's propaganda claimed that the Soviet Union was selling the few existing amounts of grain to foreign countries in exchange for hard currency to maintain its offensive rearmament. By linking this aspect to the Bolshevik ideology of world revolution it underlined the threat posed by the expansionist character of the Comintern.

Simultaneously, the ProMi employed select intermediaries to conduct a 'charitable' propaganda campaign. In view of the misery of the people in Russia – 'whole regions are deserted' – the aid organization 'Brothers in Need' was founded. It emphasized above all Christian compassion and asked for donations to help the one-and-a-half million 'German national and religious comrades' in the East. In a report, a ProMi official later admitted that the two activities were causally related. His claim might have been exaggerated that the priests in, for instance, Germany, Austria and Britain had been 'puppets' of Germany's propaganda. It is a fact, however, that, in spring 1934 in Britain, Dr Ewald Ammende, General Secretary of the European Congress of Nationalities and member of the Innitzer-Committee, succeeded in his untiring efforts to form a committee to aid Russia with the help of representatives of various churches and denominational organizations, and thus to start a kind of moral offensive against the Soviet Union. It was, however, a mistake to believe that such efforts of a humanitarian nature would divert the attention of the world public from Germany to the Soviet Union.

The suppression of the 'Röhm revolt', the disruptions in the religious sector, the intervention in Austria, the martial spirit, and the doctrine of the 'Nordic Master Race' in Germany, all had a much more lasting effect on the British public than the reports from the Soviet Union.

In reaction, the ProMi tried to find means and ways to replace the 'defamation' of Germany with that of the Bolshevik system. The 'Pro-Deo-Commission' (Graf Keyserlingk) took on the struggle against the 'movement of the godless' in Russia. By highlighting the anti-religious policies of the Soviet regime as an expression of the 'destruction of occidental culture', priests of different denominations and politicians in Portugal, Ireland, Poland, Greece and Switzerland were enlisted and influenced in an anti-Communist manner. When the Soviet Union was accepted into the League of Nations in 1934, protests, as ordered, increased though the demand for Christian states to leave the League in response to this 'affront' received little support.

The *Antikomintern*, that is to say the ProMi, intervened in the dispute about the Saar in a special manner. On the one hand, it contributed positively to the creation of the German Front as a catchment organization for 'German blood' and for the true community of fate. On the other hand, it identified the Communists as the supporters of the status quo. German support was undoubtedly strengthened by the fact that Catholic Church officials in particular were mobilized against the godless mortal enemies. Taubert later maintained that one of the unforgettable anecdotes of the *Antikomintern* had always been how the 'Saarbrücken parsons had never suspected' whose 'business' they had conducted.

After the conclusion of the Franco-Soviet and Czechoslovak-Soviet assistance pacts in 1935, Nazi Germany increased its agitation against the Bolsheviks and their 'accomplices', and, in 1936, expanded it to a press campaign which was both pursued with the greatest vigour and strictly supervised. As a first step, it was emphasized in a varying, but unambiguous tone that the aggressive militarism of the pacts was directed against the Reich. As Germany was being increasingly encircled (Soviet aircraft in Prague), peace in Europe was endangered. After the conclusion of the German-Japanese Anti-Comintern Pact all commentaries had to have as a motto: 'Through our revolution we National Socialists have saved Europe from the Communist flood. The same mission is fulfilled by the Japanese people in the Far East!' At the same time and under the seal of secrecy, Goebbels indicated to his confidants the ideological character of Nazi foreign policy. He explained that, in the long term, it would be impossible for Bolsheviks and National Socialists (including all shades of fascists) to co-exist. 'Either one or the other will have to disappear. It was not accidental that Germany's policy was already orientated towards an anti-Bolshevik line in 1935, even before the party congress of 1936.' Germany found itself 'at the beginning of a major historical conflict' in which the press had to fulfil its explanatory and indoctrinatory duty in the interest of the German people.

In the meantime, the domestic campaign against communism again gathered strength. With the propaganda apparatus highlighting the threat posed by the Bolshevik enemy, the Gestapo and the party found it easier to step in against resistance circles within Germany. Many of the ruthless domestic policies were explained with the slogan 'Every opponent of the Third Reich is an ally of Bolshevism.' It was argued that the 'most dangerous spokesmen of Bolshevism' would always find a home among the *Stahlhelm*, in political Catholicism and in the Confessing Church. In addition, the example of Communism in the Soviet Union was used to highlight the dangers from which Hitler had saved the German people. In news reports and commentaries, journalists referred to Bolshevism as the 'world destroyer' and 'world enemy'. The Soviet Union was portrayed in the bleakest colours.

By systematically contrasting the two systems all complaints of the German people were to be trivialized in the following manner: in Russia total eradication of agriculture and farmers, in the Reich *Erbhofgesetz* (Law on Hereditary Farm Entailment) of the RNS; in Russia destruction of religion, churches and priests, in Germany declared belief in positive Christianity, protection of churches and religion; in Russia elimination of political enemies, in Germany 'generous leniency against the background of the *Volksgemeinschaft*'. One of the reasons given for the increased persecution of Jews in Germany was the need to remove those elements from positions of power who were, 'as experience shows, the supporters of Bolshevism', and to stop them from subverting the people. In all this, Goebbels adroitly targeted specific propaganda messages towards specific groups in the population. To the bourgeoisie, the danger of the 'subversive activities' conducted by Communists in all countries was to be made clear; to the worker, the reality of Bolshevism (i.e. the discrepancy between wages and prices, the constant existence at starvation level, the unimaginable lack of accommodation, the absence of any social welfare, the unpaid overtime, and the total enslavement) was to be shown in the most garish colours. Farmers were told about the consequences of collectivization while priests and church groups had to be informed about the situation of the churches in the Soviet Union. Women, finally, were to be deterred by the 'breakdown of marriage' in the East. At the end of January 1936, Dr Taubert told representatives of the press to remind the population constantly that 'Adolf Hitler had saved Germany from Bolshevism' and that the Third Reich provided 'strong protection against Bolshevism'.

Compared to central and western Europe, the social conditions in the Soviet Union in the mid-1930s were to a certain extent catastrophic. The new form of serfdom experienced by workers on the collective farms, the exploitation of industrial workers, the numerous purges of party, state and military were signs of severe domestic upheaval. The population was clearly not provided with sufficient quantities of consumer goods, particularly as military expenditure had grown from 5 billion roubles in 1934 to 14.8 billion in 1939. Yet, despite vociferous ideological slogans, the rulers of the Soviet Union were primarily preoccupied with safeguarding the 'socialist gains' from the efforts of the fascist aggressors and to prevent an encirclement of the country. Such considerations led to an acceleration of rearmament.

Besides, the aim of Nazi propaganda was not to describe the situation in the Soviet Union objectively or even to arouse sympathies for the tortured individuals in the East. First and foremost, the Nazis intended to justify their own policies at home and abroad by deliberately exaggerating the conditions in the Soviet Union and the threat posed by it. In the long term, the most serious consequences arose from the systematic poisoning of German-Russian relations and from the transformation of people's minds towards an extreme 'friend-foe' image. Working with all available means and methods of modern mass communication, such propaganda, aimed at seduction, provided the breeding-ground for theories which, as a logical result of the race doctrines, reached a climax in the concept of the 'subhuman', and which were to find their terrifying and criminal application during the Second World War. This sequence of events was not significantly altered by the short phase of German-Russian cooperation. It took the propagandists of 1941 only a brief period of time to get the German people again used to the new enemy. Soon they were able to continue from the position they had abandoned in 1939. Having been fed with horror images from the East for years, most Germans had retained the memory of these vivid pictures. Linked to this was an excessive overestimation of one's own powers and an underestimation of the Russian people – for instance of their commitment to fight and their ability to improvise; and this led to a total miscalculation of the power of resistance of the enemy. After the military developments of winter 1941/42 had shown how dogged and courageous a fight the soldiers of the Red Army were putting up, a secret ProMi order to the press stated: 'On the one side, there is the rule of the hard-working, of a select elite who, supported by the moral power of an exalted *Weltanschauung*, thinks and acts heroically. On the other side there is the rule of the inferior whom it would be totally wrong to describe as heroic. In the particular case of the Soviet soldier and his criminal courage one is dealing with overbred Slavic bestiality which makes this Slav fight for his life, indeed fight to the point of self-destruction and death, on the orders of a Jewish commissar.' In another example, in the daily passwords for 6 November 1942, the 25th anniversary of the outbreak of the Bolshevik October Revolution, Goebbels demanded that the 'bloody rule' of the Bolsheviks, their merciless 'exploitation', and the enormous armaments of the Red Army, built up for the purpose of world revolution, had to be juxtaposed with the new future within the new Europe led by Germany. 'In the light of the past, the emphasis must be on the new Europe which, under the leadership of the German *Wehrmacht*, has broken down the gates of the Bolshevik peoples' prison, forever saved the peoples of the East from the mortal danger of the Bolsheviks, and [led them] towards a new order.

A propaganda campaign of this kind offered, of course, obvious advantages to the foreign policy of the Nazi regime. On the one hand, it provided for a kind of 'moral formula' to unite with other states without giving the impression that Germany pursued its own political goals. On the other, it created a useful platform from which Germany could intervene in all matters of grand policy, especially in Europe. This was evident in 1936 when Hitler commenced his support for General Franco in Spain under the banner of anti-bolshevism, and also in 1941 when the Nazi leadership called for a 'crusade' against Bolshevism.[17]

### Dienststelle Ribbentrop

While AO and *Volkstumführung* were largely active on the periphery of the foreign policy decision-making process, while APA developed ideological concepts on the basis of Rosenberg's views, and while the ProMi determinedly aimed at manipulating the German population towards the 'friend-foe' image, the *Dienststelle Ribbentrop*[18] initially moved ever closer towards the centre of the policy decision-making process. From being rather loose at the beginning, the relationship between Hitler and Ribbentrop increasingly developed towards one of personal trust. Both shared certain views, including an antipathy to the traditional diplomacy. Created in 1934 as a result of the *ad hoc* tasks which Hitler, in

---

[17]   Cf. Boelcke (ed.), *Wollt Ihr den totalen Krieg?*, 234ff; see also A. Hillgruber (ed.), *Staatsmänner und Diplomaten bei Hitler. Vertrauliche Aufzeichnungen über Unterredungen mit Vertretern des Auslandes 1939–1941*, Frankfurt/Main, 1967.
[18]   Jacobsen, *Nationalsozialistische Außenpolitik*, 252ff.

circumvention of the AA, had instructed his close associate and loyal liegeman to do, the *Dienststelle Ribbentrop* boasted an extremely heterogeneous staff of 160 in 1936. Its sphere of activity was almost unlimited, and Ribbentrop, initially an amateur and 'travelling minister' with special mission, was to rise to the position of Hitler's first adviser on foreign-policy questions by 1937. His contacts abroad, his servility, his belief in the Nazi ideology, his untiring service to a doctrinal alliance policy, and a degree of success allowed him to secure the Führer's and Reich Chancellor's favour. His work was a challenge to the AA. Although initially his ambitions were not satisfied – his desire to become Permanent State Secretary in the AA was not fulfilled nor was he made *Reichsleiter* for foreign policy – he was able to accumulate a number of posts. He reduced Bohle's influence and took control of *Volkstum* and colonial policy, in 1936 he established a party intermediary office for the supervision and disciplining of comments of a foreign political nature made by members of the NSDAP and its organizations, and, by becoming ambassador to London, he took over one of the key diplomatic positions.

As such, the *Dienststelle Ribbentrop* was not an institution to substitute or take over the AA; instead, it was the Führer's expanded planning staff for foreign-policy matters. This is shown, for instance, by the fact that, in 1938, Ribbentrop transferred only 32 per cent of his staff to the AA. With Ribbentrop and his staff, Hitler could be sure of their unconditional execution of his orders and a greater understanding of the dynamic course of his foreign policy. This was demonstrated by the naval agreement with Britain in 1935, by the Anti-Comintern Pact with Japan and Italy in 1936 and 1937 respectively, and during the Spanish Civil War. Of course, the *Dienststelle* was also the personal instrument of and springboard to power of the Extraordinary Plenipotentiary Ambassador. Supported by both Hitler's trust and Himmler's cooperation, and shielded from the party, Ribbentrop increasingly gained an influential role in the political power play, and, in February 1938, as the final reward for his tireless ambition, Hitler made him Reich Foreign Minister. From then on, however, he was to become little more than one of the executive organs of 'his master's voice'.[19] The *Dienststelle* was reduced to a shadow existence though it was never offically dissolved. The latter fate was reserved for the office of the 'Representative for Foreign Policy Questions in the Staff of the Deputy Führer'. Disbanded in February 1940, it had already lost most of its tasks in 1938 to Luther's party liaison office in the AA.

[19]    On Ribbentrop's role in the crucial period 1938 to 1940 see now Stefan Kley, *Hitler, Ribbentrop, und die Entfesselung des zweiten Weltkrieges*, Paderborn, 1996.

## Schutzstaffel (SS)

From the mid-1930s it became increasingly clear that the *Schwarzes Korps*, from 1925 *Schutzstaffel* (SS), with its power base steadily growing after the 'Röhm Putsch' (1934), was not only to be employed to safeguard order at home, but also to implement ideological objectives. *Reichsführer* Heinrich Himmler (from 1929) and Reinhard Heydrich, his deputy, left no doubt about this expanded area of responsibility for their new 'order'. Both believed that, in the long term, only 'noble blood' and the 'true race' were able to produce achievements of lasting value.[20] The intellectual training of Nazi Germany's avant-garde was therefore aimed towards the forthcoming global 'show-down'. From 1935, the two leading figures of the SS used their writings to formulate the basic principles of the future conflict: any notions of 'chivalry' towards the Jews and Bolsheviks had to be totally rejected. For the preservation of one's own people, severe measures had to be taken against the enemy. Himmler and Heydrich justified their fanatical declaration of war on the ideological enemy – what they referred to as the struggle between 'human and subhuman' – by referring predominantly to its 'historical necessity' which was more important than moral and legal dictates. Their ambitious goal was clearly outlined: in fulfilling its duty, the SS enabled Hitler to build the 'Greater German Empire', the 'greatest empire ever constructed and seen by the people of this world'. From these theoretical 'findings' and postulates, it was only a small step towards the use of force against the ideological enemy from 1938, and towards the start of eliminatory policies in 1939. Neither Goebbels nor Rosenberg, least of all the *Wehrmacht*, were able to push through their own ideas.

In addition to the political surveillance of and fight against 'enemies of the state' at home, the SS (via eleven main offices), and particularly the SD, took control of the secret intelligence service of the party. From 1934 it systematically expanded its foreign apparatus by, for instance, hiring contact men and spies, and by employing Gestapo officers in German embassies who, under the protection of extraterritoriality, observed the development of communism.

As part of the Third Reich's increased activities against world Bolshevism, the Gestapo went, in fact, one step further. It tried to create

[20]    Cf. H. Buchheim, 'Die SS – das Herrschaftsinstrument', in Buchheim et al., *Anatomie des SS-Staates* vol. 1, Munich, 1967; B. F. Smith and A. Peterson (eds), *Heinrich Himmler. Geheimreden 1933–1945 und andere Ansprachen*, Frankfurt/Main, 1974; H. Heiber (ed.), *Reichsführer! ... Briefe an und von Himmler*, Stuttgart, 1968; useful as an overview is H. Höhne, *Der Orden unter dem Totenkopf. Die Geschichte der SS*, Gütersloh, 1967, 240ff.

a united police front of 'ideologically related and geo-strategically important states' under Germany's leadership. In a series of bilateral, secret conferences between German diplomats and the SD leadership, and representatives from Italy, Finland, Bulgaria, Yugoslavia, Poland, Hungary and from other states the international activities of Bolsheviks and Freemasons were discussed, the experience gained by each country's political police was discussed, and special Gestapo facilities for the fight against the common enemy were visited. It is very likely that agreements concluded at the time later helped the SD in its measures to suppress and eliminate the ideological enemy in German-occupied Europe during the Second World War.

### Looking towards the War

Between 1939 and 1941/42 the Nazi leadership fought a war which it limited territorially and conducted in single campaigns, and which its propaganda apparatus presented as a defensive, that is to say preventative war. It appears that the regime waged war as Karl von Clausewitz, the nineteenth-century war theoretician, would have wished, as a continuation of policy by other means. Taking precedence over the creation of a European peace order, Germany's war aims culminated first in the defeat of Poland, the strategic securing of the northern flank (also for economic reasons), the elimination of the western allies as power factors on the continent, and the construction of Germany's hegemony over a so-called 'New Order' in Europe, concurrent with the political control and economic penetration of the Balkans. These events were linked to the notion that this, the 'Second Act' of the war of 1914–18, would end successfully.[21]

Hitler employed the Blitzkrieg tactic which allowed him to rely on a well-adjusted institutional machinery, and which had the advantage of avoiding drawn-out *matériel* battles and great burdens on the civilian population, of evening out the natural weakness of the German economy (avoiding the danger of total ruin), of preventing economically dangerous alliances against the Reich, and, in conjunction with diplomatic peace offers, of placing the 'moral guilt' for the 'need to continue the fight' on the enemy. In addition, the Blitzkrieg concept reflected the true scope of Germany's economy in 1939. Being laid out for 'armament in breadth' rather than for 'armament in depth', it was only

[21]   Cf. the studies by N. Rich, *Hitler's War Aims*, vols 1 and 2, New York, 1973, 1974. For the views of GDR historians see *Deutschland im zweiten Weltkrieg* vol. 1: Vorbereitung, Entfesselung und Verlauf des Krieges bis zum 22. Juni 1941, Berlin, 1974.

prepared for a nine to twelve-month conflict. Yet, the success of the Blitzkrieg dispelled widespread initial doubts about final victory, silenced criticism of the regime, assisted the growing identification of large parts of the population with those war aims which the 'Greater German Reich' had revealed to them, and thus protected the position of the Nazi elites. With the attack on the Soviet Union (June 1941) the Nazi conduct of war underwent, however, a definite qualitative transformation whose first signs had become evident in Poland in 1939/40, but which had been hidden from the population. Numerous developments (including military campaigns on several fronts, spatial expansion, the economic exploitation of the occupied territories – in part to reduce Germany's heavy burden of debt – attempts at achieving autarchy, the elimination of ideological enemies, the destruction of the Jews, and the rule of terror, all signalled a growing radicalization of the war. To this economic interest groups, most notably the large combine IG Farben, but also others, made an increasing contribution in a technological and executive way or acted as profit-driven exploiters and as henchmen heedless of others.[22] After Japan's attack on Pearl Harbour (December 1941) and Germany's declaration of war on the United States, the European conflict expanded to a global war. At the same time, the true objective of the Nazis became apparent: to make 'Greater Germany' the predominant global power via the domination of the European continent and strategically located offshore bastions (possibly by reclaiming the colonies).

Against this brief background some structural changes of the regime's foreign policy during the period 1939 to 1945 need to be outlined. 1939 undoubtedly constituted a decisive caesura, in particular because the previous revisionist policy, largely pursued by the conservative forces in the Reich, was now replaced by the expansionist policy of the Nazis. As a result, the diplomats moved more and more into the background. Only exceptionally were they still able to intervene in the course of events (e.g. the Second Vienna Award of 1940, the Three-Power-Pact of the same year, the Pact of Friendship with Turkey in 1941, and the foreign trade offensive, including arms exports, in southeastern Europe and Latin America). Instead, the AA, like so many other competing institutions, turned increasingly into an all too compliant or spineless tool for the realization of the 'New Order', for Nazi propaganda around the world, and for the regime's policy of annihilation. It did not help that, by 1942, the Reich only maintained diplomatic relations with 22 States. Nonetheless, until 1945, Hitler and Ribbentrop met numerous foreign

[22]   For a more balanced study on the role of industry see G. W. Hallgarten and J. Radkau, *Deutsche Industrie und Politik von Bismarck bis heute*, Frankfurt/Main, 1974, 225ff, but particularly 301ff.

statesmen, most frequently from Italy, Romania, Hungary, Bulgaria, Spain, Japan and Slovakia, in an effort to convince these states – with varying success – to fight alongside Germany. After the military change of fortunes in 1942/43, they tried, at times by exerting massive pressure, to stop their allies from breaking away or surrendering.[23]

Nazi Germany's expansion led to a marked increase in the number of ministries and offices that, in a wider sense (namely that of the revolutionary objective), conducted its foreign policy in the occupied, dependent or neutral states. A significant feature of these was the competition for posts and various kinds of conflicts over duties while Hitler focused almost completely on the operational conduct of war, further evidence of his desire to realize his policies largely by force of arms.[24] Tensions arose between *Wehrmacht* commanders and heads of the civilian administrations, between SS-offices and organs of the Reich Economics Ministry, the Four-Year Plan Office (Göring), the monopolies (large combines), and the Reich Ministry for the Occupied Eastern Territories (founded under Rosenberg's leadership in 1941), and between Reich commissioners, Gauleiters, the 'governors of the Greater German Reich' abroad, and the higher SS and police leaders. As before 1939, their authority was largely dependent on having access to Hitler. After Heß' flight to Britain in May 1941, control over access to the Führer was in the hands of *Reichsleiter* Bormann who consequently held a key position in the whole Nazi apparatus. Only Himmler, Ribbentrop, Goebbels, Speer (from 1942), and, during the first years of the war, Göring also had direct access to Hitler who was to leave his bunker-headquarters only rarely. Neither the internal struggles for power and the divergent ideas nor the role of the diplomatic service during the Second World War have yet been sufficiently examined.[25]

---

[23] See Hillgruber (ed.), *Staatsmänner und Diplomaten (1939–1941)* and A. Hillgruber (ed.), *Staatsmänner und Diplomaten bei Hitler*, 2nd part (1942–1944), Frankfurt/Main, 1970.

[24] See P. E. Schramm, A. Hillgruber, W. Hubatsch and H.-A. Jacobsen (eds), *Kriegstagebuch des Oberkommandos der Wehrmacht, 1940–1945* (vols I–IV), Frankfurt/Main, 1961–5.

[25] On the role of the diplomacy see B. Martin, *Friedensinitiativen und Machtpolitik im Zweiten Weltkrieg 1939–1942*, Düsseldorf, 1974. On individual institutions and offices see, among others, A. Dallin, *Deutsche Herrschaft in Rußland 1941–1945*, Düsseldorf, 1958 (on the Reich Ministry for the Occupied Eastern Territories); U. D. Adam, *Judenpolitik im Dritten Reich*, Düsseldorf, 1972 (on SS and *Volkstum* policies); P. Hüttenberger, *Die Gauleiter. Studie zum Wandel des Machtgefüges in der NSDAP*, Stuttgart, 1969 (on the heads of the civilian administrations); D. Petzina, *Autarkiepolitik im Dritten Reich. Der nationalsozialistische Vierjahresplan*, Stuttgart, 1968 (on the Four-Year Plan); K. Kwiet, *Reichskommissariat Niederlande. Versuch und Scheitern nationalsozialistischer Neuordnung*, Stuttgart, 1968 (on the Reich commissioners); G. Janssen, *Das Ministerium Speer. Deutschlands Rüstung im Krieg*, Berlin, 1968.

From 1938/39 the SS controlled two of the most important areas of Nazi foreign policy – population and *Lebensraum* policy. This organization had undoubtedly taken over the leading role in the Nazi system of rule. Himmler and Heydrich had specific ideas on what to do with those European territories eventually occupied by Germany. On the one hand, they wanted to bring Germany's land into line with its population size. This was the official aim of the considerably expanded VoMi and of the *Reichkommissar für die Festigung des deutschen Volkstums* (Reich Commissioner for the Consolidation of the German *Volkstum*), whose office was established on 7 October 1939.[26] With the largest organized 'mass migration' the Nazis intended to colonize immediately the conquered territories in order that they might become 'untouchable soil'. All countries conquered by the sword were to be turned into 'thriving Germanic provinces'. Should these territories also become insufficient, arms would simply be taken up again. At the beginning of 1943, Himmler reported to 'his' Führer that over 600,000 ethnic Germans had already been transferred back into the Reich and into the new areas of settlement. It was intended to resettle a further 400,000 (among them South Tyroleans). At the same time, the damaging influence of '*volksfremd* (non-German) population groups' was to be eliminated.

Branching out in all directions, the organs of the *Reichsführer*-SS were also given the task to move into the occupied territories behind the advancing troops and there to deal 'heavy blows to elements hostile to the Reich', 'emigrants, Freemasons, Jews, the political church opposition, and the Second and Third Internationals'.[27] This 'Special Order of the Führer' gave the SS the lead role in the systematic annihilation of political opponents. Led by the *Reichssicherheitshauptamt*, numerous German terror commandos in occupied Europe, above all in Poland and the Soviet Union (*Einsatzgruppen*), the personnel in the concentration camps, and the Gestapo left no doubt that the 'New European Order' depended essentially upon the complete execution of their task. It should be added that in those territories which suffered the most (in the East), private and semi-private companies pursued most freely their hunt for profit because it was there that the alliance between economic exploiters and the advocates of harsh resettlement policies was most strongly developed.[28]

As late as January 1944, Himmler gave assurances to his SS officers that Greater Germany would emerge from the war as 'Europe's global

[26]   On the SS see above; on VoMi see Nuremberg Doc. NO-3981, organizational and operational plan, 15 June 1944.
[27]   Cf. H. Krausnick, 'Hitler und die Morde in Polen', *Vierteljahreshefte für Zeitgeschichte* 11, 1963, 196ff.
[28]   Cf. Hallgarten, Radkau, *Deutsche Industrie und Politik*, 397ff.

power' with the task of 'giving order' to Europe with its various peoples, to be their 'wise regent' and, if necessary, their 'brutal ruler',[29]

*Summary*

For the foreign policy of the Nazi regime, the functions of ProMi, AA, AO, *Volkstumsführung, Dienststelle Ribbentrop*, above all the SS, the *Generalgouverneure*, the *Reichskommissare*, the Reich Ministry for the Occupied Eastern Territories, and the Four-Year Plan with its many subordinate offices were of dual importance: on the one hand, for the totality of foreign-policy thinking and acting, on the other for the realization of the revolutionary objective. All of these institutions saw foreign policy not simply as the assertion of national interests against other states, but also as the application of Hitler's decisions and instructions to the social and economic life of the nation and the conquered territories. With it came educational work. The population was to be made to understand foreign policy, to be made to comprehend that foreign policy measures were rightful, purposeful and achievable, and thus to prepare it, both at an organizational and intellectual level, for the forthcoming 'global either-or decision'. Accordingly, the slogan was: 'Germany will either become a global power or perish.'

These institutions propagated a particular form of friend-foe politics. Their merciless battle against the 'ultra volkish powers' was an integral part of Nazi foreign policy. Each in their own way, they all favoured a system of what they called *Volksführung* as an instrument for the implementation of foreign-policy objectives because Hitler believed that 80 million Germans within the borders of the Reich and 8 million outside its gates constituted the 'strongest national unity' in existence, stronger even than the 'largest peoples' groups' in the Soviet Union and the United States. According to Hitler this 'strength of the German people multiplied by its internal unity, its will power, and its inner worth' predestined the Reich to be the 'leading continental power the Europe'. And from it, he also drew the 'natural right' to dominate the 'space in the East which fate had assigned to the German people'.

Of course, it could not be left to the traditional, rather persistent forces and offices of the state (such as the AA) to undertake the total registration, indoctrination and control of the Germans and the elimination of political 'opponents' according to the demands of the Nazi *Weltanschauung*. This had to be the first and foremost task of the party and its organizations. However, as long as the NSDAP had failed to train

---

[29]  Jacobsen, *Nationalsozialistische Außenpolitik*, 618.

qualified experts for this task, it had to employ, *nolens volens*, members of the conservative-nationalist elite even if these were seen as lagging behind the spirit of the movement. From the beginning, the NSDAP fought, both openly and clandestinely, against those domestic groups who represented traditional, conservative or 'liberalistic' ideas of foreign policy – though, for the protection of his so-called 'peace offensive', Hitler made use of these groups until 1938. Yet, in contrast to the Central Committee of the Communist Party of the Soviet Union, he never allowed the NSDAP leadership to take control of the foreign-policy decision-making process.

Almost as important was a further aspect: due to their radical-revolutionary nature, the foreign political demands proclaimed by the Nazis prior to 1933 could not be accomplished with the help of the conservative apparatus of the AA. From the beginning, therefore, Hitler sought new organizations and unconditionally loyal henchmen to support him, against any opposition, in the gradual accomplishment of his objectives. At the same time, and supported by the AA and the Ministries of War, Economics, Finance and Air, his policies of revisionism and rearmament created the crucial preconditions for it. From early on, it was, however, left to the favour of the moment (i.e. the situation and the circumstances, that is to say the practical application of power) to decide each time on how to use the required means and methods.

If we examine the entire structure of Nazi foreign policy under this aspect, it can be argued that – in their own individual way, partly independent of each other, and frequently in circumvention of the AA – the new offices and their staff took on partial, cell-like, functions of the 'greater task' either upon a specific order or because their own initiative based on Nazi ideology had been tolerated. Among those functions, the German people were to be educated to be heroic-aggressive, indeed fanatical. Society was to be militarized while Reich Germans were to be *gleichgeschaltet*, that is the body of Germans outside the borders was to be 'steeled' into an instrument of power and a possible tool for indirect aggression. The new doctrinal alliance system, which amounted to an apparent delimitation of interests from Britain and a closer cooperation with Italy and Japan, was to be extended. Rosenberg secretly worked on plans for carving up the Soviet Union. Further functions included the fight against 'World Jewry' and Bolshevism, promoting the 'Nordic Community of Fate', and total intellectual training. During the Second World War, however, the many competing offices of SS (partly supported by *Wehrmacht* units), party (Gauleiter), the economy and the state tried, albeit with different concepts, to implement the policy of annihilation and exploitation. This policy attested to Hitler's intention to enforce the construction of the 'New Germany' and the revolutionary reorganization of Europe (along with the official and semi-official diplomacy which, for tactical reasons, constantly combined until 1938 declarations of peace with nationalistic slogans, such as the revision of the Treaty of Versailles and the right of self-determination).

In view therefore of more recent evidence we should not distinguish any longer between a revisionist and an expansionist phase of Nazi foreign policy between 1933 and 1939, but instead between a phase of concealed preparations for aggression until 1937, a period of open and violent expansion from 1938, the unleashing of war in 1939, and the plans for a step-by-step creation of a 'Greater German Reich' by way of military and terroristic violence as well as economic exploitation and financial integration.

It can be concluded from the above that any analysis of Nazi foreign policy based only on diplomatic decisions must remain one-sided and superficial. It ignores the dual character of Nazi foreign policy which needs to be seen as a parallel to the domestic development of the 'étatist' and 'actionist' state (considering the importance of the SS in the Nazi system of rule, one might even talk about a triangular relationship). Thus, one needs to refer to a traditional-conservative (i.e. revisionist) and to a revolutionary goal, and therefore to traditional and revolutionary instruments of foreign policy. The former were used, above all, as a shield against the outside world and as evidence for a 'policy of peace', but also to deceive the German people. Within the latter, Hitler made use of several forces simultaneously. Not only did this correspond to his belief in *divide et impera*, but also somehow to a tactic which he applied more specifically to the military sector from 1940; to provide each office only with as much information as he deemed necessary for the completion of the task at hand.[30] In this way, only Hitler was able to keep sight of the overall picture. Competing institutions were encouraged to be more active, ambitious officials were kept busy, and serious contenders for power were thus prevented from becoming too strong. Finally, Hitler's tactic disguised his ultimate intentions.

In addition, Hitler was able to disavow at any time policies adopted by these offices by referring to the so-called official course of foreign policy represented by the AA, even if this was ultimately only a means to an end. Only after the *de facto Gleichschaltung* of the AA and the appointment of Ribbentrop as Foreign Minister in 1938 did a development unfold which saw an increasing agreement with Hitler's original intentions and a gradual weakening of the so-called traditional-nationalistic objectives. This tactical 'disguise' during the period of

[30]    See the *Grundsätzlicher Befehl* No. 1, 11 Jan. 1940, in H.-A. Jacobsen, *Fall Gelb*, Wiesbaden, 1957, 290ff.

concealed aggression led to an unimaginable chaos of competencies which even the cell structure could not overcome in the long term.

Any critical observer will realize that, during the Second World War, the centrifugal forces, that is the diverging power blocs of state, *Wehrmacht* and party with their shifting 'game' of working with, against and alongside each other, had a much greater impact upon the structure of the totalitarian system than upon the intentions and guidelines for the ideological unity of the Third Reich and for the unity of interior and foreign-policy thinking. This picture of 'absence of system' and 'chaos of offices' is reflected in the foreign-policy sector where disputes over competency, influence and implementation of objectives were conducted with all available means. In this struggle the frontline was not simply between more conservative groups (essentially the civil service) and the Nazi leadership elite, but could also run between party offices and affiliated organizations. The Nazi leadership had neither the will nor the resources to train a new elite for the traditional foreign-policy sector alongside the civil service of the AA. Despite many competing offices its only option was essentially the 'revolution from above', that is to implement changes at the top. Neurath was replaced by his long-standing rival Ribbentrop. Although the Nazi offices contained some competent individuals with their own (frequently quite abstruse) views, those in charge and their staff were usually neither quantitatively nor indeed qualitatively able to replace the AA. Frequently, they represented a mixture of naïvety, ignorance and arrogance. Moreover, the in-fighting among the various organizations precluded joint operations against the Wilhelmstraße. Many of these 'would-be' diplomats disgraced themselves or were disgraced by the amateurish organizations they belonged to.

It is obvious that not all foreign-policy decisions in the Third Reich followed with logical consistency either the original intentions or the principle of strategy (long-term aim) and tactics (short-term aim). Frequently during the build-up phase decisions evolved from a favourable situation, from the need to experiment, and from the attempt to find a better way to achieve the set goal within the existing political power-frameworks and series of alliances.

As early as 1937, Goebbels referred to this cautious manoeuvring when he told *Wehrmacht* officers that the Nazi regime had to lead Germany gradually out of the danger zone formed by the threat of intervention by foreign countries. The regime had 'approached the goal step by step by an extremely clever manipulation of means and ordering of circumstances'. At the same time, it accustomed 'people's thinking' to the new situation.[31]

---

[31] Jacobsen, *Nationalsozialistische Außenpolitik*, 615.

Even if this policy appeared initially vacillating and full of inconsistencies and was accompanied by in-fighting over its direction, it should not be interpreted as unsystematic or purely opportunistic (though this factor was frequently of relevance). It would be wrong to underestimate the determined fanaticism of leading Nazis, above all Hitler, in the area of foreign policy. A particular 'baseline' runs though Nazi foreign policy like a thread, a kind of point of the compass towards which Hitler and his fellow leaders oriented themselves and which they eventually followed. For a time, this point may have been covered up, known only to a few. At various points, the Nazi leaders had to deviate from their course, yet their policies would always settle the compass needle back into the right direction. The greater goal, and thus the general direction, was firmly established. This did not mean, however, that the Nazi leadership had worked out definite plans with dates, phases and alternatives. At times, the Nazis deliberately refused to determine specific policies or methods for the stabilization and expansion of power. Everything depended upon the situation and circumstances in which they were able to act. For those Nazi leaders active in foreign policy this had certain consequences. Based on their own beliefs each of them (or each group) attempted to give a concrete shape to the Führer's intentions. Although they did not know how, when and under what conditions the predetermined goal was to be achieved, in their particular field of activity they contributed in part to its realization. Embroiled in disputes over competencies and restricted by temporary compromises and the tactically necessitated course of daily policy-making they displayed an attitude of restless activity. Frequently unaware of the activities of others, and the actual objective pursued by the Führer, they were simply intent (if we ignore personal ambitions) on guessing Hitler's intentions and on gaining the trust and favour of the dictator, which was necessary, in turn, to expand their own power base at home. In the process many houses of cards were constructed and the imagination stimulated (e.g. with regard to the 'Greater Space' in Europe). Much of it was idle work and a waste of human and material resources. Yet all this left Hitler cold. Only success, and the fact that he kept everybody under his control, counted.

In this context, a fundamental question arises: did this 'system' of Nazi foreign policy come about accidentally or was it deliberately planned? Very probably both at the same time. It can be argued that, despite his revolutionary élan and obvious achievements, Hitler lacked both a sufficient overview of and the mental powers for the organization of foreign policy. He also often let things go, that is to say he let things take their course, particularly as he supported the principle of struggle among his subordinates: in the long term, the stronger would gain the upper hand. There is also evidence to suggest that he deliberately strove for the establishment of a multitude of instruments for the accomplishment of his objectives, or that he at least tolerated these for certain reasons. It would have been easy for him to make a stand, that is to put an end to the chaos, to take less ambiguous decisions, and to undertake a clear demarcation of competencies. Yet, he deliberately did not do so.

Even though individuals, party and state offices may have taken a different view of the underlying principles and the speed of the foreign-policy decision-making process, until 1938 most of them were separated more by the method to be applied in each case than by the power political goal (which culminated in the creation of Greater Germany), particularly as many did not even understand, played down or only recognized during the war the revolutionary component of Nazi foreign policy. There was a wide-spread conviction among them that only each one's proposal would provide the fastest and least dangerous answer (e.g. during the period of rearmament, the departure from the League of Nations, the remilitarization of the Rhineland, the *Anschluß* or during the diplomatic steps of 1941).

Finally, one should not forget Hitler's astonishing initial foreign policy successes, his extraordinary luck until 1939, and the series of military *Blitz* victories (until 1941). Against all odds these developments consolidated Germany's growing global position year by year and helped to create the largely effective unity of people and leadership.

Today, there can be no doubt that Hitler, imbued with a special charismatic sense of mission, was ultimately determined to follow the revolutionary foreign-policy principles of the NSDAP. Since the 1920s he had worked towards the total reorganization of the European continent along racial lines. He did not shy away from anything, even a war, for which he had, since 1935, methodically prepared the German people both organizationally and mentally. From 1938 he regarded the *Wehrmacht* and the SS as the decisive instruments of his policy while the activities of other offices and organizations only fulfilled a supporting function.

Goebbels later explained the tactical approach of the Nazis by arguing that they always had to place themselves in relationship to the forces available to them. In 1933 they would not have been able to do what they did in 1934, or later, because the people would not have joined in due to a lack of preparation. It always depended on how much power one actually possessed, and how reliable this power was in overcoming intended crises. One had to understand 'what it was all about. Utopian dreams must not be pursued. Instead, if necessary, the goal was to be reached in stages.' Until now (he was referring to 1940) the Nazis had been able to deceive their enemies about the true revolutionary nature of their objectives. Precisely in the same way the Weimar politicians had been deceived until 1932 about 'where we were heading'. They had failed to realize that the commitment to legality had only been a trick. 'We did not want to tolerate parties which, after a year, might have dealt with us in the same manner as we had intended to deal with them. We could have been squashed, it would not have been difficult. Yet, it did not happen. In 1925, they could have arrested a few of us and everything would have been over. And yet, they permitted us to pass through the danger zone. Precisely the same happened in foreign policy.'[32]

The expansionist policy of the Nazis during the Second World War confirmed to a large degree this clear-cut and radical objective of Nazi foreign policy. It was the result also of the military *Blitz* victories and the growing restlessness of the dictator to achieve his 'historic mission' during his lifetime – supported by the actions of Germany's allies and the reaction of the anti-Hitler coalition, by Rosenberg's role as Minister for the Occupied Eastern Territories, by the Four-Year Plan Office, by the economy and, above all, by the SS in the occupied countries.

It may therefore make sense to refer to Germany's foreign policy from 1933 as National Socialist foreign policy, particularly as this fateful year and the subsequent development until the end of the war should be seen less in the light of the continuity of German history, and rather more under the aspect of a revolutionary change. It cannot be denied, however, that obvious parallels are to be drawn between some objectives and previous German policies in the nineteenth and twentieth centuries.

The objectives were revolutionary simply because Nazi foreign policy, with its inseparable link between ideology and power politics and its application of all available means, not only aimed at territorial expansion, the creation of geopolitically useful 'bastions' in the East and the West, and the establishment of hegemony over other people (as striven for by other other imperialist powers in previous centuries), but also at the perfectionist annihilation of its 'enemies', the total spiritual seduction of a people, and the creation of a new 'order' on the European continent based on racial principles and imbued with a qualitatively different system of values. This new 'order' was partly achieved by all those inhuman atrocities which have placed upon Germany's history a heavy burden of guilt.

[32]   Ibid., 617.

# Economy

# 4

# Germany, 'Domestic Crisis' and War in 1939

## Richard J. Overy

Originally appeared as Richard J. Overy, 'Germany, "Domestic Crisis" and War in 1939', *Past and Present*, 116 (1987) pp. 138–68.

## Editor's Introduction

Was Hitler pushed, or did he do the pushing in 1939? Richard Overy's answer as to whether Hitler was forced into war is unequivocal. Hitler wanted to attack Poland in 1939, though he would have preferred a localized conflict to the general war that followed the British and French declarations of war. According to Overy, 'it seems inherently unlikely ... that general war was a scrambled reaction in 1939 to domestic crisis'. It was not the case, as Tim Mason stated in his very critical reply to Overy's original article, 'that the leaders of the Third Reich *did* feel that they confronted a critical domestic situation, and that their foreign policy decisions *were* influenced by this awareness.'[1] Overy concedes there was 'widespread inefficiency and muddled planning', but denies that there was a crisis of such proportions that it forced the Nazi regime to escape into war.

With the unemployment problem resolved by 1936/37, the Nazi regime faced complaints about shortages of labour, most notably in the war-related industries. Industrialists also complained about insufficient allocations of raw materials, while some exporting companies expressed concern about the sluggishness of foreign trade. Other problem areas included Germany's reserves of gold and hard currency. At a societal level, the regime was clearly aware of grumbling about low wages, long working

---

[1] Tim Mason's (and David E. Kaiser's) reply to Overy's original article followed by Overy's response can be found in 'Debate: Germany, "Domestic Crisis" and War in 1939', *Past and Present* 122, 1989, 200–40.

hours, and the unavailability of consumer goods. Yet these problems and concerns, some of which were in any case deliberately overstated by those articulating them, did not amount to a crisis beyond the control of the Nazi regime. The outbreak of war in early September 1939 was not forced upon a hapless regime by a major structural crisis; it was intended.

# Germany, 'Domestic Crisis' and War in 1939

*Richard J. Overy*

The outbreak of war in 1939 is one of the most prominent issues to divide 'intentionalist' and 'functionalist' historians of the Third Reich. The former stress the individual responsibility of Hitler and his ministerial and party entourage in framing and carrying out a programme of foreign expansion, whose final goal was the achievement of world power.[1] The latter, while not ignoring the Nazis' foreign-policy objectives, emphasize the primacy of structural of functional pressures in explaining the German push for war in 1939. Such pressures are presented as the product of an increasingly bankrupt political system, which sought to stave off the inevitable social tensions between masses and leaders brought about by rapid rearmament and subsequent economic crisis. In this sense the situation is similar to that which provoked the old ruling class into risking European war in 1914, and at least one German historian has argued that the primacy of *Innenpolitik* is a key and continuous explanation for the nature of German foreign policy in the era of the world wars.[2]

These are not by any means exclusive historical categories, and there can be few historians of modern Germany who do not find themselves striking some kind of analytical balance between stated intention and the

---

[1] K. Hildebrand, *The Foreign Policy of the Third Reich* (London, 1973), esp. 91–104; id., 'La Programme de Hitler et sa réalisation', *Revue d'histoire de la deuxieme Guerre Mondiale*, 21 (1971), 7–36; A. Kuhn, *Hitlers aussenpolitisches Programm* (Stuttgart, 1970); J. Thies, *Architekt der Weltherrschaft: Die Endziele Hitlers* (Düsseldorf, 1976); M. Hauner, 'Did Hitler want a World Dominion?', *Journal of Contemporary History*, 13 (1978); F. Zipfel, 'Hitlers Konzept einer Neuordnung Europas', in D. Kurse (ed.), *Aus Theorie und Praxis der Geschichtswissenschaft* (Berlin, 1972), 154–74; M. Michaelis, 'World Power Status or World Dominion', *Historical Journal*, 15 (1972), 331–60; B. Stegemann, 'Hitlers Ziele im ersten Kriegsjahr 1939/40', *Militärgeschichtliche Mitteilungen*, 27 (1980), 93–105. There are many more.

[2] F. Fischer, *Bündnis der Eliten: Zur Kontinuität der Machtstruktur in Deutschland 1871–1945* (Düsseldorf, 1979). There is a general survey on the literature in E. Hennig, 'Industrie, Aufrüstung und Kriegsvorbereitung im deutschen Faschismus', in *Gesellschaft: Beiträge zur Marxschen Theorie 5* (Frankfurt am Main, 1975), 68–148; and also in I. Kershaw, *The Nazi Dictatorship* (London, 1985), 106–29. For a general functionalist view see H. Mommsen, 'National Socialism: Continuity and Change', in W. Laqueur (ed.), *Fascism: A Reader's Guide* (London, 1976), esp. 177ff.

circumstances and pressures which limited or diverted it. Tim Mason has argued that there is a half-way house, that Hitler's declared intentions and their flawed realization are evidence of a dialectical relationship between actors and historical context which gives primacy to neither. In Hitler's case he chooses to call this relationship 'struggle', the interplay between Hitler's crude and literal idealism and the reality of economic and administrative circumstances in the Germany of the 1930s.[3] But in the case of the outbreak of war Mason argues that Hitler could not, for once, resolve this tension, so that circumstances got the better of him. He had to choose war in 1939 'because of domestic pressures and constraints which were economic in origin and also expressed themselves in acute social and political tension'.[4] Hitler, Mason argues, did not want to fight the war he was faced with in September 1939, but he had little choice: 'These were the actions of a man who had lost control of his policies.'[5]

This is still a widely held explanation for the origins of the Second World War, and indeed has been so since these ideas were first formulated in the 1970s. In the complex politics of the Third Reich two key elements have been observed: first, the effort to push through a programme of rearmament in a short period of time to satisfy the demands of the military elites, the party hawks, and Hitler's own expansionist dreams; secondly, the desire that rearmament should not be compromised by provoking the masses into political opposition by reducing living standards and courting economic crisis. It is argued that the administrative confusion and political contradictions of the Nazi system made it increasingly difficult to deliver both arms and consumer goods/food and produced instead regular crises (foreign exchange and food in 1936, labour and the balance of payments in 1938). By 1938–9 the crisis is assumed to have reached a climax, with trade, finance, labour, and agriculture all producing irreconcilable pressures for an economy conditioned by full employment and an overvalued mark. Knowing that economic stability, and thus domestic political peace, could not be maintained under these conditions, and yet unwilling to cut back sharply on government expenditure and rearmament, Hitler launched war in 1939 in order to gain plunder with which to stave off a crisis in living standards, permit further rearmament, and

---

[3]   T. W. Mason, 'Intention and Explanation: A Current Controversy about the Interpretation of National Socialism', in G. Hirschfeld and L. Kettenacker (eds), *The Führer State: Myths and Realities* (Stuttgart, 1981), 23–40.
[4]   Ibid., 39.
[5]   T. W. Mason, conference abstract, 'Zur Funktion des Angriffskrieges 1939', 3 (conference on 'Rüstung und Wirtschaft am Vorabend des 2. Weltkrieges', Freiburg, 1974).

divert domestic political conflicts to a patriotic struggle against a new encirclement.[6]

The product of this tension between economic reality and military planning was the strategy of Blitzkrieg. Short wars would mean fewer arms and the maintenance of living standards; and would also accommodate the constraints on the military economy produced by the competing party and administrative hierarchies which, it is claimed, made it inherently difficult to prepare effectively for any larger military effort, while at the same time making war more likely. The emphasis here is on the primacy of domestic politics and economic circumstances as explanatory approaches to the outbreak of war.[7] These arguments have not been without their critics. Blitzkrieg, for example, as a coherent military and economic concept, has proved to be a difficult strategy to defend in the light of the evidence.[8] This conclusion alone must throw increasing doubt on current analyses of the relationship between domestic affairs and foreign policy in the Third Reich. The purpose of this chapter is to explore alternative ways of looking at German economic performance in the late 1930s, and to reassess the threat of serious political disorder in 1938–9. These approaches present a quite different conclusion about the outbreak of war in 1939 and Hitler's motives in attacking Poland.

I

The question of evidence is clearly crucial here, since it is on the basis of a large quantity of apparently unambiguous documentary material that the conceptual apparatus of 'domestic crisis' has been founded.

---

[6]  Mason, 'Intention and Explanation', 38–9; id., 'Some Origins of the Second World War', *Past and Present*, 10 (1964), 67–87; id., Innere Krise und Angriffskrieg', in F. Forstmeier and H.-E. Volkmann (eds), *Wirtschaft und Rüstung am Vorabend des Zweiten Weltkrieges* (Düsseldorf, 1975), 158–88; id., *Sozialpolitik im Dritten Reich* (Opladen, 1977), esp. ch. 6. For a variation on this theme see C. Bloch, 'Die Wechselwirkung der nationalsozialistischen Innen- und Aussenpolitik 1933–1939', in M. Funke (ed.), *Hitler, Deutschland, und die Mächte* (Düsseldorf, 1976), 205–21, who argues that Hitler, like Bismarck, used foreign policy manipulatively to maintain political popularity at home.

[7]  See esp. A. S. Milward, 'Hitlers Konzept des Blitzkrieges', in A. Hillgruber (ed.), *Probleme des Zweiten Weltkrieges* (Cologne, 1967), 19–40; id., 'Could Sweden have stopped the Second World War?', *Scandinavian Economic History Review*, 15 (1967), 135ff. See too W. Murray, *The Change in the European Balance of Power 1938–39* (Princeton, NJ, 1984), 18–27.

[8]  R. J. Overy, 'Hitler's War and the German Economy: A Reinterpretation', *Economic History Review*, 2nd ser. 35 (1982), 272–91; id., *Goering: The 'Iron Man'* (London, 1984), 82–9; J. Dülffer, 'Der Beginn des Krieges 1939: Hitler, die innere

And yet the evidence in question is in some important respects highly ambiguous. In the first place the absence of a body of documents expressing Hitler's recognition that foreign policy in 1938–9 was governed by domestic political priorities is taken to imply that the evidence has been lost or destroyed, rather than that it simply did not exist.[9] Though far from complete, there is a very great deal of evidence on what Nazi leaders were doing and thinking in 1939, very little of which suggests the primacy of domestic pressures. Though it does demonstrate some confusion of purpose and error of judgement (far from an exclusively German failing before 1939), there are clear strands of strategy which provide an alternative and perfectly plausible explanation for German policy. The bulk of the positive evidence for economic and domestic political crisis came either from unsympathetic conservative circles within Germany, or exiled opponents of Nazism, or, significantly, from British pre-war assessments of the nature of the Nazi regime.

The roots of the argument about domestic pressures can be traced back to the critical discussions in British political and economic circles of the nature and prospects of Hitler's Germany. The rise of economic nationalism in Germany, following on the serious credit crisis of 1930–3, inclined British politicians to view the German economy even before 1933 as a fragile structure, highly susceptible to financial and trading problems, faced all the time with serious economic difficulties, which might bring social discontent.[10] It was this situation that prompted the onset of economic appeasement. Western statesmen assumed that if Hitler were granted economic concessions, he could be brought to the conference table to work out a general European settlement. 'Might not', asked Chamberlain, 'a great improvement in Germany's economic situation result in her becoming quieter and less interested in political adventures?'[11] Cordell Hull, Roosevelt's Secretary

Krise und das Mächtesystem', *Geschichte und Gesellschaft*, 2 (1976), 443–70; M. Cooper, *The German Army 1933–1945* (London, 1978), 116–66.

[9]    Mason, 'Some Origins', 86.

[10]    On British reactions during the depression see H. James, *The Reichsbank and Public Finance in Germany 1924–1933* (Frankfurt am Main, 1985), esp. ch. 6.

[11]    Quoted in L. R. Pratt, *East of Malta, West of Suez: Britain's Mediterranean Crisis 1936–1939* (Cambridge, 1975), 158. These views underlined Chamberlain's personal belief that economic questions dominated the policy of any leader: 'The ultimate aim of this government, and I believe that it must be the ultimate aim of every government,' he told the House of Commons, 'whatever its complexion may be, is the improvement of the standard of living of the people'; in N. Chamberlain, *The Struggle for Peace* (London, 1939), 347 (debate of 1 Nov. 1938). There is evidence that the French government thought in the same way. In 1937 Paul Elbel told the French Chamber, following a Franco-German trade agreement, that 'Germany will cease to appear "a nation of dispossessed" and, with prosperity, shall return a love

of State, argued that in a freer world economy, prepared to extend concessions to Germany, 'discontent will fade and dictators will not have to brandish the sword and appeal to patriotism to stay in power'.[12] In western eyes a demonstrable relationship existed between economic prosperity and peace.

This perception of German weakness affected British strategy in a number of ways. Chamberlain's hope was that a policy of concessions to Hitler on economic questions might bring about a Grand Settlement on British terms.[13] By bolding out the prospect of economic improvement, the British government hoped to win over the moderates around Hitler, including the Reichsbank President Schacht and Hermann Göring, who would then put pressure on him to adopt a more conciliatory foreign policy. The British were alive to all kinds of rumours about political conflicts among Germany's leaders as evidence that they would finally see political good sense.[14] But at the same time the government began large-scale rearmament and a policy of increasing firmness towards Germany, in the belief that Hitler could be deterred from waging war by demonstrating the superiority of Franco-British economic resources.[15] By calling his bluff the Allies supposed that Hitler would face political hostility at home and might even be over-thrown. Carl Goerdeler, a leading member of the German conservative opposition, told the British in April 1939 that a policy of firmness might see the 'Hitler adventure . . . liquidated before the end of June'.[16]

There was, of course, much wishful thinking in all this; and such a strategy carried a considerable risk that Hitler might commit what the British Foreign Office called a 'mad-dog act' if he were pushed into an economic corner in 1939. Intelligence sources sent a stream of information to London suggesting that 'Hitler would have to ex-

of calm and a will to collaborate'; quoted in J. Gillingham, *Industry and Politics in the Third Reich* (London, 1985), 104.

[12]   A. W. Schatz, 'The Anglo-American Trade Agreement and Cordell Hull's Search for Peace 1936–1938', *Journal of American History*, 57 (1970/1), 89.

[13]   K. Feiling, *The Life of Neville Chamberlain* (London, 1946), 332–4.

[14]   C. A. Macdonald, 'Economic Appeasement and the German "Moderates", 1937–1939', *Past and Present*, 18 (1972). A good example of these rumours was the message from the British ambassador in Paris, Sir Eric Phipps, to Halifax in Jan. 1939 to the effect that Göring was about to be appointed German chancellor: see *Documents on British Foreign Policy* (HMSO, 1953), ser. 3 (hereafter *DBFP*), vi. 9–10, Phipps to Halifax, 25 Jan. 1939.

[15]   D. Dilks, 'The Unnecessary War? Military Advice on Foreign Policy in Great Britain 1931–1939', in A. Preston (ed.), *General Staffs and Diplomacy before the Second World War* (London, 1978), 120–7; G. C. Peden, 'A Matter of Timing: The Economic Background to British Foreign Policy 1937–1939', *History*, 66 (1984); 19–22; R. Shay, *British Rearmament in the Thirties* (Princeton, NJ, 1977), 228ff.

[16]   Lord Gladwyn, *The Memoirs of Lord Gladwyn* (London, 1972), 87.

plode in 1939'.[17] After Munich there was increasing evidence of what the British saw as economic crisis and social unrest in Germany. The 'X-documents', memoranda by a British businessman, A. P. Young, of conversations with Goerdeler, included the view that 'the working classes are nervous, distrustful of the leader. Their allegiance is doubtful'.[18] The second document, in September 1938, gave an even franker assessment:

> the feeling among the people against war is welling up at an alarming rate. His [Goerdeler's] recent talks with leading industrialists had satisfied X that the workers' feelings have been bitterly roused to the point where, if they were in possession of arms, they would physically revolt against the present regime.

Sending the report to British officials Young added the comment: 'We know exactly the economic and financial conditions in Germany. Nobody can deceive us. This knowledge in itself would be a big inducement to go to war, if we did not believe passionately in the divine cause of peace.'[19] Four months later Goerdeler's views hinted at imminent disaster: 'Economic and financial situation gravely critical. Inner situation desperate. Economic conditions getting worse.'[20]

Though there was some evidence to the contrary, the general drift of British strategic thinking hardened during 1939 into a conviction that Hitler was walking a tightrope. He might launch a sudden war which the Allies would win because of their greater economic resources and

---

[17]   Ibid. 86–7. The Foreign Office view was that Hitler's object 'was to divert attention away from the German economy, to suppress his own moderates, and to secure supplies of raw materials'. See too F. H. Hinsley, *British Intelligence in the Second World War*, i (HMSO, 1979), 67–9, who records Halifax's view that the sacking of Schacht was evidence that economic problems were pushing 'the mad dictator to insane adventures'.

[18]   *DBFP* vi. 708, app. I (v), enclosure in letter from Orme-Sargent to N. Henderson, 23 June 1939, 'conversation with "X" June 13 1939'. Interestingly, Henderson's response to the letter (app. I (vii), 709–10) was that the army would march behind Hitler 'as one man', and that the view that workers were unreceptive to Nazism 'rubbish, when even the most intelligent Germans believe it'. A Foreign Office note adds, however, that: 'evidence from other sources shows that the working classes are not so impressed as the intelligentsia'.

[19]   A. P. Young, *The 'X' Documents* (London, 1974), 78–82, X doc. 2, 'conversation with Carl Goerdeler, Zürich, Sept. 11th 1938'.

[20]   Ibid. 156–7, 'Memorandum based on most trustworthy information received before Jan. 15th 1939, conversation between Carl Goerdeler and Reinhold Schairer'. Goerdeler's reports were received unkindly by the Foreign Office, not because they were disbelieved, but because the British regarded him as an old-fashioned German nationalist.

the alleged inability of the German economy to sustain more than a short war once subjected to blockade and bombing; or he might back down and Germany be brought back to the conference table to complete the task of economic and political restructuring begun seriously in 1938. Either way Germany was the victim of a deep socio-economic crisis which would bring an end to Hitlerism as it then stood. Right up to the declaration of war the Allies gambled on German weakness. Indeed the French decision to declare war was allegedly influenced by a letter received by the French prime minister, Daladier, at the end of August from Berlin asking the French only to stand firm to bring Hitler to his knees.[21]

It is difficult not to conclude that British politicians, who found Nazism so hard to understand, deluded themselves into believing that Germany was much weaker and Hitler's position more precarious than was actually the case. The German economy did not collapse in 1939, nor was Hitler overthrown. Yet the British attitude is more understandable if it is remembered that much of the intelligence fed to London before 1939 came from circles within Germany, or exiles, hostile to Hitler, who had their own motives for painting a bleak picture of Germany's room for manœuvre. There were many books and pamphlets published in Britain, France, and the United States in the 1930s by German men and women with 'inside' knowledge of German conditions, most of whom were deeply hostile to Nazism.[22] This literature contributed to popular western perceptions of German difficulties, and suggested strategies for exploiting them. Contacts with prominent Germans through official channels or through intelligence added weight to the popular view. Hjalmar Schacht, the German economics minister until November 1937, tried to persuade foreign opinion that conditions in Germany would deteriorate unless the western powers made concessions.[23] There were numerous contacts with the German conservatives,

---

[21] P. Reynaud, *In the Thick of the Fight, 1930–1945* (London, 1955), 235–6. See too R. J. Minney (ed.), *The Private Papers of Hore-Belisha* (London, 1960), 216, where Hore-Belisha records his meeting with Daladier on 21 Aug. 1939: 'He thought that in the even of war we should derive great help from those hostile to the regime in Germany and attached importance to assistance by German émigrés, who were extremely anxious to disrupt the regime.'

[22] e.g. A Member of the German Freedom Party, *Hitler Calls this Living* (London, 1939); H. Hauser, *Hitler versus Germany: A survey of Present-Day Germany from the Inside* (London, 1940); H. Rauschning, *Germany's Revolution of Destruction* (London, 1939); A. Kolnai, *The War against the West* (London, 1938); E. Hambloch, *Germany Rampant: A Study in Economic Militarism* (London, 1939). There are numerous others.

[23] F. Leith-Ross, *Money Talks: Fifty Years of International Finance* (London, 1968), 232–6, 254–5; Macdonald, 'Economic Appeasement', 106–10.

who were disgruntled at being displaced by party appointees whom they thought incapable of running an economy or conducting foreign affairs sensibly, and who hoped to win friends abroad to help them reassert their influence. There were German businessmen, too, who disliked the economic controls and red tape and were seriously worried about the economic effects of rearmament and Nazi extremism. They again had their foreign contacts to whom they submitted their complaints about the new Nazi masters.[24] All of these groups contributed one way or another to building up a picture of impending economic crisis and political unrest in Germany, and it constitutes a large part of the evidence used by historians that this was so.[25]

Of course German conservatives thought their anxieties justified by what they saw around them. Even those close to Hitler in the armed forces or the government believed that by 1938–9 Hitler had gone too far. The army produced a long memorandum on the danger of inflation in December 1938, which contributed to a wider discussion of the acceptable levels of armaments expenditure and prompted some limited proposals for cutting government spending.[26] The finance minister also called for extensive cuts in government investment projects and greater rationalization in the public sector. Late in 1938 wide publicity was given abroad to a speech by the Reichsbank director Rudolf Brinkmann highly critical of Nazi economic policy. 'The situation in the private economy is critical,' he told the Reich Chamber of Industry at Dresden. 'For one thing, there are far more orders than can be filled in a lifetime. For another, production has deteriorated to a much greater extent than we can answer for. There are unmistakably genuine inflationary symptoms, and it is high time to call a halt and to promote exports.'[27] A few weeks later Schacht himself was removed as president of the bank,

---

[24] Christie Papers, Churchill College, Cambridge, 186/1 4, Rough Notes from a recent conversation with a German industrialist, 1 June 1939; 180/1 25 'Memo by members of "Big Business" in Germany, 1937'; letter from a senior industrialist to Christie, 7 July 1939; Young, 'X' Documents, 78, 137.

[25] See Mason, 'Intention and Explanation', 39, who argues that 'The view that this was a major urgent problem was common to many top military and political leaders in Germany, to top officials in Britain, to some German industrialists and civil servants, to German exiles and members of the conservative resistance, and to non-German bankers and academics', without seriously assessing the motives or interests of those involved, or evaluating their evidence.

[26] M. Geyer, 'Rüstungsbeschleunigung und Inflation: Zur Inflationsdenkschrift des OKW von November 1938', Militärgeschichtliche Mitteilungen, 23 (1981), 121–69. For Göring's response to these fears see IMT xxxii. 412–17, note on the meeting of the Reich Defence Council, 18 Nov. 1938.

[27] NA, Reichsfinanzministerium, T178, Roll 15, frames 3672058–9, Schwerin von Krosigk to Göring, May 1939; IMT xxxvi. 493–7, id. to Hitler, 1 Sept. 1938. The Brinkmann speech is reprinted in Hauser, Hitler versus Germany, 114–16.

which was used as further evidence abroad that all was far from well with the German economy. 'Very bad! Lots of repercussions in the foreign market' was the reaction of the American Treasury Secretary, Morgenthau, to the news.[28]

Underlying German worries about the financial situation was the deeper fear, evident well before 1938, that Nazi economic profligacy would endanger the currency and produce a political backlash against military spending, or might threaten to topple the regime altogether and plunge Germany back once again into political turmoil. Conservatives found Nazi economics unorthodox. They disliked excessive government control and distrusted deficit financing, as did their counterparts in the west, where fears circulated about the end of capitalism in Germany. Economic orthodoxy and political good sense seemed to indicate the need for moderation. Conservative fears for German political stability were exported to a foreign audience only too willing to believe that Nazism was a shallow, crisis-ridden movement, trying to stave off the consequences of overheating the economy.

## II

To use this conservative fear as evidence that a crisis of these proportions existed in Germany is to distort the economic reality. It also ignores other contemporary evidence which suggested the opposite: that the German economy was actually considerably stronger than its critics believed in 1939. Schacht had his own reasons for informing Hitler that the economy was facing 'desperate' problems.[29] But he told Sir Frederick Leith-Ross on a visit to London in December 1938 'in a very depressed mood' that 'the German control of wages and prices was working well and could be maintained indefinitely'.[30] Frederick Ashton-Gwatkin's report for the Foreign Office on economic conditions in Germany in February 1939 did not confirm earlier reports from

[28]  J. Blum (ed.), *From the Morgenthau Diaries: Years of Urgency, 1938–1941* (Boston, 1965), 80, Morgenthau to Roosevelt, 20 Jan. 1939. On fears for the future of capitalism in Germany see G. Hutton, 'German Economic Tensions: Causes and Results', *Foreign Affairs*, 17 (1939), 524–33; 'V', 'The Destruction of Capitalism in Germany', ibid., 15 (1937), 596–603.

[29]  Hinsley, *Intelligence*, 68.

[30]  Leith-Ross, *Money Talks*, 254. On another occasion during his visit Schacht reportedly 'pooh-poohed the suggestion that they [the German people] would not bear a good deal more than they were suffering already, and said that the standards of living could still be reduced a long way'; in Bank of England, unclassified German file, S. 89 (2), 'Germany: Notes of a Discussion which took place on the 12th Dec. 1938', 2.

the British embassy of impending economic collapse. He concluded that: 'Economic conditions inside Germany are not brilliant, but they are certainly not disastrous . . . Most Germans with whom I spoke believe that these difficulties will be surmounted; they do not think that their country is heading for the "economic collapse" which has been long prophesied. An "economic collapse" is almost impossible in a country so well regimented as Germany.'[31] British economic intelligence confirmed this picture. The research of the Industrial Intelligence Committee for the Sub-Committee on Economic Pressure on Germany suggested that Germany faced no serious financial difficulties in 1939, and would face raw-material shortages of damaging scale only after the second year of the war, if a British blockade could be made to work.[32]

Chamberlain preferred to listen to those who predicted economic disaster, since this encouraged his hope of deterring Hitler, but there were others in the administration who knew that the real picture was less hopeful. In July the Chancellor, Sir John Simon, produced a report on 'the German Financial Effort for Rearmament' which suggested that Germany was in a better economic position than Britain, with greater financial flexibility, higher taxation, and growing economic power over her eastern neighbours: 'The question of the means of payment for overseas imports in war – an ever present anxiety in our case – scarcely arises in Germany.'[33] It was the Treasury view that Germany was better prepared for a long war that Britain, who would require extensive American loans to survive, a prediction that proved to be remarkably accurate.[34]

Much of this assessment hinges on what historians mean when they talk about economic crisis. The German economy was certainly not facing a conventional economic crisis in 1938–9, with rising unemployment, sharp falls in prices and profits, widespread credit restriction, a slump in foreign trade; nothing, in other words, to match the crisis of 1929–32.[35] The words used to describe the German 'economic crisis' are general and economically imprecise – an overheated economy, forced

---

[31]   *DBFP* iv. 598–601, app. II, 'Report by Mr Ashton-Gwatkin on his visit to Germany and interviews with German Statesmen, Feb. 19th to Feb. 20th 1939'.
[32]   Hinsley, *Intelligence*, 60–4; R. J. Young, 'Spokesmen for Economic Warfare: The Industrial Intelligence Centre in the 1930s', *European Studies Review*, 6 (1976), 480–2.
[33]   Hinsley, *Intelligence*, 69–70. See too Peden, 'Matter of Timing', 23–4, who discusses in detail the Treasury assessment of Germany's financial position in 1938–9.
[34]   On the British position see W. F. Kimball, 'Beggar My Neighbour: America and the British Interim Finance Crisis 1940–41', *Journal of Economic History*, 29 (1969), 758–72.
[35]   R. J. Overy, *The Nazi Economic Recovery 1932–1938* (London, 1982), 16–21.

rearmament, economic contradictions – but they all imply that if Germany continued to pump money into military spending she would be faced with rapid inflation, serious balance-of-payments problems, financial collapse. It is important in this context, however, to distinguish between structural weaknesses and frictional problems. There is no doubt that Germany did face a difficult situation with foreign exchange and payments, and that full employment produced increasing friction in a job market with wage controls. Yet all industrial economies continually face the problems of distributing and balancing their resources. This is a characteristic feature of modern industrial states, and recent evidence suggests that the British and French economies experienced difficulties every bit as great in this respect in 1936–9 as did Germany, if not greater since they were subject to much less regulation. To see such problems, though, as evidence of economic collapse or economic chaos, as some historians have done, is to misinterpret the nature of economic life. Of the more fundamental components of economic stability none assumed what economists would regard as a critical position in 1939, and indeed it is difficult to find a contemporary economist who thought otherwise.[36]

Germany had surmounted major difficulties well before 1939. In 1933 the country had 8 or 9 million unemployed (with 6 million on the registers), trade had collapsed, credit was sharply restricted, international payments questions still unresolved. Recovery was steady, based on high government demand and close controls over trade, investment, wages, and prices. But it was by no means certain, and at points in 1934–6 there were fears of renewed crisis. By 1938–9 the worst of these fears were past. Germany's external debt was stabilized, falling in nominal terms from RM 20,000m. in 1932 to RM 9,000m. in 1938. Interest rates fell continually over the 1930s, from 6 per cent in 1932 to 3 per cent six years later. The German capital market was closely controlled by the state. Increases in state funding were covered by taxation, Reich loans, and treasury bills, which were taken up by businesses, insurance companies, and savings banks at government insistence. Up until 1938 the bulk of government expenditure was covered by taxa-

---

[36] See e.g. C. W. Guillebaud, *The Economic Recovery of Germany 1933–1938* (London, 1939), 267: 'so far as the reasonably near future is concerned . . . it would seem more probable that the German economy will grow stronger than that it will collapse or decline'. See too M. Palyi, 'Economic Foundations of the German Totalitarian State', *American Journal of Sociology*, 46 (1940/1), 472–85; T. Balogh, 'The National Economy of Germany', *Economic Journal*, 48 (1938), 490–7; S. Merlin, 'Trends in German Economic Control since 1933', *Quarterly Journal of Economics*, 57 (1943), 169–72, 185–95; G. Parker, 'Economic Outlook of Germany', *Lloyds Bank Review*, July 1937, 347–67.

tion, and only in 1939 was there a substantial increase in the cumulative government deficit. Though this alarmed Schacht, it was not an unacceptably high debt by modern standards, and certainly not for an economy under close state regulation. Firms in receipt of government contracts were also forced through dividend and profit controls to reinvest substantial industrial funds and thus carry some of the cost of rearmament themselves. By 1938 private investment once again exceeded public.[37]

At the centre of the economic strategy was control of prices and wages to prevent inflation and excessive consumer demand in competition with rearmament, and to encourage investment and savings. Although there were some limited price rises, particularly in foodstuffs, and earnings were higher in the engineering trade than in textiles, the policies were sufficiently successful to prevent any serious pressure on prices or wages, as table 4.1 demonstrates. The pressure of consumer demand was relieved by withholding goods from the shops, by high taxation, and through propaganda campaigns to encourage savings and investment. So extensive were government controls – making money into what one economist called a 'passive instrument' – that it is difficult to see how inflation could have became a factor of crisis proportions in 1939; nor did it do so until the very last stages of the war.[38]

Of course this is not to deny that the German economy faced some financial strain. Rearmament consumed very large sums of money; so too did the motorways and the Nazi Party buildings. Military expenditure in 1938 was also much higher than anticipated because of the mobilization costs in the Austrian and Sudeten crises, and the expense

[37]   On financial controls see S. Lurie, *Private Investment in a Controlled Economy: Germany 1933–1939* (London, 1947), 33–5; K. E. Poole, *German Financial Policies 1932–1939* (London, 1939), 157–66. Government revenue exceeded stated expenditure from 1933/4 to 1937/8, but fell short of it by RM 6,000 m. in 1938/9, or 4 per cent of GNP at current prices. The overall burden of government debt, RM 25,000 m, cannot be regarded as excessive in an economy where GNP had grown by 75 per cent in five years and tax revenue had almost doubled. Total government debt was considerably less than in Britain, where servicing of the debt alone consumed a substantial portion of government expenditure, equivalent to 4–5 per cent of GNP. On Germany's external debt see H. Ellis, *Exchange Control in Central Europe* (London, 1941), 231. In real terms the fall in the debt was from RM 14,000 m. to RM 7,700 m.

[38]   M. Wolfe, 'The Development of Nazi Monetary Policy', *Journal of Economic History*, 15 (1955), 398; R. Lindholm, 'German Finance in World War II', *American Economic Review*, 37 (1947), 124–8; J. J. Klein, 'German Money and Prices 1932–1944', in M. Friedman (ed.), *Studies in the Quantity Theory of Money* (Chicago, 1956), 135–6. By 1939 money supply had increased by 60 per cent over the depression level of 1932, but GNP had increased by 81 per cent over the same period (current prices).

*Table 4.1*   Wages, earnings, and cost of living, 1929–1940

|  | Money wages (1913/14 = 100) | Real wage rates | Real earnings (1925/9 = 100) | Cost-of-living index (1913/14 = 100) | Wholesale prices (1925 = 100) |
|---|---|---|---|---|---|
| 1929 | 177 | 115 | 107 | 154.0 | 96.8 |
| 1932 | 144 | 120 | 91 | 120.6 | 68.1 |
| 1933 | 140 | 119 | 87 | 118.0 | 65.8 |
| 1934 | 140 | 116 | 88 | 121.1 | 69.3 |
| 1935 | 140 | 114 | 91 | 123.0 | 71.8 |
| 1936 | 140 | 112 | 93 | 124.5 | 73.4 |
| 1937 | 140 | 112 | 96 | 125.1 | 74.7 |
| 1938 | 141 | 112 | 101 | 125.6 | 74.6 |
| 1939 | 141 | 112 | n.a. | 126.2 | 75.4 |
| 1940 | 141 | 109 | n.a. | 130.1 | n.a. |

*Sources:* G. Bry, *Wages in Germany 1871–1945* (Princeton, NJ, 1960), 331, 362; BA RD51/21–3, Deutsche Reichsbank, Statistische Tabellen, Jan. 1944, 20.

of building the *Westwall* at high speed. Plans to expand expenditure further in 1939 were revised and restrictions introduced on less essential civilian projects, though with less success than the government hoped. But all these pressures can be seen not so much as contradictions which could no longer be checked, but as problems to be coped with by adjustments in Reich financial and economic policy. The New Finance Plan, for example, introduced by Walther Funk in April 1939, was designed to see the Reich over the following three years of high state demands on the capital market.[39]

Similar controls governed the development of German trade and payments. Both were closely monitored by the state in response to the serious difficulties in this area that had developed during the 1929–33 recession. German trade revived faster after 1933 than that of Britain or the United States or France. The volume of German trade fell 50 per cent from 1929 to 1934, but recovered by 1938 to almost three-

[39]   On the 'New Finance Plan' see Lurie, *Private Investment*, 33. The core of the plan was the issue of a new type of tax certificate. All firms working on government contracts were to be paid 40 per cent in tax certificates, one type redeemable after seven months, the others after 37 months. There were tax advantages if firms held on to the certificates beyond redemption date, and they could be exchanged between firms. In this way the government could get industry involuntarily to finance a share of current arms expenditure. By Sept. 1939 certificates to the value of RM3,000 m. had been issued. See too R. Stucken, *Deutsche Geld und Kreditpolitik 1914 bis 1963* (Tübingen, 1964), 150, 155–7.

quarters of the 1929 levels. The Germans' determination to control foreign trade and payments forced them towards a policy of exchange agreements and barter trade. Though this arguably inhibited the expansion of German trade in the 1930s, it removed serious balance-of-payments difficulties, and gave Germany privileged access to markets where agreements could be reached, particularly in eastern Europe, Latin America, and the Middle East. Helped by export subsidies and a managed currency, Germany enjoyed an active trade balance for most of the 1930s, with a very modest deficit in 1934 and 1938.[40] Most important of all, controlled trade removed the need to link the Reichsmark more closely to the world market and the dollar, which would have involved devaluation, increased import prices, and produced fears at home of renewed inflation. Such fears were partly responsible for pushing Germany towards import-substitution after 1933. Though self-sufficiency was far from complete in 1939 in those areas where it was deemed feasible and strategically necessary, Germany was less dependent on the world economy and much less affected by world market fluctuations than were Britain and France, whose financial and trading position faced a range of difficulties once rearmament got seriously under way.[41] Sir Alexander Cadogan, permanent under-secretary at the Foreign Office, complained after Munich that 'Germany was far more self-sufficient than were we, who, in order to keep alive, had to import the bulk of our food and maintain the value of the pound.'[42] British gold reserves fell from £800 m. in the spring of 1938 to £460 m. in September 1939, while the pound fell sharply against the dollar, making supplies for rearmament purchased abroad even more expensive.[43]

At the core of the argument about crisis lie the questions of employment and living standards. By 1938 the German economy faced selective labour shortages which led to pressure on wages in the heavy-

[40]   H. James, *The German Slump: Politics and Economics 1924–1936* (Oxford, 1986), 332 for comparative trade performance. On controlled trade see D. Kaiser, *Economic Diplomacy and the Origins of the Second Wold War* (Princeton, NJ, 1980), esp. chs 9 and 10; H-E. Volkmann, 'Die NS-Wirtschaft unter dem "Neuen Plan"', in W. Deist et al., *Das Deutsche Reich und der Zweite Weltkrieg*, i. *Ursachen und Voraussetzungen der deutschen Kriegspolitik* (Stuttgart, 1979), 254–9; F. Child, *The Theory and Practice of Exchange Control in Germany* (London, 1958), 208–30; Palyi, 'Economic Foundations', who argued that the great strength of the German economy lay in its ability to reduce dependence on the world economy.

[41]   On Germany see D. Petzina, *Autarkiepolitik im Dritten Reich* (Stuttgart, 1968), 91–109, 183; on France R. Frankenstein, *Le Prix du réarmement français, 1935–1939* (Paris, 1982), 289–99; and on Britain, R. A. C. Parker, 'The Pound Sterling, the American Treasury and British Preparations for War 1938–39', *English Historical Review*, 98 (1983), 261–79.

[42]   Gladwyn, *Memoirs*, 86.

[43]   Parker, 'Pound Sterling', 262–3.

industrial and engineering industries. These problems led to widespread complaints about poaching of labour and some evidence of labour exploiting its improved bargaining position. The problem was alleviated to some extent by foreign labour, which had reached 435,000 by March 1939, drawn mainly from central and southern Europe. Very large-scale retraining and apprenticeship programmes were set up, reversing the shortage of skilled metalworkers by 1939, and putting 1.2 million workers through appropriate training programmes.[44] The government also responded by introducing a measure of labour conscription which proved unpopular and was used only sparingly; and by initiating efforts at rationalization, partly by reducing the competing claims of government agencies on labour resources, partly by insisting that firms modernize factory methods and reduce labour requirements that way.

All these policies were in the early stages of application when war broke out, but they do demonstrate the extent to which the government was aware of the problem and had devised strategies to cope with it. Labour problems created frictional pressures which, because they were regularly reported by the labour supervisory offices and the internal security service (SD), whose task it was to highlight such complaints, have assumed a prominence in the surviving documentation quite out of proportion to their intrinsic economic significance. Labour problems were hardly so intractable as to compel Hitler to abandon his chosen course, and opt for a war of expansion 'at any price'. If anything they suggested the opposite, that a reallocation of labour resources within the economy, and the training of additional skilled labour, was a necessary prelude to launching any major war. This is certainly what the armed forces and Göring's Four-Year Plan thought was the case with the labour strategy set up in 1938–9.[45] It might be said that any government which had successfully weathered the political and economic storms of 1933–5, and large-scale unemploy-

---

[44]   H. Volweiler, 'The Mobilisation of Labour Reserves in Germany, Part I', *International Labour Review*, 38 (1938), 448–9; the figure for foreign labour is from *Statistisches Jahrbuch für das Deutsche Reich 1939/40* (Berlin, 1940), 382. For figures on the training programmes see J. Gillingham, 'The "Deproletarianization" of German Society: Vocational Training in the Third Reich', *Journal of Social History*, 19 (1985/6), 427–8. On the labour problem in general see T. W. Mason, 'Labour in the Third Reich', *Past and Present*, 12 (1966); D. Petzina, 'Die Mobilisierung deutscher Arbeitskräfte vor und während des Zweiten Weltkrieges', *Vierteljahreshefte für Zeitgeschichte*, 18 (1970).
[45]   IMT xxxii. 150–3, Second Meeting of the Reich Defence Council, 23 June 1939, 413, Note on the meeting of the Reich Defence Council, 18 Nov. 1938; BA-MA Wi I F 5.412, results of a conference with General Göring, 16 July 1938; IWM EDS Mi 14/478, Heereswaffenamt, 'Die personelle Leistungsfähigkeit Deutschlands im Mob.-Fall', Mar. 1939.

ment, was unlikely to be thrown sharply off course by a temporary shortage of farm-hands.

The labour problem was related politically to the question of living standards. It is claimed that Hitler was particularly sensitive to the need to maintain living standards or even make concessions to the working class in order to maintain support for the regime. This was increasingly incompatible with large-scale rearmament and the impending clash of these two elements, a distributional crisis between the military and civilian economies, forced Hitler to go to war.[46] Aside from the problem of evidence, this argument fails to do justice to the nature of German strategy from 1936 onwards. The Nazi leaders knew that high government spending and rearmament would cut back on living standards but insisted that military spending took priority. Moreover, far from making concessions to the working class by maintaining civilian consumption and limiting armaments – the argument at the heart of the Blitzkrieg conception – Nazi plans were for full mobilization and armament in depth, leading already by 1938 to reductions in consumption, rationing, and shortages. Consumption as a share of National Income declined from 71 per cent in 1928 to 59 per cent in 1938. Consumer goods output increased 38 per cent between 1932 and 1938, while output of capital goods increased 197 per cent. Colonel Thomas noted that 'the Führer stands by the view that any mobilization must be a total one'.[47] The nature of Hitler's extravagant arms plans made this inevitable.

Nazi propaganda was designed to persuade the population that shortages now were necessary sacrifices for prosperity in the future. The British Embassy in Berlin reported in July 1939 that the Nazi leaders seemed well aware of the effects on living standards ('the poor quality of food and the lack of amenities which a greater supply of consumable goods would provide'), but despite this knowledge Hitler showed himself 'intolerant lately both of argument and of misgiving'. Government financial strategy, the report continued, aimed to divert 'surplus earn-

[46]   Mason, *Sozialpolitik*, 299–312.
[47]   IWM EDS Mi 14/377 (file 2), Thomas memorandum, 28 Mar. 1939, 'Gesichtspunkte für die Änderung der Mob. Vorbereitungen der Wirtschaft', 2. For a more general discussion of the effect on consumption see Overy, *Goering*, 83–7. The statistical evidence makes it clear that the growth of consumption after 1933 was restricted to the benefit of capital goods and government expenditure. See also K. Mandelbaum, 'An Experiment in Full Employment: Controls in the German Economy 1933–1938', in Oxford University Institute of Statistics, *The Economics of Full Employment* (Oxford, 1944), 189–96; Stucken, *Geld- und Kreditpolitik*, 160–1, who discusses 'indirect' rationing, controls over the quantity, and price of goods in the shops.

ings' away 'from a demand for consumable goods'.[48] Any extra pur-
chasing power available by the late 1930s was soaked up by high levels
of taxation, or by saving, which was channelled back to the government
by the banks and savings institutions to fund high government expenditure. There was, of course, no intention of allowing serious shortages
to develop, but there was no question that the workers should be given
butter before guns, or that the failure provide sufficient of both pushed
Nazi economic policies 'out of control'. By 1939 consumption and
investment were both closely controlled precisely in order to avoid this
sort of crisis.

It is possible to see the German economy in a more positive light in
1939, on as sound a footing in terms of finance, employment, output,
and balance of trade as the two western powers, increasingly shielded
from the effects of the world market, building up a powerful trading and
Reichsmark bloc, whose resources were to be used to wage a major war
in the mid-1940s. The primary goal of increasing the investment ratio
and government demand substantially, while restricting consumption
and avoiding inflation, had in large measure been achieved by 1939.
The economy was in a transitional stage as it adjusted to the demands
of large-scale war preparations. This pattern of economic development
brought its fair share of frictional difficulties, political arguments, and
evidence of mismanagement. But to claim that this is prima-facie
evidence of impending economic collapse understates the extent to
which the Nazis were able to impose their political will on economic
circumstances. The degree of planlessness and polycratic confusion
in the economic policy of the Third Reich has been much exaggerated
by measuring it against some kind of 'ideal' of rational, totalitarian
economics. To claim that political conflicts and administrative discor-
dance of themselves were a determinant of economic and social instability is to greatly distort the reality of economic policy-making, and to
underplay the powerful coercive effects of economic intervention in a
one-party state.

This was not, of course, a 'normal' economy, like those of the industrial West, any more than was Stalin's Soviet Union, with which the Nazi
control system had something in common (and whose prospects of survival the West also regularly misjudged in the inter-war years). It was
none the less a relatively stable system in the short term, which because
of its economic strength and size had by 1939 formed the major core of
the economic region of central and eastern Europe. It would be fair to

---

[48]    Bank of England, Central Bank Papers (Germany), OV 34, ix, memorandum
from British Embassy Berlin, 'Germany: Financial Position', 21 July 1939, 5, 10–11.

assume, had major war not broken out in 1939, that Germany would have established further important complementarities with neighbouring and dependent economies, and would have extended economic and political dominance over a wide area of Europe, including Poland, drawing the sinews of the continental economy inexorably towards Berlin, and preparing for the great war to the east.[49] What emerges from such a perspective is not a crisis-ridden economy dragged out of control by grumbling managers and labourers, but an economy remarkably resurgent after experiencing a real economic crisis of such severity that it brought Germany to the brink of bankruptcy and threw German politics into the melting-pot.

## III

It could well be maintained that it makes little difference to the argument whether an objective crisis existed in Germany in 1938–9 or not, but only whether the Nazi leadership, and Hitler in particular, *perceived* this as a crisis, and reacted accordingly. It is clear that German leaders knew much of what was going on in the economy, and that Hitler was closely involved in major decision-making, and in more trivial issues as well. But it is difficult to see them as passive onlookers, drifting with economic events and social pressures. Being aware of the problems, Nazi policy-makers and state officials adjusted policy to take account of circumstances, developing new instruments of economic management and social control. Hitler expected the state to intervene and solve problems as they arose, a view summed up concisely by Göring in June 1938: 'There is no place for the collapse of parts of the economy. Ways will be found. The Reich will step into the breach to help.'[50]

The development of these policy instruments dated from the early years of the regime. Indeed it could well be argued that the real period of political and economic instability was 1935–7, while the economy was still in the throes of recovery, and while the Nazis were forced to take account of popular political pressures and the interests of the

---

[49]   This was a process begun well before 1939. See Kaiser, *Economic Diplomacy*, 130–69; Gillingham, *Industry and Politics*, 90–108, 139–59; M. Broszat, 'Deutschland–Ungarn–Rumänien: Entwicklung und Grundfaktoren nationalsozialistiscer Hegemonial- und Bündnispolitik 1938–1941', *Historische Zeitschrift*, 206 (1968), 45–96; P. Einzig, 'Hitler's New Order in Theory and Practice', *Economics Journal*, 51 (1941), 1–16; S. Newman, *March 1939: The British Guarantee to Poland* (Oxford; 1976), ch. 3 and 107–20 on German economic penetration of the Balkans.
[50]   Geyer, 'Rüstungsbeschleunigung', 136.

old elites.[51] It was during the crisis over foreign exchange, imports, and rearmament in 1936 that Hitler insisted on taking a firmer grip on the economy to meet his military requirements for an active foreign-policy programme, aimed primarily at the Soviet Union. The political difficulties that Göring met in establishing the new economic framework provoked the party leaders into eliminating the conservatives as a major force in domestic politics and extending the political dominance of the movement's leaders. At the same time Himmler increased the movement's grip at a local level, extending the terror and surveillance tactics and stamping out remaining centres of resistance. From this period onwards the political influence of the non-Nazis was reduced and the population subjected to more widespread propaganda and coercion. Both sets of control, over economic and political life, were elaborated and institutionalized between 1936 and 1939, reducing the prospects of the economic strategy going wrong, and the prospects for effective political opposition. There was certainly something in Göring's claim that, 'Measures which in a state with a parliamentary government would probably bring about inflation, do not have the same results in a totalitarian state.'[52]

Although Hitler was alive to the dangers of provoking the 'home front', he was determined to forge ahead after 1936 with the plans to create a powerful economic springboard for his military adventures. This springboard was to include the industrial areas of central Europe, which were necessary to provide the Germans with continental resources for war. When diplomatic circumstances permitted expansion into Austria and Czechoslovakia, their economies were immediately integrated with the Reich, under the auspices of the Four-Year Plan.[53] This was clearly the case with Poland too, and with economic penetration of the Balkans, as Hitler made clear to his military and civilian leaders in March 1939:

> German dominion over Poland is necessary, in order to guarantee the supply of agricultural products and coal for Germany.
> As concerns Hungary and Roumania, they belong without question to the area essential for Germany's survival. The Polish case, as well as

---

[51]   Overy, *Goering*, 68–73; W. Deist, *The Wehrmacht and German Rearmament* (London 1981), ch. 3; I. Kershaw, *Popular Opinion and Political Dissent in the Third Reich* (Oxford, 1983), 120–32; A. E. Simpson, 'The Struggle for Control of the German Economy 1936/37', *Journal of Modern History*, 21 (1959).
[52]   Overy, *Goering*, 55.
[53]   Overy, *Goering*, 110–16; R. J. Overy, 'Göring's "Multi-National" Empire', in A. Teichova and P. Cottrell (eds), *International Business and Central Europe 1919–1939* (Leicester, 1983), 270–8.

appropriate pressure, will doubtless bring them round, bring them down a peg or two. Then we will have unlimited control over their immeasurable agricultural resources and their oil reserves. The same can be said of Jugoslavia.
This is the plan, which shall be completed up to 1940.[54]

There were certainly economic *motives* at work here, but these are not the same as economic *pressures* produced by impending crisis at home. This economic conception did not simply emerge as rearmament found growing difficulties, but was central to the *Lebensraum* strategy from the start. Economic expansion was as much the cause as the consequence of rearmament.

Hitler's commitment to living-space in eastern Europe dates from well before 1938–9, and was consistent with the general intention to prepare the economy for large-scale military mobilization. Neither could be achieved without cuts in living standards, and made necessary greater disciplining of the workforce. It also made it necessary to prepare the country, in Göring's words, 'psychologically for total war'. The development of a moral commitment to military expansion was the work of the armed forces and of the apparatus of propaganda, whose object was to persuade the people that guns now would mean butter later.[55] Although both efforts were less productive than the authorities might have liked, they demonstrate that Nazi leaders had a grasp of the possible consequences of their economic and military strategy from the outset, and were not caught out in 1938–9 by an unpredictable and uncontrollable social and economic crisis. Indeed they were better prepared to meet it should it occur in 1939 than perhaps at any stage since 1933.

But the truth is that there was no such crisis in 1939 for the Nazis to perceive. There is no evidence at government and ministerial level of a 'crisis' in the summer of 1939. There were no suggestions that the economy was in severe difficulties, 'out of control', in either the Finance

[54]   D. Eichholtz et al. (eds), *Anatomie des Krieges* (Berlin, 1969), 204, Doc. 88, Bericht von Wilhelm Keppler über die Rede Adolf Hitlers am 8 März 1939.

[55]   M. Balfour, *Propaganda in War 1939–1945* (London, 1979), 148, who quotes Otto Dietrich's remark in 1939: 'The German people must be roused to a readiness for sacrifice and for maximum participation.' The remark by Göring is in BA-MA Wi I F 5.412, conference with General Göring, 16 July 1938. See also W. Wette, 'Ideologie, Propaganda, und Innenpolitik als Voraussetzungen der Kriegspolitik des Dritten Reiches', in Deist et al., *Ursachen und Voraussetzungen*, 121–36, and the general discussion of efforts to mobilize the population for total war in L. Herbst, *Der Totale Krieg und die Ordnung der Wirtschaft: Die Kriegswirtschaft im Spannungsfeld von Politik, Ideologie and Propaganda 1939–1945* (Stuttgart, 1982), chs 2–3; and J. Sywottek, *Mobilmachung für den totalen Krieg: Die propagandistische Vorbereitung der deutschen Bevölkerung auf dem Zweiten Welikrieg* (Opladen, 1976), 94–103, 194–201.

Ministry, the Foreign Office, the Economics Ministry, the Four-Year Plan Office, the armed forces' economic office, or the Labour Front. Not even Schacht, least likely to disguise the amateur economics of his Nazi successors, suggested that a serious crisis existed in 1939, however much he disapproved of the way in which German finances were being run.[56] 'Crisis' is an inappropriate characterization of the German economy in the months before war.

Much the same can be said of the German working class in 1939. After six years of repression and party rule and propaganda, the working class was demoralized, powerless, and fearful. The revolutionary potential of the class was negligible. The so-called SOPADE reports, produced by SPD exiles, show the development of a mood of resignation and apathy among the working class, even of hostility towards those who preached to them of the virtues of struggle.[57] When the socialist Hilda Monte visited Germany early in 1939 she was struck by the negative attitude of workers to the political situation:

> I wish I could say that the terror alone stemmed a powerful wave of rebellion, which was ready to break out at any moment. But that would not be true . . . The terror, in common with the misery, despair, and fatigue, have worked on people's minds. It has made them acquiesce in and find excuses for the system. The result is resignation and indifference rather than rebellion . . . Since the future held out no hope or promise to them I was convinced beforehand that the masses in Germany would not, as some expected, turn round their rifles on to their leaders the moment Hitler wanted to drive them into war. The German people are not revolutionary in character, and worse things will have to happen before a rebellion breaks out.[58]

This is not to condemn the German working class for not confronting Nazism, but to understand the reality of working-class life in pre-war

---

[56]   H. Schacht, 76 *Jahre meines Lebens* (Bad Wörishofen, 1953), 495–514; Lutz Graf Schwerin von Krosigk, *Memoiren* (Stuttgart, 1974), 191ff; H. Kehrl, *Krisenmanager im Dritten Reich* (Düsseldorf, 1973), 145–55; N. Henderson, *Failure of a Mission* (London, 1940), 227–36. Interestingly there is no hint of a crisis in the detailed reports prepared on Germany in the Bank of England, though the Bank had access to a wide range of information on the state of the German economy. Yet the reports up to 1937 are full of comments on critical difficulties facing Germany.

[57]   Kershaw, *Popular Opinion*, 94–5, 108–10; J. Stephenson, 'War and Society: Germany in World War II', *German History*, 4: 3 (1986), 16–23.

[58]   H. von Rauschenplat and H. Monte, *How to Conquer Hitler: A Plan of Economic and Moral Warfare on the Nazi Home Front* (London, 1940), 190, 201. See too the letters reproduced in *Hitler Calls this Living!* (n. 22 above), 2–3, 'letter from a workman, Mar. 1938', and 4–5, 'letter from a young employee, Jan. 1939', both of which convey vividly the isolation and demoralization of the workforce.

Germany. The working class itself was far from homogeneous, and opportunities for organization and agitation almost entirely lacing. Nazi propaganda played up working-class patriotism and racialism, creating in important ways some kind of identity of interest between rulers and ruled.[59] Labour service, the Hitler Youth, and military training achieved something of the same effect. Mason himself has recently adopted Wilhelm Leuschner's argument that the condition of the working class was like life in a 'convict prison' (*Zuchthaus*), where the workers were deliberately cut off from other social groups, and from communication with the outside world, and were subjected to propaganda and coercion diluted with limited welfare concessions.[60] Though this view possibly overstates the extent to which the working class was excluded from party office and understates the degree of social mobility in a highly militarized society, there can be no doubt that the Nazi regime was particularly effective as an instrument of social control, rewarding normative actions but fiercely and deliberately repressive of dissent. 'Revolution from within', Hitler told his commanders in November 1939, 'is impossible.'[61]

Hitler's motive for controlling the working class in this way was to ensure that it should have no opportunity to repeat November 1918 – hence the efforts to maintain a reasonable minimum level of food consumption, to offer improved factory conditions, and to provide comprehensive welfare care in the event of a major war. These were not temporary concessions, extorted in the face of growing social unrest, but were a consistent component of the regime's political strategy, and also, it should be noted, of the 'social strategy' of the armed forces, equally fearful of another stab in the back. But the priority of both the party and the army was to provide only a minimum standard guaranteed for all, in contrast to the inequities of the Great War. Such a minimum had to be compatible with a high level of military expenditure and output. For those workers who objected to the restrictions involved in Nazi labour strategy by slack working, absenteeism, or veiled

[59]   D. Aigner, *Das Ringen um England: Die öffentliche Meinung 1933–1939* (Munich 1969), 349–53.

[60]   T. W. Mason, 'Die Bändigung der Arbeiterklasse im nationalsozialistischen Deutschland', in C. Sachse et al. (eds), *Angst, Belohnung, Zucht und Ordnung: Herrschaftsmechanismen im Nationalsozialismus* (Düsseldorf, 1982), 48–53. See too H. Mommsen, *Arbeiterbewegung und nationale Frage* (Göttingen, 1979), 366 who reproduces Leuschner's views in a letter to a friend on 20 Aug. 1939: 'We are imprisoned in a great convict prison. To rebel would amount to suicide, just as if prisoners were to rise up against their heavily armed overseer.'

[61]   NCA iii. 578, Doc. 789-PS, Führer conference with heads of armed forces, 23 Nov. 1939.

strikes, there were fines, work-eductation weekends with the Gestapo, the threat of conscription, or dismissal.[62]

Nazi propaganda was designed with the strategy of social control in mind. The media isolated and pilloried slackers and saboteurs. Public opinion was manipulated so that it should appear as if Germany were threatened by hostile encircling powers once again, led by capitalist enemies of the German worker. Patriotism was appealed to, particularly in the summer of 1939 when it was suggested that foreign powers were trying to break the Germans' nerve. Reluctant to appear as the unpatriotic Germans, and fearful of reprisals, it is hardly surprising that most workers chose, with resignation, to accept full employment and restricted consumption rather than confront the regime head-on. Moreover there is evidence that Hitler's personal popularity increased during 1938 and 1939, as he achieved a reversal of Versailles without war. If there was little of the overt enthusiasm of 1914 when war finally came, there was little popular hostility.[63]

The irony is that Hitler perceived crisis not in Germany in 1939, but in the democracies, precisely because they lacked the repressive political apparatus and propaganda machinery at his disposal. Henderson reported to London in January 1939 that leading Nazis thought the weakness of Britain's position lay in 'the opposition within', and one of Hitler's own arguments for pressing ahead with action against Poland was that a firm German response would lead to the overthrow of the Chamberlain and Daladier governments and plunge the Allies into political crisis.[64] There was plenty of evidence of widespread labour unrest,

[62]  S. Salter, 'Class Harmony or Class Conflict? The Industrial Working Class and the National Socialist Regime 1933–1945', in J. Noakes (ed.), *Government, Party and People in Nazi Germany* (Exeter, 1980), 84–9.

[63]  I. Kershaw, *Der Hitler-Mythos: Volksmeinung und Propaganda im Dritten Reich* (Stuttgart, 1980), 112–13, 122–6; Balfour, *Propaganda*, 49–50, 148. According to a report sent to the Bank of England from Berlin in Oct. 1939, 'there is plenty of minor grumbling but no serious discontent', Bank of England, Central Bank Papers (Germany), OV 34, ix, memorandum on German situation, 23 Oct. 1939, 2.

[64]  *DBFP* iv. 593, app. I (v), N. Henderson to Halifax, 22 Feb. 1939; E. Kordt, *Wahn und Wirklichkeit* (Stuttgart, 1948), 168, 192. Hitler was no doubt influenced by von Dirksen's reports from London which stressed the political fears of Chamberlain and the appeasers. Chamberlain realized, according to Dirksen, 'that the social structure of Britain, even the conception of the British Empire, would not survive the chaos of even a victorious war': see G. Craig and F. Gilbert (eds), *The Diplomats 1919–1939* (Princeton, NJ, 1953), 482–3, 492–3, 500–1. There is an interesting instance of Hitler's attitude in Ernst von Weizsäcker, *Memoirs* (London, 1951), 203, who records that after an interview with Henderson on 23 Aug., during which Hitler had appeared in an agitated mood, he 'slapped himself on the thigh, laughed and said: "Chamberlain won't survive that conversation: his cabinet will fall this evening"'.

political violence, and party conflict to suggest that this was a very real possibility. He was later to apply the same arguments to the Soviet Union.[65] But there is little evidence that he ever entertained the same fears about Germans, or that such fears governed his foreign-policy decisions; nor in fact did a serious threat of popular political resistance emerge at any stage between 1939 and the end of the war.

## IV

Any analysis of the relationship between domestic problems and the outbreak of war in 1939 must in the end take account of international circumstances and the conduct of foreign policy. There are strong arguments for suggesting first of all that German expansion in 1938 and 1939 was governed primarily by Hitler's exploitation of diplomatic opportunities within a strategic and ideological framework already accepted well beforehand. And secondly that, far from seeking a major war in September 1939 to avert domestic disaster, Hitler was convinced that the Polish crisis could be localized, and Poland brought within the German orbit with possibly no war at all, as had Austria and Czechoslovakia. In other words, that the main explanation for the outbreak of a war in September 1939 rather than at a future date lies with British and French decision-making rather than German.[66] If Hitler did not expect a major war in 1939, it can hardly be argued that he deliberately provoked one to avoid domestic crisis.

Hitler's strategic conception is not difficult to uncover. He wanted Germany to achieve continental hegemony, to seek living-space in an eastern empire, and to become a world power in place of the declining western 'plutocracies'. It was for that reason that he embarked on large-scale rearmament, initiated the Four-Year Plan to make Germany as nearly self-sufficient as possible in oil, chemicals, rubber, and iron ore, and began a trade and financial offensive into central and eastern Europe as a prelude to the extension there of military and political influence. *Mitteleuropa* was essential to this conception, because only very great economic resources would permit Germany to achieve world-power status, an obvious lesson Hitler drew from Germany's experience in the First World War. These resources would permit Germany to build up huge military capability. There is little hint in German planning of limited rearmament – army motorization, a fivefold increase in air

[65]    F. Taylor (ed.), *The Goebbels Diaries 1939–1941* (London, 1982), 413–15.
[66]    This is certainly the direction taken by much recent research. See A. Hillgruber, 'Zum Kriegsbeginn im September 1939', in G. Niedhardt (ed.), *Kriegsbeginn 1939* (Darmstadt, 1976), 163–77.

strength from 1938, a large battle fleet, strategic bombers, synthetic fuel and rubber production, and explosives output greater than the levels of the First World War – these were hardly the armoury for Blitzkrieg, and of course they proved more than enough to bring Germany's immediate neighbours under German influence.[67]

Much of this conception was shared by others in German society and was not exclusively Hitler's. The armed forces also argued that major war was likely to be a long-drawn-out affair, a battle of economies as well as armies. Pan-German and imperialist circles in Germany had been arguing for some such strategy since before 1914. In this sense Hitler was not an isolated actor, but was representative and spokesman of ideas about international and military questions which had a wide currency in Germany. Nor was this conception simply conjured up to cope with Germany's domestic situation in 1938–9, desperate wars of booty to stave off collapse. Nazi leaders made it plain that they wanted a free hand in eastern Europe from at least 1936 onwards: Austria first, then Czechoslovakia, then Poland.[68] There were, as we have already noted, strong economic motives in this. Lignite from the Sudetenland for synthetic fuel, the Austrian Erzberg, the coal and machinery industry of Czechoslovakia and Silesia were slotted immediately into the German economic structure under the Four-Year Plan once they were occupied by German troops.[69]

The timing of this expansion depended on circumstances: on the achievement of domestic political stability and the growth of German economic power, as well as on international conditions. Above all it was to be achieved without general war, for which Germany would not be fully prepared, as Hitler himself argued, until 1943–5.[70] That Germany

---

[67]   Overy, *Goering*, 84–6; Dülffer, 'Beginn des Krieges', 451–7, 467–8.

[68]   Christie Papers, 180/15, report of a meeting which Göring, 28 July 1937; notes of a coversation with Göring, 19 Sept. 1937; notes of a conversation with Göring, 3 Feb. 1937. Gladwyn, *Memoirs*, 66, records Göring's remark to Lady Stanley at Christmas 1937: 'You know of course what we are going to do. First we shall overrun Czechoslovakia, and then Danzig, and then we shall fight the Russians. What I can't understand is why you British should object to this.' Leith-Ross, *Money Talks*, 236–7, reports a conversation with a Romanian oil industrialist in early 1937 who told him that Hitler 'wanted to get back Danzig, reabsorb Austria, perhaps to slice off part of Czechoslovakia . . . The sort of country that he wanted for his colonies was to be found in Russia.'

[69]   Overy, 'Göring's "Multi-National" Empire', 272–8; N. Schausberger, 'Der Anschluss und seine ökonomische Relevanz', in R. Neck (ed.), *Anschluss 1938* (Vienna, 1981).

[70]   *Documents on German Foreign Policy*, ser. D, i. 3, 'Minutes of the meeting in the Reich Chancellery, Nov. 5th 1937' (Hossbach Memorandum); ser. D, vi. 580, 'Minutes of a conference on May 28th 1939': 'the armaments programme will be completed by 1943 or 1944'.

should achieve a more powerful economic and political position in central Europe was conceded by Britain and France during 1938, not without misgivings. The Czech crisis and the Munich Pact proved a vital turning-point in Hitler's calculations. He interpreted it, with some justification, as a green light for further German advances in eastern Europe. Rump Czechoslovakia was treated almost as a German satellite after October 1938; Hungary, Yugoslavia, and Romania were brought into the German economic sphere of influence. These were not the acts of a leader whose policies were out of control, but a coordinated diplomatic and economic offensive into eastern and southeastern Europe promoted by the German government and its officials, whose short-term object was to strengthen Germany's war potential, and whose long-term aim was to cement permanent German control.[71]

Munich brought two important diplomatic lessons as well. Hitler formed a conviction, underlined by the Anglophobe von Ribbentrop, that the 'men with umbrellas' had abandoned eastern Europe and were too timid and too unprepared to prevent Hitler achieving the final consolidation of eastern Europe under German domination.[72] Young reported to the Foreign Office Goerdeler's claim that

> it is vitally important to realise that Hitler is deeply and definitely convinced that after his unexpected victory at Munich, anything is possible to him . . . He says that he [Hitler] is now convinced that England is degenerate, weak, timid, and never will have the guts to resist any of his plans. No war will ever be needed against either France or England.[73]

This conviction was to stay with Hitler throughout the period leading up to war. The second lesson was that something had to be done about the Soviet Union, whose actions had been unpredictable during the Czech crisis, and who might be persuaded to join Britain's policy of encirclement. The answer was to move closer to the Soviet Union, even in the end promising her the economically less significant eastern areas

---

[71]    A. Teichova, *An Economic Background to Munich* (Cambridge, 1974), *passim*.
[72]    I. Kirkpatrick, *The Inner Circle* (London, 1959), 135. Hitler was reported as saying after Chamberlain's departure from Munich: 'If ever that silly old man comes interfering here again with his umbrella, I'll kick him downstairs and jump on his stomach in front of photographers.' 'Thank God,' he told an audience later in the year, 'we have no umbrella politicians in this country.'
[73]    Young, *'X' Documents*, 159. See too F. von Papen, *Memoirs* (London, 1952), 445: 'Hitler apparently still hoped to solve the Polish corridor question without a general war, it still being Ribbentrop's conviction that Britain was only bluffing.' Schwerin von Krosigk, *Memoiren*, 191, recalls a similar conversation with Ribbentrop in July 1939.

of Poland, in return for the promise of non-aggression by both parties. Once it became clear that Britain and France were taking the Polish crisis seriously, Hitler speeded up the moves to achieve such a rapprochement in the belief that this would lead to the collapse of British strategy and bring Poland into the German camp after a brief military campaign.

There is abundant evidence that Hitler's decision to solve the Polish question in 1939 stemmed not from domestic considerations but from diplomatic and military. He and Ribbentrop were convinced that the Polish war could be limited. The state secretary at the German Foreign Office, Ernst von Weizsäcker, recorded in his diary from February 1939 until after the outbreak of war regular assertions from Hitler that war would be localized; and he later recalled that 'on Sept. 3, when the British and French declared war, Hitler was surprised, after all, and was, to begin with, at a loss'.[74] Formal military preparations during 1939 were predicated on this assumption of a local war. As late as 21 August Hitler instructed the High Command to prepare only for limited economic mobilization against Poland.[75] The western powers were expected to make substantial gestures but not actually to fight Germany. This assessment was based on political and military intelligence which suggested first of all that the democracies were in too fragile a state politically to risk war, and secondly that they were still far too unprepared militarily.

Secret interception of British diplomatic correspondence with Warsaw and Berlin lent weight to this view, for it seemed that the British wanted the Poles to give up something, perhaps Danzig, to the Germans rather than risk major war (and there were certainly those in London and Paris who favoured just such a course).[76] The answer to the question 'why did Hitler take the risk?' lies much more in considerations of this kind than in domestic pressures. Of course the final attack on Poland did carry a greater risk than Hitler had expected, but he ran it

---

[74]   L. E. Hill (ed.), *Die Weizsäcker-Papiere 1933–1950* (Frankfurt am Main, 1974), 149 (entry for 1 Feb. 1939), 153 (entry for 16 Apr. 1939), 155–6, 159 (entry for 23 Aug. 1939), 160, 164 (entry for 7 Sept. 1939); von Weizsäcker, *Memoirs*, 205. See too M. Muggeridge (ed.), *Ciano's Diplomatic Papers* (London, 1948), 284, conversation with Ribbentrop, 6/7 May 1939: 'It is certain', said Ribbentrop, 'that within a few months not one Frenchman nor a single Englishman will go to war for Poland'; and 297–8, conversation between Ciano and Ribbentrop, 11 Aug. 1939: 'France and England cannot intervene because they are insufficiently prepared militarily, and because they have no means of injuring Germany.'
[75]   IWM EDS Mi 14/328 (d), OKW, minutes of meeting of *Wehrwirtschaft* inspectors, 21 Aug. 1939.
[76]   A. Cienciala, *Poland and the Western Powers 1938–39* (London, 1968), 241–19.

because he thought he had the measure of Chamberlain – 'Our enemies are little worms. I saw them at Munich'[77] – when in fact he had not. The answer to why war broke out in September must very largely be found by explaining British and French firmness at a time when political and military reality suggested to Hitler that they would back down; and in the British and French cases there is a good argument for saying that economic and political pressures at home played a very considerable part in that decision.

It is important to recall that with the coming of major war to Germany sooner than Hitler wanted it, the German economy had to be converted to total mobilization several years before it was ready to do so. Nevertheless Hitler proceeded as if it were now possible to have the 'big war'. To the large plans drawn up in 1938 were added economic demands even greater. Hitler authorized production programmes in the winter of 1939 that eclipsed anything achieved even by the end of the First World War.[78] By the beginning of 1941 almost two-thirds of the industrial workforce was engaged on direct military orders, a higher proportion than in Britain; living standards, already low before 1939, were cut back still further and the country smothered with controls.[79] None of this produced economic crisis, though it produced widespread inefficiency and muddled planning; neither did it prompt social or political unrest of a critical kind, because this time, unlike 1914, the government was prepared with effective rationing, welfare payments, and mechanisms of control to ensure that the home front did not crack as it had allegedly done in 1918.

[77]    NCA iii. 584–5. See too A. Speer, *Inside the Third Reich* (London, 1970), 164–5.
[78]    Hitler called for a 'programme with the highest possible figures': BA-MA Wi I F 5.412, minutes of a meeting with General Thomas, 13 Nov. 1939. The army programme (*Fertigungsplan* 1940/2) planned for artillery production four times greater than the peak level of the First World War, and machine-gun and rifle production ten times greater. See IWM EDS Mi 14/521 (part I), Munitionslieferung im Weltkrieg, Anlage 2, Munition.
[79]    On the German figure, see IWM Speer Collection, FD 5450/45, Gen. Thomas to Field Marshal Keitel, 6 July 1941; Nuremberg Trials, background documents, Case XI, Prosecution Document Book 112, 301, lecture by State Secretary Neumann at the *Verwaltungsakademie*, 29 Apr. 1941. See too R. Wagenführ, *Die deutsche Industrie im Kriege* (Berlin, 1963), 159, who gives the figures produced by Reichsgruppe Industrie during the war. The proportion working on military orders for all German industry in 1941 was 54.5 per cent if consumer industries are included, 66 per cent if they are excluded, and 58 per cent if construction is excluded, but consumer production included. The British figure is calculated from P. Inman, *Labour in the Munitions Industries* (London, 1957), 5, and H. M. Parker, *Manpower* (London, 1957), 112, 483. The figure for industry (excluding services and construction) is 50.9 per cent working on supplies and orders for the armed forces in June 1941. This is directly comparable with the figure of 58 per cent for German industry given above.

V

Interpreting the outbreak of war in this way does not impose intention over structures, though the relationship between them is different. It could well be argued that in a very general sense the rise of Nazism and the seizure of power were directly related to the failures of the world economy to cope with structural crises brought about by the First World War and the 1929 crash. These were problems that many Germans were aware of in the 1930s, as were economic nationalists in Italy or Japan. But once Hitler was securely in power he actively sought, with support among military and administrative circles in Germany, to pursue a strategy that would free Germany from the western economy and western political interests, and establish German international power. Because this could not be achieved without further economic resources, the expansion of German influence into central Europe became imperative. But before that could be begun it was necessary to establish a firm political base, to initiate rearmament, and to achieve economic recovery. It is possible to stand the structural argument on its head and to argue that domestic political peace and a more stable economy, neither of which was guaranteed before 1936, were essential *preconditions* for the period of active European expansion, rather than its consequence. Pressure of circumstances was more significant in the mid-1930s than in 1938–9.

The arguments over strategy were finally resolved in favour of the party in 1937–8, representing the triumph of the Pan-German tradition over the Prussian, and opening the way to active imperialism and racial politics. This meant the undermining of conservative influence and the strict regimentation of the working classes, and it drew its strength from the support of those party hacks and German nationalists who hoped to profit from the establishment of a wealthy German empire. In establishing the complex system of political and economic control, the subjective ambitions of the leader became a crucial reference point, holding the whole structure together, so that in the end Hitler's obsessive historical vision became willy-nilly that of Germany as a whole. In this sense the structures of the Nazi political system interlocked with the literal intentions of its leader, producing an ideological determinism that led to the Holocaust and the pursuit of world power. The more Hitler sensed this power, the more positivistic his foreign policy became, the more he risked. It seems inherently unlikely, therefore, that general war was a scrambled reaction in 1939 to domestic crisis. The acquisition of Poland was on the agenda long before this; Germany was not prepared for war with the great powers for four or five more years.

It was the obvious weakness and diplomatic ineffectualness of the Allies that tempted Hitler to solve the Polish crisis and complete the first stage of German expansion. The 'structural' pressure that really mattered at this juncture was the disintegration of the established international power constellation during the 1930s.

If domestic factors have any bearing on the outbreak of war in September 1939, they are to be found in the response of the British and French empires to the decline in their relative international strength and the cost and political difficulties of reversing this trend. For Britain in particular it soon became obvious that a sustained rearmament and increased government spending would produce crisis in the balance of payments, a decline in exports, more imports, a threat to the currency, labour difficulties, and so on.[80] By 1939 a Treasury official warned that Britain was sailing economically 'upon uncharted waters to an unknown destination'.[81] If Hitler were to be confronted militarily, while Britain and France maintained economic stability and domestic political peace, then 1939 was in some respects the best time to do so. Allied rearmament was planned to peak in 1939/40, while the advantage of using up unemployed resources and avoiding inflation was not expected to last beyond the winter of 1939. Oliver Stanley, President of the Board of Trade, concluded that 'there would come a time which, on a balance of our financial strength and our strength in armaments, was the best time for war to break out'.[82]

Neither Britain nor France was prepared to accept an end to her imperial power and world influence, though neither could really afford the military effort of defending it. Caught between these two pressures, but reasonably confident of the brittle nature of the Nazi system, they opted for war.[83] By June 1940 France was defeated and in political turmoil. By December 1940 Britain was almost bankrupt, entirely dependent on United States finance and war production to keep going. The economy and political system of the Third Reich was only brought to collapse by the combined efforts of the United States, the Soviet Union, and Britain after four years of total war.

---

[80]   R. A. C. Parker, 'British Rearmament, 1936–1939: Treasury, Trade Unions and Skilled Labour', *English Historical Review*, 96 (1981), 306–43; F. Coghlan, 'Armaments, Economic Policy and Appeasement', *History*, 57 (1972), 205–16.
[81]   Shay, *Rearmament*, 276.
[82]   Ibid., 280.
[83]   Peden, 'Matter of Timing', 15–28; P. Kennedy, *The Realities behind Diplomacy* (London, 1981), 301–16.

# Army

# 5

# Soldiers, Nazis and War in the Third Reich

## *Omer Bartov*

Originally appeared as Omer Bartov, 'Soldiers, Nazis and War in the Third Reich', *Journal of Modern History*, 63:1 (1991) pp. 44–60.

*Editor's Introduction*

One of the most enduring myths of the Third Reich is that of a German army which remained detached from the Nazi regime, of an officer corps which tried desperately to adhere to its 'chivalrous' code in the face of severe subversive pressures exerted by Nazi 'barbarians' from both the party and the SS. Consequently, the responsibility for atrocities committed during the war was attached entirely to the Nazis and not to the valiant German *Landser* and their officers. For decades after the Second World War, the myth of the 'good *Wehrmacht*' was carefully nourished by, in particular, (West) German, British and US politicians, officers and historians. 'Denigrators' remained few and far between.

Since the 1980s, however, the myth has been revealed to be precisely that. As more and more evidence emerged about the successful ideological indoctrination of soldiers and officers, the artificial separation between Nazis on one side and the *Wehrmacht* on the other has been eroded.[1] And, if that were not enough for those who used to, or continue to, believe in the myth, the *Wehrmacht* has been linked to major atrocities on the Eastern Front. As the following article reveals, Omer Bartov has been particularly adept at dissecting the mythological treatment of the

---

[1] On the *Wehrmacht*'s relationship to the Nazi State see, *inter alia*, Klaus-Jürgen Müller's seminal work *Armee, Politik und Gesellschaft in Deutschland, 1933–1945*, Paderborn, 1979; Manfred Messerschmidt, 'Die Wehrmacht im NS-Staat', in Karl-Dietrich Bracher, Manfred Funke and Hans-Adolf Jacobsen (eds), *Deutschland 1933–1945: Neue Studien zur nationalsozialistischen Herrschaft*, Düsseldorf, 1992, pp. 377–403.

*Wehrmacht* and its relationship to the Nazi regime, and at shifting our understanding of the institution. One of Bartov's concluding comments summarizes succinctly how we should now see the *Wehrmacht* – as 'the army of the people, and the willing tool of the regime, more than any of its military predecessors'.

# Soldiers, Nazis and War in the Third Reich

## Omer Bartov

From its very inception until the present day the *Wehrmacht* has presented admirers and foes alike with a series of conflicting images. This
was evident in the disagreements surrounding its character and capacities during the 1930s and the Second World War as well as in the
heated post-war debates between critics and apologists, as demonstrated
in the *Historikerstreit*.[1] Moreover, widely differing interpretations of
the *Wehrmacht* have been rooted not only in ideologically determined
positions concerning the extent of its collaboration with the Nazi
regime but also in the choice of methodological approach. Thus, while
some historians have treated the army as a separate institution,[2] this
article will emphasize the need for an anatomy of the *Wehrmacht* precisely because it increasingly came to reflect German civilian society.[3]
This will be illustrated by a brief examination of five major debates
concerning the army's image and reality: first, the issue of tradition and
modernism in the *Wehrmacht*;[4] second, the relationship between group
loyalty and ideological motivation among soldiers; third, the connection
between combat discipline and the legalization of criminality; fourth,
the contradictions between the army's image as a 'haven' from the
regime and that of being the Nazi school of the nation; and fifth, the
still contentious debate as to whether the *Wehrmacht* had retained its
'shield' untarnished or whether it had in fact served as Hitler's main
instrument.[5]

---

[1] See the most recent survey of this literature in T. Schulte, *The German Army and
Nazi Policies in Occupied Russia* (Oxford, New York, and Munich, 1989), pp. 1–27.
[2] See, e.g. K.-J. Müller, *Das Heer und Hitler: Armee und nationalsozialistisches Regime,
1933–1940* (Stuttgart, 1969).
[3] O. Bartov, *The Eastern Front, 1941–1945: German Troops and the Barbarisation of
Warfare* (London, 1985), esp. pp. 40–67; I. Welcker and F. F. Zelinka, *Qualifikation
zum Offizier? Eine Inhaltsanalyse der Einstellungsvoraussetzungen für Offiziere vom
Kaiserheer zur Bundeswehr* (Frankfurt am Main and Bern, 1982); D. Bald, *Der
deutsche Offizier: Sozial- und Bildungsgeschichte des deutschen Offizierkorps im 20.
Jahrhundert* (Munich, 1982).
[4] G. A. Craig, *The Politics of the Prussian Army, 1640–1945*, 3rd edn (London,
Oxford, and New York, 1978), pp. 468–503; M. Geyer, *Aufrüstung oder Sicherheit*
(Wiesbaden, 1980).
[5] The issues discussed here are treated at much greater length in my book, *Hitler's
Army: Soldiers, Nazis, and War in the Third Reich* (New York and Oxford, 1991).

These five issues are all concerned with the same fundamental question, namely, to what extent did the *Wehrmacht* constitute an integral part of the Nazi state? Breaking this problem into several parts is necessary simply for the sake of discussion; in reality, as far as the individuals involved were concerned, things naturally overlapped. Nevertheless, it is important to note that all the debates discussed in this reading were begun during the Third Reich itself and were not merely superimposed on the period with a view to an original interpretation. Furthermore, these issues have had a major impact on the post-war German historiography of Nazism. By analyzing them, we shall be touching both on the 'actual' historical events and on their perception by preceding generations. Finally, the *Historikerstreit* is an interesting case in point, because in raising many of the issues discussed in this reading, and in insisting on their significance for present-day Germany, it has nicely illustrated the extent to which these debates have a bearing on the German sense of national identity.

## I  Modernity and Tradition

The *Wehrmacht* presents highly conflicting images of its relationship to modernity on two different but related levels. From the technological, strategic and tactical points of view, the army was, and to some extent still is, perceived as the most modern, innovative and efficient military machine of its time. This view was not only the projection of a huge propaganda apparatus but was also derived from a great deal of concrete evidence, as the Third Reich's opponents discovered to their detriment.[6] For, once more making the most of the 'benefit of the latecomer' in the sphere of armaments, but at the same time able to draw upon its rich experience in the First World War as well as on the highly professional, albeit minuscule *Reichswehr* of the Weimar Republic, the *Wehrmacht* rapidly expanded into a formidable, well-equipped army.[7] The new army had to create its officer corps virtually from scratch, expanding the *Reichswehr's* cadre of 4,000 by enlisting Great War veterans and police officers, by making officers of professional NCOs, and especially by taking in large numbers of new recruits who were quickly made into junior officers. Naturally, this greatly accelerated promotion among the middle ranks of professional officers who had languished for years in the *Reichswehr* dreaming of the day they

[6]  See, e.g. E. K. Bramsted, *Goebbels and National Socialist Propaganda, 1925–1945* (London, 1965).
[7]  W. Deist, *The Wehrmacht and German Rearmament*, trans. E. Traynor (London and Basingstoke, 1981).

would avenge Germany's honour and be compensated finally for their patience and suffering.[8]

It was such newly promoted men who not only forged the military machine that would make Hitler's plans possible but also moulded the kind of tactics most appropriate to Germany's economic and strategic position and politically most convenient to a dictatorship anxious about retaining its domestic support.[9] In a few Blitzkrieg campaigns Germany won unprecedented victories in Poland, Scandinavia and western Europe, convincing laymen and professionals alike that the Wehrmacht's invincibility was founded upon overwhelming technological superiority. Ultimately the German generals themselves, at first quite reticent, came to believe that nothing was impossible for them, and they planned the greatest Blitzkrieg yet, operation 'Barbarossa', with much more confidence in victory than they had shown during the infamous Sitzkrieg.[10]

It is, indeed, in the momentous failure of the Russian campaign, and in Germany's consequent and predictably disastrous move toward total war, that some of the roots for the opposite view of the Wehrmacht's relationship to technology may be found, though in retrospect it became common to date the Reich's material inferiority much earlier.[11] Once the Blitzkrieg was over, the image of war as consisting of elegant Panzer sweeps and precision dive bombing was replaced by one of a huge, unstoppable steamroller, wielded by enemies who were technologically and demographically vastly superior and resisted by men whose undeniable material decline made it all the more necessary to compare their unrivaled moral supremacy to their opponents' machine-like inhumanity.[12] Among the Wehrmacht's soldiers and officers, as well as the Reich's civilians, pride in technological mastery was thus replaced by an abhorrence of industrial, anonymous destructiveness, so well symbolized by the thousand-bomber air raids on Germany's cities.[13]

---

[8]   F. L. Carsten, The Reichswehr and Politics, 1918–1933, 2nd edn (Berkeley, Los Angeles, and London, 1973).

[9]   T. W. Mason, 'Some Origins of the Second World War', in The Origins of the Second World War, ed. E. M. Robertson, 5th edn (London and Basingstoke, 1979), pp. 105–35. But see also R. J. Overy, 'Germany, 'Domestic Crisis' and War in 1939', in this volume.

[10]   E. Klink, 'Die militärische Konzeption des Krieges gegen die Sowjetunion: Die Landkriegführung', in Der Angriff auf die Sowjetunion, Das Deutsche Reich und der Zweite Weltkrieg, vol. 4 (Stuttgart, 1983), pp. 190–277.

[11]   H. Umbreit, 'Der Kampf um die Vormachtstellung in Westeuropa', in Die Errichtung der Hegemonie auf dem Europäischen Kontinent, Das Deutsche Reich und der Zweite Weltkrieg, vol. 2 (Stuttgart, 1979), p. 282.

[12]   A. S. Milward, The German Economy at War (London, 1965).

[13]   See further in O. Bartov, 'The Demodernization of the Front', in Bartov, Hitler's Army (n. 5 above).

Now even during the *Wehrmacht*'s heyday, there were those who believed that such victories had to do not so much with weapons or tactics but rather with the fighting spirit of the troops, a view ironically shared by Nazis in the Reich and profound anti-Nazis beyond its borders. As the *Wehrmacht* faltered and then lost its technological edge, the answer was sought in Germany in a further 'fanaticization' of the troops, whereas abroad the resilience of the German army against increasing odds was similarly interpreted as a sign of the soldiers' ideological commitment to Nazism.[14] Indeed, scholars have since argued that the *Wehrmacht*'s combat soldiers were among the groups most strongly attached to the Führer.[15] Similarly, the generals tended to justify their reluctance to participate in a putsch against Hitler by claiming that the lower ranks would have refused to follow suit[16] – and, judging by the widespread sense of outrage among the troops following the failed assassination attempt of 20 July 1994, they were not far off the mark.[17]

A very different view of the soldiers' ideological orientation, however, has emphasized that the *Wehrmacht* had achieved an admirable combination between the hallowed soldierly values of its Prussian ancestors and the most updated technologies of modern warfare.[18] At the same time, while the army had resisted the *Gleichschaltung* and remained immune to Nazism, its fundamental loyalty to the nation and its oath of allegiance to the state's political leadership supposedly left it with no choice but to follow orders. And as the soldiers were in any case mainly preoccupied with the defence of the Reich, and thereby of western civilization as a whole, from the 'Bolshevik menace',[19] they should be praised, rather than blamed, for their self-sacrificial devotion to duty.[20]

The discussion of the *Wehrmacht*'s attitudes toward modernism is further complicated by the fact that whereas those officers who upheld traditional values were not perforce opposed to technological innovations, Nazi rhetoric and propaganda often expressed a powerful abhorrence of modernity and made extensive use of medieval and mythical

---

[14]   M. Messerschmidt, *Die Wehrmacht im NS-Staat: Zeit der Indoktrination* (Hamburg, 1969).
[15]   I. Kershaw, *The 'Hitler Myth': Image and Reality in the Third Reich* (Oxford, 1987).
[16]   See, e.g. E. von Manstein, *Aus einem Soldatenleben* (Bonn, 1959), pp. 353–54.
[17]   M. G. Steinert, *Hitler's War and the Germans*, trans. T. E. S. De Witt (Athens, Ohio, 1977), pp. 264–73.
[18]   B. H. Liddell Hart, *The Other Side of the Hill* (London, 1948).
[19]   See, e.g. H. Guderian, *Panzer Leader*, trans. C. Fitzgibbon, 3rd edn (London, 1977), p. 440.
[20]   See, e.g. D. Brader, foreword to H-U. Rudel, *Stuka Pilot*, trans. L. Hudson, 2nd edn (Maidstone, 1973).

images.[21] Initially, an attempt was made to oppose the army's professional *Soldat* to the ideologically motivated SS *Kämpfer*. However, these simplified categories tended to overlap in practice, as the former increasingly came to rely upon ideological commitment and the latter turned out to be a highly skilled professional. This was especially the case during the last desperate phase of the war, when men belonging to both categories were united by a renewed contempt for technology and an endless trust in man's spiritual qualities – both notions that can be traced far back to their common origins.

Thus the conventional distinction between modernity and traditionalism seems rather tenuous.[22] This conclusion is not limited to the *Wehrmacht* but is a fundamental problem in interpreting the Third Reich. To take just one example, we can ask why it is that the Blitzkrieg strategy, which was based on a rational evaluation of the relation between economic means and military tactics, was considered as typically Nazi, whereas the total war strategy, which very efficiently mobilized Germany for the kind of war it had no hope of winning, was seen as representative of such clear-thinking technocrats as Albert Speer.[23] Indeed, it can be argued that an inherent tension between technology and mythology, organization and ideology, calculation and fanaticism was firmly built into the *Wehrmacht*'s relationship with society and the regime in Nazi Germany and may well have served as an important source for its tremendous, albeit destructive, energies.

## II   'Primary Group' Loyalty and Ideological Motivation

One of the most influential theses regarding morale and motivation in the *Wehrmacht* asserts that German soldiers did not fight out of ideological conviction but rather as a result of their loyalty to a so-called primary group: the close circle of comrades in their unit. The German army, it is claimed, was intentionally organized in such a manner as to satisfy the need of the individual for 'primary group' ties, and consequently, as long as these groups retained their conesion, the troops kept fighting regardless of the overall military situation. Once such groups

---

[21]   R. Dahrendorf, *Society and Democracy in Germany* (London, 1968); D. Schoenbaum, *Hitler's Social Revolution* (New York and London, 1966); and H. A. Turner, Jr., 'Fascism and Modernization', in *Reappraisals of Fascism*, ed. H. A. Turner, Jr. (New York, 1975), pp. 117–39. But see R. Zitelmann, *Hitler, Selbstverständnis eines Revolutionärs* (Stuttgart, 1987).
[22]   K.-J. Müller, *General Ludwig Beck* (Boppard am Rhein, 1980).
[23]   A. Speer, *Inside the Third Reich*, trans. R. Winston and C. Winston, 5th edn (London, 1979).

disintegrated, however, the soldiers' morale rapidly declined and they lost their value as combat troops.[24]

This line of thinking has both influenced and reflected scholars' interpretations of collaboration with and dissent from the Nazi regime in the civilian sector as well. Indeed, one might say that there exists an as yet unrecognized link between 'primary group' theory and *Alltagsgeschichte* – that is, between the notion that soldiers are motivated mainly by a desire to survive coupled with loyalty to their comrades and the increasingly popular argument that in the Third Reich most people were far too preoccupied with everyday concerns to pay much heed to the regime's rhetoric or policies. In other words, it could be said that while 'primary group' theory 'depoliticized' the *Wehrmacht*, one consequence of writing the history of the Third Reich 'from below' was to create a similar impression of a 'depoliticized' civilian society, most of whose members considered the 'normality' of daily life as far more important than the 'abnormality' of Nazi ideology and actions.[25]

And yet, as surveys of *Wehrmacht* combat formations' manpower turnover in extreme battle situations on the Eastern Front have shown, there is no room to speak of 'primary groups' surviving longer than a few weeks at a time. Nevertheless, the larger units and formations, though not constituting 'primary groups' in the sense of personal familiarity between the soldiers, did not as a rule disintegrate and showed a remarkable capacity to withstand tremendous casualties and yet remain battle worthy.[26]

Conversely, it would, of course, be just as unsound simply to claim that the troops were all committed National Socialists. Nevertheless, it should be stressed that, when speaking of a vast conscript army such as the *Wehrmacht*, the soldiers' morale and motivations were very closely related to civilian attitudes toward the regime, and both were far too complex to be explained by means of a single rather mechanistic and detached theory. In fact, we may derive some insight into the relationship between the people and the regime by suggesting that while *real* 'primary groups' do not fully explain combat motivation due to their unfortunate tendency to disintegrate just when they are most needed, the idea of attachment to an *ideal* 'primary group' composed of a certain category of human beings clearly does have a powerful integrating potential. This kind of 'primary group', however, is

---

[24]   E. A. Shils and M. Janowitz, 'Cohesion and Disintegration in the *Wehrmacht* in World War II', *Public Opinion Quarterly* 12 (1948): 280–315; M. van Creveld, *Fighting Power* (Westport, Conn., 1982).
[25]   I. Kershaw, *Popular Opinion and Political Dissent in the Third Reich* (Oxford, 1983).
[26]   O. Bartov, 'Daily Life and Motivation in War: The *Wehrmacht* in the Soviet Union', *Journal of Strategic Studies* 12 (1989): 200–14.

in some respects the precise opposite of the one presented by the original theory, for it is very much the product not merely of social ties but also of ideological internalization, whereby humanity is divided into opposing groups of 'us' and 'them'. Indeed, the sense of identification with one group, and the abhorrence of the other, are in both cases dependent on an abstraction, whereas personal familiarity may only weaken the individual's commitment by revealing the less than ideal aspects of his own side and the human face of his opponents (which is why armies dislike fraternization). This kind of categorization is, of course, just as applicable to civilians,[27] and in neither case does it necessitate any profound understanding of whatever world view one believes oneself to be fighting for. Instead, it calls for internalizing only those aspects of the regime's ideology that are based on prevailing prejudices and that readily serve to legitimize one's sufferings, elevate one's own status and denigrate one's enemies, be they real or imaginary.[28]

This interpretation may also help to clarify such otherwise perplexing phenomena as the tendency of *Wehrmacht* troops increasingly to distance themselves from the Nazi party apparatus and yet remain among Hitler's staunchest supporters almost until the end.[29] This process, similarly noted in studies of the civilian population, is at least partly explained as an expression of the German public's powerful need to believe in something or someone beyond the mundane material needs and hardships of daily life, which often were associated with the Nazi party's corruption and incompetence. It was the Führer who catered to that aspiration among the Third Reich's civilians and, to an even larger extent, among the *Wehrmacht*'s troops, whose dependence on belief in a cause was greatly enhanced by constant danger and fear. Conversely, it was the Führer's ultimate failure to go on serving as the focus of this elementary need, rather than any rational process of disillusionment from ideology, that made the collapse of his 'myth' so total, without, however, necessarily marking the disappearance of the actual need for such a myth, especially under similarly critical circumstances.[30]

[27] See a discussion of this issue as regards the 'depersonalization' and 'abstraction of the Jew' as facilitating indifference to, and participation in, the 'Final Solution', in Kershaw, *Popular Opinion and Political Dissent in the Third Reich*, p. 360; and S. Gordon, *Hitler, Germans, and the 'Jewish Question'* (Princeton, N.J., 1984), pp. 185–6.

[28] I. Kershaw, 'How Effective Was Nazi Propaganda?' in *Nazi Propaganda*, ed. D. Welch (London, 1983), p. 192.

[29] M. I. Gurfein and M. Janowitz, 'Trends in *Wehrmacht* Morale', in *Propaganda in War and Crisis*, ed. D. Lerner (New York, 1951), pp. 200–8.

[30] Kershaw, *The 'Hitler Myth'* (n. 15 above).

## III  Combat Discipline and the Legalization of Criminality

The *Wehrmacht* is generally considered to have been a highly disciplined organization. Yet this image seems to conflict with notions of ideological commitment as opposed to coercion, with the high incidence of severe punishments possibly indicating disciplinary problems, and with the troops' brutal conduct toward POWs and civilians in occupied territory – sometimes even in outright disregard of newly issued orders explicitly forbidding such behaviour. Furthermore, the idea of a faultlessly obedient military machine must also be seen in conjunction with the opinions and traditions of the Reich's civilian population. After all, Germany's authoritarian traditions provided the background not only for military discipline but also for widespread anti-democratic and dictatorial tendencies. Furthermore, domestic 'discipline' in the Third Reich, perceived by many as a return to 'normality' after the chaos of the Republic, was achieved by means not unlike those employed by the *Wehrmacht* – that is, by exploiting the regime's popularity and the public's conformism while simultaneously stamping out any opposition with the utmost brutality. Thus, quite apart from isolated manifestations of actual social or military disobedience and revolt, our understanding of the vast majority's obedience to the commands of the regime will depend to a large degree on the relative weight attributed to willing and possibly ideologically motivated support, on the one hand, and fear of punishment, on the other.

The severity of the *Wehrmacht*'s discipline was not simply part of an old Prussian tradition but, rather, the result of profound changes introduced into martial law under the Third Reich. Moreover, ideologically inspired instructions issued to the troops concerned not only offences committed within the ranks of the army but also the manner in which enemy soldiers and civilians were to be treated. Thus the question of discipline per se cannot be divorced from the new ideological determinants of martial law, and any discussion of the nature of offences and their punishment must take this factor into account if it is not totally to misinterpret the evidence. Once more, this is of course very much the case with the Third Reich's civilian society as well, and although we are speaking of two different legal systems, it must be taken into account that both were significantly altered to fit the ideological requirements of the regime.[31]

It is with this background in mind that we should consider the staggering figure of some 15,000 executions of German soldiers during the

---

[31]  M. Messerschmidt, 'Deutsche Militärgerichtsbarkeit im Zweiten Weltkrieg', in *Recht, Verwaltung und Justiz im Nationalsozialismus*, ed. M. Hirsch et al. (Cologne, 1984), pp. 553–6.

Second World War, as opposed to no more than 48 in the Great War. This was due first and foremost to the greatly expanded definition of what constituted not merely military but also political, and therefore far more serious, offences. Thus men charged with desertion, cowardice and self-inflicted wounds were also accused of treason, espionage or subversion and were likely to be sentenced to death.[32] Conversely, the 'Barbarossa' orders stipulated the curtailment of martial law as far as Soviet citizens in the occupied territories were concerned, called for the shooting of Red Army commissars, and demanded close collaboration with the *Einsatzgruppen*.[33] Thus German troops became involved, directly or indirectly, in the murder of millions of Soviet POWs and civilians. These actions were carried out, by and large, in an orderly and disciplined manner and were considered by the army as quite legal in that they were based on a concept of law and discipline particular to the Nazi regime and accepted by the *Wehrmacht*. Here was indeed a striking example of the way in which the convergence of ideology and discipline had an impact far beyond the purely military aspects of combat performance. This process, which made for compliance and agreement with orders deemed criminal by any 'normal' human standard, was well reflected in the Third Reich's civilian society and owed much of its success to the pseudo-legal posture assumed by the regime from the very beginning of Hitler's rule.[34]

The affinity between the attitudes of the German military and civilians toward 'uncontrolled' violence, as opposed to disciplined, administrative, 'legal' terror, is another important indication of the close relationship between army and society. Scholars have noted, for instance, the apparent discrepancy between the German public's critical reactions to the *Kristallnacht* pogrom and its by and large calm acceptance of the Jew's orderly 'disappearance' from the Reich to vague destinations in the East. However, these attitudes were essentially based on the same concepts of discipline and legality that prompted the army command's anger at the growing incidence of 'wild requisitions' and indiscriminate shootings among the troops, while at the same time it issued orders for the 'eradication' of millions of human beings and

---

[32]   M. Messerschmidt, 'German Military Law in the Second World War', in *The German Military in the Age of Total War*, ed. W. Deist (Leamington Spa, N.H., 1985), pp. 323–35.

[33]   C. Streit, *Keine Kameraden: Die Wehrmacht und die sowjetischen Kriegsgefangenen, 1941–1945* (Stuttgart, 1978), pp. 28–61; H. Krausnick and H.-H. Wilhelm, *Die Truppe des Weltanschauungskrieges: Die Einsatzgruppen der Sicherheitspolizei und des SD, 1938–1942* (Stuttgart, 1981).

[34]   See, e.g. K. D. Bracher, *The German Dictatorship: The Orgins, Structure, and Effects of National Socialism*, trans. J. Steinberg (New York and London, 1970), pp. 191–8.

based the entire logistical apparatus of 'Barbarossa' on a wholesale exploitation of the occupied territories.[35] Discriminating between categories was based not only on designating organized crimes as legal and 'wild' actions as illegal but on geographical (and consequently also racial and political) criteria as well. The relatively few cases of armed robbery and rape that occurred in occupied France in 1940–41 were punished by death;[36] but in Russia, though officers constantly complained of 'wild requisitions' by their troops, charges of plunder rarely appeared on the courts-martial lists. Similarly, while 'contact' with Russian women was frowned upon as a potential cause of racial 'contamination', 'mutilation', and venereal disease and as fraternization with the enemy, charges of rape almost totally vanished – not so much because such acts were not committed but because it was impossible to accuse a German soldier of a 'moral offence' against '*Untermenschen*'.[37] However, as by 1944 many of the troops serving in France had been brutalized by their previous experience in the East, the impossibility in the long run of setting geographical limits to barbarism was rapidly revealed, whether we speak of orders from above or of local initiatives.[38]

Such differentiating attitudes were, of course, neither limited to the *Wehrmacht* nor reserved to occupied populations, as may clearly be seen from the euthanasia and racial campaigns within the borders of the Reich.[39] Furthermore, the obedient and uncritical participation of millions of soldiers in 'legalized' crimes was also significant in that it probably both reflected the moral values these young men had internalized before their recruitment and affected their state of mind and conduct upon returning to civilian society following the collapse of the Third Reich. One aspect of this impact could be seen in the content and uncritical public reception of the numerous personal memoirs and formation chronicles published in Germany in the 1950s and 1960s, which revealed an alarming sympathy with the distorted norms of discipline and obedience, law and criminality that characterized the *Wehrmacht*.[40]

[35] R.-D. Müller, 'Das Scheitern der wirtschaftlichen "Blitzkriegstrategie"', in *Der Angriff auf die Sowjetunion*, Das Deutsche Reich und der Zweite Weltkrieg, vol. 4 (Stuttgart, 1983), pp. 936–1029.

[36] See, e.g. document RH126-12/99, 25 October 1940, Bundesarchiv-Militärarchiv (Federal Archive), Freiburg.

[37] Bartov, *The Eastern Front, 1941–1945* (n. 3 above), pp. 126–7.

[38] See, e.g. M. Hastings, *Das Reich: Resistance and the March of the Second SS Panzer Division through France, June 1944* (London, 1981).

[39] E. Klee, '*Euthanasie' im NS Staat: Die 'Vernichtung lebensunwerten Lebens'* (Frankfurt am Main, 1983), *Dokumente zur 'Euthanasie'* (Frankfurt am Main, 1985), and *Was sie taten – was sie wurden: Ärzte, Juristen und andere Beteiligte am Krankenoder Judenmord* (Frankfurt am Main, 1986).

[40] van Creveld (n. 24 above).

## IV  A 'Haven' from the Regime or the School of the Nation?

One of the most prevalent images of the *Wehrmacht* during the Third Reich was that of a 'haven' from the regime. Indeed, the fact that to the present day this idea has retained so much force seems to indicate that it continues to serve a variety of needs and purposes both in Germany and abroad. This is particularly striking in view of the abundant information regarding the ideological penetration of the *Wehrmacht* by the Nazis made available to the public as early as the Nuremberg trials and the richly documented studies published since then on the army's institutional and ideological *Gleichschaltung*.[41]

The origins of this view date back to the *Wehrmacht*'s own efforts to continue propagating its previous image of '*Überparteilichkeit*', implying both moral 'cleanliness' and institutional autonomy. However, while gratefully accepting Hitler's proposal of a so-called two-pillar state, which put the NSDAP and the army on equal standing,[42] the generals did their utmost to gain the regime's favour by initiating a process of political indoctrination among the troops, which was given great impetus with the reintroduction of compulsory conscription in 1935. Paradoxically, by trying to preserve its former autonomy the *Wehrmacht* thus adopted more and more of National Socialism's ideological tenets.[43]

Many ordinary civilians also shared this notion of the army as a 'haven', not least because they soon found themselves closely attached to it, either as conscripts or as parents and spouses to soldiers. Once in uniform, the young recruits may well have believed that they were simply being made into soldiers. But thanks to the combined efforts of the regime and the generals, they were in fact increasingly moulded in accordance with the new National Socialist ideal of the political warrior. Yet this was not a process most contemporary young Germans could have been aware of, because they came to the army not tabula rasa but from a system of schooling and paramilitary youth training that had made this new type of soldiering seem quite natural to them.[44]

Now, while recent research has shown that indoctrination material of all kinds did in fact reach even the most distant combat units fighting

---

[41]  See, e.g. A. Hillgruber, *Zweierlei Untergang: Die Zerschlagung des deutschen Reiches und das Ende des europäischen Judentums* (Berlin, 1986); and O. Bartov, 'Historians on the Eastern Front: Andreas Hillgruber and Germany's Tragedy', *Tel Aviver Jahrbuch für deutsche Geschichte* 16 (1987): 325–45.

[42]  K.-J. Müller, *The Army, Politics and Society in Germany, 1933–1945: Studies in the Army's Relation to Nazism* (New York, 1987), pp. 16–53.

[43]  R. J. O'Neill, *The German Army and the Nazi Party, 1933–1939* (London, 1966).

[44]  See, e.g. H. Scholtz, *Erziehung und Unterricht unterm Hakenkreuz* (Göttingen, 1985).

under the most adverse conditions,[45] it remains difficult to gauge the manner in which this schooling affected the men's state of mind and conduct. Nevertheless, on the basis of these studies one can no longer speak of the army as a 'haven' but, at most, of the individual as being his own potential 'haven' or 'shelter', perhaps in the rather popularized sense of what has come to be known in post-war Germany as 'inner resistance', a kind of opposition which by its very obscurity and passivity will inevitably defy empirical study.

Resistance to the assumption that the *Wehrmacht* had in fact undergone a profound process of Nazification is also rooted in its implications for post-war German society. For this would mean not only that the men who founded the FRG and GDR had internalized National Socialist modes of thought and conduct during the formative years of their youth but also that possibly no other sector in Hitler's Germany could have remained entirely immune to the impact of Nazism.[46] Moreover, the widespread reluctance to consider seriously the role of abstract ideas in men's actions may well be seen as a disillusioned reaction to an era whose great ideological promises had moved millions of men to inflict untold destruction on each other.[47] Ironically, as a consequence, serious discussion of ideological factors has been avoided, not because such factors could positively be shown to have been historically negligible but merely because they could neither be quantified nor fitted into convenient explanatory models.[48] More recently, works concerned with presenting a 'history from below' have tended to stress the centrality of everyday life, implying that matters ideological were almost totally irrelevant for the average, 'normal' individual.[49]

The idea of the army as a 'haven' must be qualified on several other counts apart from its ideological exposure. First, it should be remembered that for domestic and foreign purposes alike the *Wehrmacht* symbolized the Third Reich's revival of German power, based on an alliance between the conservative elites and the new Nazi party. Thus the army both legitimized Hitler's rule and, as his armed instrument, added a highly concrete dimension to the Führer's wildest plans. Consequently,

[45]   Messerschmidt, *Die Wehrmacht im NS-Staat* (n. 14 above). pp. 354–5, 483; Bartov, *The Eastern Front, 1941–1945*, pp. 68–105.
[46]   O. Bartov, 'The Missing Years: German Workers, German Soldiers', *German History* 8 (1990): 46–65.
[47]   See survey of literature in I. Kershaw, *The Nazi Dictatorship: Problems and Perspectives of Interpretation*, 2nd edn (London and New York, 1989).
[48]   T. W. Mason, 'Intention and Explanation: A Current Controversy about the Interpretation of National Socialism', in *Der 'Führerstaat': Mythos und Realität*, ed. G. Hirschfeld and L. Kettenacker (Stuttgart, 1981), pp. 23–40.
[49]   M. Broszat, 'Plädoyer für eine Historisierung des Nationalsozialismus', *Merkur* 39 (1985): 373–85.

even if no attempt had been made to indoctrinate its ranks, the *Wehrmacht* as an institution had a tremendously important propagandistic, political and psychological value.

Second, on the personal level, many of the middle-ranking officers, some of whom where soon to become Germany's most celebrated generals, were to a large degree creatures of the regime. This was not only because they owed allegiance to Hitler as Führer, commander in chief, and the man responsible for their rapid promotion but also because they believed that had it not been for him they would never have been able to realize their dreams of a highly modern, total war of expansion. The combined gratification of personal ambitions, technological obsessions and nationalist aspirations greatly enhanced their identification with Hitler's regime as individuals, professionals, representatives of a caste and leaders of a vast conscript army. Men such as Beck and Guderian, Manstein and Rommel, Doenitz and Kesselring, Milch and Udet cannot be described as mere soldiers strictly devoted to their profession, rearmament, and the autonomy of the military establishment while remaining indifferent to and detached from Nazi rule and ideology.[50] The many points of contact between Hitler and his young generals were thus important elements in the integration of the *Wehrmacht* into the Third Reich, in stark contradiction of its image as a 'haven' from Nazism.

Third, the view of the army as a 'haven' greatly misrepresents the social implications of rapidly building a huge military force based primarily on conscripts and then conducting an increasingly total war which within a few years devoured large portions of the nation's manpower. By absorbing so many men into its ranks the *Wehrmacht* both reflected society to a growing extent and, even more important, came to be perceived by the civilian sector as an integral part of the nation. For, as we have already noted, almost every family had at least one member in uniform, a fact which greatly enhanced the average individual's sense of attachment to the army. Civilians suffered and gained from the war in several unexpected ways; but whatever their fate, they were well aware of the fact that it had become closely tied to that of the soldiers.[51]

[50] M. Geyer, 'Professionals and Junkers: German Rearmament and Politics in the Weimar Republic', in *Social Change and Political Development in Weimar Germany*, ed. R. Bessel and E. Feuchtwanger (London, 1981), pp. 77–133, and 'Etudes in Political History: Reichswehr, NSDAP, and the Seizure of Power', in *The Nazi Machtergreifung*, ed. P. D. Stachura (London, 1983), pp. 101–23. Also see Guderian (n. 19 above), pp. 18–46.

[51] J. Stephenson, '"Emancipation" and Its Problems: War and Society in Württemberg, 1939–1945', *European History Quarterly* 17 (1987): 345–65. Also see M. Schmidt, 'Krieg der Männer – Chance der Frauen? Der Einzug von Frauen in

## V   The 'Untarnished Shield' or Hitler's Instrument?

The *Wehrmacht*'s apologists have always maintained that it was not involved in any of the murder operations which took place 'behind' the front. However, this portrayal contradicts not only the revelations made at Nuremberg but also the findings of numerous studies which have since shown that both the top echelons of the *Wehrmacht* and the fighting troops at the front had a major share in the crimes committed by the Third Reich during the Second World War. Nevertheless, the debate continues regarding the causes, scope and historical 'uniqueness' of the *Wehrmacht*'s actions, as well as concerning the legality of either executing or disobeying the so-called criminal orders, if not of actually trying to topple the regime whose policies they were designed to implement.[52]

The fact that calls to preserve the *Wehrmacht*'s 'shield' untarnished originated in the army is an indication not only of some officers' moral scruples but also of their awareness of the damage such collaboration with an inherently criminal regime would ultimately inflict upon their own status. Indeed, even those officers who plotted against Hitler seem to have been motivated mostly by institutional, political and strategic rather than moral and legal concerns. Moreover, the uncharacteristic clumsiness with which they conducted their actions seems to raise doubts about their priorities; one almost feels as if these plots were designed more to calm uneasy consciences and to please posterity than to achieve any immediate results. In this the conspirators succeeded admirably, for the attempted putsch provided post-war apologists with proof the *Wehrmacht*'s opposition to the Nazi regime, while its failure to materialize saved the army from becoming the focus of another 'stab in the back' legend, as many of the officers had indeed feared.[53]

Another element in the ambiguity surrounding the *Wehrmacht*'s actual conduct in occupied Europe can be traced back to events in newly occupied Poland. Here it was General Blaskowitz who, shocked and angered by the actions of the SS, lodged official complaints about their crimes and demanded that the army be kept out of them. This reaction, conventionally portrayed as a symbol of the upright *Wehrmacht* officers' morality, simultaneously implied, however, an agreement not to do anything to prevent SS atrocities as long as the military did not have

die Büros der Thyssen AG', pp. 133–62; A.-K. Einfeldt, 'Auskommen – Durchkommen – Weiterkommen: Weibliche Arbeitserfahrungen in der Bergarbeiterkolonie', pp. 267–96, both in *'Die Jahre weiss man nicht, wo man die heute hinsetzen soll': Faschismus im Ruhrgebiet*, ed. L. Niethammer (Berlin, 1983).

[52]   See, e.g. Schulte (n. 1 above); E. Nolte, 'Vergangenheit, die nicht vergehen will', *Frankfurter Allgemeine Zeitung* (6 June 1986); Hillgruber (n. 41 above).

[53]   See, e.g. H. C. Deutsch, *Hitler and His Generals* (Minneapolis, 1974).

to get their own hands dirty. In this sense, Blaskowitz was actually legitimizing murder, just as his colleagues had done in the brutal 'purge' of the SA in 1934. And, murder having become legitimate, it was difficult to find arguments against taking an active part in it. This was not limited to the generals, for once the rank and file observed their officers tolerating SS operations they often tended to behave in the same manner, as indeed Blaskowitz had point out. On the organizational level, too, the effect of events in Poland was to enhance and institutionalize rather than limit contacts between the *Wehrmacht* and the SS. Thus on the eve of 'Barbarossa' the *Wehrmacht* ordered close cooperation between its own formations and the *Einsatzgruppen*; and, having failed to defeat the Russians, the army came to perceive Himmler's soldiers as welcome assistants in protecting its rear from partisan activities by uprooting the Reich's alleged political and biological enemies.[54]

The most powerful and successfully disseminated argument regarding the aims and nature of the *Wehrmacht*'s war in the East, however, was based on relegating the issue of the army's criminal involvement to a position of secondary importance while simultaneously placing the *Wehrmacht* firmly in the anti-communist camp. Indeed, this approach strove both to 'balance' the barbarities of the *Wehrmacht* with Soviet atrocities and, even more significant, to shift the emphasis to the vast service rendered by the troops of the Third Reich to western civilization as a whole in damming the 'Asiatic-Bolshevik flood'. The origins of this image of the *Wehrmacht* as the bulwark of *Kultur* date back to Nazi Germany's invasion of the Soviet Union in the summer of 1941. Presented at the time as a crusade against Bolshevism, this action achieved a certain popularity in occupied western Europe.[55] But the greatest gains for this image of the *Wehrmacht* were made when the Third Reich was already in its death throes, at a time when Nazi propaganda did its utmost to convince the troops that they were defending humanity against a demonic invasion, while simultaneously hoping to sow dissent between the Soviet Union and its western allies. Though not successful in preventing the total collapse of the Reich, these efforts did bear fruit in another important sense, for they both prepared the ground for the FRG's eventual alliance with the West and provided the *Wehrmacht*'s apologists with a forceful and politically useful argument, even if it conveniently confused cause and effect.

[54]  Krausnick and Wilhelm (n. 33 above).
[55]  J. Förster and G. R. Ueberschär, 'Freiwillige für den "Kreuzzug Europas gegen den Bolschewismus"', in *Der Angriff auf die Sowjetunion, Das Deutsche Reich und der Zweite Weltkrieg*, vol. 4 (Stuttgart, 1983), pp. 908–35; B. Wegner, 'Auf dem Wege zur pangermanischen Armee', *Militärgeschichtliche Mitteilungen* 2 (1980): 101–36.

The astonishing persistence of this new/old image of the *Wehrmacht* was given powerful expression in the *Historikerstreit*. Indeed, it may be that not enough attention has been focused on the bizarre inversion of the *Wehrmacht*'s roles proposed by all three major exponents of the new revisionism, whereby overtly or by implication the army is transformed from culprit to saviour, from an object of hatred and fear to one of empathy and pity, from victimizer to victim. Thus Michael Stürmer's geopolitical determinism added a measure of scientific inevitability (and continuity) to Germany's historical mission to serve as a bulwark against barbarian invasions from the East; Ernst Nolte's thesis about the horrors of the gulags and the fear of Bolshevism as having 'originated' Auschwitz made it possible to rearrange chronology and imply that the *Wehrmacht*'s invasion of the Soviet Union was essentially a preventive attack, just as the atrocities it committed were merely intended to anticipate even worse barbarities by the 'Asiatic hordes'; and Andreas Hillgruber's awe at the *Wehrmacht*'s self-sacrificing struggle to halt the 'orgy of revenge' about to be unleashed by the Bolsheviks made him insist on the need to 'empathize' with the troops of East Prussia in conscious detachment from the inmates of the death camps whose continued extermination the *Ostheer* thus assured. Martin Broszat's much-debated 'plea' for a historicization of the Third Reich was therefore answered by Stürmer's and Nolte's attempts to place Nazi Germany within a larger historical context and by Hillgruber's insistence on empathy with the individual *Landser*. The fact that many of the above arguments made ample use of the National Socialist terminology prevalent in the period to which they addressed themselves only added another peculiar dimension to these allegedly necessary and innovative, but in fact far from useful and mostly rather worn out, ideas and methodologies.[56]

From everything we have said, it appears that just as we cannot speak of the *Wehrmacht* as an institution in isolation from the state, it is impossible to understand the conduct, motivation and self-perception of the individual officers and men who made up the army

---

[56] *'Historikerstreit': Die Dokumentation der Kontroverse um die Einzigartigkeit der nationalsozialistischen Judenvernichtung*, ed. Serie Piper, 3rd edn (Munich, 1987); E. Nolte, *Das Vergehen der Vergangenheit: Antwort an meine Kritiker im sogenannten Historikerstreit* (Frankfurt am Main, 1987); H.-U. Wehler, *Entsorgung der deutschen Vergangenheit? Ein polemischer Essay zum 'Historikerstreit'* (Munich, 1988); C. S. Maier, *The Unmasterable Past: History, Holocaust, and German National Identity* (Cambridge, MA, 1988); and Bartov, 'Historians on the Eastern Front' (n. 41 above).

without considering the society and regime from whence they came.[57] And, as the relationship between the military and civilian society was mutual rather than one-sided, it is also necessary to take into account the impact not merely of the *Wehrmacht* establishment but also of the millions of soldiers who went through its ranks upon all aspects of life in the Third Reich.

If we accept this premise, it becomes clear that it is not enough to say that the army was forced to obey the regime by terror and intimidation, that it was manoeuvered into collaboration by the machinations of a minority of Nazi and opportunist officers, or, finally, that its support for the regime was based on a profound misunderstanding of what National Socialism really meant and strove for. All these explanations will appear insufficient once we realize that, particularly and increasingly in the Third Reich, the army as an institution formed an integral part of rather than a separate entity from the regime, while as a social organization it was composed of a rapidly growing number of former civilians and consequently reflected civilian society to a greater rather than a lesser extent than in the past. The *Wehrmacht* was the army of the people, and the willing tool of the regime, more than any of its military predecessors.

It is in this manner too that the connection recently emphasized between the *Wehrmacht*'s criminal conduct in the East and the extermination of the Jews should be understood, whether we speak of the generals or the privates.[58] Indeed, although differences of age, social background and education, political tradition and religion all played a part in each individual's actions, the soldiers were more, not less, likely than the civilians to belong to those categories supportive of the regime, its ideology and its policies,[59] while the army's top echelons, their raison d'être being the direction and application of violence, found it relatively easy to legitimize the execution of Nazi policies with what seemed to be purely military arguments. It is thus in large part the tendency to overlook or underestimate the importance of the intimate ties between the army, the regime and society, rather than any 'objective'

---

[57]  J. Förster, 'Das Unternehmen "Barbarossa" als Eroberungs- und Vernichtungskrieg', in *Der Angriff auf die Sowjetunion. Das Deutsche Reich und der Zweite Weltkrieg*, vol. 4 (Stuttgart, 1983), pp. 440–7, and 'New Wine in Old Skins? The *Wehrmacht* and the War of "Weltanschauungen", 1941', in *The German Military in the Age of Total War*, ed. W. Deist (Leamington Spa, N.H., 1985), pp. 304–22.

[58]  G. Hirschfeld, ed., *The Policies of Genocide: Jews and Soviet Prisoners of War in Nazi Germany* (London, Boston, and Sydney, 1986).

[59]  Bartov, *The Eastern Front, 1941–1945* (n. 3 above), pp. 40–67; Schulte (n. 1 above), p. 288 and sources quoted therein.

lack of documentary evidence, which has hitherto made for posing the wrong questions and offering unsatisfactory interpretations as to the functions, influences and historical importance of the *Wehrmacht* in the Third Reich.

# Working Class and
*Volksgemeinschaft*

# 6

# The Appeal of Exterminating 'Others': German Workers and the Limits of Resistance

*Alf Lüdtke*

Originally appeared as Alf Lüdtke, 'The Appeal of Exterminating "Others": German Workers and the Limits of Resistance', *Journal of Modern History*, 64, Supplement (1992) pp. S46–67.

*Editor's Introduction*

To the same extent that millions of working-class Germans voted for the NSDAP before and during 1933, many workers remained attracted to the regime after 1933. While there was some scepticism about propagandistic pronouncements about the reorganization of German society into a *Volksgemeinschaft*, workers could often not avoid being impressed by some of the achievements of the new regime, nor remain unaffected by such blatant propaganda ploys as *Kraft durch Freude* (Strength through Joy) and *Schönheit der Arbeit* (Beauty of Labour).

Without any doubt, the Nazi police apparatus proved to be very successful in suppressing active working-class resistance. Other workers maintained a passive political detachment from the regime, but were nonetheless forced into fulfilling their allotted role, in the economy and in the military. But many others 'rendered their services' quite willingly. Some workers became fanatical supporters of the regime and its ideology.

This reading complements some of the conclusions drawn by Omer Bartov. While Bartov's work has been instrumental in debunking the myth(s) of an 'ideology-free' and 'untarnished' *Wehrmacht* (a view hallowed by the political right), Lüdtke dissipates the myth of a German working-class overwhelmingly resistant to the Nazi regime and its ideology (a view revered by the political left).[1] Lüdtke argues that 'an interpretation of workers as victims and leaders as the sole agents, comforting as it might be, is not sufficient'. The letters Lüdtke examined support his uncomfortable interpretation – workers 'became both victims and accomplices of Nazism'.

[1]   Cf. Mason, *Nazism, Fascism and the Working Class*, and his *Social Policy in the Third Reich; The Working Class and the National Community*, Providence, RI, 1993.

# 6

# The Appeal of Exterminating 'Others': German Workers and the Limits of Resistance

## Alf Lüdtke

I

This chapter was triggered by the shock of reading through large stacks of letters that German soldiers had sent to their employers during the Second World War.[1] The authors were blue-collar workers or lower-level clerks in middle- if not large-size machine tool factories located primarily in the Saxon city of Leipzig. What I found particularly striking was how intensely the authors of the letters seemed to identify with both the Nazi policy of utter contempt for 'peoples of the East' and the actual killing of 'enemies' at the front line or in the *Hinterland*. To be sure, historical reconstruction is bound to reveal the 'otherness' of its 'objects'. At first glance these 'others' had shown a rather familiar face. They were single or married males who occupied good jobs in industry. In their letters they gave testimony to the duress and dangers of military life in war times. As I read on, though, this seeming familiarity increasingly became blurred.

Two aspects stand out. Fundamentally, these writers did not define themselves by their industrial work and their relations to other workers. On the contrary, their identity was completely framed by what they encountered as the profile of the military man. These letters dismantle notions both of the homogenous workers' consciousness and of social class as the primary focus of peoples' efforts to place themselves in society and history. Second, these letters raise doubts about the claim that the 'masses' in Nazi Germany were completely subdued and thus made victims to the dominant cliques and bureaucracies of state and

[1]  Staatsarchiv Leipzig (StAL), Rudolf Sack, nos 353, 356, 358, 371, 397–400; Meier und Weichelt Eisen und Stahlwerke, nos 322, 323 (esp. 298); Braunkohlenwerk Sarzdetfurth AG, nos. 184, 185.

party. In view of these letters the question arises to what extent the 'ordinary people' were involved in or aware of what actually happened at the front.

## II

After 1933 most Germans readily accepted the Führer, Adolf Hitler, and many actively supported him.[2] In general, the goals of Nazi leaders such as 'restoring' the grandeur of the Reich and 'cleaning out' alleged 'aliens' in politics and society were widely cheered. Critical comments about, for instance, the demonstrative brutality of the *Sturmabteilungen* (SA) or the arrogance of party functionaries were only rarely pushed into the public consciousness. This popular mode of coping with demands and incentives from above by no means contested the Nazi mode of domination. The vast majority of industrial workers tried to pursue their immediate interests by obtaining jobs and earning higher wages. Only a very few extended their criticism beyond mismanagement or injustice on the shop floor or, in their respective neighbourhoods, to the political regime or the social order as a whole. And after 1939 notions of the Germans at war and their 'people's community' tended to absorb the remnants of skepticism that remained. It was no longer the party but the 'fatherland' that called most urgently.[3]

Such perspectives on Nazi Germany focus on the 'grand total'. They do not pay particular attention to the specificity of each single decision, which always involved a moment of uncertainty even, for instance, if the co-workers on the shop floor or the distinctive features of a job have been known quantities for many years. In such broad perspectives the historian perceives individual action or passivity only in summation, that is, only in hindsight. Accordingly, this perspective elides those ambiguities which distinctively mark each moment of action. It underrates, if not totally neglects, the very openness of situations which turns counter to its structured and analytically accurate outcome. For this much is certain: even inside 'total institutions' choices were possible.

[2]   Ian Kershaw, *The Hitler Myth: Image and Reality in the Third Reich* (Oxford, 1987).
[3]   Ulrich Herbert, 'Arbeiterschaft im "Dritten Reich": Zwischenbilanz und offene Fragen', *Geschichte und Gesellschaft* 15 (1989): 320–60, esp. 349, 'Die guten und die schlechten Zeiten: Überlegungen zur diachronen Analyse lebensgeschichtlicher Interviews', in *'Die Jahre weiß man nicht wo man die heute hinsetzen soll': Lebensgeschichte und Sozialkultur im Ruhrgebiet, 1930–1960*, ed. L. Niethammer (Bonn, 1983), pp. 67–96.

The inmates of concentration camps constantly made decisions which had wide-ranging effects on life and death.[4]

In Nazi Germany, rigorous efforts to control 'the masses' were not limited to the institutions of repression and confinement. The Nazi authorities invested enormous energy in regulating the labour markets.[5] Workers, however, still seized space and time to manoeuver for choices about job and employer. Closer to home, each day each worker decided how to perform his or her task, when or how to turn his or her back on someone. To those who time and again made these decisions this was nothing but routine. Simultaneously, the question of whom to approach and whom to avoid on the shop floor, on the street or in the pub posed not small but big and intensely political problems: how was one to assert one's needs and interests? We can clarify this point by considering the recollections of three workers. These demonstrate clearly both the room for choice and the implied permanence of decisions.

In 1934 Walter Uhlmann worked as a toolmaker in a middle-sized machine construction company in Berlin. He recalls that most of his co-workers shared anti-Nazi attitudes and that people could trust each other.[6] Before 1 May 1934, which was the first anniversary of the National Socialist Labour Day, they reassured each other that 'nobody will force us to participate at this May-Day parade'. Thus, they made sure of showing up at the meeting place but then left in another direction. According to this recollection a considerable number of co-workers abstained from the official parade. In other words, they went but simply decided to follow a different route.

During an interview with the operator of a drilling machine, I asked him how he encountered enforced labour during wartime in the big locomotive production and armament construction works of Henschel.[7] He recalled, 'Well, there were lads from concentration camps. At work, they were kept in separate cages within the same workshops. However, we just saw them, we didn't have contact, and we were not allowed to

---

[4] See the account by Primo Levi, *Se questo è un uomo?* (Turin, 1986). On efforts to sustain a 'way of one's own' and, in particular, to withstand the brutality of the SS, see Otto Dov Kulka, 'Ghetto in an Annihilation Camp: Jewish Social History in the Holocaust Period and Its Ultimate Limits', in *The Nazi Concentration Camps: Proceedings of the Fourth Yad Vashem International Historical Conference* (Jerusalem, 1984), pp. 315–30.

[5] Timothy W. Mason, *Arbeiterklasse und Volksgemeinschaft* (Opladen, 1975), passim, and 'The Workers' Opposition in Nazi Germany', *History Workshop Journal* 11 (1981): 120–37.

[6] Walter Uhlmann, 'Antifaschistische Arbeit', *Aus Politik und Zeitgeschichte* B 18/80 (1980), pp. 7–15, esp. p. 8.

[7] Interview with H. N. Kassel, 13 September 1987.

[have contact]. When we took our breaks we sat amongst ourselves. I just don't know how it was and who they were. We also had *Fremdarbeiter* from Russia; to them we once in a while passed a piece of bread which was strictly prohibited.' The assertion is that there was no choice in the case of the inmates of the concentration camp but that non-obedience/resistance to authority existed in respect to the *Fremdarbeiter*.[8]

The final recollection, from another company, does not question the possibility of choices. Rather, this anonymous former *Fremdarbeiter* from Russia recalled different decisions of the German workers. Not only did he remember constant clubbing at different workshops – something which had vanished from the memory of the Henschel worker – but he also mentioned that during breaks at Daimler-Benz the German workers sat down to eat their lunch which was a sandwich (*Butterbrot*).[9] The Russians, however, were not allowed to eat anything; they could only get cold water. In his opinion the *Butterbrot* which many Germans pretended or claimed to have passed to Russians or Poles was not worth mentioning.

As in German society on the whole, the range and impact of resisting behaviour was limited during the whole period of Nazi rule to a small minority among the working classes. However, until 1935–6 thousands of people from proletarian neighbourhoods illegally laboured to make audible the voices of non- and anti-Nazi Germans. The Gestapo ruthlessly persecuted most of the people who repeatedly engaged in such action, putting them under tremendous pressure and threatening them. But the impression which these cases convey can be mistaken: the shift from non-compliance to compliance and even to active, if not enthusiastic, support was no linear change. On the contrary, these cases indicate the permanence of different modes of behaviour. Individuals did not pursue one straight line. Rather, many zigzagged back and forth; the traces of their practices may be imagined as distinct 'patchworks' which do not show a clear-cut profile of either unqualified support or constant resistance. To reconstruct crucial features of this

[8]   As to the policies of enforced labour during the Second World War, see the general account by Ulrich Herbert, *Fremdarbeiter: Politik und Praxis des 'Ausländer-Einsatzes' in der Kriegswirtschaft des Dritten Reiches* (Berlin and Bonn, 1985), Herbert, ed., *Europa und der 'Reichseinsatz': Ausländische Kriegsgefangene und KZ-Häftlinge in Deutschland, 1939–1945* (Essen, 1991) and, esp., *A History of Foreign Labor in Germany, 1880–1980: Seasonal Workers/Forced Labourers/Guest Workers* (Ann Arbor, Mich., 1990), pp. 131–92.

[9]   '"Wir waren ja niemand": Ein ehemaliger Zwangsarbeiter berichtet über die Jahre 1942 bis 1945 in Genshagen-Obrigheim', in *Das Daimler-Benz-Buch: Ein Rüstungskonzern im 'Tausendjährigen Reich'*, ed. Hamburger Stiftung für Sozialgeschichte des 20. Jahrhunderts (Nördlingen, 1987), pp. 471–81.

patchwork mode of decision, it is necessary to trace the diverse elements of people's behaviour in specific situations. Reconstructing the bricolage of everyday life enables the historian to explain both compliance and non-compliance.


III


Opinions about workers' attitudes and behaviours during Nazism are overwhelmingly based upon a common set of assumptions. According to this view, factory workers tended to resist the demands and incentives of Nazi rule from the very outset. Recently, however, closer investigation of certain industries and specific regional contexts has questioned this long-standing and widespread belief. Günther Mai and Wolfgang Zollitsch among others have pointed out that in the elections to the newly established Nazi-*Vertrauensräte* (factory councils), in spring 1933, large groups of wage earners showed their support of Nazism. For instance, in the steel mills and the mines of the Ruhr as well as in the public transportation industry in Berlin, the first *Vertrauen-sratswahlen* in April 1933 yielded remarkable results for candidates nominated by the Nationalsozialistische Betriebszellen-Organisation (NSBO).[10] And not all of those who voted nay seem to have rejected Nazism in general. Rather, they expressed their anger over and critique of the incompetence of certain candidates of the NSBO to improve wages, as Martin Rüther convincingly argues for the consumption industries of Cologne.[11]

The range and forms of actual compliance in the 'proletarian masses', however, were recognized only when the secret reports on local Social Democracy in Exile (SOPADE) activists to their party's leaders in exile were published in 1980. In these reports the comrades recorded the *Stimmung* (sentiment) of cooperation with Nazism and the support for Hitler in factories and working-class neighbourhoods in Germany. If they did not encounter actual enthusiasm for Hitler, these correspondents time and again sensed attitudes that they interpreted

[10] These elections still provided a secret ballot. W. Zollitsch, 'Die Vertrauens-ratswahlen von 1934 und 1935: Zum Stellenwert von Abstimmungen im "Dritten Reich" am Beispiel Krupp', *Geschichte und Gesellschaft* 15 (1989): 361–81, esp. 375; esp. Günther Mai, 'Die Nationalsozialistische Betriebszellen-Organisation', *Viertel-jahrshefte für Zeitgeschichte* 31 (1983): 573–613, *passim*; V. Kratzenberg, *Arbeiter auf dem Weg zu Hitler: Die nationalsozialistische Betriebszellen-Organisation, ihre Entste-hung, ihre Programmatik, ihr Scheitern, 1927–1934* (Frankfurt am Main, 1987), pp. 195ff, 272–3.
[11] Martin Rüther, *Arbeiterschaft in Köln, 1928–1945* (Cologne, 1990), pp. 173ff.

as 'total passivity' in their co-workers and colleagues.[12] They emphasized that one had to face the fact that people stubbornly shied away from any activity which might even smell of opposition to the National Socialist regime.

The expectation that workers fundamentally would oppose Nazism can be traced back to the fierce political struggles of the Weimar Republic. Before 1933 both social democratic and communist organizations claimed that the proletariat would fight and ultimately conquer fascism. But the Christian workers' associations also demonstratively reassured their clientele that every 'true workingman' would rally around the strongholds of faith and good order, the church and its associations. The approaches of these groups differed widely: after 1929 the communists followed the line of the Communist International, accusing the Sozialdemokratische Partei Deutschlands (SPD) of pursuing 'social fascism' while, simultaneously, the social democrats denounced what they perceived as the similarity of Nazi and *Kozi* (the communists).[13] Nevertheless, the leadership and the functionaries of the left mass organizations as well as of the Christian associations remained convinced that National Socialism did not appeal to any 'true' worker.

The notion of the 'true workingman' who displayed inexhaustible self-reliance had an enormous impact. It reached far beyond the boundaries of social class and political camps. Even the fiercest enemies shared this view, as is reflected by the policies of the Gestapo after 1933. Persecution of 'communist/marxist' adversaries outdistanced by far that of other opponents and ranked highest with the Gestapo throughout the whole Nazi period.[14] It was in this vein that Gestapo and communist or

[12]   Deutschland-Berichte der Sozialdemokratischen Partei Deutschlands (SOPADE) (Frankfurt, 1980), 4: 1937, p. 1238; for the following quotation, see ibid., p. 777: 'One can discern not only widespread toleration of Nazism but also an increase of its positive acceptance since 1934 among the workforces of big companies of the heavy industries in the areas at the Rhine and the river *Ruhr* (*Gutehoffnungshütte,* Oberhausen, *Bochumer Verein*), in the mining industries at the *Ruhr,* and also at one of the largest companies of the chemical industry (*Bayer* at Leverkusen).' See also Zollitsch, esp. pp. 369ff, pp. 375ff; and E. Wolff, *Nationalsozialismus in Leverkusen* (Leverkusen, 1988), pp. 196ff.

[13]   Eike Hennig, 'Anmerkungen zur Propaganda der NSDAP gegenüber SPD und KPD in der Endphase der Weimarer Republik', *Tel Aviver Jahrbuch für Deutsche Geschichte* 17 (1988): 209–40, esp. 215ff.

[14]   Detlev J. K. Peukert, 'Der deutsche Arbeiterwiderstand, 1933–1945'; in *Der deutsche Widerstand, 1933–1945,* ed. K.-J. Müller (Paderborn, 1986), pp. 157–81, esp. p. 176 and, more generally, *Die KPD im Widerstand: Verfolgung und Untergrundarbeit an Rhein und Ruhr, 1933–1945* (Wuppertal, 1980); see also Horst Duhnke, *Die KPD von 1933–1945* (Cologne, 1972). So far a comparable study on social democratic resistance activities has not been written. See, however, esp. Herbert Obenaus, 'Probleme   der   Erforschung   des   Widerstandes   in   der   Hannoverschen Sozialdemokratie 1933 bis 1945', *Niedersächsisches Jahrbuch für Landesgeschichte* 62 (1990): 77–95.

social democratic activists alike aimed at tracing every hint of non-compliance among the working masses. Thus, oppressors and victims focused on almost identical images of the true workingman and his presumed resistance. As a result, any sign of protest was picked up and amplified. By 1935–6 most of the resisters from the working classes were arrested by the Gestapo or ordinary police, brought to jail, or detained in concentration camps.

## IV

'Proletarians' would tenaciously fight Nazism. At least during the 1920s both the social democratic and the communist party conceived of workers as the implacable enemies of Nazism. Thus, what else could they do but stand up and combat all efforts to draw them into the sphere of the Nazi? This view prevailed among analysts inside and outside Germany even after 1945. Then the stereotype of proletarian resisters fitted even more perfectly into that bipolar model which informed most explanatory approaches to German fascism. Accordingly, only a few people like Hitler or Himmler (aside from bureaucratic apparatuses) 'acted'; everyone else became 'victims' including the brave but desperately small groups of resisters.

Most of the surviving inmates of prisons and concentration camps shared those views which minimized individual agency. Their experience of suffering surely entitled them to such a reading of history: if anybody had been victims of Nazi domination, they had, whether they were active communists or social democrats or had other backgrounds. Simultaneously, however, even major perpetrators like Albert Speer claimed victimization.[15] And on the political plane the Allied efforts to organize de-Nazification of German society only too quickly turned into what Lutz Niethammer has called the production of *Mitläufer* (fellow travellers).[16]

The term *Mitläufer* was widely used and gained currency almost immediately. 'Just to follow along': the emphasis on being only one among millions reverberated with the almost desperate efforts of many Germans not to be reminded of their mode of coping with Nazism. Nobody wanted to deal with the seamless continuity by which

[15]   Albert Speer, *Erinnerungen*, 8th edn (Frankfurt, 1972), p. 522.
[16]   L. Niethammer, *Die Mitläuferfabrik: Die Entnazifizierung am Beispiel Bayerns*, 2nd edn (Berlin and Bonn, 1982); for a general account, esp. Klaus-Dieter Henke and Hans Woller, eds, *Politische Säuberung in Europa: Die Abrechnung mit Faschismus und Kollaboration nach dem Zweiten Weltkrieg* (Munich, 1991), especially the contributions by Henke (pp. 21ff) on the western zones, and by Helga A. Welsh, who depicts the developments in the Soviet zone after 1945.

sustaining oneself in many instances turned into accepting (if not sustaining) state-organized mass murder. Precedents of exclusion facilitated these attitudes. The labeling of so-called aliens and the 'dangerous' (*Gemeinschaftsfremde*) was a commonly accepted and established practice for a long time,[17] one closely linked to the emergence of a modern police state. Continual discrimination by the state may have fostered people's eagerness to forget their multiple ways of not perceiving seemingly minor acts of discrimination, from the boycott of the Jewish stores on 1 April 1933, to the expulsion of Jews from 'German' forests, street cars or benches, to the pogrom of 9–10 November 1938. And how did people encounter the deportations from 1942 until 1944 and even 1945? Of course, there were noises, there was screaming; and people listened to the hammering boots of marching troops as well as to the shuffling feet of hundreds and thousands of desperate people pushed through the streets of towns which had been home to them. But did not every war impose harsh measures? Especially in wartime, many people felt on safe moral ground; they claimed that after 1939 it was not Hitler but the *Vaterland* that called.[18]

## V

Against this background the vigorous attack of Hannah Arendt in the early 1960s stood out in sharp contrast. A victim herself, forced into exile in the 1930s, she followed closely the Eichmann trial in 1961. In this context she pointed to the widespread *Mittäterschaft* or complicity of most Germans with Nazism.[19] In her view, the overwhelming majority of Germans condemned the crimes of the Nazis but obviously almost all had been ready to participate. When questioned about their complicity, most people displayed an innocent conscience. Did not every social and political organization rely on obedience? In addition, people commonly argued that their acceptance and participation in the Nazi regime prevented even 'worse' evils. People pointed out that they accepted or cooperated in order to rescue Germany from what they perceived as the 'red menace'.[20]

[17] Detlev Peukert, *Volksgenossen und Gemeinschaftsfremde: Anpassung, Ausmerze und Aufbegehren unter dem Nationalsozialismus* (Cologne, 1982), pp. 219ff.
[18] Gabriele Rosenthal, ed., *'Als der Krieg kam, hatte ich mit Hitler nichts mehr zu tun': Zur Gegenwärtigkeit des 'Dritten Reiches' in Biographien* (Opladen, 1990), pp. 223ff.
[19] Hannah Arendt, *Eichmann in Jerusalem: A Report on the Banality of Evil* (London, 1963), esp. p. 134.
[20] The fear of 'the menace from the East' concomitantly remained vague and stark. After the Russian revolutions of 1917 and 1918, large segments of German society including the working class had identified revolutionary violence with 'Cossack'

According to Arendt, the overwhelming majority of Germans were 'accomplices' between 1933 and 1945. Arendt's point was made without further specification of particular groups, classes or strata of German society. However, since the Eichmann trial revealed the 'banality of evil' in the inner workings of the Schutzstaffel (SS), Arendt's point particularly pertained to the bureaucracies of state and party as well as to the functional elites of the Third Reich. Of course, the question remains as to whether other segments and layers of society were affected by the same attitude. How did wage-earning women and housewives perceive the situation in the 1930s and 1940s? How did they act when they faced the constraints or attractions of Nazism in power? Moreover, how did male industrial workers – a segment of society treated with enormous respect but also suspicion by the Nazi authorities – interpret Nazi Germany?

Questions about German complicity with Nazism were ignored for a long time. Only the focus on the practices of the everyday revealed the enormous degree of routine involvement of the many with the execution of both war and holocaust. The very routines of bureaucratic formality or paperwork directly involved many lower-level officials with practices of extermination: those numerous pedantic railway conductors, for instance, searched every passenger; innumerable city clerks kept books carefully registering everyone, including those who had been declared 'Jews' by Nazi laws and decrees.[21] These studies began to reveal that the majority of Germans in their daily practices not only accepted but also actively contributed to sustaining Nazism and its terror. Thus, 'the masses' can no longer appear as passive objects or as victims of the brutal visions and fatal organizational skills of only a few 'dominant' people.

Like the analyses of state and polities, historical studies of labour focused overwhelmingly on the institutions of power or, in this case, of

brutality. Thus, long-standing popular clichés were revitalized and redesigned to cover the presumed 'red' or 'Bolshevik menace'. This view enhanced other notions of the endangered 'order of German things'. To save the German people if not Europe and its values from the 'savage hordes of – Jewish – Bolsheviks' by any means at hand appeared justified. Such views were not confined to some classes or milieus; see similar perceptions among leading social democrats. See Peter Lösche, *Der Bolschewismus im Urteil der deutschen Sozialdemokratie, 1903–1920* (Berlin, 1967); especially the intriguing approach to male attitudes which closely linked abhorred images of 'the female' and the 'reds' after 1917–18, particularly among volunteers of the paramilitary Freikorps; Klaus Theweleit, *Männerphantasien* (Frankfurt, 1977), vols 1, 2.

[21]    See the general account by Uwe Dietrich Adam, *Judenpolitik im Dritten Reich* (Düsseldorf, 1972). The actual steps of being labelled are shown in painstaking detail by Hazel Rosenstrauch with photographs by Abraham Pisarek in *Aus Nachbarn wurden Juden* (Berlin, 1988).

protest, the organized labour movements. Parties and trade unions seemed the only important topic of labour history because they seemingly allowed historians to perceive workers as able to contest discrimination and exploitation. Accordingly, studies related the catastrophic collapse of the labour movement in 1933 to a mixture of petrification within the higher echelons of the party and trade-union bureaucracies with personal incompetence if not betrayal among leading functionaries. This view also tended to emphasize the difference between rank-and-file members and the elite: ordinary workers, in spite of the bleak outlook, relentlessly strove to set up organizations and activities of resistance.

Since many of these alleged resisters 'without a [well-known] name' were communists, historical research followed the pattern of the respective political camps during the Cold War. While they were declared the only heroes in the East, studies in the West almost completely neglected their hardship and suffering – that is, the history of their defeat by the Gestapo in 1935–6. At the same time, adherents of social democracy were rendered faceless and voiceless. In East Germany they were labelled as traitors to the communists, while westerners did not care too much for differences within the left. Studies on the rank and file of workers' resistance under the Nazis started only in the late 1970s.[22] Then the partial opening to social and, finally, cultural and everyday-life studies in West German historiography also began to have an impact on research on National Socialism. It was at the intersection of increasing awareness of the everyday with renewed interest in the consolidation of German fascism that more studies focused on the everyday behaviour and politics of workers. Timothy Mason's magisterial book on industrial workers in the 1930s fueled this turn to a large extent as did the publication of the reports of the SOPADE.

---

[22]   The only exception was and remained for a long time Günter Weisenborn, *Der lautlose Aufstand: Bericht über die Widerstandsbewegung des deutschen Volkes, 1933–45* (Frankfurt, 1953). As to more recent research which has expanded the focus from resistance onto the realms of practices of resisting, see esp. Martin Broszat, 'Resistenz und Widerstand: Eine Zwischenbilanz des Forschungsprojekts', in *Bayern in der NS-Zeit* (Munich and Vienna, 1981), 4: 691–709; Peukert, *Volksgenossen und Gemeinschaftsfremde*, chs 3, 5–7. Hans Mommsen, 'Der Widerstand gegen Hitler und die deutsche Gesellschaft', in *Der Widerstand gegen den Nationalsozialismus*, ed. Jürgen Schmädecke and Peter Steinbach (Munich and Zürich, 1985), pp. 3–23. He underlines that not institutions, organized movements, or even 'the masses' 'defended Germany against Hitler' but 'outcasts', esp. pp. 17–18. Ian Kershaw, 'Widerstand ohne Volk? Dissens und Widerstand im Dritten Reich', in Schmädecke and Steinbach, eds, pp. 779–98; Peter Steinbach, 'Widerstandsforschung im politischen Spannungsfeld', in *Aus Politik und Zeitgeschichte* B 28/88, pp. 3–21.

# VI

Mason argued that the dominant Nazi cliques and agencies pursued three parallel policies regarding industrial workers: repression, neutralization and integration.[23] From the outset, police and the Nazi militia (SA) were allowed to exercise almost unlimited violence in their furious search for active opponents, in particular members of the socialist and communist but also Christian labour organizations, the SPD and Kommunistische Partei Deutschlands (KPD), and Allgemeiner Deutscher Gewerkschaftsbund (ADGB) (and Rote Gewerkschaftsopposition [RGO]) and Catholic Workers' Associations.[24] While particularly intense during the initial years of the Nazi seizure of power, brutal repression remained a constant feature of the Nazi regime. After 1936, the encroachment of the SS on society became not only crucial for the development of the state apparatus but also severely impinged upon the experience of the masses.

Repression was conceived of as the task of the public domain, or of the state.[25] In contrast, tactics of neutralization and integration of workers primarily worked through the realm and practices of industry. The introduction of *Leistungslohn* and increasing differentiation of wage scales figured prominently among respective managerial strategies. They were designed to promote or, at least, trigger processes of internal segmentation within the factories; individuals could improve not only their incomes but also their ranking among their co-workers by 'climbing the ladder'.[26] Of course, efforts to increase fissures and differentiations within respective work forces were not invented in the Third

---

[23] Timothy W. Mason, 'Die Bändigung der Arbeitklasse in Deutschland: Eine Einleitung', in *Angst, Belohnung, Zucht und Ordnung: Herrschaftsmechanismen im Nationalsozialismus*, eds C. Sachse et al. (Opladen, 1982), pp. 11–53, esp. pp. 18ff.

[24] The most comprehensive study focusing on the communist resistance is Peukert, *Die KPD im Widerstand* (n. 14 above).

[25] However, especially large companies from the sector of heavy industry had invoked the legitimacy of state and police when they called for and installed *Werkspolizei*, which meant in practice they paid for the employment of state or communal policemen rather often within the company's private confines, esp. Ralph Jessen, 'Unternehmerherrschaft und staatliches Gewaltmonopol. Hüttenpolizisten und Zechenwehren im Ruhrgebiet (1870–1914)', in *'Sicherheit' und 'Wohlfahrt': Polizei, Gesellschaft und Herrschaft im 19. und 20. Jahrhundert*, ed. Alf Lüdtke (Frankfurt, 1992), pp. 767–86.

[26] Tilla Siegel, *Leistung und Lohn in der nationalsozialistischen 'Ordnung der Arbeit'* (Opladen, 1989); esp. Rüdiger Hachtmann, *Industriearbeit im 'Dritten Reich': Untersuchungen zu den Lohn- und Arbeitsbedingungen in Deutschland, 1933–1945* (Göttingen, 1989). The latter focuses on the phases of rationalization since 1933 and scrutinizes its disciplinary effects. Both studies emphasize rewards instead of repressive measures. However, they still share the assumption that the majority of workers

Reich. They can be traced to previous stages of industrialization. But throughout the 1930s a new drive for modernization and rationalization intensified the remodelling of both the material bases and the social relations of industrial production.[27]

At the same time, Nazi authorities presented their own goals and simultaneously denounced the alleged 'foes of the German people', using a specific rhetoric. To a large extent they borrowed styles and icons of representation from their declared enemies: well-ordered marching columns resonated with the paramilitary units as well as with demonstrations as they were staged by the political right and the left (and, not least, the church); the colour red was appropriated from the labour movement.[28] However, the Nazis connected these elements in new ways; in particular, they employed features that would convey feelings of 'modernity'. Thus, they developed new modes of approaching the proletarian masses. Walter Benjamin interpreted this as an 'aestheticization of politics', a previously unknown form of 'representation'. The Nazis offered the masses attractive opportunities to express themselves but did not give them any chance to assert their rights.[29]

Detailed analyses of concrete settings reveal, however, that the government and in particular the Deutsche Arbeitsfront (DAF) imple-

did not agree with either the goals or politics of Nazism. Thus, the politics of companies as well as of Nazi party or of the state toward labour is still perceived as part of the larger efforts to 'tame' the working class. The working class appears as an entity relying on potential rebelliousness as did the *classes dangereuses* in the nineteenth century.

[27] This did not stop at the factory walls. Carola Sachse argues that factory and family politics in the 1930s and 1940s displayed structural identity. In the Siemens company, for example, the notion of family would unite home and workplace. In addition, it conveyed the seeming necessity of unequal work and pay for male and female workers. The hierarchical differences between occupational denominations and differential wages of men and women would directly reflect the different status of men and women within the family and in the public realm. But it was not a traditional image of family which managers and functionaries tried to invoke. Instead, the 'modern' family was appraised. Company interests in a large workforce of inexpensive female workers and the goal of the Nazi state to promote an industrial boom but also to strengthen the ties of the presumed (nuclear) family worked in the same direction. However, modes of coping and possible 'deviations' from the prescribed path of family are not considered here; see Carola Sachse, *Siemens, der Nationalsozialismus und die moderne Familie: Eine Untersuchung zur Rationalisierung in Deutschland im 20. Jahrhundert* (Hamburg, 1990).

[28] However, this may not exhaust the meaning of flying red banners in late Weimar Germany. Sexual connotations are emphasized by Klaus Theweleit, *Männerphantasien*, vol. 2, *Männerkörper: Zur Psychoanalyse des weißen Terrors*, 2nd edn (Rheinbek, 1980), pp. 281ff.

[29] Walter Benjamin, 'Das Kunstwerk im Zeitalter seiner technischen Reproduzierbarkeit', in his *Gesammelte Schriften* (Frankfurt, 1974) 1, pt. 2: 471–508, esp. 506ff.

mented programmes that offered both material benefits and satisfaction of representational needs. Pay for second holidays at Easter of Pentecost and expansion of vacation but also spectacular events on the national and local level or the promise of travel, Kraft durch Freude (KdF), the Nazi organization of and for leisure: at least in the opinion of the DAF, these and other measures would tie people to the state and state politics. Entrepreneurs, however, seemed to read integration and *Volksgemeinschaft* primarily as an attempt to bind a core group of workers to their particular company. In this way, activities that had mostly been developed during the First World War were renewed or extended. Then, enterprises of all sizes had organized support of workers at home for 'their people' at the front. Parcels and letters were sent to show demonstratively the connectedness of the work force at the 'home front' with their co-workers 'out there' on the 'firing line'. Simultaneously, this policy reflected the immediate concerns of enterprises and of government to keep workers and soldiers quiet and to sustain their compliance. Thus, state agencies did not interfere with firms that, for instance, openly circumvented the rationing system.[30]

The claim of *Burgfriedenspolitik* or 'civic truce' on the level of central government had its spin-offs within the factory workshops themselves. Social relations of production were to be redesigned. 'Works community' (*Werksgemeinschaft*) would supersede traditional hierarchical relations at work. The cooperation of workers, instead of their subordination to the factory's owner (*Fabrikherr*), promised constant flow of production and increased returns. This new trend was favoured particularly by bigger companies. In fact, the often cited difference between the especially harsh treatment of workers in heavy industry and the 'softer' methods in other branches such as machine construction or electrical engineering seemed to be diminished. During the 1920s the notion of 'works community' increasingly overcame its initial flavour of mere propaganda. Bigger companies set up support systems for workers' nuclear families that provided child care, medical services, or practical training in good housekeeping.[31]

[30]  For the 'home-front' aspects see esp. the painstaking case study of respective developments and administrative attitudes in the Ruhr area by Anne Roerkohl, *Hungerblockade und Heimatfront: Die kommunale Lebensmittelversorgung in Westfalen im Ersten Weltkrieg* (Stuttgart, 1991).
[31]  Alf Lüdtke, 'Deutsche Qualitätsarbeit: "Spielereien" am Arbeitsplatz und "Fliehen" aus der Fabrik; industrielle Arbeitsprozesse und Arbeiterverhalten in den 1920er Jahren', in *Arbeiterkulturen zwischen Alltag und Politik*, ed. F. Boll (Vienna and Munich, 1986), pp. 155–97, esp. pp. 188ff. While during most of the 1920s companies eagerly engaged in some form or other of 'works community', the majority of workers still were employed by smaller firms. The majority also did not live in the industrial centres of the Rhine and Ruhr or in Saxony, nor did they populate the

During the Weimar Republic, industry interfered with government and party politics primarily to foster policies which protected their own sphere. It was in this vein that companies and associations of industrial entrepreneurs or managers supported various authoritarian pressure groups and perspectives even more intensely after 1930, that is, under the impact of the depression and mass unemployment. Thus, industry either approved or even strongly supported the takeover of the Nazis in 1933.[32] Again, industry's first priority was to maintain or restore a realm of its own. However, most companies only reluctantly cooperated with Nazi efforts to develop measures aimed at integrating workers into the *Volksgemeinschaft* that the latter were attempting to recreate. Most managers perceived campaigns for the improvement of the workplace environment (*Schönheit der Arbeit*) and even for adding better lighting for the machines and installing new security equipment as interference with their own affairs.[33]

## VII

Workers also seemed to remain at a distance regarding DAF and wider appeals of *Volksgemeinschaft* even if they were the ones to benefit the most. However, the illegal reports to the SOPADE also hinted at a widespread fascination among workers for Nazi or DAF incentives and activities. Many workers ridiculed refurbishments of washrooms and toilets – measures that had been imminent anyway. Nevertheless, they were impressed because these activities proved that at least some of the concerns of their everyday lives were taken seriously.

The actual effects of these improvements should not be overestimated. Only a small percentage of workers actually encountered

conglomerates of Berlin, Hamburg or even Stuttgart. Here 'works community' remained a foreign term. Those who represented the majority of workers either experienced old style paternalism, i.e. unregulated arbitrariness of the boss, or they could pursue life trajectories in which household structures allowed for seasonal detachment from industry since they earned incomes from different sources, mostly as peasant-workers; cf. Jean Quataert, 'The Politics of Rural Industrialization: Class, Gender, and Collective Protest in the Saxon Oberlausitz of the Late Nineteenth Century', *Central European History* 20 (1987): 91–124, esp. 105ff.

[32]   David Abraham, *The Collapse of the Weimar Republic: Political Economy and Crisis*, 2nd edn (New York and London, 1986); Reinhard Neebe, *Großindustrie, Staat und NSDAP, 1930–1933: Paul Silverberg und der Reichsverband der Deutschen Industrie in der Krise der Weimarer Republik* (Göttingen, 1981); esp., for the mid-1920s, Bernd Weisbrod, *Schwerindustrie in der Weimarer Republik: Industrielle Interessenpolitik zwischen Stabilisierung und Krise* (Wuppertal, 1979).

[33]   Ch. Friemert, *Produktionsästhetik im Faschismus: Das Amt 'Schönheit der Arbeit' von 1933 bis 1939* (Munich, 1980).

practical results of the Nazi activities. Mostly they had to do the work themselves: news spread from above by means of newsreels and illustrated papers. Rumours played an important role, too. The imagination overwhelmed the reality on the shop floor. Nevertheless, claims by Nazi leaders that only their policies asserted the 'honour of labour' could be confirmed in the daily experiences of workers.[34] For the first time issues were taken up such as washrooms which the former unions and other workers' organizations had considered too petty to pursue. In addition, *Schönheit der Arbeit* was only one among other efforts that were experienced as re-establishing order within the community as well as in state and society at large. In the context of the buildup of the armed forces and the *Vierjahresplan*, after 1935–6 employment increased as did wages. For younger people especially the future appeared brighter. They would be able to feed a family or, at least, to buy a motorbike or a radio.[35]

German workers in the 1930s and 1940s did not strictly distinguish between 'economic' and 'political' interests. Their socio-economic wellbeing was kept separate neither from assertion of needs on the shop floor or in the neighbourhood nor from official politics as proclaimed through the media. As the SOPADE correspondent bitterly noted: workers remained 'passive', if they did not applaud the regime.[36]

But for the most part, workers did not keep their distance from the cheering masses. They joined them, for instance, at the Nazi May Day of 'national labour', or when Hitler's voice was heard on the radio, or in the newsreel celebrating another 'great day' in the 'nation's history'. Distanced curiosity might also turn into fascination when Hitler denounced, for instance, the Treaty of Versailles (1934), or when he officially presented rearmament plans and declared Germany's military sovereignty (1935). It seems that, at least at these moments, workers

[34] In historical research the impact of material and symbolic satisfaction of workers' presumed need for respect is mostly considered to be highly limited. This supposition is, however, rarely tested in studies of particular local or industrial settings. For a different view, see my article 'Ehre der Arbeit: Industriearbeiter und Macht der Symbole: Zur Reichweite symbolischer Orientierungen im Nationalsozialismus', in *Arbeiter im 20. Jahrhundert*, ed. K. Tenfelde (Stuttgart, 1991), pp. 343–92. See also the detailed analysis and painstaking documentation of the Saar area in Klaus-Michael Mallmann and Gerhard Paul, eds, *Herrschaft und Alltag: Ein Industrierevier im Dritten Reich* (Bonn, 1991).
[35] See the results provided by intensive interviews that focused on the cycles of people's life experiences; Niethammer, ed. (n. 3 above).
[36] Deutschland-Berichte, Bd. 4: 1937, p. 1238; for the following, ibid., p. 777. The rather homogenous distance toward Nazism these workers of Bremen dockyards displayed does not represent a 'typical' case. See, e.g. the intense support of Nazism which prevailed in aircraft and automobile construction at Bremen, esp. Inge Marßolek and René Ott, *Bremen im Dritten Reich*, p. 152. Also, see n. 12 above.

applauded no less enthusiastically than most other *Volksgenossen.*[37] Moreover – and this is an issue the historian of the everyday can amply buttress – it would be misleading to assume that positive assessments and articulations would only have distorted people's 'real' needs and interests. For one thing, many life trajectories of males and male groups provided experiences that intimately connected individual lives with the nation as a whole. To these people, who were either soldiers during the war or who had grown up listening to the stories of their fathers, uncles and brothers, internationalism and anti-militarism had no appeal. Their attitude of heroic pride did not necessarily call for another war. Nonetheless, in their view of manly conduct the nation and its army figured most prominently.

Attitudes of this kind are not simply products of out-and-out manipulation. Instead, workers undoubtedly 'read' official politics according to their individual preferences and experiences. Thus, they interpreted and reshaped if not 'privatized' politics. But this did not happen in isolation. Their everyday life had been reframed and, increasingly, politicized. Home and workplace had been incorporated into networks of supralocal communication, dependency and control since well before 1933.[38]

Most important, in the 1920s almost all notions of an alternate order of society directly reflected crucial features of the existing ones, even among fervent adherents of societal change. Socialist and communist, but also Catholic, workers' organizations also clung to the discipline of military units. To all of them, the shine of polished machinery appealed and triggered immediate and almost unlimited approval: the 'better future' would look like an efficiently executed blowup enlargement of the present.[39] And personal longings for any kind of private future were

---

[37]  Gerhard Paul, *'Deutsche Mutter, heim zu Dir!'* (Bonn, 1986). While positive sentiments may be less surprising in matters of 'national' or 'German' questions, Mallmann and Paul have recently argued that, at least in the Saar area, even workers' dissent remained within the confines of a 'loyal antipathy'; see Mallmann and Paul, eds, *Herrschaft und Alltag,* pp. 327ff.

[38]  For this point see my article, 'Cash, Coffee-Breaks, Horseplay: Eigensinn and Politics among Factory Workers in Germany circa 1900', in *Confrontation, Class Consciousness, and the Labor Process,* ed. M. Hanagan and C. Stephenson (New York, 1986), pp. 65–95, esp. pp. 82ff; as to the domain of 'popular culture', see the overview by Adelheid von Saldern, 'Arbeiterkulturbewegung in der Zwischenkriegszeit', in Boll, ed. (n. 31 above), pp. 29–70; or, from another angle, the explorations by Victoria de Grazia, 'Mass Culture and Sovereignty: The American Challenge to European Cinemas, 1920–1960', *Journal of Modern History* 61 (1989): 53–8.

[39]  On the proneness to military forms and rituals in social democracy, see Gerhard Hauk, ' "Armeekorps auf dem Weg zur Sonne": Einige Bemerkungen zur kulturellen Selbstdarstellung der Arbeiterbewegung', in *Fahnen, Fäuste, Körper: Symbolik und*

intricately woven into aspirations of restored national greatness. Thus, when people referred to 'German quality work', the emphasis lay equally on both terms: 'German' and 'quality', a claim that united not only workers but most Germans against the 'others'.

## VIII

Official and unofficial efforts to (re)construct a 'works community' gained momentum with the war in 1939. Many employers developed networks of communication with and support of their previous employees who were drafted into the army. Businesses regularly mailed newsletters conveying the developments within the company, but they also collected parcels (so-called *Liebesgaben*) and distributed them at occasions like birthdays or Christmas. In many cases the blue-collar or clerical workers who received these gifts or newsletters responded by writing long letters home. Several companies from Leipzig whose work force in 1939 consisted of five to six hundred or, in one case, of more than two thousand workers, regularly received such letters from soldiers whose peacetime employment was suspended during the war. Some of the letter writers obviously used this occasion because they did not have a circle of friends or relatives back home who would be open to reading about their life in the military. Others mentioned in their letters that they primarily wrote to their kin and friends. However, most of these former or, as it were, suspended employees obviously developed a sense of commitment to their respective work community.

Field-post letters had to pass the military censor before they were mailed. The writers were accustomed to orders of the German military command that strongly emphasized that 'field-post letters are weapons, too, comrades'.[40] Military authorities provided further guidance, distributing to the troops time and again specific formulations which should be used when writing field-post letters. The military aimed at turning these letters into 'vitamins of the psyche' which would rejuvenate anybody who became tired. The foremost recommendation was 'to display a manly attitude and to write in a strong and clear language'.

*Kultur der Arbeiterbewegung*, ed. D. Petzina (Essen, 1986), pp. 69–89; on the Catholic movement, see the hitherto unpublished research on its public appearances by Josef Mooser, esp. his exploratory outline: Josef Mooser, 'Arbeiter, Bürger und Priester in den konfessionellen Arbeitervereinen im deutschen Kaiserreich, 1880–1914', in *Arbeiter und Bürger im 19. Jahrhundert*, ed. Jürgen Kocka (Munich, 1986), pp. 79–105.

[40]   O. Buchbender and R. Sterz, eds, *Das andere Gesicht des Krieges: Deutsche Feldpostbriefe, 1939–1945* (Munich, 1982), p. 26.

Close reading of dozens of field-post letters that had been sent to former employers gives the impression that the writers did not strictly obey these rules. To be sure, one topic was the similarity between being a soldier and life as a worker at home. For instance, the soldier Emil Caspar wrote on 31 October 1943, that they just had marched three hundred kilometres in nine days. It had been hard, but in fact, 'it is as if you are working at home'. A hand at a shale mine wrote on 8 October 1943, from Norway that he had quickly adjusted to the military 'and if you only show obedience and good will everything is fine'.[41] Another solider from the Braunkohlenwerk, obviously also a blue-collar worker, wrote on 8 December 1943, that 'I never felt as good on my job as I do now with the military'.[42]

As might be expected, field-post letters to former employers were most explicit and detailed when soldiers gave an account of the foreignness if not the alienness of their present situation. A very limited set of stereotypes regarding foreign countries surfaced time and again. For instance, Walter Feurig wrote on 24 November 1942, from Italy that there was 'poverty and filth all over'. This was not 'home' to him – although he told his audience that he liked the picturesque scenery. And more than a year later, on 12 December 1943 (that is, after Italy had declared a cease-fire under Badoglio in July), he told his Leipzig correspondents that the people in Italy 'seem to be nice and display an enormous hospitality, they are always happy and gay, of course, they do not labour as the Germans are used to do, but they seem to be unpretentious and always make the best of things'.[43] This went along with remarks like Rudolf Harmann's abrupt note from 18 August 1944, that 'we mop up with Italy'.[44]

The picture was different when soldiers wrote from Poland or the Russian territories. The soldier Heinz Dübner noted on 21 November 1939, that 'the Poles played havoc while we had to restore order and by doing this we became real men'.[45] Almost the same attitude emerges in the letter of Edmund Heinzel who served in November 1940 with the *Reichsarbeitsdienst* in occupied Poland. He told his readers that houses and streets at his place 'are very deficient, that is, houses are built

---

[41]    StAL (n. 1 above), Braunkohlenwerk 184, fols 33, 37. See also Curzio Malaparte, *Die Wolga entspringt in Europa* (Cologne, 1989), pp. 32, 44; in these reports to Italian newspapers, written in the summer of 1941, he refers to the Russian and German armies as 'mobile steel mills' and also sees an identity in both armies regarding the merger of military discipline and of inudstrial discipline.
[42]    StAL, Braunkohlenwerk 184, fol. 115, Gerhard Melzig.
[43]    Ibid., Sack 397, fols 21, 18.
[44]    Ibid., fol. 111.
[45]    Ibid., Villeroy and Boch, Steingutfabrik Torgau, no. 67.

from wood and mud and, to put it in one word, it is really a *polnische Wirtschaft*'.[46]

Stereotypes of the Russians were almost identical. The private O. Müller wrote on 27 August 1941, from northeastern Russia that 'one sees only huts and not houses and you had better not step into them because of the "odour"; you don't find curtains, there is neither electric light nor [running] water'.[47] During the war in Russia many of those who survived the first weeks stayed continuously for one or two years with their unit since leave was granted only rarely. As private first class Rolf Goebeler wrote on 21 June 1943, 'many folks develop a stubborn doggedness, it grows during the on-going fighting, and they aim at crushing the enemy at any rate. The mates swear but this is good!'[48] The toil of soldiering re-emphasized notions of being 'thrown' into an alien and hostile environment. Encounters with the natives in the hinterland only too often fostered the image of their total otherness. At the same time, enduring the dangers of battle stimulated emotional fury which, in turn, became intricately connected with the routines of the military. Thus, soldiers increasingly conceived of the enemy as not only the 'other' but also the 'subhuman'.

The 'others' of the distant front, however, were also approaching 'home': since 1941, foreign labour was increasingly forced to work in German industry. The companies conveyed this information to their employees who had been drafted as soldiers; the soldiers responded to it. One of the main concerns that worried the employees who were far away was the quality of work. The soldier Roland Groß offered a consolation to himself and to his mates when he wrote on 18 August 1941, that 'although the best quality workers are drafted I think the foreign helpers will not degrade the quality of the machine [tools]' which were the products of this particular factory.[49] In contrast, another displayed furious hatred. Karl Schreiber wrote on 21 July 1942, that 'we have too much sympathy with the Russians but they do not have any with us. These foreign workers will not accomplish anything. And if they do not work, the best world be to put up a machine gun and to shoot them all'. It appears that this man had been in bitter fights. He referred to the Russian mode of fighting and paid it respect, saying that 'the Russian fights to the last man, unlike the Tommy'. This stood in sharp contrast to the impressions of a cook who had a job with the military staff somewhere in the hinterland of the Russian front. His letter revealed a more joyful tone. He wrote that he could 'imagine lots

[46]    Ibid., Sack 397, fol. 157.
[47]    Ibid., Sack 353, fols 2–3.
[48]    Ibid., fols 44–5.
[49]    Ibid., Sack 397, fol. 193.

of trouble at work [at home] with foreign workers. But with good will and sign language one can get along pretty well. At least that is what I do with the Russians here'.[50]

These few examples indicate a range of opinions, observations and reactions. Yet it is noteworthy that the letter writers frequently employed notions and images that had been launched or, more commonly, reshaped by the agencies of propaganda. It is unlikely that they employed these formulas only because a censor or some other public eye might look at their writing. In addition, it should be granted that the audience which they addressed was different from family, relatives or friends at home. These letters had to impress workmates while at the same time playing to their supervisors. Thus, there is a certain public quality to these letters that shaped their style. Most writers seem to have aimed at striking the pose of experience and success. In stark contrast to this jovial moderation is the intensity with which most writers engaged in accounts of their hatred, bitterness and condescension toward the enemy. Yet the two topics reveal a remarkable similarity between public rhetoric and private perception. This conjunction both reflects support of Nazism and simultaneously triggers an alignment with Nazi ideas.

There was, for instance, Herbert Habermalz, a sergeant who had been employed as a clerk with the sales department of the company of Rudolf Sack. This machine construction factory produced farm equipment, in particular plows. Habermalz was a member of a flight crew in the air force and was stationed in southern Poland, mostly in Cracow. In a letter of 7 August 1943, he gave a detailed account of the detection of a mass grave by German authorities. 'The people who had been buried were, in his words, victims of the GPU [the soviet secret police]. This grave was in the middle of a "Volkspark", only ten metres next to a swing. . . . Of course, I was eager to see the graves. You really can say that the GPU did a very good job – which we, of course, cannot grasp at all. One could see rather well-kept corpses of males, but also of females. All of them with their hands on the backs. . . . Next to the site a group of physicians was at work. The smell was not the best as you may imagine. In addition, there were those many many people who cried and looked for their people among the corpses and the physical remains.'[51] Just a few days earlier he had written a letter in which he described painstakingly the environment of the air base. Accordingly, it was 'very nice, the Wisla is really close. . . . It is only a pity that this quiet

---

[50]   Ibid., Sack 399, fols 167–8.
[51]   Ibid., Sack 353, fol. 31.

scenery is occasionally disturbed by "Iwan" with his artillery. Apart from that one can believe to be in a spa.'[52]

In early July of 1943 the firm of Rudolf Sack received a letter from a colleague of Habermalz, Gerd Sauer. He had also been stationed in Poland and for some time in Warsaw. There he encountered 'real metropolitan life', as he put it. He felt quite happy and relaxed, especially since he had found a large group of people to mix with, most of them SS and *Volksdeutsche*: 'The *Volksdeutsche*, mostly ladies, are very nice, friendly and intelligent and also very well-educated.' In June 1943, Habermalz had sent a letter to the Sack firm in which he described a flight from Cracow to Warsaw. 'We flew several circles above the city. And with great satisfaction we could recognize the complete extermination of the Jewish Ghetto. There our folks did really a fantastic job. There is no house which has not been totally destroyed. This we saw the day before yesterday. And yesterday we took off for Odessa. We received special food, extra cookies, additional milk and butter, and, above all, a very big bar of bittersweet chocolate.'[53]

## IX

These letters, to be sure, also reflect perceptions of 'being turned into' objects of those who occupy the 'heights of command' of policy, economy and society. However, an interpretation of workers as victims and leaders as the sole agents, comforting as it might be, is not sufficient. The very texture of these letters indicates that the authors did not encounter military draft and participation in war as totally 'alien' situations. The intense descriptions of various situations and encounters which these letters contain reflect efforts to 'ban' the permanent uncertainties and the dangers to one's own life. At the same time, though, the letters indicate that anxieties were transformed into an intensified loyalty to military superiors. Even more, the experience of being part of the war machinery itself enhanced attachment to the goals the Nazi leadership proclaimed time and again. These soldiers tried to 'get by' under enormous hardship and suffering. Thus, they tried to cope with and appropriate the given situation; but in this very practice of 'coping and appropriating' the authors turned into actors. This is true even for those privates who wrote angry or artificial letters home. They all documented how they became both victims and accomplices of Nazism.

[52]    Ibid., Sack 352, fol. 32.
[53]    Ibid., fol. 46.

The letter writers were trained in (or, at least, socialized to) factory life in large German cities. Their self-images, however, permitted them to easily connect the experiences of civilian work and military life, to accept the dangers as well as the attractions of war. The humiliating rituals of military drill during basic training were very frightening to most people. To be able to 'stand it' and, in the end, to master the situation provided an enormous boost to the person's self-esteem.[54] No direct line connected military life under peacetime conditions with the dangers and opportunities of war. But given that the war had begun, it was not merely travelling and 'touring hitherto unknown' places that seemed to justify any toil and danger at the front or in the hinterland. To be a soldier did not only mean to be linked to an enormous organization and to modern weaponry. Those at the front or with the units behind actually used their guns; they time and again employed the capabilities of the machinery of war to kill. War was work.

These letters reveal that many individuals perceived their masculinity in military terms and images. To these people, their original claim to perform a 'clean' job at home increasingly became linked to the efficient killing operations of the army.[55] In the end, participation in the exter-

---

[54]    Workers who had been claimed by 'their' companies as indispensable for sustaining armament production were those who continued to work 'at home'. They encountered relative though different experiences of confrontation with 'the others'. After 1940–1 they increasingly encountered *Fremdarbeiter, Ostarbeiter*, prisoners of war, and inmates of concentration camps within their workshops. Of course, industrial and political authorities suspiciously watched and strictly forbade any contact between Germans and these foreigners. Instances of Gestapo intervention show that even handing over a small sandwich or a few grams of tobacco was treated as a serious crime. Violators were sent to prison if not to work camps, and usually they had to serve between one and six months. After they had served their sentences, in a number of cases inmates were also transferred to concentration camps; see Herbert, *Fremdarbeiter* (n. 8 above), *passim*. The point is, however, that the registered cases of 'prohibited contact' and their sharp increase from 1941 to 1942 (see Herbert, p. 123) cannot be interpreted as disobedience not to mention resistance. The same figures rather indicate those persons who had given the information to the authorities. They might have longed for a premium or aspired to other benefits; but did not many share the presumption that only harsh treatment would protect *Führer und Reich?* On aspects of closing the gaps between classes at the German 'homefront' as a response to 'total war' efforts and Allied air raids after 1943, see Mark Roseman, 'World War II and Social Change in Germany', in *Total War and Social Change*, ed. Arthur Marwick (Houndsmill and London, 1988), pp. 58–78, esp. pp. 68ff.
[55]    On the invasion of the Soviet Union and the aspects of extermination on the level of political military planning and leadership, see esp. *Das Deutsche Reich und der Zweite Weltkrieg*, ed. Militärgeschichtliches Forschungsamt (Stuttgart, 1983), 4: 18ff, 413ff. For the military occupation army in the East, see the excellent account

mination of 'others' might appear to many as the ultimate fulfillment of those cherished notions of 'German quality work'.

by Theo Schulte, *The German Army and Nazi Policies in Occupied Russia* (Oxford, 1989). In my opinion, only historical reconstruction of everyday life provides the opportunity to explain the (relative) attractiveness of the military not only in peace but also in war. This perspective reveals the relationships between and ambivalences of ideology and the daily experiences of people. See Lutz Niethammer, 'Heimat und Front: Versuch, zehn Kriegserinnerungen aus der Arbeiterklasse zu verstehen', in *'Die Jahre weiß man nicht'* (n. 3 above), pp. 163–232. See also the critique of this assumed connectedness in Omer Bartov, 'The Missing Years: German Workers, German Soldiers', *German History* 8 (1990): 46–65.

# Police State

# 7

# Surveillance and Disobedience: Aspects of the Political Policing of Nazi Germany

## Robert Gellately

Originally appeared as Robert Gellately, 'Surveillance and Disobedience: Aspects of the Political Policing of Nazi Germany' in *Germans against Nazism: Nonconformity, Opposition and Resistance in the Third Reich (Essays in Honour of Peter Hoffmann)* (1990) pp. 15–36.

*Editor's Introduction*

The introduction to the previous chapter briefly refers to the success of the Nazi police apparatus in suppressing resistance activities. Central to these repressive activities were the operations of the Gestapo. Following upon the establishment of the Nazi secret police and its first ruthless interventions against opponents of the regime, a perception evolved (abetted by the Nazi propaganda machinery) of an 'omniscient, omnipotent, omnipresent'[1] organization.

Both historical and fictionalized accounts, particularly in a multitude of films and television series, have perpetuated this image of the Gestapo. But, just as perceptions of the role of the *Wehrmacht* have changed, recent research on the Gestapo presents a rather different picture of the organization and, crucially, of its relationship to German society.

[1] See the title of an important recent contribution on the Gestapo, Klaus-Michael Mallmann and Gerhard Paul, 'Omniscient, Omnipotent, Omnipresent? Gestapo, Society and Resistance', in David F. Crew (ed.), *Nazism and German Society, 1933–1945*, London, 1994, 166–96.

As Robert Gellately points out, 'membership in the Gestapo was remarkably small', so small, in fact, that the organization was absolutely dependent on the cooperation of individual Germans. While the Gestapo was undoubtedly feared by many, fear is an insufficient explanation for the level of information passed on to the secret police by members of the public. A second explanation, that of a network of paid informers, also fails to account for the success of the Gestapo. Neither coercion nor reward provide an adequate explanation for the flow of information the Gestapo used when tracking down resisters, 'community aliens', and other 'target groups'. Instead, we should consider Gellately's conclusion that 'the population at large internalized the norms of the regime to the point where they acted as unofficial extensions of the terror by keeping their eyes and ears open, and by informing the authorities of what they saw and heard'.

# Surveillance and Disobedience: Aspects of the Political Policing of Nazi Germany

*Robert Gellately*

Studies of resistance, opposition or dissent in Nazi Germany have had little to say about the process by which the country was brought under surveillance and control by the Gestapo (Secret State Police). This neglect is surprising since the Gestapo, which stood at the head of an extensive police and Party network, represented the most important formal–institutional obstacle faced by conspiracies against Hitler. This body did not only attempt to search out and destroy serious threats to the regime; it also endeavoured to suppress all non-compliance by the population at large. Within a remarkably short time, this concerted effort severely reduced the possibilities for even the most innocuous forms of disobedience, all of which were politicized, characterized as 'opposition' and, therefore, criminalized. Historians are beginning to see that the Gestapo's activities played a vital role in establishing and enforcing the strictest possible parameters on behaviour, so that there emerged in Germany an extreme example of what Michel Foucault calls a 'surveillance' or 'panoptic' society.[1] However, though historians might agree that these terms represent a more or less apt description of post-1933 Germany, they have not explored the nature of this development and its implications for everyday life. As a consequence, they have failed to understand the structural limitations placed upon possible expressions of disobedience in Nazi Germany.

## Review of the Literature

The Institute for Contemporary History in Munich has contributed greatly to our understanding of 'resistance and persecution' in Bavaria.

---

[1]  M. Foucault, *Discipline and Punish: The Birth of the Prison*, trans. A. Sheridan, NY, 1979, pp. 217, 301. See also his 'The Subject and Power' in H. L. Dreyfus and P. Rabinow (eds), *Michel Foucault: Beyond Structuralism and Hermeneutics*, Chicago, 1982, pp. 208ff. Foucault disagrees with the 'materialist' interpretation of G. Rusche and O. Kirchheimer, *Punishment and Social Structure*, NY, 1939, reissued 1967, but this neglected work offers valuable insights into the treatment of crime under fascism. They note (p. 179) that the Gestapo operated 'by the general doctrine

Although its six-volume study completed several years ago touches on some aspects of the Gestapo and the court system, it never addresses the persecutors in any depth.[2] One might have expected that oral histories, such as the recent three-volume study yielded by the research project on the Ruhr workers,[3] would highlight the role of controlling organizations of the Party and state, since terroristic elements of Nazism ought to have stamped indelible impressions on the memories of non-Nazis, especially in such a working-class milieu. Yet that series, too, is practically silent when it comes to the Gestapo and how it operated.

At the opposite end of the spectrum, some accounts of working-class resistance exaggerate the role of the Gestapo as an explanation for the failure of workers' resistance; they tend to overestimate the numbers formally and informally part of the Gestapo and attribute comprehensive abilities to it.[4] In fact, given the conception of Nazism held by the Left, which saw it primarily as a kind of conspiracy of the capitalists and the Nazis against the workers instead of a social movement with broad (if by no means universal) support *also* in the working-class milieu, it is not so surprising that the Left pictured the Gestapo and Nazism in general as a kind of foreign apparatus imposed on German society.[5] The

that politically relevant acts are not subject to judicial review'. I discussed some of the comparative literature at a conference at the University of Pennsylvania in April 1988; see 'Enforcing Racial Policy in Nazi Germany', in T. Childers and J. Caplan (eds), *Re-evaluating the 'Third Reich': New Controversies, New Interpretations*, NY, 1993.

[2]  M. Broszat et al. (eds), *Bayern in der NS-Zeit*, 6 vols, Munich, 1977–83 (hereafter cited as *Bayern*, with the appropriate volume number).

[3]  See L. Niethammer (ed.), *'Die Jahre weiß man nicht, wo man die heute hinsetzen soll.' Faschismus-Erfahrungen im Ruhrgebiet*, Berlin, 1983, especially the contribution by U. Herbert, ' "Die guten und die schlechten Zeiten." Überlegungen zur diachronen Analyse lebensgeschichtlicher Interviews', pp. 67ff. See also L. Niethammer (ed.), *'Hinterher merkt man, daß es richtig war, daß es schiefgegangen ist.' Nachkriegs-Erfahrung im Ruhrgebiet*, Berlin, 1983; also L. Niethammer and A. von Plato (eds), *'Wir kriegen jetzt andere Zeiten.' Auf der Suche nach der Erfahrung des Volkes in Nachfaschistischen Ländern*, Berlin, 1985, particularly Niethammer's remarks on the causes of the silences in his 'Fragen – Antworten – Fragen. Methodische Erfahrungen und Erwägungen zur Oral History', pp. 392ff. Some of the remarks by a participant in the Ruhr project are available now in U. Herbert, 'Good Times, Bad Times: Memories of the Third Reich', in R. Bessel (ed.), *Life in the Third Reich*, Oxford, 1987, pp. 97ff. Denunciations and the Gestapo are mentioned at several points in B. Wenke, *Interviews mit Überlebenden. Verfolgung und Widerstand in Südwestdeutschland*, Stuttgart, 1980, pp. 20ff.

[4]  See the document from 1936 from a Bochum area trade unionist reprinted in full in D. J. K. Peukert and F. Bajohr, *Spuren des Widerstands. Die Bergarbeiterbewegung im Dritten Reich und im Exil*, Munich, 1987, pp. 133ff.

[5]  See D. J. K. Peukert, *Die KPD im Widerstand. Verfolgung und Untergrundarbeit an Rhein und Ruhr 1933 bis 1945*, Wuppertal, 1980, pp. 116ff. See also his *Volksgenoßen und Gemeinschaftsfremde. Anpaßung, Ausmerze und Aufbegehren unter dem*

repeated suggestion that the working class was reluctant to volunteer information to the authorities does not stand up under closer inspection, although such contentions echo the perceptions of the Left at the time, both inside Germany and abroad.[6] Without diminishing the role of the Gestapo, there is a need here for some demythologizing.

For the most part, the police and other control organizations are either not mentioned at all or taken for granted in studies of resistance. At an international conference on the fortieth anniversary of the July 1944 plot to assassinate Hitler, for example, there were some 65 papers presented which dealt with virtually every conceivable kind of resistance, but not a single contribution was devoted to *any* control organizations.[7] Why is it that works on resistance do not see fit to examine how the persecutors went about their daily tasks? Certainly, such neglect cannot be attributed simply to an oversight on the part of any particular historian, but is rather a result issuing in large measure from the ways in which these studies have been conceptualized. The Gestapo – to the limited extent that it receives attention at all – is mostly a synonym for ruthless, arbitrary and inescapable terror, the quintessence of the 'police state'. Peter Hoffmann's observation in his latest account of the resistance is representative. He states that 'the Gestapo terrorized dissidents with the mere possibility of a knock on the door at five o'clock in the morning and two leather-coated figures standing outside saying, "Come with us".[8] Although such widely held perceptions of the 'ubiquitous Gestapo' certainly contain some truth, it is high time to examine, more systematically and in depth, the many issues surrounding the policing of Nazi Germany. As Tim Mason points out, it is insufficient merely to attribute the absence of resistance 'to the unique power of the totalitarian state'; that is to use 'a sort of shorthand rather than to offer

*Nationalsozialismus*, Cologne, 1982, pp. 233ff. Contemporary socialists' interpretations of Nazism can be found in the *Deutschland-Berichte der Sozialdemokratischen Partei Deutschlands (SOPADE) 1934–1940*, Salzhausen, 1980. However, that there was *more* than merely a misperception behind the Left's impotence after 1933 is made clear by T. W. Mason, 'The Third Reich and the German Left: Persecution and Resistance', in H. Bull (ed.), *The Challenge of the Third Reich*, Oxford, 1986, pp. 95ff.
6    See Peukert, *Die KPD im Widerstand*, pp. 121ff.
7    J. Schmädeke and P. Steinbach (eds), *Der Widerstand gegen den Nationalsozialismus. Die deutsche Gesellschaft und der Widerstand gegen Hitler*, Munich–Zürich, 1985. For other examples of the same neglect, see R. Löwenthal and P. von zur Mühlen (eds), *Widerstand und Verweigerung in Deutschland 1933 bis 1945*, Berlin, 1982, and H. Graml (ed.), *Widerstand im Dritten Reich. Probleme, Ereignisse, Gestalten*, Frankfurt am Main, 1984.
8    P. Hoffmann, *German Resistance to Hitler*, Cambridge, MA, 1988, p. 30; cf. his 'The War, German Society and Internal Resistance', in M. Laffan (ed.), *The Burden of German History 1949–45*, London, 1988, p. 197.

an explanation'.[9] It is certainly true that the emergence of the Gestapo and the obliteration of most opposition were directly related.

Barrington Moore has pointed out that in the final analysis the 'one prerequisite' for expressions of disobedience to take place anywhere is the existence of 'social and cultural space' which 'provides more or less protected enclaves within which dissatisfied or oppressed groups have some room', so that a minimum of mobilization can occur.[10] The Gestapo, and the other negative inducements to obey, the awareness of the widespread incidence of tip-offs to the authorities, in conjunction with the so-called positive accomplishments of the regime (such as curing unemployment or tearing up the Treaty of Versailles) and 'self-coordination', worked to reduce to a minimum the space for any kind of disobedience to blossom.[11]

The effectiveness of any enforcement body is to a greater or lesser extent dependent upon the cooperation or collaboration it receives from the society of which it is a part. This was certainly true in Nazi Germany, in which general surveillance was felt to be inescapable, so that it became increasingly difficult for any disobedience to be expressed, let alone for resistance and opposition to crystallize.[12] Clearly, accounts of resistance cannot afford to over-look the extent and nature of organizations of surveillance and suppression.

### Local Organization of the Gestapo and its Spy Network

According to the recollections of many who once lived in Nazi Germany, the effectiveness of the Gestapo and the surveillance system rested on a numerically large police force and an 'army' of spies and paid informers.[13] It is true that no one felt far from the scrutiny of the Nazi state whether in public, at work or even at home. However, this sense of being watched could not have been due to the sheer physical presence

---

[9]   T. W. Mason, 'Injustice and Resistance: Barrington Moore and the Reaction of German Workers to Fascism', in R. J. Bullen et al. (eds), *Ideas into Politics: Aspects of European History 1880–1950*, London–Totowa, NJ, 1984, p. 115.

[10]   B. Moore, Jr, *Injustice: The Social Bases of Obedience and Revolt*, White Plains, NY, 1978, p. 482.

[11]   Ibid., p. 483.

[12]   See, for example, H. Zeisel, *The Limits of Law Enforcement*, Chicago, 1982, pp. 83ff; also G. Aly and K. H. Roth, *Die restlose Erfaßung. Volkszählen, Identifizieren, Aussondern im Nationalsozialismus*, Berlin, 1984, pp. 36ff.

[13]   The classic example of the emphasis on numbers is E. Kogon, *Der SS-Staat. Das System der deutschen Konzentrationslager*, Munich, 1974, p. 28. Cf. F. Dröge, *Der zerredete Widerstand. Zur Soziologie und Publizistik des Gerüchts im 2. Weltkrieg*, Düsseldorf, 1970, pp. 54ff. See also n. 38, below.

of Gestapo officials, because membership in the Gestapo was remarkably small. By the end of 1944 there were approximately 32,000 persons in the force, of whom 3,000 were administrative officials, 15,500 or so executive officials and 13,500 employees and workmen, 9,000 of them draftees. 'Administrators' had the same training as other civil servants, and dealt with personnel records, budgets, supplies and legal problems such as those stemming from passport law. Especially trained 'executive officials' were assigned tasks according to the various desks (*Referate*) into which the State Police was sub-divided, and they 'executed the real tasks of the Gestapo', although 'a number of these officials also were engaged in pure office work'.[14] The Gestapo also took over other organizations and some of their personnel, such as the customs frontier guards, but these had little to do with day-to-day policing inside Germany and can be left out of account here. Otto Ohlendorf, head of the *Sicherheitsdienst* (Security Service, SD), estimated that there was 'one specialist' or executive official 'to three or four persons' in the Gestapo.[15]

Given the small number of officials in the Gestapo, their distribution had to be thin on the ground. A March 1937 survey of personnel in the Düsseldorf Gestapo region, for example, showed a total of 291 persons, of whom 49 were concerned with administrative matters and 242 involved more directly with police work (in the *Außendienst*). At that time 126 officials were stationed in Düsseldorf, a city with a population of approximately 500,000. Other cities within the overall jurisdiction of the Düsseldorf headquarters were assigned additional personnel: Essen had 43 officials to cover a population of about 650,000, while Wuppertal had 43 and Duisburg 28 each for populations in excess of 400,000. Oberhausen had 14 officials and Mönchen-Gladbach 11, while Kleve and Kaldenkirchen, with 8 each, were the smallest two of the eight cities in the jurisdiction to have their own Gestapo posts. In comparison with the rest of the country, numbers for Düsseldorf were relatively large, partly because of the 165 kilometres of national border for which it was responsible.[16] Still, given the demands made by the regime, this was a small force to police the roughly four million inhabitants of a jurisdiction known for its support of opposition parties such as the Social Democratic (SPD) and Communist (KPD) parties, for being

[14] See International Military Tribunal, *Trial of the Major War Criminals before the International Military Tribunal, Nuremberg, 14 November 1945 to 1 October 1946* (hereafter IMT), vol. 21, Nuremberg, 1947–9, pp. 294ff. See also the testimony of Werner Best in IMT, vol. 20, pp. 123ff.
[15] See IMT, vol. 4, p. 345.
[16] Bundesarchiv/Koblenz (hereafter BAK): R58/610, Personalstatistik der Staatspolizei, 31 March 1937.

a haven of 'political Catholicism', and for its relatively large Polish and Jewish populations.

Information from other localities indicates that the personnel in each post were divided into officials, teletypists, assistants, clerks, typists, drivers and so on. These were normally subdivided into departments and separate subsections (*Referate*) more or less on the ever-changing patterns of Berlin headquarters.[17] Moreover, the range of political behaviour that came within the sphere of the Gestapo was varied and constantly growing. For example, the desk in the Düsseldorf Gestapo concerned with Polish and Eastern European workers in July 1943 had twelve separate subsections dealing with everything from 'refusal to work' and 'leaving the workplace without permission', to 'forbidden sexual relations'. The section on the 'Economy' was divided into eight subsections. While the regular police were in charge of enforcing economic regulations enacted for the duration of the war, the Gestapo was to be called in when, for example, the deed caused unrest in the population or when the perpetrator was a public figure.[18]

Outside the largest cities such as Berlin, Hamburg or Munich, the various desks (*Referate*) in any given local Gestapo post could consist of a single official, and in many cases this person had to look after more than one desk.[19] The numbers of the officials in the Gestapo survey of 1937 may even be inflated, if the example of the town of Eutin in Schleswig-Holstein is any guide. The 1937 survey counted three Gestapo men there, but Lawrence Stokes maintains that three local civic administrators in succession looked after political police matters along with their other tasks. They had to take care of between 15 and 25 areas of administration (*Referate*), a number of which had nothing whatsoever to do with police work. Thus, the 1937 survey may exaggerate the numbers in the Gestapo and convey a false impression of the extent of its professionalism.[20]

A number of additional organizational and personnel questions that are especially important to studies of resistance might also be discussed if space permitted. For example, mention might be made of the police network beyond the Gestapo, such as the Criminal and Order Police, and

[17]   See P. R. Black, *Ernst Kaltenbrunner: Ideological Soldier of the Third Reich*, Princeton, 1984, pp. 297ff.

[18]   Hauptstaatsarchiv/Düsseldorf (hereafter HStA-D): RW 36/3, 6ff. Plan of Gestapo – Düsseldorf.

[19]   On the Gestapo organization see BAK: R58/1112, 145–6 and R58/242, 101. Cf. the testimony of Karl Heinz Hoffmann in IMT, vol. 20, p. 160; also Ibid., vol. 21, pp. 293–4; and K. Moritz and E. Noam, *NS-Verbrechen vor Gericht 1945–1955. Dokumente aus hessischen Justizakten*, Wiesbaden, 1978, pp. 272–3.

[20]   See Landesarchiv/Schleswig-Holstein: Regierung Eutin, A II 2 (260/17 462), and L. D. Stokes, *Kleinstadt und Nationalsozialismus. Ausgewählte Dokumente zur Geschichte von Eutin, 1918–1945*, Neumünster, 1984, p. 504.

also the part played by the Nazi Party and the Security Service of the SS in the surveillance of the country. It would also be useful to consider the limited purge of the Weimar Republic's state political police forces, because the 'cleansing' was not nearly as complete as is often claimed in the literature.[21] One topic which must be addressed, however, is the Gestapo spy network, so often the subject of speculation in resistance circles at the time.

Little information has survived on Gestapo spies, thought to be so numerous that it was all but impossible to escape from their 'silent, mysterious, unperceived vigilance'.[22] In fact, there seem to have been far fewer than believed then and since. The most important of the agents were 'V-persons' (contacts), often, but not always, paid and recruited by the various 'desks' or specialists in the local Gestapo branches; there were also 'G-persons' (informants), occasional tellers of tales; and, finally, 'I-persons' (informants), who were not part of the spy network proper, but kept track of the public mood and reported to the police. Not much is known about such people, their number, turnover, occupations and contributions. One Bavarian locality where some information has come to light is Nuremberg. As of 1 September 1941, a total of 150 Gestapo officials were centred there, responsible for a population which totalled 2,771,720 distributed over 14,115 square kilometres.[23] Elke Fröhlich discovered that in the years 1943–4 six of these officials were in charge of the informers' department – section IVn – and that there were some 80–100 people regularly informing the Gestapo.[24] The ratio of informers to full-time officials in Nuremberg was therefore at the very most one paid informer for every official. Normally these people conveyed information on a specific area of concern to the police while continuing their regular jobs and professions. Thus the Gestapo was far from being at the head of an 'army' of agents.[25]

The Gestapo's confidential informants have been the subject of a study by Walter Weyrauch.[26] In 1945, under the auspices of the United

[21]  For a discussion of these and other issues, see Gellately, 'Enforcing Racial Policy', and the volume cited in n. 40 below.
[22]  The quotation (from 1847 but equally apt for the Third Reich) is in Foucault, *Discipline and Punish*, p. 280. Cf. IMT, vol. 20, p. 128.
[23]  BAK: R58/856, 1 September 1941.
[24]  E. Fröhlich, 'Die Herausforderung des Einzelnen. Geschichten über Widerstand und Verfolgung', in Broszat et al. (eds), *Bayern*, vol. 6, 1983, p. 212. Cf. G. Meyer, *Nacht über Hamburg. Berichte und Dokumente*, Frankfurt am Main, 1971, p. 81.
[25]  Cf. I. Marßolek and R. Ott, *Bremen im Dritten Reich. Anpaßung, Widerstand, Verfolgung*, Bremen, 1986, p. 183; and H. Schwarzwälder, *Geschichte der Freien Hansestadt Bremen*, vol. 4, *Bremen in der NS-Zeit (1933–1945)*, Hamburg, 1985, pp. 407–8.
[26]  W. O. Weyrauch, 'Gestapo Informants: Facts and Theory of Under-cover Operations', *Columbia Journal of Transnational Law*, vol. 24, 1986, pp. 554ff.

States military government, Weyrauch analysed a collection of the Frankfurt Gestapo card files on informers. His up-dated summary deals only with the 1,200 or so cards of people who at one time or another were paid to inform. He deliberately excludes other kinds of collaborators such as those he calls 'spite informers', even though, as indicated below, they were of far greater significance in generating police investigations than those who were paid and/or who worked regularly for the Gestapo on a voluntary basis. Weyrauch sees the 'typical Nazi informant in the Frankfurt data as 'unconnected with the Nazi party or the official German government structure', and known 'as unsympathetic' to Nazism: the sort of person who 'sometimes seemed suited for a leadership position after the war'.[27] Informants were also drawn from among foreigners in the country, from known opponents to the regime, and from those considered 'tainted' for 'ethnic or religious reasons'.[28] Weyrauch notes that some priests even turned over to the police confidential information gained via the confessional.[29]

Presented with these facts, Weyrauch's account loses its plausibility when he continues to insist that the primary motive for collaboration was what he terms 'circumstantial coercion'. He himself maintains that 'the index cards were silent about specific threats', that the extent to which these putative threats 'amounted to duress as a legal defence is a matter of speculation', and that 'significantly the vast majority of suspect persons seem to have been able to avoid becoming confidential informants after having been interrogated and detained by Gestapo officials'.[30] It is strange that such evidence, provided by Weyrauch himself, did not lead him to suspect that many collaborators might also have had their own reasons for cooperating with the Gestapo.[31]

Such an impression is confirmed by material on several Gestapo agents that survives from Aachen. It is clear that the Gestapo and its regular informers were always on the lookout for recruits. An Aachen report to the Cologne Gestapo on 24 August 1942 stated that an agent on holiday chanced to meet a priest whom he had known for some time. The priest was characterized as 'suitable' for the job of informant

[27]  Ibid., p. 560.
[28]  Ibid., pp. 577ff. Cf. BAK: R58/610.
[29]  Weyrauch, 'Gestapo Informants', p. 579.
[30]  Ibid., pp. 565, 567, 568.
[31]  Cf. M. Maschmann, *Fazit. Mein Weg in der Hitler-Jugend*, Munich, 1981, pp. 43ff;
C. Klessmann and F. Pingel, *Gegner des Nationalsozialismus*, Frankfurt am Main, 1980, pp. 195ff; and R. Giordano, *Die zweite Schuld oder von der Last Deutscher zu sein*, Hamburg, 1987, pp. 30ff.

because of his favourable disposition toward the regime. Other agents' files in the Düsseldorf archive give the distinct impression that many responded positively to working for the Gestapo, and those who wished to discontinue doing so, or who failed to show the requisite enthusiasm, were dropped or quit of their own accord.[32]

Detlev Peukert also believes that the information passed on to the Gestapo from planted spies was not as useful as the tips received from the population at large or the reports of 'the smaller agents on the periphery of the Communist milieu'.[33] Still, there is evidence that planted agents at times played an important role. The Aachen Gestapo, for example, wrote in October 1944, that one of them was working undercover on the Communist Party; he is described as 'very gifted' in making contacts with 'enemy circles', 'intelligent, cautious, but nevertheless unerring'. He could be regarded as 'reliable . . . his reports were flawless and led to the greatest success'. 'His active and gifted collaboration' is mentioned in a letter to Cologne headquarters. On the basis of one of his reports, it was possible to destroy a very large 'terror organization of mixed character'.[34]

Gertrud Meyer's account of Gestapo methods of tracking the workers' movement in Hamburg shows that, in a number of instances, undercover agents were crucial in the arrest of Communist functionaries.[35] A Gestapo spy in Würzburg, acting as an *agent provocateur* in the autumn of 1934 were so far as to initiate and organize an underground KPD group, even getting the needed illegal literature from the police, only then to turn in those who could be recruited.[36] A number of other works also show that the Gestapo had to make greater efforts in planting spies in the working-class movement than was usually the case when it came to dealing with other 'opponents'. However, while some collaborators may have had to be intimidated to work with the police, this was not invariably the case.[37] And it may well be that a few spectacular 'successes' led to an over-estimation of the strength of the Gestapo and its agents, especially within the underground opposition movements.[38]

[32]   See HStA-D: RW 34 Nr. 33, Staatspolizeistelle Köln.
[33]   Peukert, *Die KPD im Widerstand*, p. 123.
[34]   HStA-D: RW 34 Nr. 33.
[35]   Meyer, *Nacht über Hamburg*, pp. 77ff.
[36]   H. Mehringer, 'Die KPD in Bayern 1919–1945', in Broszat et al. (eds), *Bayern*, vol. 5, 1983, pp. 228–9.
[37]   Cf. Marßolek and Ott, *Bremen im Dritten Reich*, p. 183; also Peukert, *Die KPD im Widerstand*, pp. 125ff.
[38]   A. Merson (*Communist Resistance in Nazi Germany*, London, 1985, p. 51) believes the numbers of spies 'must have totalled a high number'; while only a few infiltrated the KPD successfully, they were 'of great individual significance.'

## The Everyday Operation of the Gestapo

Many studied of resistance tend to focus on isolated and fragmentary arrest statistics, which necessarily convey an inaccurate picture both of the resistance and the energy the Gestapo had to devote to combating it.[39] Firmer generalizations about the resistance can be made by exploiting the resources of the Gestapo files which have survived for Düsseldorf and Würzburg. Some interesting findings emerge from Reinhard Mann's work, even though he was not particularly concerned with the question of resistance. Mann studied a random sample of 825 cases drawn from the 70,000 surviving Düsseldorf Gestapo files. His results have the advantage of taking reflections about the general preoccupations of the Gestapo out of the realm of pure speculation and uninformed impressions.

Table 7.1, which is based on Mann's investigations,[40] shows the preoccupations of the Düsseldorf Gestapo over the course of the Nazi dictatorship. Thirty per cent of his sample (245 cases) pertained to tracking prohibited, mostly left-wing organizations. Of the 204 cases of people involved in illegal political parties or organizations, 61 were suspected of having links with the KPD and 44 with the SPD. In 49 cases, it was not possible to establish specific political affiliation. When it came to organized political parties, the main opponents were clearly the Marxists, while the pursuit of religiously oriented or youth organizations took up a much smaller share of all Gestapo activities.

Efforts to destroy illegal organizations increased after 1933, when only 14 of the 245 cases came to light, while the highest number of such proceedings began in 1935 with 57 cases, up from 30 the year before. Thereafter a more or less steady decline set in. In 1937, 42 cases were opened, but the number fell the next year to 18, and the following year to only 13; after a brief flurry in 1940, the drop continued with only 2 in 1941. There were 7 cases in 1942, 4 in 1943, and 1 in 1944. The declining number of cases in the sample after 1935 in part reflects the success of the Gestapo in eliminating organized opposition.[41]

[39]   Isolated figures on 'protective custody' and related matters are summarized in Hoffmann, 'The War', pp. 192–3.
[40]   See R. Mann, *Protest und Kontrolle im Dritten Reich. Nationalsozialistische Herrschaft im Alltag einer rheinischen Großstadt*, Frankfurt am Main, 1987, p. 180. Mann rounded off his percentage figures; their total exceeds 100 per cent. For further comments on this work, and on the strengths and weaknesses of Gestapo files as historical sources, see R. Gellately, *The Gestapo and German Society: Enforcing Racial Policy, 1933–1945*, Oxford, 1990. This work is based primarily on a study of the Gestapo case files in the Staatsarchiv/Würzburg.
[41]   Mann, *Protest und Kontrolle*, p. 182 (chart 1).

*Table 7.1*   Proceedings of the Düsseldorf Gestapo between 1933 and 1945

|  | Number | Total | % |
|---|---|---|---|
| Continuation of forbidden organization: |  |  |  |
| Political parties and associations | 204 |  |  |
| Forbidden religious associations and sects | 15 |  |  |
| Dissolved associations and activity for forbidden youth groups | 26 |  |  |
|  |  | 245 | 30 |
| Non-conforming behaviour in everyday life: |  |  |  |
| Verbal utterances | 203 |  |  |
| At work or in leisure activities | 38 |  |  |
|  |  | 241 | 29 |
| Other forms of nonconformity: |  |  |  |
| Acquiring or spreading of forbidden printed matter | 37 |  |  |
| Listening to foreign radio | 20 |  |  |
| Political passivity | 7 |  |  |
| Assorted others | 75 |  |  |
|  |  | 139 | 17 |
| Conventional criminality |  | 96 | 12 |
| Administrative control measures |  | 104 | 13 |
| Totals |  | 825 | 100 |

*Source*: R. Mann, *Protest und Kontrolle im Dritten Reich*, Frankfurt, 1987, p. 180.

The Düsseldorf Gestapo pursued nearly as many persons suspected of 'non-conforming everyday behaviour' – 29 per cent of all its cases – as it did those involved in outlawed organizations. Much energy was expended to control the spoken word, and the majority of cases of this kind of nonconformity brought to the Gestapo's attention (203 cases out of 241) pertained to airing opinions in public. Many of these kinds of investigations must have depended on the observations of people beyond the ranks of the Gestapo, since it simply had too few members to keep watch or to listen in on its own.

The Gestapo was also keen to enforce policies with regard to obtaining and/or spreading information disallowed by the regime: 7 per cent of the sample (57 instances) concerned such matters. Other forms of nonconformity – 'political passivity' and a wide variety of deviations lumped together as 'other kinds' of nonconformity – constituted nearly 10 per cent of the Gestapo case-load. The last named category, with 75 investigations, is a catch-all which contains everything from the anti-Hitler caricaturist, to the reluctant military recruit of 'mixed race', to the Catholic school rector denounced for insufficient Nazi zeal.[42] It is evident that the Gestapo was operating with a concept of opposition and security which went well beyond conventional definitions. A further 13 per cent of all proceedings (104 cases) were commenced by the Gestapo upon suspicion that someone had broken 'administrative control measures', such as bending or breaking rules on residency requirements. Because crime in the third Reich was to a great extent politicized, the Gestapo spent much time (12 per cent of all the cases in the sample) dealing with what in table 7.1 was called 'conventional criminality'. It investigated accusations involving 'morals charges' such as homosexual activity[43] and supplying false information to the authorities; but the largest single category of 'conventional crime' was 'economic' charges of various kinds.[44]

A brief comparison of the Gestapo offices in Düsseldorf and Würzburg reveals a remarkable similarity in organization and *modus operandi*.[45] This finding is to be expected, given the efforts that were made to achieve central control. But the preoccupations of each Gestapo post varied according to local circumstances. One obvious and persistent concern of the Düsseldorf Gestapo, which emerges with special clarity in contrast to Würzburg, is that the former had to police both the Rhine river and the border with respect to the flow of people, goods and money. The border was located far from Würzburg, and is hardly mentioned in the files. Nor were the illegal Communist and Socialist movements as important in the largely agricultural and rural Würzburg area as in the Rhineland, and the Gestapo divided its time accordingly. Other variations undoubtedly existed, for example, in places which had neither Jews nor much of an illegal workers' movement. In both Düsseldorf and Würzburg Catholicism and policing the pulpit were also of great importance.

It would appear that the activity, even the effectiveness of the Gestapo, if measured in terms of the quantity of new cases undertaken,

---

[42]  Ibid., pp. 266ff.
[43]  Note the case of one of the Gestapo heads in Würzburg, Josef Gerum, and his pursuit of such matters; besides the file on him in the Berlin Document Centre, see Fröhlich, pp. 76ff.
[44]  See Mann, *Protest und Kontrolle*, p. 252 (table 3).
[45]  For details, see Gellately, *The Gestapo*, chs 1 and 2.

began to fall off after 1941. Mann's statistics can be read to show that, with important exceptions (namely concerning foreign workers, on which more is said below), virtually every form of disobedience it tracked began to decline from 1942 onwards. This reading is troubling in that, for example, it indicates a decrease in the frequency of 'non-conforming expressions of opinion' handled after 1941 by the Düsseldorf Gestapo, while data from other (non-quantifiable) sources and secondary accounts suggest that across the country grumbling, rumour-mongering, and even 'malicious' gossip probably began to grow at precisely that time.[46] Moreover, although Mann's figures show that 'conventional criminality' handled by the Gestapo declined after 1940, there are indications from other writers that certain kinds of crime, especially in the broad area of the economy, almost certainly increased.[47] It is clear that the Gestapo's vigilance continued right to the bitter end; yet it was becoming less successful in picking up disobedience at the very moment it is likely to have been increasing. While the number of Gestapo cases dropped after 1941, those which were initiated on the basis of information received from the population declined even more precipitously, and virtually ceased by 1944.[48]

No reliable statistics on Gestapo arrests from 1933 to 1945 appear to have survived. There are indications in the admittedly fragmentary statistics of arrests during the war years which suggest that a major transformation took place in its activities. It may well be, as Mann's figures for Düsseldorf establish, that after 1941 the *absolute* number of new Gestapo cases declined. However, national figures for several wartime years show that the Gestapo then began to devote increasing energy to controlling a new 'race enemy' within the country, namely the army of foreign workers, whose *relative* importance to the Gestapo increased dramatically. In order to supervise these persons and

---

[46]  Mann, *Protest und Kontrolle*, p. 241. For the growth of all types of dissent, see I. Kershaw, *Popular Opinion and Political Dissent in the Third Reich: Bavaria 1933–1945*, Oxford, 1983, pp. 281ff; and M. G. Steinert, *Hitler's War and the Germans: Public Mood and Attitude during the Second World War*, trans. T. E. J. de Witt, Athens, Ohio, 1977, pp. 117ff. Negative rumours about the impending war with the USSR began to circulate widely across Germany in the spring of 1941; see H. Boberach (ed.), *Meldungen aus dem Reich 1938–1945*, vol. 6, Herrsching, 1984, pp. 2273–5. See also the overview of M. Broszat, 'Vom Widerstand: Bedeutungswandel in der Zeitgeschichte', in his *Nach Hitler. Der schwierige Umgang mit unserer Geschichte*, Munich, 1987, pp. 320ff.

[47]  Mann, *Protest und Kontrolle*, p. 252. For a local example, see J. Stephenson, 'War and Society in Württemberg, 1939–1945: Beating the System', *German Studies Review*, vol. 8, 1985, pp. 89ff.

[48]  See R. Gellately, 'The Gestapo and German Society: Political Denunciation in the Gestapo Case Files', *Journal of Modern History*, vol. 60, 1988, pp. 654–94. Cf. Mann, *Protest und Kontrolle*, p. 294.

segregate them from the German population, especially when they were employed outside work-camps or the camps attached to factories proper, the police was to a large extent dependent upon the provision of information from attentive citizens, and in the first years of the war apparently had no difficulty in obtaining it. Thus by the summer of 1942 (between May and August) the Gestapo made a total of 107,960 arrests, 79,821 of them foreigners; in addition, there were 4,962 cases in which Germans were caught in forbidden contact with such individuals. While not all those arrested were informed upon by a civilian – a supervisor or Labour Front official in a camp could readily call in the Gestapo – local studies suggest that a substantial proportion of arrests probably resulted from tip-offs from the public. To be sure, it is also clear that the Gestapo continued its drive to recruit informers inside even the smallest clusters of foreign workers scattered around the country.

In short order, the bulk of the Gestapo's effort went into dealing with the new 'racially foreign' threat inside the country. The police continued to uncover various kinds of German 'opposition', but in relative terms such arrests represented a declining percentage of the Gestapo's workload. Given that in all likelihood non-compliance (broadly defined) was growing, it is plausible to suggest that a large part of the reason for the failure to turn up more of it was that citizens were becoming less inclined to inform on others. By comparison, therefore, the arrests of opponents such as communists and socialists began to assume a relatively smaller place in the Gestapo workload. Thus some 5,161 people had been arrested in those same summer months of 1942 on suspicion of communist or socialist activity; a handful of people (416) were thought guilty of listening to foreign radio stations; and 286 were taken into custody for protesting at official church policies. There were other forms of miscellaneous opposition; but these and others just mentioned paled in comparison to the police problem posed by the foreign workers.[49] The figures for January to June 1943, indicate that of 241,968 arrests, 155,145 pertained to foreign workers and an additional 10,773 to Germans suspected of outlawed contact with them. In the same period, 8,850 people were arrested on suspicion of communist or socialist activities; and there were other opponents caught, such as the 1,314 who were suspected of listening to a foreign radio station, and 638 who protested against Nazi church policy. It is clear, however, that numerically the emphasis of the Gestapo's work was shifting to the workplace – 12,249 Germans were also arrested for

---

[49]   W. Schumann et al., *Deutschland im Zweiten Weltkrieg*, vol. 2, Berlin (East), 1975, p. 412. The figures are for Germany and its incorporated areas.

shirking on the job – and that the greatest effort was reserved for policing foreigners inside the country.[50]

Between July and September 1943 the figures show a continuation of the trend: of the total of 146,217 arrests, 105,262 were foreigners charged with refusal to work or shirking; 6,549 Germans were also accused of this 'crime'. There were, in addition, 4,637 arrests of Germans for breaking regulations by socializing with these foreigners. Some 5,757 people were arrested for suspected communist or socialist activity, and another 404 for protesting against church policy.[51]

It would be useful to have more information on these statistics, which are known to be flawed, because (among other things) when it came to the despised foreigners, especially those from eastern Europe, the Gestapo grew inclined to adopt Draconian methods and, before very long, to apply lynch justice.[52] Even so, the figures suggest a reorientation in Gestapo activity, the vast bulk of which pertained to the economy, mostly focused on the foreigners and on keeping them at work and racially segregated. The figures probably underestimate the involvement of the Gestapo with these workers; in 1944 and 1945, as the war was carried into Germany, not all dealings with them were registered, and reports of executions, quite aside from arrests, went astray. As Germans became increasingly reluctant to inform the authorities about the 'criminality' of foreign workers, the Gestapo grew more ruthless in dealing with them, and meted out punishment on its own authority. An examination of cases brought to the attention of the Gestapo in Würzburg shows a gradual decline, beginning with the diffusion of knowledge about the German losses suffered at Stalingrad; and by 1944 and 1945

---

[50]   Schumann et al., *Deutschland im Zweiten Weltkrieg*, vol. 3, Berlin (East), 1982, p. 241.

[51]   Schumann et al., *Deutschland im Zweiten Weltkrieg*, vol. 4, Berlin (East), 1984, p. 407.

[52]   As early as August, 1942, the Gestapo executed without trial foreigners (Poles) considered 'guilty' of having sexual relations with German women. See, for example, the detailed local SD report in the Staatsarchiv/Bamberg: M30/1048. Cf. U. Herbert, *Fremdarbeiter. Politik und Praxis des 'Ausländer-Einsatzes' in der Kriegswirtschaft des Dritten Reiches*, Berlin, 1986, pp. 327ff. For case studies of the Special Courts see K. Bästlein, 'Die Akten des ehemaligen Sondergerichts Kiel als zeitgeschichtliche Quelle', *Zeitschrift der Gesellschaft für Schleswig-Holsteinische Geschichte*, vol. 113, 1988, pp. 157ff; and B. Schimmler, *Recht ohne Gerechtigkeit. Zur Tätigkeit der Berliner Sondergerichte im Nationalsozialismus*, Berlin, 1984. For an important local study, and a review of the East German literature, see especially W. Bramke, 'Der unbekannte Widerstand in Westsachsen 1933–1945', *Jahrbuch für Regionalgeschichte*, vol. 13, 1986, pp. 220ff, and his 'Der antifaschistische Widerstand in der Geschichtsschreibung der DDR in den achtziger Jahren. Forschungsstand und Probleme', *Aus Politik und Zeitgeschichte. Beilage zur Wochenzeitung Das Parlament*, 8 July 1988, pp. 23ff.

the flow of information from the population simply evaporated. Isolated evidence from elsewhere in Germany suggests that in the last months of the war the Gestapo dispensed even with the appearance of following procedures and, for example, liquidated foreign workers in their area to eliminate witnesses who might offer testimony on Gestapo misdeeds.[53]

Before concluding, it is useful to provide several specific remarks on denunciations, such a prominent feature of the Nazi era and, until recently, not investigated by historians. Political denunciations, or the provision of information on suspected criminality by the population at large, were the single most important factor behind the initiation of all Gestapo cases.[54] As indicated in table 7.2, which is also taken from Reinhard Mann's study, 26 per cent of the random sample of 825 cases he examined began with an *identifiable* denunciation from the population, and another 3 per cent came from businesses.

Mann believed that the incidence of information coming from the population was actually much greater, and suggested that the German people had been won over to Nazism. He could not have meant that denouncers as a whole acted out of loyalty to the Nazi system, because his own figures (on which more presently) reveal that they cooperated for all kinds of reasons.[55] Still, the extent of the reliance on denunciations from the population is a dramatic revelation, since it suggests a substantial degree of accommodation, adjustment or even collaboration – a term that denotes active rather than passive participation – by Germans in the workings of the Nazi terror system. This behaviour has hitherto not been fully appreciated. The figures would suggest that the regime's most dreaded enforcer would have been seriously hampered without public cooperation. To be sure, the files themselves have gaps and are far from exhaustive in providing background information. The files on 13 per cent of the cases are silent about what moved the Gestapo into action. The observations of the Gestapo and its net of regular informers launched a surprisingly small proportion of cases on their own, namely 15 per cent; but once the authorities

[53] This issue is discussed in Gellately, *The Gestapo*, ch. 8. On the gaps in the statistics, even those on executions, see M. Messerschmidt and F. Wüllner, *Die Wehrmachtjustiz im Dienste des Nationalsozialismus. Zerstörung einer Legende*, Baden-Baden, 1987, pp. 63ff. See also H. Obenaus, ' "Sei stille, sonst kommst Du nach Ahlem!" Zur Funktion der Gestapostelle in der ehemaligen Israelitischen Gartenbauschule von Ahlem (1943–1945)', *Sonderdruck* from *Hannoversche Geschichtsblätter*, Neue Folge, vol. 41, 1987, pp. 1–32.
[54] See the literature cited in Gellately, 'Political Denunciation'; note especially M. Broszat, 'Politische Denunziationen in der NS-Zeit: Aus Forschungserfahrungen im Staatsarchiv München', *Archivalische Zeitschrift*, vol. 73, 1977, pp. 221ff.
[55] Ibid., pp. 287ff.

*Table 7.2*   Causes for the Initiation of a Proceeding with the Gestapo –
Düsseldorf, 1933–44

| | | | |
|---|---|---|---|
| 1 | Reports from the population | 213 (= | 26%) |
| 2 | Information from other control organizations | 139 (= | 17%) |
| 3 | Own observations of Stapo-Düsseldorf, V-persons | 127 (= | 15%) |
| 4 | Information via communal or state authorities | 57 (= | 7%) |
| 5 | Statements of interrogations | 110 (= | 13%) |
| 6 | Information from businesses | 24 (= | 3%) |
| 7 | Information via NS organizations | 52 (= | 6%) |
| 8 | No information | 103 (= | 13%) |
| | Total | 825 (= | 100%) |

Source: R. Mann, *Protest und Kontrolle im Dritten Reich*, Frankfurt, 1987, p. 292.

proceeded with their own interrogations, they uncovered further incriminating evidence which led to almost as many new investigations. On its own, however, the Gestapo was clearly not in a position to deal with the political policing of the country. It received help both from other 'control organizations', such as the Criminal, Order and Military Police, which together provided information in 17 per cent of the cases the Gestapo pursued, and from the Nazi Party (6 per cent). Other evidence shows that these organizations, in turn, had often been informed by someone from the population at large, so that even greater participation from the public took place than might be deduced from Mann's statistics.[56] It is also clear that local Nazi Party officials received many more denunciations from the population, but sometimes handled these on their own, and did not pass on all the information they acquired to the Gestapo.

Although the Gestapo's power became nearly unchecked, Tim Mason suggests that this does not explain how it was implemented.[57] When one looks in greater detail at its efforts to police the more private spheres of social and sexual life, such as for example to create barriers between Jews and non-Jews and, after 1939, between foreign workers and the German people, it can be shown that in doing so the reliance on tips from the population was even greater than the general picture painted by Mann. To give but one example based on a study of the Gestapo files in Würzburg, over half of all the suspected transgressions of the September 1935 Nuremberg laws forbidding marriage and

[56]   Cf. Gellately, 'Political Denunciation', pp. 661ff.
[57]   Mason, 'Injustice', p. 115.

extra-marital sexual relations between Jews and non-Jews began with a denunciation from the population. Given that Würzburg and the surrounding district of Lower Franconia were among the most reluctant to vote Nazi before 1933, had little or no tradition of anti-Semitism, and remained staunchly Catholic, it is reasonable to suppose that the situation was worse elsewhere. Without the flow of information from the population the regime's attempts to enforce such racial policies would have been severely hampered. According to one recent account, Gestapo surveillance and control was extended down to the shop-floor in factories such as the Volkswagen Works because employees were willing to pass along information about non-compliance. Thus, for example, a foreman turned in a German worker in 1943 for listening to foreign radio broadcasts and expressing doubts about the war's outcome. His reasons for doing so had little to do with the 'political' content of the remarks. Instead, he seems to have informed because he feared that, having over-heard the 'treasonous' words, he might himself be denounced by those who worked under him, men whom he knew resented his often demanding approach to daily tasks.[58]

On the question of assessing the motives of those who denounced others to the police, Mann was not able to determine any reason whatever in 39 per cent of all the cases which began with a tip from someone in the population. He claims that of the rest, 37 per cent had identifiable 'private' or instrumental motives, but only 24 per cent what he terms 'system-loyal' ones.[59] Even if one were to allow the latter figure to stand – and it is problematical – such statistics suggest that the Gestapo was repeatedly utilized for purposes completely unintended by the regime. The country's leaders might have preferred to receive tip-offs from loyal Nazis; but all denunciations were structurally useful, even when they were based on the most self-serving motives, were utterly without foundation, and were even consciously false. Nazi leaders from Hitler on down were troubled about how to cope with the denouncers, especially those who laid careless and/or knowingly erroneous charges. After much vacillation and many second thoughts, the attitude prevailed that it was advisable to have too much information rather than too little, so that even at times when the flood of tips threatened to become

---

[58]   On Lower Franconia, see the detailed examination in Gellately, *The Gestapo*, chs 3–6. On the VW Works see K.-J. Siegfried, *Das Leben der Zwangsarbeiter im Volkswagenwerk 1939–1945*, Frankfurt am Main, 1988, pp. 72–3; see also his *Rüstungsproduktion und Zwangsarbeit im Volkswagenwerk 1939–1945. Eine Dokumentation*, Frankfurt am Main, 1986, pp. 92ff.

[59]   Mann, *Protest und Kontrolle*, p. 295.

dysfunctional, the snoopers were not overmuch discouraged nor the false denouncers punished too severely.[60]

Fritz Stern rightly points out that too much should not be made of the negative factors which led to compliance and accommodation.[61] The same kind of desire to get on-side is mentioned in William S. Allen's study of Northeim where, for example, a local non-Nazi school principal 'prompted solely by his awareness of the new atmosphere' suspended a student for spreading a rumour that the Nazis were responsible for burning the Reichstag.[62] These informal reinforcements of the terror system brought the Gestapo to life, because suddenly towns were flooded by 'amateur "Gestapo" operatives', who thereby helped to undermine the resolve of anyone wishing to swim against the tide.[63] Even a brief look at specific instances of resistance, such as that offered by the 'White Rose' group in Munich, reveals the many ways in which the population at large internalized the norms of the regime to the point where they acted as unofficial extensions of the terror by keeping their eyes and ears open, and by informing the authorities of what they saw and heard.

## Conclusion

This chapter has explored several aspects of the surveillance society in Nazi Germany by focusing on how the Gestapo operated outside the gaols and concentration camps. It is clear that the elimination of relatively safe enclaves in which disobedience might have developed structurally required information from the population at large. While the majority might, as some writers would have it, remain silent, apathetic or passive – on the 'Jewish Question',[64] for example – the Gestapo

[60] The response of Nazi leaders to denunciations is discussed in Gellately, *The Gestapo*, ch. 5. For a telling remark from Hitler in 1933, in which he noted that 'we are presently living in a sea of denunciations and human evil', see L. Gruchmann, *Justiz im Dritten Reich 1933–1940. Anpaßung und Unterwerfung in der Ära Gürtner*, Munich, 1987, p. 835.

[61] F. Stern, 'National Socialism as Temptation', in his *Dreams and Delusions: The Drama of German History*, NY, 1987, pp. 147ff. Cf. H. B. Gisevius, *To the Bitter End*, trans. R. and C. Winston, London, 1948, pp. 101ff.

[62] W. S. Allen, *The Nazi Seizure of Power: The Experience of a Single German Town 1922–1945*, rev. edn, NY, 1984, p. 157.

[63] Ibid., p. 189.

[64] See I. Kershaw, 'German Popular Opinion and the "Jewish Question", 1939–1943: Some Further Reflections', in A. Paucker (ed.), *Die Juden im Nationalsozialistischen Deutschland/The Jews in Nazi Germany 1933–1945*, Tübingen, 1986, p. 384.

could continue to enforce anti-Semitic policies as long as it could count on a substantial number of people to come forward. Germans – both those who cooperated and those who thought it best to keep their distance – were actively engaged in the policing process, and such 'auto-policing' or 'auto-surveillance' needs to be kept firmly in mind in any study of opposition, resistance, dissent or any other kind of disobedience.

The emergence of an extreme example of a surveillance society in Nazi Germany simultaneously eliminated several of the most important preconditions for the existence of disobedience, let alone opposition or resistance. Other and related factors frequently mentioned in the literature also continued to play a role. The 'atomization' of society persisted, so that solidarities were difficult to maintain or to form anew. Political 'criminality' could be tracked down in short order, and the demoralizing perception was that there was little chance of success. Not only did all these factors reduce the possibility for some sort of underground to emerge; but also a cardinal fact of life for the citizens in Nazi Germany after 1939 was that the fatherland was at war. The terror bombings of the Reich, and the decision to insist upon unconditional surrender, robbed the Allied cause of much of the moral edge it might otherwise have enjoyed over the Nazi regime.[65]

Given the lack of encouragement from outside Germany and the fortress mentality within, as well as the likelihood of failure, those who would disobey – let alone press on to offer opposition or to organize resistance – were bound to be few in number. Even in the occupied countries, where there were less severe limitations on the space for disobedience, most opposition and resistance did not get under way until after the Nazi grip began to slacken. It should come as no surprise that inside Germany, where secure enclaves remained smaller and more fragile, disobedience was slower to take shape, more restricted in scope and carried the troubling consequence, unique to Germany, of being difficult to dissociate from treason.

Even though there were few enclaves in Nazi Germany, moments of disobedience, of non-compliance, even of opposition and resistance materialized at one point or another. Accounts testify to the courage of many individuals and groups who swam against the tide, who were not swept away by the powerful momentum to comply. Any evaluation of the courage and commitment of such people must reflect on the nature of the situation they faced and the strength of the odds against them.

[65]   See the perspective offered by C. Bielenberg, *Ride Out of the Dark*, London, 1968, pp. 119ff.

One should also not forget that, in Peter Hoffmann's words, 'on the whole, at all times from 1933 to 1945 the majority of German voters, indeed of the entire population, supported the government, albeit with varying degrees of willingness.'[66]

---

[66]   Hoffmann, *German Resistance*, p. 51. A similar point is made by G. van Roon, *Widerstand im Dritten Reich*, 4th edn, Munich, 1987, pp. 12ff.

# Women

# 8

# Victims or Perpetrators? Controversies about the Role of Women in the Nazi State

*Adelheid von Saldern*

Originally appeared as Adelheid von Saldern, 'Victims or Perpetrators? Controversies about the Role of Women in the Nazi State' in *Nazism and German Society*, 1933–1945, ed. David F. Crew (1994) pp. 142–60.

*Editor's Introduction*

Nazi propaganda reels of the 1930s constantly bombarded viewers with pictures of Hitler surrounded by adoring German women and girls. These images cannot be explained away simply as a stage-managed ploy or as an expression of Hitler's obsession with young women. Although the leadership of the NSDAP and its organizations was entirely male in its composition, totally committed to a male-dominated society, and therefore strictly opposed to the emancipation of women, the party managed to attract considerable support from German women. About one third of female voters opted for the Nazi party in the elections of November 1932. It is clear that this level of support did not decrease after 1933.

In the following contribution, Adelheid von Saldern provides a succinct summary of the reasons why many women were so enthusiastic first about Hitler and his party, and from 1933 about Hitler and his regime. This particular issue is, however, subsumed into the main concern of the reading: are women in the Third Reich 'to be seen more as victims or as accomplices?'

Saldern's verdict echoes the conclusions reached by Lüdtke in his article on the role of German workers. Like Lüdtke, Saldern rejects a simplistic division into either victim or accomplice/perpetrator. Instead, she invites the reader to distinguish between degrees of variations, or 'types', of victims and accomplices. In Saldern's words, 'in the everyday realities produced by German fascism, ordinary men and women became complex and contradictory combinations of both victims *and* perpetrators'. Saldern does concede that 'this mixture of roles probably displayed gender-specific features because women were confined to minor political offices and to the less overtly Nazified everyday life of the private sphere.'

# Victims or Perpetrators?
## Controversies about the Role of Women in the Nazi State

*Adelheid von Saldern*

For a long time women were more or less excluded as subjects of historical research on the Third Reich, but the situation has begun to change during the past few years. Historians have not, however, been able to agree in their evaluations of the role of women in the Nazi period; are women to be seen more as victims or as accomplices?[1] This controversial question has been posed and answered in quite conflicting ways with regard not only to Nazi Germany but for contemporary society as well.[2] The discussion of the role of women in the Third Reich has been stirred up by Claudia Koonz's book, *Mothers in the Fatherland*, published in 1987, which argues that the 'emotional work' done by women for men contributed to the stability of the Nazi system. Her arguments have certainly not gone unchallenged and in what follows I want to sketch the main outlines of the current debate.[3]

---

[1] Critical surveys of the historiography of women in the Third Reich are presented by Haubrich and Gravenhorst and – with somewhat different conclusions – by Reese and Sachse: Karin Haubrich and Lerke Gravenhorst, 'Wie stellen wir heute moralische Wirklichkeiten von Frauen im Nationalsozialismus her?' in Lerke Gravenhorst and Carmen Tatschmurat (eds), *Töchter-Fragen. NS-FrauenGeschichte* (Freiburg, i. Br., 1990) and Dagmar Reese and Carola Sachse, 'Frauenforschung und Nationalsozialismus. Eine Bilanz' also in *Töchter-Fragen*, pp. 73–107; Gudrun Brockhaus also presents a critical discussion of the literature in which the thesis of 'women as victims' dominates; see Gudrun Brockhaus, 'Opfer, Täterin, Mitbeteiligte. Zur Diskussion um die Rolle der Frauen im Nationalsozialismus' in *Töchter-Fragen*, pp. 107–27.

[2] See Christina Thurmer-Rohr, *Vagabundinnen. Feministische Essays* 3rd edn (Berlin, 1987); Beate Schaeffer-Hegel (ed.), *Frauen und Macht. Der alltägliche Beitrag der Frauen zur Politik des Patriarchats*, 2nd edn (Pfaffenweiler, 1988).

[3] Gisela Bock, 'Die Frauen und der Nationalsozialismus: Bemerkungen zu einem Buch von Claudia Koonz', *Geschichte und Gesellschaft*, vol. 15, no. 4, 1989, pp. 563–79. I intend in this chapter not to review Koonz's book, but rather to present her main arguments, which I have sometimes exaggerated and sharpened so as to be able to work out more precisely the differences, both methodological and interpretive, between Koonz and Bock.

## Women as Victims

In the existing literature, women have often been portrayed as the victims of National Socialism;[4] the Nazi system oppressed women, reduced them to mere objects who were therefore not able actively to defend themselves from National Socialism. It is certainly true that there were many women who were undeniably victims of the Nazi regime, above all Jewish women, but also Gypsy women, women in the resistance, and so on. There is also no doubt that, in general, women were the victims of structural discrimination in politics, society and the economy.[5] For example, the few women who occupied responsible positions in state and society before 1933 were forced out of their offices and professions.[6] Women's chances of being admitted to university and thus to the future functional elite of the Third Reich mostly declined (at least until the outbreak of the war).[7] Many young women had to work in badly paid agricultural jobs or as housemaids.[8] The list of discriminatory measures against women could be enlarged considerably and in so far as the term 'victim' refers to these kinds of structural sexual discrimination it is quite applicable.

This, however, is not the core of the controversy among women's historians which becomes more evident when we take a look at Gisela Bock's discussion of sterilization. Bock argues that compulsory sterilization affected women more than men – especially in qualitative terms. Because women's identities were more closely connected to their sexual fertility, Bock thinks that forced sterilization did greater existential damage to women than to men. Bock sees an aggressive anti-feminism in Nazi sterilization practices which she thinks must be placed in the larger context of the Holocaust. Both Jews and women were to be regarded as 'inferior.' According to Bock, sterilization was a component of racial policy, which was supposed to purify the 'racial body' by 'removing the racially inferior'; here, Bock refers, in particular, to the estimated 4,500 women who died as a result of forced sterilization.

[4]   See, for example, Annette Kuhn and Valentine Rothe (eds), *Frauen im deutschen Faschismus* (Düsseldorf, 1982); Gerda Szepansky, *'Blitzmädel', 'Heldenmutter', 'Kriegerwitwe'* (Frankfurt, 1986).

[5]   See, for example, Ute Frevert, *Frauen-Geschichte. Zwischen Bürgerlicher Verbesserung und Neuer Weiblichkeit* (Frankfurt, 1986), p. 209; Georg Tidl, *Die Frau im Nationalsozialismus* (Wien/München/Zurich, 1984), pp. 35–41.

[6]   See, for example, Rita Thalman, *Frausein im Dritten Reich* (München/Wien, 1984), pp. 94–104.

[7]   Ibid., p. 104.

[8]   This change was produced by the introduction of the 'Hauswirtschaftliches Jahr' (Housekeeping Year) and by the 'Arbeitsdienst für Mädchen' (Labour Service for Girls).

One of the merits of Bock's book is that it demonstrates the breadth of the application of eugenic ideas, all stemming from a common basic assumption, namely that it was both 'necessary' and 'possible' to cleanse a people of alleged 'racial inferiors', either by preventing their reproduction or by isolating and killing them. Problems arise, however, from Bock's attempts to generalize and to extend her conclusions to all women. The Nazis did indeed think that women were, in general, inferior to men, but Bock fails to recognize that women's 'inferiority' was a relative matter which did not imply evaluation in the sense of a racial policy. Aryan women might allegedly be 'inferior' to Aryan men but both were members of a supposedly 'superior race'. By jumbling together very different meanings of 'inferiority', Gisela Bock arrives at a conceptual equation of anti-feminism and anti-Semitism that is not convincing.[9]

Nevertheless, the evaluation of someone as 'inferior' was based on different criteria for men and for women. Under certain conditions, promiscuous women were much more vulnerable than men to being labeled 'inferior' – above all, if they came from a so-called 'anti-social milieu'. But, this sort of classification was, in any case, connected more with conservative-bourgeois values than with racist-fascist ideas. Bock supports her thesis that Nazi sterilization affected women more deeply than men by arguing that it damaged or destroyed women's social identity, which was based primarily on motherhood and fertility. Bock presumes that all women found their identity in child-bearing and motherhood, an argument which applied to some of the women who were sterilized but certainly not to all of them. As Atina Grossmann puts it, Bock comes 'curiously close to implying that non-mothers are not really women'.[10] Bock overstates her characterization of sterilization as a general policy of anti-natalism. She argues that 1.6 million births were prevented by sterilization.[11] But this birth-deficit was, however, supposed to be compensated by increasing the number of children born to 'valuable' parents, by tolerating illegitimate births (from 'valuable' women) and by a strictly enforced prohibition of abortion. Thus the Nazi regime can equally well be seen as a pro-natalist racial welfare state.

---

[9]    Claudia Koonz draws a similar conclusion; see Claudia Koonz, 'Erwiderung auf Gisela Bocks Rezension von "Mothers in the Fatherland"', *Geschichte und Gesellschaft*, vol. 18, no. 3, 1992, p. 396; see also Lerke Gravenhorst, 'Nehmen wir National-sozialismus und Auschwitz ausreichend als unser negatives Eigentum in Anspruch? Zu Problemen im feministisch-sozialwissenschaftlichen Diskurs in der Bundes-republik Deutschland' in *Töchter-Fragen*, p. 29.

[10]   Atina Grossmann, 'Feminist debates about women and National Socialism', *Gender and History*, vol. 3, no. 3, 1991, p. 355.

[11]   Gisela Bock, *Zwangssterilisation im Nationalsozialismus* (Opladen, 1986), p. 462.

Bock's interpretation of Nazi policy leads to the conclusion that all women were potential victims with the result that it is all too easy to argue that the number of women who shared direct responsibility for the Third Reich was negligible and that their involvement with the Nazi dictatorship was only a secondary phenomenon, purely a process of accommodation.[12]

Another key element in the present controversy is the question of whether women who were (co-)perpetrators can also be seen as victims. It is well known that the norms and values which had regulated the system of justice up until the Nazi era were replaced by their opposites, which, however, had become legitimate. The fascist system made it possible for people to commit certain crimes without facing punishment; indeed, these people were rewarded, even promoted. Only if the Nazi regime had gone so far as to force people to commit criminal acts could they be seen, in any meaningful sense, as victims of the dictatorship rather than as (co-)perpetrators. But in very few cases can this type of overt coercion be documented; even male and female concentration camp guards were usually allowed to change their jobs if they wanted to.[13] So when, for example, Helga Schubert describes women who made denunciations to the Gestapo (*Denunziantin*) as 'victims of the dictatorship',[14] we should ask whether this is not an inappropriate confusion of the perpetrators with the real victims, even if this was not Schubert's original intention. Dagmar Reese argues, however, that the precondition for becoming a perpetrator is 'a person's freedom of choice' and 'the ability to act as a responsible subject'. In her case study of a woman worker at Siemens, who transferred to a job at the Ravensbrück concentration camp, Reese argues that this woman's social milieu, her gender-specific upbringing and education, as well as the political system, did not allow her to act as a responsible subject.[15] But what might be true in this one case becomes problematic when generalized because then we risk not finding any subjects who were (co-)responsible for their deeds.

---

[12]   Ibid., p. 139. See also Helga Schubert's argument that denouncers were victims; Helga Schubert, *Judasfrauen: Zehn Fallgeschichten weiblicher Denunziation im 'Dritten Reich'*, 3rd edn (Frankfurt, 1990).

[13]   This information was given to me by Claus Füllberg-Stolberg (History Department, University of Hanover) who is directing a research project on women in Nazi concentration camps.

[14]   Schubert, *Judasfrauen*, p. 9; Schubert's intention (which can, however, be questioned) is to present denunciation as a 'typically female' form of participation in the crimes of the Third Reich.

[15]   Dagmar Reese, 'Homo homini lupus-Frauen als Täterinnen?' in *Internationale Wissenschaftliche Korrespondenz für die Geschichte der deutschen Arbeiterbewegung (IWK)*, vol. 27, no. 1, 1991, p. 34.

## The Public Sphere and the Private Sphere

Much of the discussion of women in Nazi Germany revolves around the relationship between the public sphere and the private sphere.[16] Historians usually proceed from the assumption that the private, reproductive sphere was determined more by women and the public sphere more by men. The interrelationship between the public sphere and the private sphere has become a central issue in historical debates; were these two spheres intertwined or basically separate from each other? Was the private sphere infiltrated by the public? In the following comments, I will discuss the main interpretations that appear in recent literature and, at the same time, present some of my own thoughts on these issues.

### Changes in the private sphere and the interconnections between public and private

Koonz claims that in the private sphere, women played a role that requires us to speak of guilt or at least of 'complicity', rather than of innocence. But by focusing upon women's guilt, Koonz has laid herself open to attack.[17] As Gisela Bock puts it, 'As long as the "guilt" of women is seen as bearing and raising children, in the work done for the family and in the "traditional" role of women, who were said to be at the centre of National Socialist racial policy, there is hardly a chance of achieving a new view'.[18] In particular, the following statement by Koonz has received much attention and criticism: 'Far from remaining untouched by Nazi evil, women operated at its very centre'.[19] More specifically and concretely, Koonz argues that 'When the SS man returned home, he entered a doll's house of *ersatz* goodness in which he could escape from his own evil actions.[20] But as Koonz does not differentiate sharply

[16] Of course, the concept of the two spheres is an analytical construction which reflects the complexities of reality only in very approximate terms. In this discussion, I have omitted consideration of the professional realm, the sphere of production and other parts of the public sphere, because this does not touch upon this controversy. Although Jürgen Habermas has also worked on the private and public spheres, his focus differs from that of the *Historikerinnenstreit*; see Jürgen Habermas, *Strukturwandel der Öffentlichkeit* (Neuwied/Berlin, 1962).

[17] This criticism is made not only by Bock ('Historikerinnenstreit', *Geschichte und Gesellschaft*) but also by Reese and Sachse ('Frauenforschung' in *Töchter-Fragen*, p. 101).

[18] Bock, 'Historikerinnenstreit', *Geschichte und Gesellschaft*, p. 404.

[19] Claudia Koonz, *Mothers in the Fatherland. Women, the Family and Nazi Politics* (New York, 1987), p. 6.

[20] Ibid., p. 420.

between the structural entanglement of the two spheres and the more subjective question of individual guilt and responsibility, her text lays itself open to misunderstanding.

Ernst Fraenkel's insights can be helpful in approaching the structural side of the problem. Fraenkel differentiated between the 'prerogative state' (*Massnahmenstaat*), by which he meant the sphere dominated by Nazi illegality and injustice, and the 'normative state' (*Normenstaat*), or the sphere under Nazism where the norms of pre-Nazi bourgeois society still survived. According to Fraenkel these two spheres were by no means insulated from one another; rather they were arranged in a hierarchy which always allowed the 'prerogative state' to infiltrate the 'normative state;' yet the *Massnahmenstaat* 'only' partially utilized its hegemony.[21]

If we were to apply such an analysis to the situation of women – which Fraenkel did not do in his book[22] – we would have to conclude that women lived and acted in the *Massnahmenstaat* less than in the *Normenstaat*, which included the private sphere, the sphere of reproduction, family and housework, but which was infiltrated by the *Massnahmenstaat*. Indeed, Dagmar Reese and Carola Sachse argue that during the Third Reich, the private sphere was so radically invaded by the *Massnahmenstaat* that it makes little sense to speak of a 'female space; what remained was only an empty shell, which no longer enclosed differentiated concepts'.[23] Fraenkel's approach may be more useful because he worked not with a picture of an empty shell, but rather two overlapping spheres, in which one dominated the other in an incalculable manner. Neither sphere was independent of the other; in the private sphere (*Normenstaat*), women (and men) were repeatedly confronted with regulations imposed by the public sphere, the *Massnahmenstaat*, when, for example, Jewish shops were boycotted, when the 'block warden' (*Blockwart*) system was constructed in the neighborhoods,[24] when a neighbour was taken away or when the family was

---

[21]    Ernst Fraenkel, *Der Doppelstaat* (Frankfurt, 1974), 1st edn (New York, 1940); the terms 'prerogative state' and 'normative state' are used in the 1941 English translation of Fraenkel's book by E. A. Shils, Edith Lowenstein and Klaus Knorr; see *The Dual State. A Contribution to the Theory of Dictatorship* (New York/London/Toronto, 1941), Introduction, pp. xiii–xiv: 'By the Prerogative State we mean that governmental system which exercises unlimited arbitrariness and violence unchecked by any legal guarantees, and by the Normative State an administrative body endowed with elaborate powers for safeguarding the legal order as expressed in statutes, decisions of the courts, and activities of the administrative agencies.'

[22]    Fraenkel was concerned 'only' with legal issues.

[23]    Reese and Sachse, 'Frauenforschung' in *Töchter-Fragen*, p. 102.

[24]    A 'block warden' (*Blockwart*) was a person who had to observe and report on the behaviour of the inhabitants of several houses.

pressured to let their child join the Hitler Youth. Thus women could experience the *Massnahmenstaat* even when they were not directly connected with it as either victim or as perpetrator; a non-political, private sphere simply did not exist. As the deputy principal, *Studiendirektorin* Hedwig Forster, a committed Nazi, put it, the housewife should even boil fish in a National Socialist way.[25]

### Separate spheres and an innocent private sphere? Arguments and counter-arguments

If analysing the structural interconnections between the public and the private sphere is not thought to be a legitimate exercise, then arguments will have to be based solely on the examination of individual or group behaviour. However, the existing literature displays certain methodological inconsistencies; some women's historians retain a structural approach instead of examining individual and group behaviour. But rather than emphasizing the connections between the public and private spheres, these women's historians insist upon their separation, a division drawn along more or less gendered lines. They argue that women acted primarily in a 'sane', non-political, private arena, an assumption which sometimes leads to a positive evaluation of women's activities in the Third Reich. Women are shown to have been able to cope with difficult situations, especially during the war, when women adapted to the steadily worsening conditions of everyday life so as to ensure the survival of their families. This literature stresses women's strength and ability to endure their own suffering.[26] Women's work in the Third Reich is presented as having been primarily oriented to 'practical value' (*Gebrauchswert*) and involved with the natural resources of society, which are thought to have humanizing functions:[27] for example, Kuhn and Rothe stress women's 'use-oriented' dealings with the 'natural resources' of the society 'in their social necessity and their humanizing functions'.[28]

Windaus-Walser rejects such generalizations: 'Was it not the race hygienists and eugenists of both sexes who claimed that their specific "use-value orientation" in their dealings with the "natural resource" of human beings was necessary for the society and had a humanizing

---

[25] Also cited in Adelheid von Saldern, 'Die Situation der Frau im Dritten Reich', in *Historisches Museum am Hohen Ufer* (ed.), *1933 und danach. Hannover* (Hannover, 1983), p. 52.
[26] Szepanksy, *Blitzmädel*, p. 9.
[27] Kuhn and Rothe, *Frauen*, p. 18.
[28] Ibid., p. 15.

function?'[29] Reese and Sachse disagree: 'Modern race-hygiene was shaped by men as a science, as was its relationship to state and society . . . National Socialist racial policy was, doubtless, a male policy on the levels of scientific conceptualization, political decisions and administrative implementation.'[30]

But can we really be so sure? Should we not also ask whether many women did not also support these 'scientific' conceptualizations, these political decisions and administrative implementations? Did women really 'only' endure such a policy because they were relatively powerless and were they 'only' passively involved in the practical realization of racial eugenics?[31]

Just as there could be no completely innocent private sphere, so, too, the existence of any general cultural resistance, based upon 'feminity', against the Nazi regime must be questioned. In the Third Reich, the original ideal of a life bound to natural resources suffered massive deformations – as did many other ideals – especially as a result of its connections with eugenic concepts. Female social workers provide one example of this process. They had initially wanted to transform the natural resource of 'motherliness' into a humanitarian profession. But under the Nazis they often ended up preparing the way for the 'selection' and elimination of so-called 'inferior life', a process which was also justified on purportedly 'humanitarian' grounds, such as 'decreasing suffering' or 'preventing damage to society'.[32]

*Different spheres, different values: two sides of the same coin*

Ute Daniel describes a drifting apart of the norms and values which dominated in each sphere. While the private sphere was characterized by values such as personal intimacy and mutual responsibility, the public sphere, which included the political, was dominated by instrumental rationalization (*Zweckrationalität*), or, in other words, an 'in order to' mode of thinking. For example: 'In order to gain world power status, war had to be waged; in order to maintain the "German race", Jews and

---

[29]   Karin Windaus-Walser, 'Gnade der weiblichen Geburt? Zum Umgang der Frauenforschung mit Nationalsozialismus und Anti-semitismus', *Feministische Studien*, vol. 6, no. 1, 1988, p. 105.

[30]   Ibid., p. 94.

[31]   Bock does not systematically analyse the role of women in the practical implementation of this policy but some of her references give the impression that women were reluctant to participate; Bock, *Zwangssterilisation*, pp. 208, 298, 302, 344, 392.

[32]   Examples in Angela Ebbinghaus (ed.), *Opfer und Täterinnen. Frauenbiographien des Nationalsozialismus* (Nördlingen, 1987); see also p. 7.

others had to be exterminated.'[33] In such a system of 'instrumental rationalization', people were used as means to an end; the end itself was usually of a supra-individual nature. Moreover, in this system of instrumental rationalization, most Germans were given the impression that the negative side of the Third Reich 'only' affected 'aliens' and 'outsiders' such as 'non-Aryans', the opponents of the regime, homosexuals and, during the war, foreign workers and forced labourers. For most Germans, both men and women, private life continued to be 'livable', even when, for the 'others', it was not.[34] One of the compensations, the semblance of a relatively intact private sphere – at least until the loss of fathers and sons at the front and the long nights of bombing at home – and the relatively strong integration of women within this private sphere might explain women's toleration of the Nazi system.

At first glance, it appeared that nothing had changed in the private sphere in comparison with the preceding decades. But, in fact, a great deal had changed. The Nazi state which many women tolerated was a barbaric system, a system made possible by the passive acquiescence of the overwhelming majority of the German people. The continued existence of a seemingly intact private sphere made it easier for the Nazi system to wield power. But in uncovering this structural and functional interconnection between the private sphere and the public sphere, between a seemingly 'pure and safe private world' (*heile Welt*) and 'barbarism', it is not necessary to assume individual guilt. People's behaviour did not have to change: although behaviour in the private sphere may have remained 'the same', its impact changed as an automatic consequence of the transformation of the public-political sphere.

### The special female public sphere

In addition to the private sphere, women in the Third Reich were also given their own public sphere, although with very limited influence. Here a relatively autonomous field of activity within the general framework of National Socialist values and norms became possible for women, even though they were under the leadership of men at the very top. In 1936, for example, 11 million of the 35 million women in Germany were members of the *NS-Frauenschaft*.[35] By and large, these

---

[33] Ute Daniel, 'Über die alltäglichen Grenzen der Verantwortung: Industriearbeit 1933–1945' in *SOWI/Sozialwissenschaftliche Informationen*, vol. 20, no. 2, 1991, p. 85.

[34] Ibid., p. 87.

[35] Koonz, *Mothers in the Fatherland*, p. 457.

women, and especially those who were leaders, accepted the role allotted to them by the Nazi system. Many were more or less positively inclined to National Socialism. Although there was some grumbling and criticism in certain areas, this did not usually amount to serious (political) opposition. Of course, not all historians agree with this view, preferring, instead, to argue that women were 'peculiarly resistant to National Socialism'.[36]

In a rather different assessment, Claudia Koonz argues that: 'The state support of the female public "sphere" offered women a counterbalance to the authority of husbands and fathers, of priests and pastors.'[37] Similarly, Schmidt-Waldherr maintains that in the Nazi state it was women themselves who 'were allowed' to transpose the Nazi concept of 'mothers of the home' (*Hausmütter*) into the concept of 'mothers of the folk' (*Volksmütter*) which was combined with a female public sphere although it remained relatively distinct from other fields of public activity.[38] And through their responses to the problems of everyday life, which were generally seen as women's tasks in the private sphere now transformed into public issues, the Nazis tried to fuse the private with the public spheres and to define women's roles in both. Such an intermingling meant that the private sphere became politicized. Carrying Schmidt-Waldherr's arguments further, we might say that women did not see this infiltration of politics into the private sphere as illegitimate or as a form of subordination. It may rather have been regarded as a welcome termination of a senseless division between the two spheres which enhanced women's social status and constructed an apparently productive synthesis between the 'public' and the 'private'.

## Women as Perpetrators

The terms 'innocence' and 'guilt', 'victim' and '(co-) perpetrator' refer primarily to individual subjects, not to [social or political] structures. Ute Daniel and others have rightly pointed out that terms such as 'victim' and 'perpetrator' distract attention from more important questions, rather than focusing upon them. Such terms can at best be employed only as very rough descriptions of women as individuals responsible for their own actions.

[36]   See, for instance, Jill Stephenson, *The Nazi Organisation of Women* (London, 1981), p. 170.
[37]   Koonz, 'Erwiderung', *Geschichte und Gesellschaft*, p. 395.
[38]   Hiltraud Schmidt-Waldherr, 'Konflikte um die "Neue Frau" zwischen liberalbürgerlichen Frauen und den Nationalsozialisten' in *Töchter-Fragen*, p. 181.

*Voting*

'Hitler came into power through women': this has been a widely accepted stereotype.[39] Although the claim that women voted in disproportionate numbers for Hitler has been refuted or, at least, greatly relativized by historians,[40] it cannot be denied that women did vote for conservative parties, above all for the German National People's Party (DNVP) and the Catholic Centre Party (*Zentrum*). In a period of deepening crisis in state and society, the conservative political parties promised to protect the family and thus to maintain what many women regarded as the only quasi intact female sphere. Women's decision to vote conservative has to be seen as an act of 'social logic'. Moreover, church and religion appealed to many women. The strong, if contradictory, affinity of conservatism for National Socialism, particularly in the early 1930s, and the possible implications of such an affinity for women's history have, however, usually not been considered seriously. Neither has the fact that one third of female voters voted for the NSDAP in the last democratic election before Hitler's take-over.[41] How was it possible that in 1932 one-third of women voted for a party which, from our present point of view, was as anti-female as the NSDAP? Much of the existing literature talks in terms of deception and manipulation.[42] More sophisticated arguments suggest that a certain 'social logic' was at work here and that many of the same reasons that moved women to vote conservative also caused them to support the Nazis. For example, Nazi propaganda for enhancement of the status of housewives and mothers met with some success among women to whom the Great Depression had denied alternative prospects. Claudia Koonz suggests that many women, especially those from the lower but also the middle classes rejected the type of emancipation symbolized by the 'New Woman' of the 1920s, because it was at odds with their mentality, their view

[39] Annemarie Tröger and Jürgen Falter have commented critically upon this stereotype; see Annemarie Tröger, 'Die Dolchstosslegende der Linken. "Frauen haben Hitler an die Macht gebracht"' in Gruppe Berliner Dozentinnen (eds), *Frauen und Wissenschaft. Beiträge zur Berliner Sommeruniversität für Frauen*, July 1976 (Berlin, 1977), p. 326 and Jürgen W. Falter, *Hitlers Wähler* (München, 1991), p. 136.

[40] Tröger, 'Dolchstosslegende', *Frauen und Wissenschaft*, p. 327; see also Falter, *Hitlers Wähler*, pp. 136–46.

[41] A precise analysis cannot be constructed, because gender was often not taken into consideration when the election data was originally collected; see Falter, *Hitlers Wähler*, p. 139.

[42] The current trend in historical studies is to attempt to replace the 'manipulation thesis' with other explanations, directed more at the analysis of social interests, milieux, mentalities and 'social logics'; see also Frevert, *Frauen-Geschichte*, p. 207.

of society and their idea of the proper 'gender-order'. Helen Boak concludes that the Nazi movement 'was not anti-woman, but against the emancipation of woman which it was thought took her away from her age-old role of wife and mother'.[43] Koonz argues convincingly that Nazi women and even many conservative women approved of the possibility of expanding the 'female sphere' in the Nazi system.[44] Despite its male-bonding culture, Nazism must also have appealed to women and to female 'social logic'. Windaus-Walser takes Nazi propaganda elevating the status of (Aryan) women as mothers seriously and she tries to decode the ways in which it might have addressed the interests and identities of many women, especially those who were mothers. She suggests that the 'enhancement of female merits in the production of "worthy" lives, as it was expressed in the National Socialist cult surrounding the Aryan mother' probably played an important role.[45] Windaus-Walser's argument could hardly be more at odds with Bock's interpretation of Nazism as fascist anti-natalism. But Windaus-Walser does of course assume that women acted exclusively or primarily as 'women' and 'mothers', a position questioned by Dorothea Schmidt and Helen Boak.

Both Schmidt and Boak ask whether it was necessarily only gender-specific points of view which led women to vote for the NSDAP or the conservative parties.[46] Making use of both Weimar and present-day voting analyses, Schmidt suggests that it is not so much a party's specific position on women, but rather its general *Weltanschauung* that determines women's voting behaviour. Boak claims that 'Women chose to vote NSDAP for the same reasons men voted for the party – out of self-interest, out of a belief that the party best represented their own idea of what German society should be, even if they may have disagreed with the party's stand on individual issues'.[47] Boak thinks that the party's attitude to women's role in society 'did not play a decisive part in voters' choice and that what the Nazis had to say on this subject was to a large extent a reflection of the views held by the DVP, DNVP, Centre party and BVP'.[48]

[43]   Helen L. Boak, ' "Our last hope": Women's votes for Hitler – A reappraisal', *German Studies Review*, vol. 12, no. 2, 1989, p. 303. Boak refers to Thomas Childers, *The Nazi Voter. The Social Foundations of Fascism in Germany, 1919–1933* (London, 1983), p. 267.

[44]   Koonz, *Mothers in the Fatherland*, p. 55.

[45]   Windaus-Walser, 'Gnade', *Feministische Studien*, p. 112.

[46]   Dorothea Schmidt, 'Die peinlichen Verwandtschaften-Frauenforschung zum Nationalsozialismus' in Heide Gerstenberger and Dorothea Schmidt (eds), *Normalität oder Normalisierung* (Münster, 1987), p. 58.

[47]   Boak, ' "Our last hope",' *German Studies Review*, p. 303.

[48]   Ibid., p. 302.

*Female anti-Semitism*

In her book, *Die friedfertige Frau*,[49] published in 1983, Margarete Mitscherlich contends that, as a rule, women who were anti-Semites or racists had taken over a male point of view. This argument has been widely accepted by women's historians. Projection of hate for the fathers (*Vaterhass*), the shifting of incestuous wishes on to Jews (*Rassenschändung*), rivalry, aggression and so on, these unconscious psychological motives for the development of anti-Semitism were 'relevant above all for the male psyche'.[50] As a result of super-ego deformation, the ego-ideal of male anti-Semites was narcissistic. Because women generally had a weakly developed super-ego, female anti-Semitism could only be evaluated as a secondary phenomenon. Female anti-Semitism arose when the suppressed woman wanted to identify herself with the (anti-Semitic) male suppressor and adapted to his prejudices: 'The tendency to adapt is in turn connected with her great fear of losing love.'[51]

But Windaus-Walser has, with good reason, challenged this gender-specific interpretation of social psychological processes; weakly developed super-egos, a sufficient 'pre-condition' for anti-Semitism, can be found among both men and women. Conflicts stemming from the Oedipus Complex can be found in women too; although the mother becomes the object of hate and rivalry, this mother hate can be transferred to men. Super-ego deformations, projections, idealizations and rejection mechanisms also appear in women. In short, Windaus-Walser cannot subscribe to any notion of the 'blessing of female birth' and insists instead upon investigating women's contribution to the Nazi system: 'What if National Socialism corresponded to the unconscious needs and inner psychological mechanisms of these women as well as to their conscious ideas? What if the hate felt by female anti-Semites did not differ from that of their male counterparts? What if women had not simply adapted to ('male') National Socialism but had made their own contribution to it?'[52] Women might, in fact, have delegated their murderous intentions to men: 'Men then would have acted not only in their own name, but also in the name of women.'[53] There was no specific female or male libido (or aggression), and, according to Windaus-Walser, there was only one anti-Semitism, which could of course be

---

[49] Translated into English as *The Peaceable Sex: On Aggression in Women and Men* (New York, 1987).
[50] Margarete Mitscherlich, *Die friedfertige Frau* (Frankfurt, 1985), p. 152.
[51] Ibid., pp. 160, 156.
[52] Windaus-Walser, 'Gnade', *Feministische Studien*, p. 111.
[53] Ibid.

expressed in different ways.[54] Windaus-Walser does not want to relativize the 'deeds of the (male) actors', but rather to explore the broadly
associated field, to which the attitudes and behaviour of women also
belonged, which made these deeds possible.

### The issue of 'female guilt'

Finally, we need to ask whether women as individuals shared the guilt of
the Nazi regime, whether we can speak of a 'specifically female guilt', a
guilt, as Gisela Bock puts it, which should be looked for 'in specifically
female activities' in the traditionally separate private sphere.[55] Bock
herself refuses to accept the notion of a 'specifically female guilt' because
she thinks that Nazi racial policy must not be confused with either the
norms or with the reality of the 'traditionally female sphere' and because
the 'real contribution of women to the Nazi crimes occurred in non-
traditional functions external to the home'.[56] But, once again, this argument neglects the structural interconnection of the private sphere and
the public sphere. And while women certainly had less influence than
men, they were by no means powerless, even though the particular scope
for action and influence depended upon class and ethnic differences.
Thus we cannot be satisfied with a description of women as merely the
victims and the objects of Nazi policy who were simply forced to adapt to
reality. The private sphere was by no means a safe and sane refuge; some
women denounced their husbands.[57] Many mothers educated their children in the Nazi spirit; in other words, we must think in terms not only of
the 'power of the father' but of the mother as well.[58] The evaluation of
female behaviour is particularly complicated when it comes to women
who supported their 'Nazi-men' morally and psychologically.[59] The Nazis
had a predilection for a pleasurable and cosy family life which became
more important the more these men committed crimes in their work but

---

[54]   These differences result from a 'typical' female 'mechanism of delegation' or
'indirect participation', as well as from the relatively strict division which obviously
exists between female wishes or phantasies, on the one hand, and female deeds, on
the other.
[55]   Bock, 'Historikerinnenstreit', *Geschichte und Gesellschaft*, p. 400.
[56]   Ibid., p. 401.
[57]   See Klaus-Michael Mallman and Gerhard Paul, *Herrschaft und Alltag. Ein Industrierevier im Dritten Reich* (Bonn, 1991), p. 233.
[58]   See Windaus-Walser, 'Gnade', *Feministische Studien*, p. 11.
[59]   See Claudia Koonz, 'Mothers in the Fatherland: Women in Nazi Germany' in
Renate Bridenthal and Claudia Koonz (eds), *Becoming Visible. Women in European
History* (Boston, 1977), p. 470.

did not want to lose the 'decency' which they supposedly demonstrated at home in their role as good husbands and fathers. The influences that shaped inter-sexual relations were often complex and multi-layered. Because attitudes and gestures were frequently more important than 'high-sounding phrases', there are few documentary sources which would allow us to explore this dimension of support for National Socialism; even oral history is often deficient when it comes to the subtle nuances of the intimate, private sphere.

There is no clear-cut answer to the problem of conducting empirical historical research on women's guilt. One reasonable approach involves constructing a socio-cultural reappraisal of individual or group biographical backgrounds and thereby reconstructing as exactly as possible the components which were self-determined *and* those which were determined by exterior forces, as well as the mixture of both.[60] Bock's attempt to make women as wives and mothers free of guilt is not very productive. Mothers' and wives' experiences were defined not only by the private but also by the public sphere. And the attitudes of women and also of juveniles in the female public sphere can often only be explained by looking at experiences formed in the private sphere.

It might be useful to look more closely at the women who were committed to the Nazi movement and its female public sphere. Activist women wanted to enlarge their own domain – children, kitchen, church, hospital and culture – and thus to influence society as women. For example, Renate Finkh, born in 1926, joined the Hitler Youth (*Hitlerjugend*) and assumed a leading position as *Jungmädelführerin* in 1940. Ambitious and proud of belonging to the elite of the so-called German 'national community' (*Volksgemeinschaft*), she tried to influence the private sphere of other daughters and mothers so as to convince them of the Nazi ideology.[61] In her life, then, there was a mutual interaction between the female public sphere and the private sphere.

In her article on girls who were leaders of the League of German Girls (*Bund deutscher Mädel*), Dagmar Reese talks about 'entanglement and responsibility' (*Verstrickung und Verantwortung*) but doubts that these particular teenagers can be seen as 'mature individuals'.[62] Yet Reese also defines her task as

---

[60]   See, for example, Inge Marssolek's book about Helene Schwärzel's denunciation of Carl Goerdeler: *Die Denunziantin: Helene Schwärzel, 1944–47* (Bremen, 1993).
[61]   See Charles Schüdekopf (ed.), *Der alltägliche Faschismus. Frauen im Dritten Reich* (Berlin/Bonn, 1981), p. 68; further examples can be found in Renate Wiggershaus, *Frauen unterm Nationalsozialismus* (Wuppertal, 1984).
[62]   Dagmar Reese, 'Verstrickung und Verantwortung. Weibliche Jugendliche in der Führung des Bundes Deutscher Mädel', *SOWI/Sozialwissenschaftliche Informationen*, vol. 20, no. 2, 1991, p. 90.

showing that active involvement in the League of German Girls made, or could have made, sense in the life situation of female juveniles – at the same time, however, emphasizing that this involvement had and still has a political dimension: women remain responsible for their behaviour.[63]

Reese presents four types of women: (a) the politically oriented leader; (b) the young woman prepared to adapt who primarily focused upon protecting her social status; (c) the rebellious type who wanted to escape from home; (d) the social climber. With the possible exception of the first category, each of these different types of young women joined the BdM for reasons that derived more or less from their position in the private sphere. Again we are led to the issue of the entanglement of private and public spheres.

Reese is of course correct when she differentiates between the extent of the responsibility of each type. She holds the politically oriented leaders (type (a)) fully responsible for their acts. Reese analyses the behaviour of the other types and especially of those in group (b) who were prepared to adapt, in terms of the relationship between the individual and a modern, sectionally organized system in which individuals are only 'cogs in a wheel' (a relationship to which Hannah Arendt had earlier drawn attention). The system could be maintained because individuals limited their perceptions and made obedience their maxim.[64] Agreeing with Hannah Arendt, Reese states 'that, in the case of adults, obedience means support, with the result that a system which appears to be passively tolerated' is in fact 'actively maintained'.[65] Men were, in general, more involved in political thought and action than were women. But we must also consider how narrowly the term 'political' was defined at the time. Should 'politics' perhaps not also include the societal norms and values of the Nazi regime [which both women and men helped to reproduce], such as the ideal of a 'pure *Volk*' or the specifically Nazi development of 'modernization?'[66]

---

[63]    Ibid., p. 91.
[64]    Ibid., p. 95.
[65]    Hannah Arendt, *Nach Auschwitz. Essays & Kommentare* (Berlin, 1989), Reese concludes from her interviews that it is usually only the 'social climber' and 'the rebellious type' who are prepared, after 1945, to reflect seriously upon their participation in the Nazi system; those who were willing 'just' to adapt, tend to make light of the Nazi system because they were supposedly neither emotionally involved with the system nor existentially integrated into it; Reese, 'Homo homini lupus' in *Internationale Wissenschaftliche Korrespondenz*, p. 96.
[66]    Ute Frevert takes the issue of 'modernization' into consideration and – as a result – the possible positive impacts upon women's attitudes toward the Nazi regime: 'Many reforms were absolutely attractive . . .' Frevert mentions youth policy, the divorce law reform and the female NS organizations; Frevert, *Frauen-Geschichte*,

Finally, there are strong arguments in favour of abandoning the search for 'pure types' (i.e. for those who were 'only' victims or 'only' perpetrators) so as to focus more attention upon what can be called 'mixed types'. In the everyday realities produced by German fascism, ordinary men and women became complex and contradictory combinations of both victims *and* perpetrators, although this mixture of roles probably displayed gender-specific features because women were confined to minor political offices and to the less overtly Nazified everyday life of the private sphere. This meant that women were commonly co-observers, co-listeners and co-possessors of 'guilty' knowledge, rather than co-perpetrators; their 'complicity' consisted of passivity and toleration in the face of an action, but not the action itself. The investigation of such mixtures of opposites, of such 'sites of contradiction' in their gender-specific forms can be productive not only because it reveals the complex subjectivity of women but also the complexity of all individual reactions, whether male or female, to Nazi attitudes and decisions.

### 'Negative Property?'

Female historians have the same right as male historians to different understandings of history and society and to different epistemologies. Female historians cannot and should not expect to achieve a homogeneous interpretation of the role of women in the Third Reich. The differences that separate historical assessments have, in part, arisen from differing viewpoints on the question of whether the disadvantages and subordinations to which women have been historically subjected can only be properly understood by those who identify 'as much as possible' with the female gender. Some female historians certainly appear to think this type of identification is absolutely necessary. Consequently, women's history has been written with the aim of constructing a homogeneous gender history, free of contradictions, with which contemporary women can uncritically identify. The negative aspects have been left out, even though the price has sometimes – as in the case of the Third Reich – been high, amounting, indeed, to a denial that women acted as responsible subjects. Women's deeds have usually been evaluated 'only' with regard to their inherent 'social logic'. Although this approach has

p. 242. The question of 'modernization' should be examined more closely in future research, although the term 'modernization' must be disconnected from the 'concept of enlightenment'. Unless the Janus-face of modernization, i.e. the potential in 'modernization' for barbarism, is made a central theme, the Third Reich could appear in an unwarranted positive light.

provided an extremely worthwhile enrichment of the modern historiography of women, it should not allow us to ignore the impact of women's attitudes and actions upon the Nazi system as a whole.

Exactly why the 'history of women in German fascism' should be integrated into a strategy of gender identification, as, for example, Kuhn and Rothe have done, remains a puzzle.[67] Nazi propaganda spoke of 'the' women in general, but the real lives and experiences of women under Nazism varied greatly. Should we not rather identify with particular individual females or groups of women – for instance, with the many female political opponents of Nazism and the women resistance fighters, with Jewish women and the other real female victims of the Third Reich – while at the same time not ignoring 'the others' who were structurally involved in the Nazi system or who, as individuals, were more or less 'guilty?'[68]

Only a critical, as well as empathetic, approach to the history of women can produce the capacity for understanding which promotes the emancipation of women. And (female) historians should also discuss a question which Jean Amery asks about Germans in general and which Lerke Gravenhorst now addresses to women – namely, whether the history of women in the Third Reich must be appropriated as a kind of 'negative property'.[69] Whether the Nazi regime is presented primarily as a dictatorship exercised by men or by both men and women – with, of course, due recognition of the fact that power and responsibility were by no means equally shared – cannot be a small concern. Future research must discover how and to what extent the Nazi regime managed to integrate women. It must also explain why, as Hanna Lauterbach puts it, 'most women [felt] that they themselves and all they valued were not suppressed by the regime and its ideology'.[70] Was it all 'just' a great historical misunderstanding? Did women mistakenly see fascism as a special type of 'emancipation?'[71] Or had the decisive steps already been taken in the Weimar Republic as a result of widespread authoritarianism which, as Komann points out, prevented women from seeing the realistic chances offered them for emancipation and using them for the transformation of their wishes into social and economic

[67]   Kuhn and Rothe, *Frauen*.
[68]   In this chapter, there is, unfortunately, not room to discuss the rich history of politically motivated women who were part of the opposition to Nazism.
[69]   Jean Amery, *Jenseits von Schuld und Sühne* (München, 1980; 1966), p. 124; Gravenhorst, 'Negatives Eigentum' in *Töchter-Fragen*, pp. 21, 25.
[70]   Hanna Lauterbach, ' "Aber dann hätten wir ja nur noch Verbrecherinnen . . ." Kommentar zur Diskussion über den Anteil von Frauen am "Handlungskollektiv Deutschland"' in *Töchter-Fragen*, p. 143.
[71]   See Gudrun Brockhaus, 'Opfer' in *Töchter-Fragen*, p. 123.

autonomy?[72] Heilbrun argues that religions which 'train women to accept an inferior status, to exist only for the support and nurturance of men and children, are simultaneously training them for an authoritarian world'.[73] Did religion play this role in the Weimar Republic and in the Third Reich and what role does religion play today?

The highly controversial interpretations of women's roles in the Third Reich which I have discussed in this chapter can be seen as the 'female' side of the '*Historikerstreit*'.* This '*Historikerinnenstreit*' [conflict among historians of women] has focused, in particular, upon the question of whether one half of the population (women) can be absolved of any real responsibility for the crimes of the (male) Nazi regime. Many women historians (but hardly any men) have participated in this '*Historikerinnenstreit*'. On the other hand, it is quite remarkable that few women have contributed to the '*Historikerstreit*.'[74] It will be important in the future to overcome these kinds of gendered divisions with regard to the most central issues of German historiography.

[72] Margot Komann, '"Wie ich Nationalsozialistin wurde." Eine kritisch-feministische Lektüre der Theodore Abel-Akten' in *Töchter-Fragen*, p. 165.

[73] Carolyn C. Heilbrun, 'Women, Jews, and Nazism', *The Yale Review*, vol. 77, no. 1, 1987, p. 78. The relevance of this statement for the Catholic Church must be amended in one important respect; Catholicism was (and is) a form of authoritarianism that is not state-oriented. In many cases, this led to a special type of cultural resistance to the Nazi regime.

* The *Historikerstreit* or 'historians' conflict' was a heated controversy in the late 1980s in which the German historian, Ernst Nolte, and the social theorist, Jürgen Habermas, played leading roles. Nolte claimed that the Holocaust was by no means a unique event in twentieth-century history and that genocide and totalitarian terror had not been invented by Hitler but by Stalin. Led by Habermas, Nolte's critics charged that his attempts to 'relativize' the Holocaust, by comparing it to other genocides, amounted to nothing less than the 'trivialization' of Nazi atrocities. The *Historikerstreit* did not produce a single piece of new evidence about the Holocaust or the Nazi regime. But it did show that certain historians were prepared to argue, as also were many leading conservative politicians, that the Nazi era should no longer be allowed to cast its shadow over the rest of Germany's modern history and over the identities of contemporary Germans.

[74] See Mary Nolan 'The *Historikerstreit* and social history', *New German Critique*, vol. 44, Spring/Summer 1988, pp. 51–80; Adelheid von Saldern, 'Hillgrubers "Zweierlei Untergang" – der Untergang historischer Erfahrungsanalyse?' in *Normalität oder Normalisierung*, pp. 160–70; Adelheid von Saldern and Irmgard Wilharm, 'NS-Geschichtsbild und historisch-politische Kultur am Wendepukt' in Hannoversche Hochschulgemeinschaft (ed.), *Uni Hannover. Zeitschrift der Universität Hannover*, vol. 14, no. 1, 1987, pp. 36–48.

# Hitler as Dictator

# 9

# 'Working Towards the Führer.' Reflections on the Nature of the Hitler Dictatorship

## Ian Kershaw

Originally appeared as Ian Kershaw, 'Working Towards the Führer: Reflections on the Nature of the Hitler Dictatorship', *Contemporary European History*, 2:2 (1993) pp. 103–18.

### Editor's Introduction

There is a wide span of opinion about Hitler's role and position in the Third Reich. While Hans-Adolf Jacobsen, for instance, emphasizes Hitler's 'belief in *divide et impera*' (see Reading 3 in this collection), Ian Kershaw, in the following article, denies that there was any 'systematic "divide and rule" policy'. On the one hand, Jacobsen stresses 'Hitler's tactic' of creating 'an unimaginable chaos of competencies'; on the other, Kershaw denies there was any 'sustained attempt to *create* the administrative anarchy of the Third Reich'.

Setting himself against the crude division of historians of the Third Reich into 'intentionalists' and 'structuralists/functionalists', a dichotomy also referred to in other sections of this Reader, Kershaw makes a case for a more sensible approach. As he stated elsewhere[1]: '"Intention" and "structure" are both essential elements of an explanation of the Third Reich, and need synthesis rather than to be set in opposition to each other.' In the following reading, Kershaw puts his demand for synthesis into practice by combining elements of both 'intentionalism' and 'structuralism'. While Kershaw emphasizes the importance of Hitler's central goals, 'territorial expansion and "removal of the Jews"', and 'the function of

---

[1] Ian Kershaw, 'Hitler: "Master in the Third Reich" or "Weak Dictator"?', ch. 4 in Kershaw, *The Nazi Dictatorship; Problems and Perspectives of Interpretation*, London, 3rd edn, 1993.

Hitler's "charismatic" Führer position . . . : that of unifier, activator, and of enabler in the Third Reich', he also argues that the radicalization stimulated by Hitler was 'largely brought about by others, without Hitler's clear direction'.

This synthesis of interpretations will provoke discussion. Kershaw's reading invites further debate by contrasting Hitler's rule with that of Stalin. In the light of the debate surrounding the publication of *Le Livre noir* (see General Introduction) this has, of course, become a subject of particular interest.

# 'Working Towards the Führer.' Reflections on the Nature of the Hitler Dictatorship

*Ian Kershaw*

The renewed emphasis, already visible in the mid-1980s, on the inter-twined fates of the Soviet Union and Germany, especially in the Stalin and Hitler eras, has become greatly intensified in the wake of the upheavals in eastern Europe. The sharpened focus on the atrocities of Stalinism has prompted attempts to relativize Nazi barbarism – seen as wicked, but on the whole less wicked, than that of Stalinism (and by implication of communism in general).[1] The brutal Stalinist moderniz-ing experiment is used to remove any normative links with humanizing, civilizing, emancipatory or democratizing development from modern-ization concepts and thereby to claim that Hitler's regime, too, was – and intentionally so – a 'modernizing dictatorship'.[2] Implicit in all this is a reversion, despite the many refinements and criticisms of the concept since the 1960s, to essentially traditional views on 'totalitarianism' and to views of Stalin and Hitler as 'totalitarian dictators'.

There can be no principled objection to comparing the forms of dictatorship in Germany under Hitler and in the Soviet Union under Stalin and, however unedifying the subject matter, the nature and extent of their inhumanity.[3] The totalitarianism concept allows comparative analysis of a number of techniques and instruments of domination, and this, too, must be seen as legitimate in itself.[4] The

---

[1] Ernst Nolte's contributions to the *Historikerstreit* reflect this tendency. See '*Historikerstreit*'. *Die Dokumentation der Kontroverse um die Einzigartigkeit der nation-alsozialistischen Judenvernichtung*. (Munich: Piper, 1987), 13–35, 39–47, and his book *Der europäische Bürgerkrieg 1917–1945* (Frankfurt am Main/Berlin: Proplyäen Verlag, 1987).

[2] See, for instance, the essay collection produced by Michael Prinz and Rainer Zitel-mann, eds, *Nationalsozialismus und Modernisierung* (Darmstadt: Wissenschaftliche Buchgesellschaft, 1991), especially the editors' foreword (vii–xi) and Zitelmann's own essay, 'Die totalitäre Seite der Moderne', 1–20.

[3] See on this the thoughtful comments of Charles Maier, *The Unmasterable Past. History, Holocaust, and German National Identity* (Cambridge, MA/London: Harvard University Press, 1988), 71–84.

[4] The Deutsche Forschungsgemeinschaft is currently investigating the structures of differing authoritarian systems in twentieth-century Europe in a major research project, 'Diktaturen im Europa des 20. Jahrhunderts: Strukturen, Erfahrung, Überwindung und Vergleich'.

underlying assumption that both regimes made *total* claims upon society, based upon a monopolistic set of ideological imperatives and resulting in unprecedented levels of repression and attempted indoctrination, manipulation and mobilization – giving these regimes a dynamic missing from more conventional authoritarian regimes – again seems largely incontestable. But the fundamental problem with the term 'totalitarianism' – leaving aside its non-scholarly usage – is that is a descriptive concept, not a theory, and has little or no explanatory power.[5] It presumes that Stalinism and Hitlerism were more like each other than different from each other. But the basis of comparison is a shallow one, largely confined to the apparatus of rule.[6]

My starting point in these reflections is the presumption that, despite superficial similarities in forms of domination, the two regimes were *in essence* more *unlike* than like each other. Though seeing greater potential in comparisons of Nazism with other fascist movements and systems rather than with the Soviet system. I would want to retain an emphasis upon the unique features of the Nazi dictatorship and the need to explain these, alongside those characteristics which could be seen as generic components of European fascism in the era following the First World War, through the specific dominant features of German political culture. (In this I admit to a currently rather unfashionable attachment to notions of a qualified German *Sonderweg*).[7]

Sometimes, however, highlighting contrasts can be more valuable than comparing similarities. In what follows I would like to use what, on an imperfect grasp of some of the recent historiography on Stalinism, I understand to be significant features of Stalin's dictatorship to establish some important contrasts in the Hitler regime. This, I hope, will offer a basis for some reflections on what remains a central problem of interpretation of the Third Reich: what explains the gathering momentum of radicalization, the dynamic of destruction in the Third Reich? Much of the answer to this question has, I would suggest at the outset, to do with the undermining and collapse of what one might call 'rational' structures of rule, a system of 'ordered' government

---

[5]   I argue this case in chapter 2 of my *Nazi Dictatorship. Problems and Perspectives of Interpretation*, 3rd edn (London: Edward Arnold, 1993).

[6]   The comparison becomes even more shallow where the focus shifts from Stalin's own regime to later 'Stalinist' systems. The revelations of the extent of repression in the German Democratic Republic have, for example, prompted simplistic notions of essential similarities between the Honecker and Hitler regimes. See on this the comments of Eberhard Jäckel, 'Die doppelte Vergangenheit', *Der Spiegel*, 23 Dec. 1991, 39–43.

[7]   On the *Sonderweg* debate, see the sensible comments of Jürgen Kocka, 'German History before Hitler: The Debate about the German *Sonderweg*', *Journal of Contemporary History*, vol. 23 (1988), 3–16.

and administration. But what caused the collapse and, not least, what was Hitler's own role in the process? These questions lie at the centre of my enquiry.

First, however, let me outline a number of what appear to me to be significant points of contrast between the Stalinist and Hitlerist regimes.
• Stalin arose from *within* a system of rule, as a leading exponent of it. He was, as Roland Suny puts it, a committee man, chief oligarch, man of the machine;[8] and, in Moshe Lewin's phrase, 'bureaucracy's anti-Christ', the 'creature of his party',[9] who became despot by control of the power which lay at the heart of the party, in its secretariat. In a sense, it is tempting to see an analogy in the German context in the position of Bormann rather than Hitler. It is possible to imagine Stalin echoing Hitler's comment in 1941: 'I've totally lost sight of the organizations of the Party. When I find myself confronted by one or other of these achievements, I say to myself: "By God, how that has developed!"'?[10]
At any rate, a party leader and head of government less bureaucratically inclined, less a committee man or man of the machine, than Hitler is hard to imagine. Before 1933 he was uninvolved in and detached from the Nazi Movement's bureaucracy. After 1933, as head of government he scarcely put pen to paper himself other than to sign legislation put in front of his nose by Lammers. The Four-Year Plan Memorandum of 1936 is a unique example from the years 1933–45 of a major policy document composed by Hitler himself – written in frustration and fury at the stance adopted during the economic crisis of 1935–6 by Schacht and some sectors of business and industry. Strikingly, Hitler only gave copies of his memorandum to two persons, Göring and Blomberg (much later giving a third copy to Speer). The Economics Minister himself was not included in the short distribution list! Business and industrial leaders were not even made aware of the existence of the memorandum.[11]
Hitler's way of operating was scarcely conducive to ordered government. Increasingly, after the first year or two of the dictatorship, he

[8]   Ronald Suny, 'Proletarian Dictator in a Peasant Land: Stalin as Ruler' (thereafter Suny, Dictator') (unpublished), 10–11.
[9]   Moshe Lewin, 'Bureaucracy and the Stalinist State' (unpublished), 26.
[10]   Werner Jochmann, ed., *Adolf Hitler. Monologe im Führerhauptquartier* (thereafter Jochmann, *Monologe* (Hamburg: Albrecht Knaus Verlag, 1980), 158; trans. *Hitler's Table Talk* thereafter *Table Talk*, intro. H. R. Trevor-Roper (London: Weidenfeld and Nicolson, 1953), 153.
[11]   Dieter Petzina, *Autarkiepolitik im Dritten Reich* (Stuttgart: Deutsche Verlags-Anstalt, 1968), 48–53; Peter Hayes. *Industry and Ideology. IG Farben in the Nazi Era* (Cambridge: Cambridge University Press, 1987), 164–7.

reverted to a lifestyle recognizable not only in the party leader of the 1920s but even in the description of the habits of the indolent youth in Linz and Vienna recorded by his friend Kubizek.[12] According to the post-war testimony of one of his former adjutants:

> Hitler normally appeared shortly before lunch, quickly read through Reich Press Chief Dietrich's press cuttings, and then went into lunch. So it became more and more difficult for Lammers [head of the Reich Chancellory] and Meissner [head of the Presidial Chancellory] to get him to make decisions which he alone could make as head of state. . . . When Hitler stayed at Obersalzberg it was even worse. There, he never left his room before 2.00 p.m. Then, he went to lunch. He spent most afternoons taking a walk, in the evening straight after dinner, there were films. . . . He disliked the study of documents. I have sometimes secured decisions from him, even ones about important matters, without his ever asking to see the relevant files. He took the view that many things sorted themselves out on their own if one did not interfere.[13]

As this comment points out, even Lammers, the only link between Hitler and the ministries of state (whose heads themselves ceased definitively to meet around a table as a cabinet by early 1938), had difficulty at times with gaining access to Hitler and extracting decisions from him. Lammers himself, for example, wrote plaintively to Hitler's adjutant on 21 October 1938 begging for an audience to report to the Führer on a number of urgent matters which needed resolution and which had been building up since the last occasion when he had been able to provide a detailed report, on 4 September![14]

Hitler's increasing aloofness from the State bureaucracy and the major organs of government seems to mark more than a difference of style with Stalin's *modus operandi*. It reflects, in my view, a difference in the essence of the regimes, mirrored in the position of the leader of each, a point to which I will return.

• Stalin was a highly interventionist dictator, sending a stream of letters and directives determining or interfering with policy. He chaired all important committees. His aim appears to have been a monopolization of all decision-making and its concentration in the Politburo, a

---

[12]   See August Kubizek, *Adolf Hitler, mein Jugendfreund*, 5th edn (Graz/Stuttgart: Leopold Stocker Verlag, 1989).

[13]   Fritz Wiedemann, *Der Mann, der Feldherr werden wollte* (Kettwig: Velbert, 1964), 69; trans. Jeremy Noakes and Geoffrey Pridham, eds, *Nazism 1919/1945. A Documentary Reader* (thereafter Noakes and Pridham, *Nazism*) (Exeter: Exeter University Press, 1984), ii. 207–8.

[14]   Institut für Zeitgeschichte, Munich, Nuremberg Document no. NG-5428; trans. Noakes and Pridham, *Nazism*, ii. 245.

centralization of state power and unity of decision-making which would have eliminated Party–State dualism.[15]

Hitler, by contrast, was on the whole a non-interventionist dictator as far as government administration was concerned. His sporadic directives, when they came, tended to be delphic and to be conveyed verbally, usually by Lammers, the head of the Reich Chancellory, or, in the war years (as far as civilian matters went), increasingly by Bormann.[16] Hitler chaired no formal committees after the first years of the regime, when the Cabinet (which he hated chairing) atrophied into non-existence.[17] He directly undermined the attempts made by Reich Interior Minister Frick to unify and rationalize administration, and did much to sustain and enhance the irreconcilable dualism of Party and State which existed at every level.[18]

Where Stalin appeared deliberately to destabilize government (which offered the possibility of a bureaucratic challenge),[19] Hitler seems to have had no deliberate policy of destabilization, but rather, as a consequence of his non-bureaucratic leadership position and the inbuilt need to protect his deified leadership position by non-association with political infighting and potentially unpopular policies, to have presided over an inexorable erosion of 'rational' forms of government. And while the metaphor of 'feudal anarchy' might be applied to both

[15]   Suny, 'Dictator', 11–13, 24, 34–5, 38.

[16]   Dieter Rebentisch, *Führerstaat und Verwaltung im Zweiten Weltkrieg* (thereafter, Rebentisch, *Führerstaat*) (Stuttgart: Franz Steiner Verlag Wiesbaden, 1989), has clearly shown that Hitler involved himself in civilian affairs to a far greater extent than was once thought. However, when he intervened it was usually at the prompting of one of the few favoured Nazi leaders graced with regular access to his presence, and providing him with one-sided information on specific issues of concern to them. He remained at all times alert to any extension of their power which could undermine his own. Other than this, there was nothing in his haphazard interventions to indicate any systematic grasp of or clear directives for coherent policy-making. In military matters and armaments production, from the middle of the war onwards, Hitler's involvement was on a wholly different scale. Here, his interventions were frequent – at daily conferences – and direct, though his dilettante, arbitrary and intransigent interference was often disastrously counter-productive. See Helmut Heiber, ed., *Hitlers Lagebesprechungen. Die Protokollfragmente seiner militärischen Konferenzen 1942–1945* (Stuttgart: Deutsche Verlags-Anstalt, 1962), and Willi A. Boelcke, ed., *Deutschlands Rüstung im Zweiten Weltkrieg. Hitlers Konferenzen mit Albert Speer 1942–1945* (Frankfurt am Main: Verlagsgesellschaft Athenaion, 1969).

[17]   See Lothar Gruchmann, 'Die "Reichsregierung" im Führerstaat', in Günther Doecker and Winfried Steffani, eds, *Klassenjustiz und Pluralismus* (Hamburg, Hoffmann und Campe Verlag, 1973), 192.

[18]   See Peter Diehl-Thiele, *Partei und Staat im Dritten Reich* (Munich: Beck Verlag, 1969), 61–9.

[19]   Suny, 'Dictator', 28, 32.

systems,[20] it seems more apt as a depiction of the Hitler regime, where bonds of personal loyalty were from the beginning the crucial determinants of power, wholly overriding functional position and status.

• Personalities apart, Hitler's leadership position appears to have been structurally more secure than Stalin's. If I have followed the debates properly, it would seem that there was some rational basis for Stalin's purges even if the dictator's paranoia took them into the realms of fantasy.[21] As the exponent of one party line among several, one set of policies among a number of alternatives, one interpretation of the Marx-Lenin arcanum among others, Stalin remained a dictator open to challenge from within. Kirov, it appears, had the potential to become a genuine rival leader in the early 1930s, when dissatisfaction and discontent with Stalin's rule was widespread.[22] Stalin's exaggerated feeling of insecurity was then to some measure grounded in reality. The purges which he himself instigated, and which in many instances were targeted at those closest to him, were above all intended to head off a bureaucratic challenge to his rule.

Hitler thought Stalin must be mad to carry out the purges.[23] The only faint reflections in the Third Reich were the liquidation of the SA leadership in the 'Night of the Long Knives' in 1934, and the ruthless retaliation for the attempt on Hitler's life in 1944. In the former case, Hitler agreed to the purge only belatedly and reluctantly, after the going had been made by Himmler and Göring, supported by the army leadership. The latter case does bear comparison with the Stalinist technique, though by that time the Hitler regime was plainly in its death-throes. The wild retaliation against those implicated in the assassination attempt was a desperate measure and aimed essentially at genuine opponents, rather than being a basic technique of rule.

Down to the middle of the war, Hitler's position lacked the precariousness which surrounded Stalin's leadership in the 1930s. Where Stalin could not believe in genuine loyalty even among his closest supporters, Hitler built his mastery on a cultivated principle of personal

---

[20]   *Ibid.*, 30; Robert Koehl, 'Feudal Aspects of National Socialism', *American Political Science Review*, vol. 54 (1960), 921–33.

[21]   My main orientation was gleaned from the debates in *The Russian Review*, vols 45–6 (1986, 1987), as well as from J. Arch Getty, *Origins of the Great Purges. The Soviet Communist Party Reconsidered* (Cambridge: Cambridge University Press, 1985); Moshe Lewin, *The Making of the Soviet System* (New York: Methuen, 1985); Robert C. Tucker, ed., *Stalinism: Essays in Historical Interpretation* (New York: Norton, 1997); and the unpublished papers by Ronald Suny and Moshe Lewin (see above notes 8–9).

[22]   Suny, 'Dictator', 20, 27.

[23]   Elke Fröhlich, ed., *Die Tagebücher von Joseph Goebbels* (Munich: K. G. Saur Verlag, 1987), iii. 198 (entry for 10 July 1937).

loyalty to which he could always successfully appeal at moments of crisis.[24] He showed a marked reluctance to discard even widely disliked and discredited satraps like Streicher, who had in Hitler's eyes earned his support through indispensable loyalty and service in the critical early years of the movement.[25] And he was in the bunker visibly shaken by news of Himmler's treachery – the 'loyal Heinrich' finally stabbing him in the back.[26]

A dangerous challenge to Hitler, especially once Hindenburg was dead, could effectively come only from within the armed forces (in tandem with an emergent disaffected, but unrepresentative, minority among the conservative elites) or from a stray attack by a lone assassin (as came close to killing Hitler in 1939).[27] Even in 1944, the leaders of the attempted coup realized their isolation and the lack of a base of popular support for their action.[28] Hitler, it has to be accepted, was, for most of the years he was in power, outside the repressed and powerless adherents of the former working-class movements, sections of Catholicism, and some individuals among the traditional elites, a highly popular leader both among the ruling groups and with the masses.

And within the Nazi Movement itself, his status was quite different from that of Stalin's position within the Communist Party. There are obvious parallels between the personality cults built up around Stalin and Hitler. But whereas the Stalin cult was superimposed upon the Marxist-Leninist ideology and Communist Party, and both were capable of surviving it, the 'Hitler myth' was structurally indispensable to, in fact the very basis of and scarcely distinguishable from, the Nazi Movement and its *Weltanschauung*.

Since the mid-1920s, ideological orthodoxy was synonymous with adherence to Hitler. 'For us the Idea is the Führer, and each Party member has only to obey the Führer,' Hitler allegedly told Otto Strasser

---

[24]   A good example was his successful appeal to his old comrades, the *Gauleiter*, to close ranks at the moment of deep crisis following the sudden departure of Gregor Strasser in December 1932. see Noakes and Pridham, *Nazism*, i. 112–14 (based on an unpublished vivid, post-war account by Hinrich Lohse held in the Forschungsstelle für die Geschichte des Nationalsozialismus, Hamburg). I am grateful to Jeremy Noakes for letting me see a photocopy of this document.
[25]   See Jochmann *Monologe*, 158–60; *Table Talk*, 153–6.
[26]   H. R. Trevor-Roper, *The Last Days of Hitler* (London: Pan Books, 1973), 202.
[27]   See Anton Hoch, 'Das Attentat auf Hitler im Münchner Bürgerbräukeller 1939', *Vierteljahreshefte für Zeitgeschichte*, vol. 17 (1969), 383–413; and Lothar Gruchmann, ed., *Autobiographie eines Attentäters. Johann Georg Elser* (Stuttgart: Deutsche Verlags-Anstalt, 1970).
[28]   See Hans Mommsen, 'Social Views and Constitutional Plans of the Resistance', in Hermann Graml, et al., *The German Resistance to Hitler* (London: Batsford, 1970), 59.

in 1930.[29] The build-up of a 'Führer party' squeezed heterodox positions onto the sidelines, then out of the party. By the time the regime was established and consolidated, there was no tenable position within Nazism compatible with a fundamental challenge to Hitler. His leadership position, as the font of ideological orthodoxy, the very epitome of Nazism itself, was beyond question within the movement. Opposition to Hitler on fundamentals ruled itself out, even among the highest and mightiest in the party. Invoking the Führer's name was the pathway to success and advancement. Countering the ideological prerogatives bound up with Hitler's position was incompatible with clambering up the greasy pole to status and power.

• Stalin's rule, for all its dynamic radicalism in the brutal collectivization programme, the drive to industrialization and the paranoid phase of the purges, was not incompatible with a rational ordering of priorities and attainment of limited and comprehensible goals, even if the methods were barbarous in the extreme and the accompanying inhumanity on a scale defying belief. Whether the methods were the most appropriate to attain the goals in view might still be debated, but the attempt to force industrialization at breakneck speed on a highly backward economy and to introduce 'socialism in one country' cannot be seen as irrational or limitless aims.

And despite the path to a personalized dictatorship, there was no inexorable 'cumulative radicalization'[30] in the Soviet Union. Rather, there was even the 'great retreat' from radicalism by the mid-1930s and a reversion towards some forms of social conservativism before the war brought its own compromises with ideological rectitude.[31] Whatever the costs of the personal regiment, and whatever the destructiveness of Stalin in the purges of the party and of the military, the structures of the Soviet system were not completely broken. Stalin had been a product of the system. And the system was capable of withstanding nearly three decades of Stalin and surviving him. It was, in other words, a system capable of self-reproduction, even at the cost of a Stalin.

It would be hard to claim this of Nazism. The goal of national redemption through racial purification and racial empire was chimeric, a utopian vision. The barbarism and destructiveness which were inherent in the vain attempt to realize this goal were infinite in extent, just as the expansionism and extension of aggression to other peoples were boundless. Whereas Stalinism could 'settle down', as it effectively did after

[29]   Noakes and Pridham, *Nazism*, i. 46.
[30]   The term is that of Hans Mommsen. See his article, 'Der Nationalsozialismus: Kumulative Radikalisierung und Selbstzerstörung des Regimes', in *Meyers Enzyklopädisches Lexikon*, vol. 16 (1976), 785–90.
[31]   Suny, 'Dictator', 21–2.

Stalin's death, into a static, even conservative, repressive regime, a 'settling down' into the staid authoritarianism of a Francoesque kind, is scarcely conceivable in the case of Nazism. Here, the dynamic was ceaseless, the momentum of radicalization an accelerating one incapable of having the brakes put on – unless the 'system' itself were to be fundamentally altered.

I have just used the word 'system' of Nazism. But where Soviet communism in the Stalin era, despite the dictator's brutal destabilization, remained recognizable as a *system* of rule, the Hitler regime was inimical to a rational order of government and administration. Its hallmark was *systemlessness*, administrative and governmental disorder, the erosion of clear patterns of government, however despotic.

This was already plain within Germany in the pre-war years as institutions and structures of government and administration atrophied, were eroded or merely bypassed, and faded into oblivion. It was not simply a matter of the unresolved Party–State dualism. The proliferation of 'special authorities' and plenipotentiaries for specific tasks, delegated by the Führer and responsible directly to him, reflected the predatory character and improvised techniques immanent in Nazi domination.[32] Lack of coherent planning related to attainable middle-range goals; absence of any forum for collective decision-making; the arbitrary exercise of power embedded in the 'leadership principle' at all levels; the Darwinian principle of unchecked struggle and competition until the winner emerged; and the simplistic belief in the 'triumph of the will', whatever the complexities to be overcome: all these reinforced each other and interacted to guarantee a jungle of competing and overlapping agencies of rule.

During the war, the disintegration of anything resembling a state *system* rapidly accelerated.[33] In the occupied territories, the so-called Nazi 'new order' drove the replacement of clearly defined structures of domination by the untramelled and uncoordinated force of competing power groups to unheard of levels. By the time Goebbels was writing in his diary, in March 1943, of a 'leadership crisis'[34] – and speaking privately of a 'leader crisis'[35] – the 'system' of rule was unrescuable. Hitler's leadership was at the same time absolutely pivotal to the regime but

[32] See Martin Broszat, *Der Staat Hitlers* (thereafter Broszat, *Staat*) (Munich: dtv, 1969), esp. chs 8–9.
[33] The internal government of Germany during the war has now been systematically examined by Rebentisch, *Führerstaat* (see n. 16 above).
[34] Louis D. Lochner, ed., *Goebbels Tagebücher aus den Jahren 1942–43* (Zürich: Atlantis Verlag, 1948), 241, 274, 296.
[35] Albert Speer, *Erinnerungen* (Frankfurt am Main/Berlin: Propyläen Verlag, 1969), 271.

utterly incompatible with either a rational decision-making process or a coherent, unified administration and the attainment of limited goals. Its self-destructive capacity was unmistakeable, its eventual demise certain.

Hitler was irreplaceable in Nazism in a way which did not apply to Stalin in Soviet Communism. His position was, in fact, irreconcilable with the setting up of any structures to elect to select a successor. A framework to provide for the succession to Hitler was never established. The frequently mooted party senate never came about.[36] Hitler remained allergic to any conceivable institutional constraint, and by 1943 the deposition of Mussolini by the Fascist Grand Council ruled out once and for all any expectation of a party body existing quasi-independently of the Leader in Germany. Though Göring had been declared the heir apparent, his succession became increasingly unlikely as the Reich Marshal's star waned visibly during the war. None of the other second-rank Nazi leaders was a serious alternative candidate to succeed Hitler. It is indeed difficult to see who could have taken over, how the personalized rule of Hitler could have become systematized. The regime, one is compelled to suggest, was incapable of reproducing itself.

The objection that, but for a lost war there was nothing to prevent this happening, seems misplaced. The war was not accidental to Nazism. It lay at its very core. The war had to be fought and could not be put off until a more favourable juncture. And by the end of 1941, even though the war dragged on a further three and a half years, the gamble for 'world power' was objectively lost. As such, the dynamism of the regime and its self-destructive essence could be said to have been inseparable.

This brings me back to the questions I posed at the beginning of the chapter. If my understanding of some of the recent discussion on Stalinism is not too distorted, and if the points of contrast with the Hitler regime I have outlined above have some validity, then it would be fair to conclude that, despite some superficial similarities, the character of the dictatorship, that is, of Stalin's and Hitler's leadership positions within their respective regimes, was fundamentally different. It would surely be a limited explanation, however, to locate these differences merely in the personalities of the dictators. Rather, I would suggest, they should be seen as a reflection of the contrasting social motivations of the followers, the character of the ideological driving force and the corresponding nature of the political vanguard movement upholding each regime. The Nazi Movement, to put the point bluntly, was a classic

---

[36]   See Broszat, *Staat*, 262, 361–2; Rebentisch, *Führerstaat*, 101, 421–2.

'charismatic' leadership movement; the Soviet Communist Party was not. And this has a bearing on the self-reproducing capacity of the two 'systems' of rule.

The main features of 'charismatic authority' as outlined by Max Weber need no embroidering here: the perceptions of a heroic 'mission' and presumed greatness in the leader by his 'following'; the tendency to arise in crisis conditions as an 'emergency' solution; the innate instability under the double constant threat of collapse of 'charisma' through failure to meet expectations and of 'routinization' into a 'system' capable of reproducing itself only through eliminating, subordinating or subsuming the 'charismatic' essence.[37] In its pure form, the personal domination of charismatic authority' represents the contradiction and negation of the impersonal, functional exercise of power which lies at the root of the bureaucratic legal-rational authority of the 'ideal type' modern state system.[38] It cannot, in fact, become 'systematized' without losing its particular 'charismatic' edge. Certainly, Max Weber envisaged possibilities of institutionalized 'charisma', but the compromises with the pure form then become evident.

The relevance of the model of 'charismatic authority' to Hitler seems obvious.[39] In the case of Stalin it is less convincing. The 'mission' in this latter case resides, it could be argued, in the Communist Party as the vehicle of Marxist-Leninist doctrine. For a while, it is true, Stalin hijacked the 'mission' and threatened to expropriate it through his personality cult. But this cult was a gradual and belated product, an excrescence artificially tagged on to Stalin's actual function. In this sense, there was a striking contrast with the personality cult of Hitler, which was inseparable from the 'mission' embodied in his name practically from the beginning, a 'mission' which from the mid-1920s at the latest did not exist as a doctrine independent of the leader.

Weber's model of 'charismatic authority' is an abstraction, a descriptive concept which says nothing in itself of the content of any specific manifestation of 'charismatic authority'. This is determined by the relationship of the leadership claim to the particular circumstances and 'political culture' in which it arises and which give it shape. The essence

---

[37]   Max Weber, *Economy and Society*, eds Guenther Roth and Claus Wittich (Berkeley/Los Angeles: University of California Press, 1978), 241–54, 266–71, 1111–57.
[38]   See André Gorz, *Farewell to the Working Class* (London: Pluto Press, 1982), 58–9, 62–3.
[39]   The model is interestingly deployed by M. Rainer Lepsius, 'Charismatic Leadership: Max Weber's Model and its Applicability to the Rule of Hitler', in Carl Friedrich Graumann and Serge Moscovici, eds, *Changing Conceptions of Leadership* (New York: Springer-Verlag, 1986). My own attempt to use it is in my short study *Hitler. A Profile in Power* (London: Longman, 1991).

of the Hitlerian 'charismatic claim' was the 'mission' to achieve 'national rebirth' through racial purity and racial empire. But this claim was in practice sufficiently vague, adaptable and amorphous to be able to mesh easily with and incorporate more traditionalist blends of nationalism and imperialism, whose pedigree stretched back to the *Kaiserreich*.[40] The trauma of war, defeat and 'national disgrace', then the extreme conditions of a state system in a terminal stage of dissolution and a nation wracked by chasmic internal divisions, offered the potential for the 'charismatic claim' to gain extensive support, stretching way beyond the original 'charismatic community', and for it to provide the basis for an altogether new form of state.

In a modern state, the replacement of functional bureaucracy through personal domination is surely an impossibility. But even the co-existence of 'legal-rational' and 'charismatic' sources of legitimacy can only be a source of tension and conflict, potentially of a seriously dysfunctional kind. What occurred in the Third Reich was not the supplanting of bureaucratic domination by 'charismatic authority', but rather the superimposition of the latter on the former. Where constitutional law could now be interpreted as no more than 'the legal formulation of the historic will of the Führer – seen as deriving from his 'outstanding achievement'[41] – and where Germany's leading constitutional lawyer could speak of 'state power' being replaced by unrestrained 'Führer power',[42] the result could only be the undermining of the basis of impersonal law on which modern 'legal-rational' state systems rest and the corrosion of 'ordered' forms of government and institutionalized structures of administration through unfettered personal domination whose overriding source of legitimacy was the 'charismatic claim', the 'vision' of national redemption.[43]

The inexorable disintegration into 'systemlessness' was, therefore, not chiefly a matter of 'will'. Certainly, Hitler was allergic to any semblance of a practical or theoretical constraint on his power. But there was no systematic 'divide and rule' policy, no sustained attempt to

---

[40]   For the imperialist traditions on which Nazism could build, see Woodruff D. Smith, *The Ideological Origins of Nazi Imperialism* (Oxford: Oxford University Press, 1986). The ways in which Nazism could exploit 'mainstream' nationalism are stressed by William Sheridan Allen, 'The Collapse of Nationalism in Nazi Germany', in John Breuilly, ed., *The State of Germany* (London: Longman, 1992), 141–53.
[41]   Hans Frank, *Im Angesicht des Galgens* (Munich/Gräfelfing: Beck Verlag, 1953), 466-7; trans. Noakes and Pridham, *Nazism*, ii. 200.
[42]   Ernst Rudolf Huber, *Verfassungsrecht des Großdeutschen Reiches* (Hamburg, Hanseatische Verlagsanstalt, 1939), 230; trans. Noakes and Pridham, *Nazism*, ii. 199.
[43]   For a compelling analysis of 'national rebirth' as the essence of the fascist doctrine, see Roger Griffin, *The Nature of Fascism* (London: Pinter, 1991).

*create* the administrative anarchy of the Third Reich. It was, indeed, in part a reflection of Hitler's personality and his style of leadership: as already pointed out, he was unbureaucratic in the extreme, remained aloof from the daily business of government and was uninterested in complex matters of detail. But this non-bureaucratic style was itself more than just a personal foible or eccentricity. It was an inescapable product of the deification of the leadership position itself and consequent need to sustain prestige to match the created image. His instinctive Darwinism made him unwilling and unable to take sides in a dispute till the winner emerged. But the need to protect his infallible image also made him largely incapable of doing so.

It was not in itself simply the undermining of 'rational' structures of government and proliferation of chaotic, 'polycratic' agencies that mattered. It was that this process accompanied and promoted a gradual realization of ideological aims which were inextricably bound up in the 'mission' of the 'charismatic' Leader as the 'idea' of Nazism, located in the person of the Führer, became translated between 1938 and 1942 from utopian 'vision' into practical reality. There was, in other words, a symbiotic relationship between the structural disorder of the Nazi state and the radicalization of policy.

The key development was unquestionably the growth in autonomy of the authority of the Führer to a position where it was unrestrained in practice as well as theory by any governmental institutions or alternative organs of power, a stage reached at the latest by 1938.[44] After the Blomberg – Fritsch affair of February 1938 it is difficult to see where the structures or the individuals capable of applying the brakes to Hitler remained. By this date, the pressures unleashed in part by the dictator's own actions, but even more so by diplomatic and economic developments beyond his control, encouraged and even conditioned the high-risk approach which was in any case Hitler's second nature.

Meanwhile, in conjunction with the expansion into Austria and the Sudetenland in 1938, race policy, too, shifted up a gear. The *Reichskristallnacht* pogrom in November, instigated by Goebbels not Hitler – though carried out with the latter's express approval[45] – was the culmination of the radicalization of the previous year or so, and ended

---

[44] See Broszat, *Staat*, ch. 8.
[45] The recently discovered, formerly missing, parts of Goebbels' diaries make explicitly clear Hitler's role in approving the most radical measures both as regards to pogrom itself and its aftermath. See the extracts published in *Der Spiegel*, no. 29 (1992), 126–8; an abbreviated version of the diary entry for 10 Nov. 1938 is available in Ralf Georg Reuth, ed., *Joseph Goebbels. Tagebücher* (Munich: Piper, 1992), iii. 1281–2.

by handing over effective centralized coordination of the 'Jewish Question' to Heydrich.

Territorial expansion and 'removal of the Jews', the two central features of Hitler's *Weltanschauung*, had thus come together in 1938 into sharp focus in the foreground of the picture. The shift from utopian 'vision' to practical policy options was taking shape.

It would be mistaken to look exclusively, or even mainly, to Hitler's own actions at the source of the continuing radicalization of the regime. Hitler was the linchpin of the entire 'system', the only common link between its various component parts. But by and large he was not directly needed to spur on the radicalization. What seems crucial, therefore, is the way in which 'charismatic authority' functioned in practice to dissolve any framework of 'rational' government which might have acted as a constraint and to stimulate the radicalization largely brought about by others, without Hitler's clear direction.

The function of Hitler's 'charismatic' Führer position could be said to have been threefold: that of unifier, of activator, and of enabler in the Third Reich.

As *unifier*, the 'idea' incorporated in the quasi-deified Führer figure was sufficiently indistinct but dynamic to act as a bond not only for otherwise warring factions of the Nazi Movement but also, until it was too late to extricate themselves from the fateful development, for non-Nazi national-conservative elites in army, economy and state bureaucracy. It also offered the main prop of popular support for the regime (repeatedly giving Hitler a plebiscitary basis for his actions) and a common denominator around which an underlying consensus in Nazi policy could be focused.[46]

As *activator*, the 'vision' embodied by Hitler served as a stimulant to action in the different agencies of the Nazi Movement itself, where pent-up energies and unfulfilled social expectations could be met by activism carried out in Hitler's name to bring about the aims of Leader and Party. But beyond the movement, it also spurred initiatives within the state bureaucracy, industry and the armed forces, and among the professionals such as teachers, doctors or lawyers where the motif of 'national redemption' could offer an open door to the push for realization of long-cherished ambitions felt to have been held back or damaged by the Weimar 'system'.[47] In all these ways, the utopian 'vision' bound up with the Führer – undefined and largely undefinable – provided 'guidelines

---

[46]   I have attempted to present the evidence in my study *The 'Hitler Myth'. Image and Reality in the Third Reich* (Oxford: Oxford University Press, 1987).

[47]   For an excellent study of how the medical profession exploited the opportunities offered by National Socialism, see Michael H. Kater, *Doctors under Hitler* (Chapel Hill/London: University of North Carolina Press, 1989).

for action'[48] which were given concrete meaning and specific content by the voluntary 'push' of a wide variety of often competing agencies of the regime. The most important, most vigorous and most closely related to Hitler's ideological imperatives of these was, of course, the SS, where the 'idea' or 'vision' offered the scope for ever new initiatives in a ceaseless dynamic of discrimination, repression and persecution.

Perhaps most important of all, as *enabler* Hitler's authority gave implicit backing and sanction to those whose actions, however inhumane, however radical, fell within the general and vague ideological remit of furthering the aims of the Führer. Building a 'national community', preparing for the showdown with Bolshevism, purifying the Reich of its political and biological or racial enemies, and removing Jews from Germany, offered free license to initiatives which, unless inopportune or counter-productive, were more or less guaranteed sanction from above. The collapse in civilized standards which began in the spring of 1933, and the spiralling radicalization of discrimination and persecution that followed, were not only unobstructed but invariably found legitimation in the highest authority in the land.

Crucial to this 'progress into barbarism'[49] was the fact that in 1933 the barriers to state-sanctioned measures of gross inhumanity were removed almost overnight. What had previously been unthinkable suddenly became feasible. Opportunities rapidly presented themselves; and they were readily grasped. The Sterilization Law of July 1933 is an early instance of such a dropping of barriers. Ideas long cherished by proponents of eugenics in biological-social engineering found all at once a climate in which they could be put into practice without the constraints still taken for granted in proposals – in themselves inhumane enough, but still confined to *voluntary* sterilization – for legislation put forward by the German Doctors' Association just weeks before Hitler's takeover of power.[50]

By 1939 the erosion of civilized values had developed far enough to allow for the possibilities of liquidating as 'useless life' those deemed to be harmful to the propagation of 'healthy comrades of the people'.[51] And, illustrating how far the disintegration of the machinery of

---

[48]   Martin Broszat, 'Soziale Motivation und Führer-Bindung des Nationalsozialismus', *Vierteljahreshefte für Zeitgeschichte*, vol. 18 (1970), 405.

[49]   Michael Burleigh and Wolfgang Wippermann, *The Racial State. Germany 1933–1945* (Cambridge: Cambridge University Press, 1991), back cover.

[50]   See Jeremy Noakes, 'Nazism and Eugenics: The Background of the Nazi Sterilisation Law of 14 July 1933', in R. J. Bullen, et al., eds, *Ideas into Poitics* (London/Sydney: Croom Helm, 1984), 75–94, esp. 84–5.

[51]   See the documentation by Ernst Klee, *'Euthanasie' im NS-Staat. Die 'Vernichtung lebensunwerten Lebens'*, 2nd edn (Frankfurt am Main: Fischer Verlag, 1983).

government had progressed, when written authorization was needed, it took the form not of a government law or decree (which Hitler expressly ruled out) but a few lines typed on Hitler's private headed paper.[52] The few lines were enough to seal the fate of over 70,000 mentally ill and physically disabled persons in Germany by mid-1941 in the so-called 'euthanasia action'.

After 1939, in the parts of Poland annexed by Germany and incorporated into the Reich, prompted by Hitler's exhortation to brutal methods in a 'racial struggle' which was not to be confined by legal considerations,[53] the constraints on inhumanity to the Polish population, and of course to the Jewish minority in Poland, disappeared completely. Hitler needed to do nothing to force the pace of the rapidly escalating barbarism. He could leave it to this satraps on the spot. Characteristically, he said he asked no more of his *Gauleiter* in the East than that after ten years they should be able to announce that their territories were completely German.[54] The invitation was in itself sufficient to spark a competition in brutality – though allegedly this was the opposite of what Hitler wanted – between the arch-rival provincial chieftains Albert Forster in West Prussia and Arthur Greiser in the Warthegau to be able to report to the Führer in the shortest time that the 'racial struggle' had been won, that complete Germanization had been achieved.[55]

The licence which Hitler as 'enabler' offered to such party bosses in the East can be illustrated graphically through the 'initiative' taken by Greiser in May 1942 recommending the liquidation of 35,000 Poles suffering from incurable tuberculosis.[56] In the event, Greiser's suggestion encountered difficulties. Objections were raised that it would be hard to maintain secrecy – reference was made here to the impact of the earlier 'euthanasia programme' in Germany itself – and was likely, therefore, to arouse unrest among the Polish population as well as presenting foreign propaganda with a gift. It was regarded as necessary to consult Hitler himself if the 'action' were to go ahead. Greiser's enlightening response ran: 'I myself do not believe that the Führer needs to be asked

---

[52]   *Ibid.*, 100–1.
[53]   Martin Broszat, *Nationalsozialistische Polenpolitik 1939–1945* (Frankfurt am Main: Fischer Verlag, 1965), II. 25.
[54]   *Ibid.*, 200 n. 45.
[55]   *Ibid.*, 122.
[56]   The correspondence between Greiser and Himmler on the subject, dated between 1 May and 3 Dec. 1942, is in the personal file of Arthur Greiser in the Berlin Document Center (thereafter BDC). For a more extended discussion, see my article, 'Improvised Genocide? The Emergence of the "Final Solution" in the "Warthegau"', *Transactions of the Royal Historical Society*, 6th series, vol. 2 (1992), 51–78, here 71–3.

again in this matter, especially since at our last discussion with regard to the Jews he told me that I could proceed with these according to my own judgement'.[57] This judgement had already, in fact, been to recommend to Himmler the 'special treatment' (that is, killing), of 100,000 Jews in the Warthegau – the start of the 'final solution' there.[58]

Greiser thought of himself throughout as the direct agent and instrument of the Führer in the crusade to create his 'model Gau'. Any hindrance was met by the claim that his mandate to Germanize the Warthegau rested on plenipotentiary powers bestowed on him personally by the Führer himself.[59]

The relationship between the Führer, serving as a 'symbol' for actionism, and ideological radicalization, and the drive 'from below' on the part of so many agencies, non-Nazi as well as Nazi, to put the 'vision' or parts of it into operation as practical policy is neatly captured in the sentiments of a routine speech of a Nazi functionary in 1934:

Everyone who has the opportunity to observe it knows that the Führer can hardly dictate from above everything which he intends to realize sooner or later. On the contrary, up till now everyone with a post in the new Germany has worked best when he has, so to speak, worked towards the Führer. Very often and in many spheres it has been the case – in previous years as well – that individuals have simply waited for orders and instructions. Unfortunately, the same will be true in the future; but in fact it is the duty of everybody to try to work towards the Führer alone the lines he would wish. Anyone who makes mistakes will notice it soon enough. But anyone who really works towards the Führer along his lines and towards his goal will certainly both now and in the future one day have the finest reward in the form of the sudden legal confirmation of his work.[60]

[57]   BDC, Personal File of Arthur Greiser, Greiser to Himmler, 21 Nov. 1942.
[58]   BDC, Personal File of Arthur Greiser, Greiser to Himmler, 1 May 1942.
[59]   Examples in the Archive of the Polish War Crimes Commission, Ministry of Justice, Warsaw, Greiser Trial Documents, File 11, fol. 52, File 13, fol. 15. According to the post-war testimony of one of the heads of regional administration in the Warthegau, Greiser never missed an opportunity in his speeches to insist that he was 'persona gratissima' with the Führer (File 36, fol. 463). Another contemporary commented that his gratitude knew no bounds once Hitler had granted him this special plenipotentiary authority. See Carl J. Burckhardt, *Meine Danziger Mission 1937–1939* (Munich: dtv, 1962), 79. I have provided a short pen-picture of Greiser for the second volume of Ronald Smelser, et al., eds, *Die braune Elite und ihre Helfer* (Darmstadt: Wissenschaftliche Buchgesellschaft, 1993).
[60]   Niedersächsisches Staatsarchiv, Oldenburg, Best. 131, nr. 303, fol. 131v, speech Werner Willikens, State Secretary in the Ministry of Food, 21 Feb. 1934; trans. Noakes and Pridham, *Nazism*, ii. 207.

These comments hint at the way 'charismatic authority' functioned in the Third Reich – anticipation of Hitler's presumed wishes and intentions as 'guidelines for action' in the certainty of approval and confirmation for actions which accorded with those wishes and intentions.

'Working towards the Führer' may be taken in a literal, direct sense with reference to party functionaries, in the way it was meant in the extract cited. In the case of the SS, the ideological executive of the 'Führer's will', the tasks associated with 'working towards the Führer' offered endless scope for barbarous initiatives, and with them institutional expansion, power, prestige and enrichment. The career of Adolf Eichmann, rising from a menial role in a key policy area to the manager of the "Final Solution', offers a classic example.[61]

But the notion of 'working towards the Führer' could be interpreted, too, in a more indirect sense where ideological motivation was secondary, or perhaps even absent altogether, but where the objective function of the actions was nevertheless to further the potential for implementation of the goals which Hitler embodied. Individuals seeking material gain through career advancement in party or state bureaucracy, the small businessman aiming to destroy a competitor through a slur on his 'aryan' credentials, or ordinary citizens settling scores with neighbours by denouncing them to the Gestapo, were all, in a way, 'working towards the Führer'. Doctors rushing to nominate patients of asylums for the 'euthanasia programme' in the interests of a eugenically 'healthier' people; lawyers and judges zealous to cooperate in the dismantling of legal safeguards in order to cleanse society of 'criminal elements' and undesirables; business leaders anxious to profit from preparations for war and, once in war, by the grabbing of booty and exploitation of foreign slave labour; thrusting technocrats and scientists seeking to extend power and influence through jumping on the bandwagon of technological experimentation and modernization; non-Nazi military leaders keen to build up a modern army and restore Germany's hegemony in central Europe; and old-fashioned conservatives with a distaste for the Nazis but an even greater fear and dislike of the Bolsheviks: all were, through their many and varied forms of collaboration, at least indirectly 'working towards the Führer'. The result was the unstoppable radicalization of the 'system' and the gradual emergence of policy objectives closely related to the ideological imperatives represented by Hitler.

Time after time, Hitler set the barbaric tone, whether in hate-filled public speeches giving a green light to discriminatory action against

---

[61]   See Hannah Arendt, *Eichmann in Jerusalem* (London: Faber and Faber, 1963).

Jews and other 'enemies of the state', or in closed addresses to Nazi functionaries or military leaders where he laid down, for example, the brutal guidelines for the occupation of Poland and for 'Operation Barbarossa'. But there was never any shortage of willing helpers, far from being confined to party activists, ready to 'work towards the Führer to put the mandate into operation. Once the war – intrinsic to Nazism and Hitler's 'vision' – had begun, the barbarism inspired by that 'vision' and now unchecked by any remnants of legal constraint or concern for public sensitivities plumbed unimaginable depths. But there was no prospect, nor could there have been, of the 'New Order' settling into a 'system' of government Competing fiefdoms, not structured government, formed the grim face of Nazi rule in the occupied territories. The rapaciousness and destructiveness present from the start within Germany now became hugely magnified and intensified with the conquered peoples rather than the Germans themselves as the main victims.

Through the metaphor of 'working towards the Führer'. I have tried to suggest here that the 'vision' embodied in Hitler's leadership claim served to funnel a variety of social motivations, at times contradictory and conflicting, into furthering – intentionally or unwittingly – Nazi aims closely associated with Hitler's own ideological obsessions. The concept of charismatic authority' in this interpretation can be taken as useful in helping to depict the bonds with Hitler forged by various social and political forces, enabling the form of personalized power which he represented to free itself from all institutional constraints and to legitimize the destructive dynamic intrinsic to the Nazi gamble for European hegemony through war.

The model of 'charismatic authority', which I have suggested is applicable to the Hitlerian but not to the Stalinist dictatorship, not only helps to characterize the appeal of a quasi-messianic personalized form of rule embodying national unity and rebirth in the context of the collapse of legitimation of the democratic system of Weimar. It also, given the irreconcilable tension between 'charismatic authority' and bureaucratic rule in the Third Reich, offers insights into the inexorable crosion of anything resembling a *system* of domination capable of reproducing itself. Within this 'Behemoth' of governmental disorder,[62] 'working towards the Führer' amounted to a selective push for the radicalization and implementation of those ideological lines most closely associated with Hitler's known broad aims, which could gradually take shape as policy objectives rather than distant goals.

---

[62] See Franz Neumann, *Behemoth. The Structure and Practice of National Socialism* (London: Victor Gollancz, 1942).

Above all, the 'charismatic' model fits a form of domination which could never settle down into 'normality' or routine, draw a line under its achievements and come to rest as conservative authoritarianism, but was compelled instead to sustain the dynamism and to push ceaselessly and relentlessly for new attainments in the quest to fulfil its chimeric goal. The longer the Hitler regime lasted, the more megalomaniacal the aims, the more boundless the destructiveness became. But the longer the regime went on, the less it resembled a governmental *system* with the capacity to reproduce itself.

The inherent instability of 'charismatic authority' in this manifestation – where the specific content of the 'charismatic claim' was rooted in the utopian goal of national redemption through racial purification, war and conquest – implied, then, not only destructiveness but also self-destructiveness. Hitler's own suicidal tendencies could in this sense be said to reflect the inbuilt incapacity of his form of authoritarian rule to survive and reproduce itself.

# Resistance

# 10

# German Society and the Resistance against Hitler, 1933–1945

## *Hans Mommsen*

Translation by Christian Leitz of Hans Mommsen, 'Die Opposition gegen Hitler und die deutsche Gesellschaft 1933–1945', in Klaus-Jürgen Müller (ed.), *Der deutsche Widerstand 1933–1945*, Ferdinand Schöningh, Paderborn et al., 2nd edn, 1990, pp. 22–39.

*Editor's Introduction*

Hans Mommsen's article is a tribute to the small minority of Germans who risked their lives by opposing the Nazi regime. Yet it is certainly not an uncritical eulogy of the resistance. Instead, in an effort to explain the resounding failure of all attempts to eliminate Hitler and overthrow the Nazi regime, Mommsen highlights the problems, shortcomings and weaknesses which affected the resistance.

Not only was the resistance small in numbers, it also lacked a reliable support base among the German population. The passive, indeed often openly hostile, attitude of most Germans to the idea of opposition and to the proponents of this idea made it extremely difficult for resistance groups to operate and relatively easy for the Nazi police apparatus to track them down. In addition, it certainly did not help that the various resistance groups never managed to come together in a joint movement (though, as Mommsen points out, cooperation between groups sometimes facilitated the work of the Gestapo). Even the 20 July 1944 coup attempt, which brought together the widest social and political spread of resisters, did not include all groups, the most notable absence being the Communists.

The 20 July 1944 plot, usually lauded as the most significant attempt to overthrow the regime, reveals two of the major difficulties that confronted the resistance. First, most members of the conservative resistance involved in the plot had either supported, cooperated with, or at least tolerated the Nazi regime in its early years. Communists and Social Democrats, on the other hand, faced severe persecution soon, in some cases immediately after Hitler's appointment as Chancellor. And second, in view of their varied political backgrounds, the plotters were faced with the problem of agreeing on a political system with which to replace the Nazi dictatorship.

Obstacles clearly abounded. Yet, to conclude with Mommsen, 'faced with constant setbacks, with arrests and torture, with anxieties about family, friends and fellow resisters' the German resistance determined to continue their struggle, 'if necessary until the bitter end'.

# German Society and the Resistance against Hitler, 1933–1945

*Hans Mommsen*

## I Change of Perspectives

The history of the German resistance against Hitler constitutes a string of efforts by people who, inadequately equipped and surrounded by a highly unfavourable environment, tried to put an end to the madness of the National Socialist regime and save Germany from total internal and external collapse. In hindsight we know that these efforts had little chance of success. Without any doubt, it was frequently a matter of chance that attempts to assassinate Hitler failed,[1] attempts which, if successful, would certainly have changed the course of events. In a deeper sense, however, the resistance should not be judged by its potential outcome. There are logical explanations why repeated attempts on Hitler's life failed. Even if we assume that the resisters had been blessed with success, it is still doubtful whether they could have implemented their plans. Would they not have created a civil war-like situation which would have resulted in Germany's political and military collapse, an outcome which, judged by the objectives of the conspirators, would not have been markedly different to the one which followed the suicide of the dictator. The coup attempt of 20 July 1944 is above all marked by the fact that it was undertaken in the awareness of being in a borderline situation in which, regardless of success or failure, the main aim was to make a gesture against the continuation of the Nazi regime of terror.

It would be wrong to judge the essence of the resistance struggle by the likelihood of its success and to derive from this criteria that distinguish between 'legitimate' acts of opposition and simple revolt. The men and women who, under largely different circumstances and with changing political goals, opposed the Nazi terror were primarily concerned with an inner attitude of not succumbing to the mental and physical pressure so successfully applied against most of their fellow citizens. Safeguarding their own social and political identity against the unifor-

---

[1] Cf. Peter Hoffmann's comprehensive account *Widerstand, Staatsstreich, Attentat: Der Kampf der Opposition gegen Hitler*, Munich, 1969, 297ff; see also idem, *Die Sicherheit des Diktators. Hitlers Leibwachen, Schutzmaßnahmen, Residenzen, Hauptquartiere*, Munich, 1975.

mity created by indoctrination constituted the essential basis for the decision to resist the regime. Additional motivating factors included social moulding, political interests, religious ties and ideological attitudes. Of less importance was the question whether it was really possible to achieve a political *coup d'état* and what the chances of success really were.

Resistance in the Third Reich should therefore not be judged purely in relation to the question whether the relationship between means and objective was 'realistically' weighed up. Nor should the resistance be trivialized by pointing at its outward failure and the hopelessness of some of its operations. Both point at its moral-political centre: the struggle against a system of rule which destroyed the individual by turning him into a pure functionary of its inhuman objectives.[2] To act in such a way demanded the conviction that it was worthwhile to fight for a fundamentally different system. Not without good reason did Helmuth James von Moltke declare that the first priority had to be to restore 'the image of humanity in the hearts of our fellow citizens'.[3]

These considerations make it questionable to allot more weight to the resistance 'from above' just because, under the prevailing conditions, it enjoyed a greater chance of success and to condemn as irresponsible attempts by the political left to create a mass resistance movement. The artificiality of such a distinction is revealed by the fact that, from 1942; the bourgeois-conservative resistance became aware of its lack of support among the broad masses and, belatedly, it attempted to rectify the situation through the creation of a non-partisan people's movement.[4] Even then, however, it remained antagonistic towards the communist resistance whose attempts to maintain an illegal cadre organization as a basis for a broad oppositional people's movement was barely more successful.

There is also little ground for judging the legitimacy of the various diverging factions of resisters by the extent to which their long-term political aims differed from the standards of a democratic constitutional state. In the continental Europe of the 1930s and 1940s parliamentary democracy was, after all, regarded as a largely obsolete political system. At the same time, students of the resistance should not be forced into the straitjacket of a simply moralizing way of examination even though the central theme of the resistance had been to uphold the principles of

[2]   This is emphasized in particular in the classic study by Hans Rothfels, *Die deutsche Opposition gegen Hitler. Eine Würdigung*, Frankfurt/Main, 3rd edn, 1969.
[3]   Helmut James von Moltke, *Letzte Briefe*, Berlin, 8th edn, 1959, 18ff.
[4]   Cf. Hans Mommsen, 'Gesellschaftsbild und Verfassungspläne des deutschen Widerstands', in Walter Schmitthenner and Hans Buchheim (eds), *Der deutsche Widerstand gegen Hitler*, Cologne, 1966, 152ff.

humanity against the escalation of ideological indoctrination and systematic terror. Socio-political and spiritual tendencies of a frequently contrasting nature within the resistance against Hitler reflect possible alternatives for the development of Germany, or at least alternatives which had not been historically exhausted. A proper understanding of the inner structure of the Third Reich is impossible without a good knowledge of the efforts of an opposition which frequently reached deep into the Nazi apparatus.[5]

## 2  Resistance without People

In contrast to the *résistance* in countries occupied by Germany the German resistance found itself perforce in opposition to the nationalistic attitude of the population – especially under the conditions of the Second World War. In broad terms, resistance was always both high treason and treason against one's country.[6] Some members of the bourgeois-conservative resistance were initially reluctant to face up to that fact. The opposition justly claimed to represent the true interests of the German people against the Nazi party. Yet, those average citizens who conformed with the demands of the regime and served it loyally had difficulties recognizing these facts even though they found some aspects of the regime such as its *Bonzenwirtschaft*[7] and Himmler's and the Gestapo's terror methods generally repugnant. By carefully exploiting the Hitler cult and by undermining or eliminating the office of the Reich President, the army and the governmental apparatus the Führer was made the only point of reference of the nation's need for identity.[8] No secondary sources of legitimation – such as the monarchy in Italy or governments-in-exile elsewhere – could be used to derive

[5]  A growing atmosphere of internal criticism of decisions taken in part by competing officials strengthened both the illusion that Hitler was not responsible for the suicidal direction of the regime, and the common self-deception that it was possible to return to a stabilization of the system and 'normality'. Cf. my article 'Ausnahmezustand als Herrschaftstechnik des NS-Regimes', in Manfred Funke (ed.), *Hitler, Deutschland und die Mächte. Materialien zur Außenpolitik des Dritten Reiches*, Düsseldorf, 1976, 30–45.

[6]  Basically mistaken was the initial attempt to distinguish between both types of treason and to remove treason against one's country from those methods which the resistance regarded as legitimate. Oster in particular arrived at a conflicting conclusion; cf. Romedio Galeazzo von Thun-Hohenstein, *Der Verschwörer. General Oster und die Militäropposition*, Berlin, 1982.

[7]  Corrupt system of 'bigwigs'.

[8]  Of fundamental importance is Ian Kershaw's study *Der Hitler-Mythos. Volksmeinung und Propaganda im Dritten Reich*, Stuttgart, 1980, esp. 190ff.

the right to act in the name of the nation. By terminating one's loyalty to Hitler – and this included blaming the 'little Führers' and not Hitler for the reality of the regime – the individual chose to put himself outside the nation.

Among bourgeois-conservative resisters in particular it required a drawn-out learning process before these facts were understood. Carl Goerdeler's persistence in hanging on to his illusion of getting Hitler to alter his war policy by a united front of generals was influenced by the thought that a new stab-in-the-back theory must not be created. At the same time Goerdeler's Prussian-Protestant roots help to explain his fundamental moral objections to political murder.[9] For a considerable length of time resisters such as Goerdeler were blinded by the illusion that Hitler's unscrupulous subordinates, among them Himmler, Goebbels and Göring, were largely responsible for the destruction of public and legal order. Helmuth von Moltke, on the other hand, rejected an assassination in principle because he was convinced that, as the Nazi system constituted the final stage of a faulty development which had started with the Reformation, it needed to 'burn out' to allow the anticipated secular new beginning.[10] With the escalation of National Socialist crimes and the destruction experienced during the final phase of the war immediate action became an absolute necessity. After Moltke's arrest and in recognition of the fact that to overthrow the regime the dictator had to be assassinated, the majority of the Kreisau Circle committed itself fully to Stauffenberg's plans for a coup. From 1942 Moltke himself had, in fact, worked towards the overthrow of Hitler and his government. As the events immediately prior to the collapse of the Third Reich show, only the dictator's death destroyed the integrating power of the Hitler-myth. The latter had temporarily grown in strength in the aftermath of the 20th July, but started to disintegrate during the last year of the war.[11]

Despite the great range of levels and social backgrounds the resistance remained a resistance without people. Initially, this development evolved from the conspiratorial circumstances under which oppositional activities were undertaken. The KPD, and to a more limited extent

---

[9]  To the very end Goerdeler maintained his opposition to an assassination. Cf. Gerhard Ritter, *Carl Goerdeler und die deutsche Widerstandsbewegung*, Stuttgart, 2nd edn, 1964, 366.

[10]  Cf. Mommsen, 'Gesellschaftsbild', 116ff, 153. Many publications maintain erroneously that the Kreisau Circle restricted itself to planning for a new order. Important insights into Moltke's views can be found in the collection of materials by Freya von Moltke, Michael Balfour and Julian Frisby, *Helmuth James von Moltke. 1907–1945. Anwalt der Zukunft*, Stuttgart, 1975.

[11]  Cf. Marlis G. Steinert, *Hitlers Krieg und die Deutschen. Stimmung und Haltung der deutschen Bevölkerung im Zweiten Weltkrieg*, Düsseldorf, 1970, 471ff.

also the SPD, suffered woefully when they tried to organize public mass demonstrations during the initial phase of the regime. As a result the police apparatus managed to penetrate the illegal cadre organization of the KPD. Politically experienced Social Democrats such as Emil Henk distanced themselves from the semi-conspiratorial organizational activities of the SPD of which the Gestapo, as we know today, was generally well informed. The latter used to intervene only, however, if contacts to the KPD had been established or if supraregional networks had been created.[12]

Apart from groups such as the KPD which were to some extent prepared for conspiratorial activities, resistance groups were forced to develop on the basis of personal contacts and private circles of friends. Although the left was able to build upon an understanding of conspiratorial organizations, its resistance activities often originated in the initiative of individuals. Initially, the recruitment of conspirators was therefore restricted to those groups of people who, prior to 1933, had been in political or social, occasionally also professional, contact with each other. Repeated efforts by the KPD to establish contacts with Social Democrats or with oppositionally minded priests were rarely successful. The party depended on former party members to revitalize a conspiratorial network which was regularly battered by the Gestapo. If we consider how many sacrifices were suffered for the maintenance of the conspiratorial network alone, it is remarkable that, again and again, the party attempted to overcome its heavy setbacks. Preserving the network overtook illegal propaganda activities as the top priority, particularly as the latter, if badly executed, regularly brought the Gestapo onto the scene. At no time did the KPD succeed in recruiting groups of non-communist workers, least of all among the younger generation – unless they had grown up in a traditionally communist environment.[13]

Conspiratorial socialist groups such as the *Rote Stoßtrupp* (Red Raiding Party), *Neubeginnen* (New Beginning), *Deutsche Volksfront* (German Popular Front) or the *Internationale Sozialistische Kampfbund* (International Socialist Combat League) fared no better and were largely

[12]   This is clearly shown in surviving *V-Mann* reports; cf. Emil Henk, *Die Tragödie des 20. Juli 1944*, Heidelberg, 2nd edn, 1946. See also Hans Mommsen, 'Aktionsformen und Bedingungen des Widerstands in der Arbeiterschaft', in *Widerstandsbewegungen in Deutschland und in Polen während des Zweiten Weltkrieges*, Braunschweig, 2nd edn, 1983, 70ff.

[13]   On the Communist resistance see Horst Duhnke, *Die KPD von 1933 bis 1945*, Cologne, 1971; Arnold Sywottek, *Deutsche Volksdemokratie. Studien zur politischen Konzeption der KPD 1935–1946*, Düsseldorf, 1971; Detlev Peukert, *Die KPD im Widerstand. Verfolgung und Untergrundarbeit an Rhein und Ruhr 1933–1945*, Wuppertal, 1980; and Heinz Kühnrich, *Die KPD im Kampf gegen die faschistische Diktatur*, East Berlin, 1983.

wiped out by the mid-1930s.[14] Bourgeois-conservative resistance groups generally experienced similar difficulties though they found themselves in a somewhat more favourable position as the Gestapo approached them with much more caution, not so much because the regime feared a possible decline in its prestige, but because it did not believe members of the upper class to be capable of serious oppositional action. The conspiratorial activities of Carl Goerdeler and other representatives of civilian opposition groups were to a certain extent disguised by the fact that from late 1941 negative comments about the political situation and the behaviour of party officials, including high-ranking ones, proliferated everywhere.[15]

As chancellor-presumptive Goerdeler lived for a time in the hope that a majority of Germans would support a new government once the Nazi crimes had been revealed. Hassell and Popitz, however, regarded this notion with far more scepticism while the *Kreisauer* discovered that they could not count on the support of the mass of the working class. Hence, prior to the coup, the conspirators felt justified to do without a mass organization though, in anticipation of communist activities, they worked towards gaining backing from the trade unions as well as those sections of the working class which had formerly supported the Social Democrats. All available evidence seems to indicate that sections of the population, indoctrinated as they were by rallying calls, would have opposed the transitional government. Still, the decision to attempt the coup was the correct one even if it led to military instability. The relative isolation of the conspirators, however, would have remained a problem.

## 3   Supporters and Examplars

The bourgeois resistance was strongest when it could build on those surviving social elements which had not been affected by the external

---

[14]   Overview accounts in Peter Grassmann, *Sozialdemokraten gegen Hitler 1933 bis 1945*, Munich, 1976; and Richard Löwenthal and Patrik von zur Mühlen (eds), *Widerstand und Verweigerung in Deutschland 1933–1945*, Berlin, 1982; see also Mommsen, 'Aktionsformen', 71ff; and Tim Mason, 'Arbeiteropposition im nationalsozialistischen Deutschland', in Detlev Peukert and Jürgen Reulecke (eds), *Die Reihen fast geschlossen*, Wuppertal, 1981, 293ff.

[15]   Cf. Hedwig Maier, 'Die SS und der 20. Juli', *Vierteljahreshefte für Zeitgeschichte* 14, 1966, 299ff; Hoffmann, *Widerstand*, 349ff. For a summary see Ger van Roon, *Widerstand im Dritten Reich*, Munich, 4th edn, 1985, 182ff. That the Gestapo rarely intervened can be explained by the fact that the resisters of the 20th July shunned the creation of conspiratorial networks (as preferred by the left) and instead opted for partly close, but nonetheless informal contacts.

nazification of society. This conclusion also applied to the solidarity among those sections of the officer corps whose ideas had been shaped by Prussian traditions and who had not fallen for the kind of military-technical efficiency goals which, from 1933, had led to a significant consolidation of the close alliance between military and Nazi leadership.[16] Such sociological preconditions for membership of the resistance produced a certain social and political exclusiveness of the budding resistance circles even though Helmuth von Moltke in particular tried to overcome this by recruiting representatives of the working class (first Mierendorff and Haubach, later Julius Leber) into the Kreisau Circle.[17]

The 20 July resistance movement thus boasted a rather strange social mixture. On the one hand it contained personalities especially from the Kreisau Circle (and less so from the military resistance) who had acquired political experience chiefly in the late 1920s. In a way they had been political outsiders who had either emerged from the youth movement or been influenced by it, they believed in neo-conservative or neo-romantic ideas and had only exceptionally (for instance, in the case of Haubach and Mierendorff) had experience of practical politics.[18] There were others, such as Fritz-Dietlof von der Schulenburg, Claus Schenk von Stauffenberg or Henning von Tresckow, whose professional careers had developed under the Nazis. This group was faced with a circle of much older dignitaries among whom Ludwig Beck, Erwin von Witzleben and other outstanding officers were outnumbered by senior civil servants and diplomats who had initially held important positions in the regime some of which they consciously retained.

That professional politicians, in particular members of parliament, were almost completely absent was not an accident. After the manifest failure of Weimar's parliamentary system its representatives were to some extent politically neutralized. Politicians such as Konrad Adenauer or Theodor Heuss, while detached from the regime, did not see a starting-point for any effective opposition. Nearly all resistance groups agreed in their opposition to a return to Weimar conditions. This may also explain why, especially after the elimination of those circles pushing for a coup, Social Democrats were comparatively more weakly represented in the conspiratorial resistance than Communists and the Social Democratic left. Apart from the fact that conspiratorial action conflicted

[16] See Klaus-Jürgen Müller's fundamental study *Das Heer und Hitler. Armee und nationalsozialistisches Regime 1933–1940*, Stuttgart, 1969; see also Manfred Messerschmidt, *Die Wehrmacht im NS-Staat. Zeit der Indoktrination*, Hamburg, 1969.

[17] Cf. Ger van Roon, *Neuordnung im Widerstand. Der Kreisauer Kreis innerhalb der deutschen Widerstandsbewegung*, Munich, 1967, 226ff; and Moltke et al., *Helmuth James von Moltke*, 218.

[18] Cf. Mommsen, 'Gesellschaftsbild', 77ff.

with social democratic mentality, the SPD's leadership-in-exile did not manage to develop political goals which went beyond the defensive attitude of late Weimar.[19] Although the SOPADE leaders-in-exile used revolutionary language, the restoration of the parliamentary system was of more importance to them than the goal of a socialist revolution. Efforts to create a united front with the KPD foundered on the usual mutual reservations, on the special tactical demands of the KPD, and on the sad fact that contacts with illegal Communist cadres endangered the SPD's own resistance activities. While the KPD distanced itself from its former 'social fascism' slogan in 1935, it continued to hold on to its demand for a 'united front from below'.[20]

Although the Social Democratic members of the Kreisau Circle had been actively involved in party work before 1933, they were largely outsiders due to their intellectual calibre and their political convictions. This was even true of Julius Leber in spite of his many years of service to the Lübeck branch of the party and his experience as a member of the Reichstag.[21] Wilhelm Leuschner and others in the Goerdeler circle who shared his views were more concerned with trade-unionist concepts. When, in April 1933, they had come together in the *Führerkreis der deutschen Gewerkschaften* (Leadership Circle of German Trade Unions), it became clear to what extent they had turned away from Weimar's parliamentary system.[22] As a potential minister in the new government Leuschner too was faced with the difficulty of having to use older officials who, according to Leber's somewhat disparaging remark, had largely lost touch with the workers.[23]

Plans by the Goerdeler Circle largely followed on from the period of Weimar's presidential governments though clear differences emerged between the more strongly conservative-authoritarian position of Ulrich von Hassell and Johannes Popitz, Goerdeler's liberal ideology

---

[19] Cf. Grassmann, *Sozialdemokraten gegen Hitler*, 36ff; Lewis J. Edinger, *Sozialdemokratie und Nationalsozialismus. Der Parteivorstand im Exil 1933–1945*, Hanover, 1960, 28ff.

[20] Cf. Peukert, *KPD im Widerstand*, 222ff.

[21] Dorothea Beck, *Julius Leber, Sozialdemokrat zwischen Reform und Widerstand*, Berlin, 1983, 162ff, 177ff; see also Joachim G. Leithäuser, *Wilhelm Leuschner, Ein Leben für die Republik*, Cologne, 1962; James L. Henderson, *Adolf Reichwein. Eine politisch-pädagogische Biographie*, Stuttgart, 1958; and the short biographies of Mierendorff and Haubach in van Roon, *Neuordnung*, 123ff and 181ff.

[22] Gerhard Beier, 'Zur Entstehung des Führerkreises der vereinigten Gewerkschaften Ende April 1933', *Archiv für Sozialgeschichte* XV, 1975, 365ff; Hans Mommsen, 'Die deutschen Gewerkschaften zwischen Anpassung und Widerstand', in idem, *Arbeiterbewegung und nationale Frage*, Göttingen, 1979, 376ff.

[23] *Spiegelbild einer Verschwörung. Die Kaltenbrunner-Berichte an Bormann und Hitler über das Attentat vom 20. Juli 1944*, Stuttgart, 1961, 218.

tinged with a *deutschnational* bias and the more corporative views of the Christian and free trade unionists. The group of conspirators, including Fritz-Dietlof von der Schulenburg and the *Kreisauer* Adam von Trott zu Solz, which established closer links to Stauffenberg in 1943, found itself 'between both fronts' and tried to act as a mediator. Like Stauffenberg and some members of the military opposition this inner leadership circle of the 20th July, which was also joined by Julius Leber, was influenced by neo-conservative ideas with a strong social emphasis. This helps to explain the group's subsequent detachment from Goerdeler's views even though this did not have any direct effect on the preparations for the coup.[24]

In summary, it can be said that the national-conservative resistance consisted largely of individuals whose social environment, professional background and religious attachment had helped them to preserve their inner independence and social identity despite progressive National Socialist indoctrination. In the process they usually reverted to political attitudes which had stood in opposition to Weimar's republicanism. This was made worse by the spiritual isolation of the resistance. In contrast to *emigrés* and illegal organizations in the concentration camps, and despite the cosmopolitan attitudes of some of the conspirators of 20 July, the latter were far less influenced by western European political traditions.[25] This may account for the political objectives of the bourgeois-conservative resistance which, despite markedly different views on individual issues, was shaped by the concept of building a bridge between East and West, between Socialism and Capitalism – in other words a continuation of Germany's *Sonderweg* ('special path').[26]

## 4   Resistance as an Act of Survival

Initially, the 20th July resistance movement appeared to develop in a politically neutralized environment. It was barely affected by factional dispute as the conceptions of individual groups were all marked by a belief in a 'revolution from above'. The arrival of the *Nationalkomitee Freies Deutschland* (National Committee for a Free Germany)[27] made it

---

[24]   Cf. Mommsen, 'Gesellschaftsbild', 155ff; see also Christian Müller, *Oberst i. G. Stauffenberg. Eine Biographie*, Düsseldorf, date not known (possibly 1970), 303ff.
[25]   Cf. Hermann Brill, 'Gegen den Strom', *Wege zum Sozialismus* issue 1, Offenbach, 1946.
[26]   On the *Sonderweg* concept see Ernst Fraenkel, *Deutschland und die westlichen Demokratien*, Stuttgart, 1964.
[27]   See Bodo Scheurig, *Freies Deutschland. Das Nationalkomitee und der Bund Deutscher Offiziere in der Sowjetunion 1943–44*, Munich, 2nd edn, 1961; cf. Kurt

apparent that the Communist movement had become a serious factor. Resistance leaders such as Moltke, Schulenburg and Stauffenberg faced this challenge head on. That differences emerged within the bourgeois-conservative resistance over the political direction it ought to take was therefore not a sign of weakness, but rather an acknowledgment of the political reality. As a result, an attempt was made to create a popular movement which was to provide political backing to the insurgent government. Eventually, however, under pressure of time no agreement was reached on the movement's political direction and its foreign policy objectives. For political rather than conspiratorial reasons some conspirators expressed concerns that Leber and Reichwein had established contacts with the Communist resistance movement. Even though such contacts eventually led to intervention by the Gestapo and consequentially both threatened and accelerated the execution of the coup, they indicate that despite many differences all groups shared the same motivation. The future looked bleak and earlier illusions had clearly faded away; but Hitler was to be overthrown, the total occupation of Germany thus prevented and the nation state saved within the borders of 'the German people'.

It would go beyond the scope of this chapter to examine either the diverse range of initiatives and their motivational bases or the lack of ties among them due to an absence of conspiratorial means of communication. In the first instance, the decision to resist sprang from the personal experience and insight of the individual. From the outset of the regime some conservatives, such as Ewald von Kleist-Schmenzin, were committed to resist it with all available means. With regard to the initial situation in 1932/33, a typology of different political groups can be identified. It is not surprising that socialist and communist resistance commenced before that of denominational circles and the civilian and military resistance which eventually merged into the conspiracy of the 20th July. Illusions which the traditional elites held about the possible collusion between their own aspirations and the policies of the Nazis help to explain the comparatively belated formation of the bourgois-conservative resisance. Confronted with the regime's violent actions against Poland, the systematic liquidation of the Jews[28] and the extermination policies applied in the Soviet Union it became apparent that the Nazi regime could not be transformed into an authoritarian system by, on the one hand, removing the influence of the NSDAP and eliminating Hitler while, on the other hand, adopting elements of Nazi societal changes.

Finker, *Stauffenberg und der 20. Juli 1944*, Cologne, Berlin, 1967, 203ff. For an opposing view see Müller, *Stauffenberg*, 418.

[28] Cf. Christof Dipper, 'Der deutsche Widerstand und die Juden', *Geschichte und Gesellschaft* 9, 1983, 349–80.

Despite growing areas of conflict the churches, for their part, tried to come to an arrangement with the regime. Yet, the euthanasia programme in particular forced individual Christian groups to conclude that the preservation of institutional and theological integrity was no longer enough and that political action against the regime was required. This raises, of course, the issue of how to distinguish between resistance that intended to overthrow the system, and active *Resistenz* (though judged from the angle of the convictions of the individual, this constitutes an artifical separation). Those who risked their lives to hide Jewish fellow citizens and acquire forged exit permits for them, those who tried to help Russian prisoners-of-war, those who, at their workplaces, fought for the rights of workers and refused to be indoctrinated by the German Labour Front, those who protested against the treatment of the Jewish population or publicly denounced the euthanasia programme, those who refused to obey criminal orders, those who as a powerless protest against Nazi war policies daubed slogans on walls at night-time, those who protected the persecuted and shared their ration cards with them – in a wider sense they all belonged to the resistance.[29]

Within the active resistance the degree of opposition against policies and methods of the National Socialist regime also varied as even insiders became only gradually aware that the regime's deeply criminal traits were actually its essential components. The decision to carry out the coup at any price (even if this, in the sarcastic words of Julius Leber,[30] demanded a readiness to sign a pact with the devil) gathered strength among many from their critical assessment of particular aspects of the regime and from moral outrage about its criminal acts. Communists and socialists as well as many *Kreisauer* and some representatives of the Christian churches, however, were committed to total opposition against the Nazi regime from its outset. Yet, even these groups had to arrive at a resolution on whether to await passively the decline of the regime or to intervene actively in order to replace it with a new, more just system.

## 5    Phases and Changes in the Shape of the Resistance

The evolution of the resistance interacted with the progressive radicalization of the system and the escalation of its foreign and military

---

[29]    On the concept of resistance see Peter Hüttenberger, 'Vorüberlegungen zum "Widerstandsbegriff" ', *Geschichte und Gesellschaft*, special issue 3, 1977, 117–34; Klaus-Jürgen Müller, 'Die deutsche Militäropposition gegen Hitler. Zum Problem ihrer Interpretation und Analyse', in idem, *Armee, Politik und Gesellschaft in Deutschland 1933–1945*, Paderborn, 4th edn, 1986, 101ff.
[30]    See Beck, *Julius Leber*, 178.

policies. The occupation of neighbouring countries altered the conditions of the resistance struggle as it drastically reduced the smuggling in of propaganda material, the conspiratorial courier services as well as contacts to the western powers. The intensification of terroristic attacks by the Gestapo and other police organizations, the transformation of the psychological conditions of the fight after the outbreak of war, and the modification of foreign- and domestic-policy objectives owing to the increasing likelihood of military defeat created greater burdens for the resistance, yet they also strengthened its determination to risk the overthrow of the regime in an almost hopeless situation.

Germany's resistance experienced a bitter learning process. It is obvious that it required substantial energies just to adapt to the changing circumstances both at home and abroad. During its formative stage, roughly the period 1933 to 1935, the resistance had to force itself to a decision to avoid semi-public action and to create conspiratorial forms of association rather than to rely on pre-1933 organizations such as youth associations, trade unions, political parties or church organizations.

During the second stage of its evolution, from 1935 to 1938, the resistance is marked by both the growth of conspiratorial forms of association (in particular among working-class resistance groups), and the consolidation of organizations in exile in Czechoslovakia, the Netherlands and France. Yet, even during this period most resisters continued to deceive themselves by their belief that an anti-fascist mass movement would emerge and overthrow the Nazi regime. This kind of self-deception would find its reflection in illegal propaganda and information material such as, for instance, the SOPADE-reports.[31] By the end of the period it had, however, become clear that illegal groups which attempted to expand beyond the close circle of known like-minded individuals were doomed to be crushed.

The year 1938 is in many ways seen as a turning-point in the radicalization of the regime's policies, including most notably the transition towards active preparations for war. Even though the resistance had predicted from its outset that Hitler meant war, the third stage of its evolution, from 1938 to 1940, was dominated by a new aspect, the fight against the war and, after the attack against Poland, against its expansion into global conflict. To Hitler's chagrin, the Munich Agreement of 1938 temporarily delayed his plans for war. Initially for military reasons, these plans were opposed by General Beck who subsequently resigned

---

[31] *Deutschland-Berichte der Sozialdemokratischen Partei Deutschlands 1934–1940 (Sopade)*, 7 vols, Salzhausen, 1980.

from his post as Chief of General Staff.[32] At the same time, the evolution of the military opposition led by Beck and von Witzleben was linked to conflicts at the military leadership level which had become increasingly obvious since the Fritsch crisis and which were affected by the contrasting views on foreign and military policy held by the conservative *Reichswehr* leadership and Hitler. The military opposition subsequently made contact with Admiral Canaris' *Abwehr*. The Fritsch crisis also induced Fritz-Dietlof von der Schulenburg to move towards total opposition against a regime which he now regarded as unreformable, corrupt and criminal.[33]

In a parallel development, an opposition group was formed in the Foreign Ministry largely owing to an initiative by Germany's former ambassador in Rome, Ulrich von Hassell. Through contacts with the western powers Hassell and his group attempted to back the coup which military leaders repeatedly strived for prior to the attack on France. The group also established contacts with the Vatican.[34] Interrelated to Hassell's group was the formation of the core of a group subsequently known as the Goerdeler Circle. Over the coming years it established contacts with former Christian and Social Democratic trade-union leaders and thus gradually rid itself both of the original exclusivity of its 'dignitary' membership and of the strongly authoritarian answers proposed by Popitz and von Hassell.[35]

Already severely weakened by the Gestapo the Communist cadres experienced a certain disorientation due to the Nazi-Soviet Non-Aggression Pact of August 1939. After Hitler's decision not to postpone the attack on France any longer, the restless efforts of the bourgeois opposition groups to achieve Hitler's elimination followed by an authoritarian remodelling of the Nazi regime – though not a revolutionary rupture – failed not only because the military forces which were

---

[32]   Cf. Klaus-Jürgen Müller, *General Ludwig Beck. Studien und Dokumente zur politischen Vorstellungswelt und beruflichen Tätigkeit des Generalstabschefs 1933–1938*, Boppard, 1980; see also 'Generaloberst Ludwig Beck. Generalstabschef des Deutschen Heeres 1933 bis 1939', in idem, *Armee, Politik und Gesellschaft*, 76ff.

[33]   Cf. Hans Mommsen, 'Fritz-Dietlof Graf von der Schulenburg und die preußische Tradition', *Vierteljahreshefte für Zeitgeschichte* 32, 1984, 213–39, esp. 234ff; see also Albert Krebs, *Fritz-Dietlof Graf von der Schulenburg. Zwischen Staatsräson und Hochverrat*, Hamburg, 1965.

[34]   On the foreign policy of the resistance see Hermann Graml, 'Die außenpolitischen Vorstellungen des deutschen Widerstands', in Schmitthenner and Buchheim (eds), *Der deutsche Widerstand*, 15–72. An overview of early plans for a coup is given in Hoffmann, *Widerstand*, 69ff; see also Peter Ludlow, 'Papst Pius XII., die britische Regierung und die deutsche Opposition im Winter 1939/40', *Vierteljahreshefte für Zeitgeschichte* 22, 1974, 299–341.

[35]   Cf. Mommsen, 'Gesellschaftsbild', 131ff.

supposed to lead the coup found themselves tied down, but also because the victory over France, which was achieved unexpectedly quickly and without large numbers of casualties, led the dictator to the height of his popularity and brought him the unconditional loyalty of a previously hesitant officer corps. It should, however, be remembered that acts of resistance by individuals – Georg Elser's bomb attack in the Bürger-bräukeller on 8 November 1939 being the outstanding example – could have changed the course of things.[36]

In early summer 1940 the resistance was faced with a completely new situation. No longer could it hope that a quick elimination of Hitler would win it support among the public at large. The hard, tenacious and self-sacrificing resistance struggle which followed was no longer imbued with the hope of rapid successes. From then on firmness of conviction became more important than unrealistic actionism which had previously helped to fill the ranks of the resistance. Not only was careful planning of the intended coup now required, but also the devising of a lasting and credible alternative to the existing regime. Sections of the resistance therefore concentrated their energies upon the long-term planning of the political and social constitution for an anti-fascist Germany.

The subsequent period of reorganization is marked on the one hand by the notable reactivation of the Communist resistance, on the other by the emergence of the Kreisau Circle.[37] The Communists repeatedly suffered heavy losses and the destruction of entire resistance groups. Attempts to establish a new leadership at home after operating from occupied western European countries had barely reduced the risks, were blessed with little success and invited increased counteractivities by the Gestapo. After drawn-out efforts the latter even managed to uncover the espionage activities of the *Rote Kapelle* (Red Orchestra).[38]

The bourgeois resistance also came to feel the cruelty of the Nazi persecution apparatus. A lack of conspiratorial protection led to the uncovering and liquidation of the student resistance group *Weiße Rose* (White Rose).[39] Canaris was only partly able to foil Gestapo incursions into the resistance activities of *Abwehr* members. Consequentially, the

---

[36]   Cf. Anton Hoch, 'Das Attentat auf Hitler im Münchner Bürgerbräukeller 1939', *Vierteljahreshefte für Zeitgeschichte* 17, 1969, 383–413.

[37]   Apart from van Roon, *Neuordnung im Widerstand*, see also Kurt Finker, *Graf Moltke und der Kreisauer Kreis*, East Berlin, 1978.

[38]   On the KPD see Peukert, *KPD im Widerstand*, 342ff; on the 'Red Orchestra' see Heinz Höhne, *Kennwort Direktor. Die Geschichte der Roten Kapelle*, Frankfurt/Main, 1970.

[39]   See Richard Hanser's (rather uncritical and novel-like) *Deutschland zuliebe. Die Geschichte der Weißen Rose*, Munich, 1982.

*Abwehr* ceased to be a centre of coordination. The largely accidental uncovering of the Solf Circle resulted in the arrest of Helmuth James von Moltke and thus put an end to the planning activities of the Kreisau Circle. Those *Kreisauer* who continued to remain active joined the resistance group around Claus Schenk von Stauffenberg. Partly in reaction to the Kreisau plans the Goerdeler Circle intensified its own planning. Efforts to devise a joint programme were, however, not completed prior to 20 July 1944, especially as the increasingly catastrophic military situation urgently demanded immediate action.

The period 1941 to 1943 is characterized by the repeated failure of attempts to either arrest or assassinate Hitler. That the civilian opposition led by Goerdeler became increasingly impatient about the absence of a military putsch can partly be explained by a lack of information about the growing difficulties under which the military plotters had to labour. As a colonel in the *Ersatzheer* (home army) Claus von Stauffenberg organized the decisive change by preparing *Unternehmen Walküre* (Operation Valkyrie). Under the pretense of making advance preparations for the suppression of a possible rising of forced labourers and prisoners-of-war in the Reich, Stauffenberg was able to plot the putsch meticulously. The greatest difficulty consisted, however, in the execution of Hitler's assassination. The coup attempt of 20 July 1944 was considerably weakened by the fact that Stauffenberg was forced to act both as assassin and as indispensable leader of the military coup.

The attempted assassination took place against the background of a desolate domestic situation. The effects of Allied bombing attacks had impaired the communication network of the conspirators while the threat of Gestapo interference made it almost impossible for the civilian resistance and the action centre of the military opposition in the Bendlerstraße to finalize arrangements. This led to a heightening of misunderstandings which had emerged above all among those around Goerdeler about Stauffenberg's domestic- and foreign-policy objectives, in particular about the opening up towards the left so consciously intended by Leber and Stauffenberg.

The coup attempt failed notably because, against all expectations, Hitler survived the explosion in the Wolfsschanze with only minor injuries, but also more importantly because the precondition for the execution of 'Operation Valkyrie', the takeover of the executive power by the commander of the *Ersatzheer* and the smooth enforcement of orders by Bendlerstraße officials, was only achieved in exceptional cases (in Vienna and Paris). It became evident that the inner homogeneity of Germany's officer corps on which Stauffenberg had relied for his plans had vanished. Subordinate military sections first adopted a wait-and-see policy and then obeyed the countercommands which arrived soon after from the Führer's headquarters. Crucially, the resistance had failed to interrupt the communication lines in and out of the Wolfsschanze and to occupy Berlin radio in order to eliminate Joseph Goebbels.[40]

The humiliating treatment of the conspirators and like-minded individuals highlighted how badly the regime's inner prestige had been hit by the coup. *Exekutivkommandos* (executive commandos) were active until just before the capitulation of 8 May 1945 while the special commission in the *Reichssicherhauptamt* had not yet completed its work. Even cold-blooded Gestapo officials were shocked by the constantly growing number of conspirators which emerged from their investigations, even more so as the questioning of high-ranking supporters of the regime such as Graf Helldorf and Fritz-Dietlof von der Schulenburg revealed thoughts similar to their own; that the regime was perishing not least because its corruption and irresponsibility had reached unheard-of levels. And the 7,000 individuals named by the Gestapo in connection with the 20th July did not even include all those who, either indirectly or in part directly, had knowledge of the conspiracy.

The resistance did not end with the 20th July. Alongside Communist operations the regime was faced with efforts by those (as in Munich[41]) who opposed the senseless continuation of the war and the extension of scorched-earth policies upon Reich territory. Yet, the terroristic police apparatus of the regime continued to function until the bitter end. Its operational range widened to include youth groups such as the *Edelweißpiraten* (Edelweiss Pirates) which from being basically apolitical were politicized by the oppressive methods applied against them.[42]

## 6  Taking Stock of the Resistance

In drawing a 'balance sheet' of the German resistance against Hitler we arrive at the conclusion that it drew support only from a quantitatively small proportion of the population. The circumstances of the National

---

[40]  See Hoffmann, *Widerstand*, 479ff, 507ff; see also idem, 'Zum Ablauf des Staatsstreichversuches des 20. Juli 1944 in den Wehrkreisen', *Wehrwissenschaftliche Rundschau* 14, 1964, 377–97.

[41]  Cf. Hildebrand Troll, 'Aktionen zur Kriegsbeendigung im Frühjahr 1945', in Martin Broszat, Elke Fröhlich and Anton Grossmann (eds), *Bayern in der NS-Zeit*, vol. IV, Munich, 1981, esp. 660ff.

[42]  Although no links existed between these youth groups and earlier political groups, stylistic elements of the *bündisch* youth were sometimes copied. Cf. Detlev Peukert, *Die Edelweißpiraten. Protestbewegung jugendlicher Arbeiter im Dritten Reich. Eine Dokumentation*, Cologne, 1980; Arno Klönne, 'Jugendliche Opposition gegen Hitler-Jugend und NS-Staat', in Klaus-Jürgen Müller (ed.), *Der deutsche Widerstand 1933–1945*, Paderborn, 2nd edn, 1990, 182–207.

Socialist system of power and the inability of much of the population to mount political criticism did not permit, however, a channelling into one united movement of the many impulses directed against the regime or individual representatives of it. Anyone resisting the regime had to accept that the mass of deceived 'national comrades' would regard him or her as a traitor against the nation. Resistance forced the individual to be cautious even in conversations with close confidants. Attitudes towards the regime divided entire families, and not just the young from the old. In practice, institutional backing did not exist; the few exceptions included the Walberberg Monastery which offered a retreat for Catholic resisters and permitted an open exchange of ideas.

Those joining the resistance were influenced by differing, indeed sometimes even contrasting reasons, circumstances and interests. The *milieu* of working-class resisters was far removed from that of the bourgeois-conservative opposition. Views on the future political order differed hugely among the individual resistance groups. Yet, this was far less important than the fact that the resistance was prepared to think beyond the increasingly horrifying reality of the Nazi regime and to offer alternatives, even if these contained many utopian aspects. The groups shared the conviction that a system of power which was constructed upon lies, deception, corruption, naked violence and an accumulation of crimes could not survive and that beyond it there would be a social order in which, irrespective of its ideological framework, justice, human dignity and free self-determination were guaranteed.

Faced with constant setbacks, with arrests and torture, with anxieties about family, friends and fellow resisters it was this vision which enabled the members of the German resistance to continue their struggle, if necessary until the bitter end. Through their actions they demonstrated that human dignity could be preserved in the midst of a sea of inhumanity. This inspires at once hope and obligation. The legacy of the German resistance against Hitler, and indeed that of the *résistance* in countries occupied by Germany, continues to present us today with a challenge that was by no means fully met by the creation of constitutional democracies.

# Holocaust/ 'Final Solution'

# 11

# Nazi Resettlement Policy and the Search for a Solution to the Jewish Question, 1939–1941

## *Christopher Browning*

Originally appeared as Christopher R. Browning, 'Nazi Resettlement Policy and the Search for a Solution to the Jewish Question, 1939–1941', *German Studies Review*, 9:3 (1986) pp. 497–519.

*Editor's Introduction*

As Ian Kershaw has suggested (see the introduction to Reading 9), the division between 'intentionalist' and 'functionalist' interpretations of the Third Reich needs to be superseded by a synthesis of the two approaches. This view is clearly endorsed by Christopher Browning in his discussion of Nazi Jewish policy, an area in which the 'intentionalist-functionalist' debate has had a particularly strong impact.[1] After a brief summary of the debate Browning concludes that 'these contrasting positions are unduly polarized', and that a 'middle position' is possible.[2]

[1]  On the functionalist interpretation see Hans Mommsen, 'The Realization of the Unthinkable: The "Final Solution of the Jewish Question" in the Third Reich', in Hans Mommsen, *From Weimar to Auschwitz*, Princeton, 1991; and Martin Broszat, 'Hitler and the Genesis of the "Final Solution"', *Yad Vashem Studies* 13 (1979), 73–125. Strongly 'intentionalist' are Philippe Burrin, *Hitler and the Jews: The Genesis of the Holocaust*, London, 1994; Gerald Fleming, *Hitler and the Final Solution*, Berkeley, Cal., 1984; and Lucy Dawidowicz, *The War against the Jews, 1933–1945*, Toronto, 1976.
[2]  See also Christopher Browning, 'Beyond "Intentionalism" and "Functionalism": A Reassessment of Nazi Jewish Policy from 1939 to 1941', in Thomas Childers and Jane Caplan (eds), *Reevaluating the Third Reich*, New York, 1993, 211–33.

In practice, such a 'middle position' means that Browning rejects the 'intentionalist' argument that has 'Hitler awaiting the opportune moment to implement programmatic ideological goals that had crystallized in the 1920s'. Hitler, Browning maintains, did not possess an established programme for systematic mass murder, a policy which only surfaced in direct correlation to 'Operation Barbarossa', the war against the Soviet Union. Browning does concede, however, that Hitler came to power with a firm conviction that Jews mush be 'removed'. While this 'removal' was not necessarily tantamount to systematic mass murder, it did encompass the possibility of a large-scale loss of Jewish lives.

This last point is particularly relevant to the resettlement schemes which the Nazi regime tried to implement after the attack on Poland. For Browning these schemes, which are outlined in the central part of the following reading, had Hitler's 'explicit endorsement and support'. While the policy of resettlement cannot be viewed simply as a diversionary tactic or an 'opportunistic detours' on the pre-planned road to mass murder (as 'intentionalists' would argue), it is also wrong to play down or even ignore the key role Hitler played in the regime's Jewish policy during the period 1939 to 1941 (as 'functionalists' do).

# Nazi Resettlement Policy and the Search for a Solution to the Jewish Question, 1939–1941

*Christopher Browning*

In recent years the historiographical discussion of Nazi Jewish policy has reflected the wider debate on National Socialism between so-called 'intentionalists' and 'functionalists' and the even broader division within the historical profession between those who explain history through the ideas and decisions of individuals and those who explain history through the impersonal and underlying structures of society and institutions that limit and shape the actions of individuals.[1] The intentionalists concentrate for the most part on political and diplomatic history and have focused their interpretation of the Nazi period on the central role of Hitler and the continuity of his ideological goals from their crystallization in the 1920s through their realization in the early 1940s. The functionalists (also referred to as 'structuralists') are generally social and institutional historians. They have emphasized the polycratic nature of the Nazi regime and have sought to explain the course of events during this period in terms of the improvisation and cumulative radicalization produced by the contradictory nature and chaotic decision-making process of this regime rather than by the dominant role of Hitler and the calculated pursuit of his ideological goals.[2]

Initially the debate on Nazi Jewish policy focused on the 1930s, with the intentionalists arguing that this policy was a conscious and calculated preparation for the realization of Hitler's 'unalterable' programme and the functionalists portraying it as a 'planless' radicalization along the 'twisted road' to Auschwitz.[3] More recently this controversy has

---

[1] The research for this work was undertaken while I had the privilege of being a Fellow of the Institute for Advanced Studies of the Hebrew University of Jerusalem.

[2] The terms 'intentionalist' and 'functionalist' were coined by Tim Mason, 'Intention and Explanation: A Current Controversy about the Interpretation of National Socialism', Gerhard Hirschfeld and Lothar Kettenacker, eds, *Der Führerstaat: Mythos und Realität* (Stuttgart, 1981), pp. 21–40. Two articles starkly contrast the two approaches: Hans Mommsen, 'Hitlers Stellung im nationalsozialistischen Herrschaftssystem', pp. 43–72; and Klaus Hildebrand, 'Monokratie oder Polykratie? Hitlers Herrschaft und das Dritte Reich', pp. 73–97.

[3] For contrasting views, see for instance: Lucy Dawidowicz, *The War Against the Jews* (New York, 1975), Karl Dietrich Bracher, *The German Dictatorship* (New York,

centred on the events of 1941 and Hitler's particular role in the decisions and orders for the Final Solution in that year.[4] By the time these issues were debated at a conference in Stuttgart in May 1984, the lines of polarization, at least among German historians, had been clearly drawn.[5]

The functionalists who argued for an evolutionary view of Nazi Jewish policy in the 1930s claimed either that Hitler made no decision and issued no orders for the Final Solution in 1941 (Broszat and Mommsen) or did so only in the fall of 1941 (Adam). In either case the Final Solution resulted primarily from the dashed expectations of the Russian campaign. Plans to solve the Jewish question by expulsion into the wastelands of conquered Russia has been thwarted. The eastward movement of Jews already underway was backing up, and whether by Hitler's decision or local initiative, mass murder emerged as the way out of the *cul-de-sac* into which the Nazis had manoeuvered themselves.

For the intentionalists, in this case Eberhard Jäckel and Andreas Hillgruber, there was a fundamental connection in Hitler's mind between the acquistion of *Lebensraum* through the invasion of Russia and a solution to the Jewish question through systematic mass murder, which together constituted the nucleus or *Kernstück* of Hitler's racist ideology and were his conscious goals since the 1920s.[6] The Final Solu-

1968), and Helmut Krausnick, 'The Persecution of the Jews', *Anatomy of the SS State* (New York, 1968) on the one hand, and Karl Schleunes, *The Twisted Road to Auschwitz* (Urbana, Illinois, 1970) and Uwe Dietrich Adam, *Judenpolitik im Dritten Reich* (Düsseldorf, 1972) on the other.

[4] Uwe Adam first articulated the functionalist side of this aspect of the debate in *Judenpolitik im Dritten Reich*, pp. 303–16. It was developed further by Martin Broszat, 'Hitler und die Genesis der "Endlösung". Aus Anlaß der Thesen von David Irving', *Vierteljahrshefte für Zeitgeschichte* (hereafter cited as *VfZ*), 25/4 (1977), pp. 739–75. A 'moderate functionalist' reply to Broszat can be found in Christopher R. Browning, 'Zur Genesis der "Endlösung". Eine Antwort an Martin Broszat', *VfZ*, 29/1 (1981), pp. 97–109. A starkly intentionalist stand, which took aim at David Irving rather than Broszat, appeared with Gerald Fleming, *Hitler und die Endlösung. 'Es war des Führers Wunsch ...'* (Wiesbaden and Munich, 1982). A further articulation of the functionalist interpretation followed with Hans Mommsen, 'Die Realisierung des Utopischen: Die "Endlösung der Judenfrage" im "Dritten Reich"', *Geschichte und Gesellschaft*, IX/3 (Autumn, 1983), pp. 381–420.

[5] The conference proceedings, both papers and debate, have now been published as Eberhard Jäckel and Jürgen Rohwer, eds, *Der Mord an den Juden im Zweiten Weltkrieg: Entschlußbildung und Verwirklichung* (Stuttgart, 1985).

[6] Andreas Hillgruber, 'Die "Endlösung" und das deutsche Ostimperium als Kernstück des rassenideologischen Programms des Nationalsozialismus', *VfZ*, 20 (1972), pp. 133–53, reprinted with updated footnotes in Manfred Funke, ed., *Hitler, Deutschland und die Mächte* (Düsseldorf, 1978), and 'Die ideologisch-dogmatische Grundlagen der nationalsozialistischen Politik der Ausrottung der Juden in den besetzten Gebieten der Sowjetunion und ihre Durchführung 1941–1944', *German*

tion emerged in 1941 from a series of decisions taken by Hitler during the preparations for Barbarossa in the spring of 1941 and the euphoria of victory in the following summer that inaugurated policies to achieve these long-held and inextricably connected goals simultaneously.

In my opinion these contrasting positions are unduly polarized. A middle position that views the development of Nazi Jewish policy as evolutionary rather than programmatic but at the same time credits Hitler with making the key decisions in the spring and summer of 1941 in close connection with the preparations for and initial euphoria of the Russian campaign is not contradictory. What might seem a reckless jumping from the functionalist to the intentionalist horse in midstream turns out not to be a jump at all if one looks more closely at the relatively ignored interim years of 1939 and 1940 that lie between the two periods that have hitherto been the centre of attention, that is the development of Nazi Jewish policy in the 1930s and the fateful events of 1941.[7]

Nazi Jewish policy in this interim period centred on the resettlement or expulsion schemes of the Lublin Reservation and the Madagascar Plan. For many historians these schemes have seemed too bizarre and feckless from the post-Auschwitz perspective to be taken seriously. For instance, the first historian to make a scholarly study of this subject, Philip Friedman, concluded in 1953 that '[a]midst all these projects for population transfers the deportation of the Jews could easily pass as a part of the general plan. There was therefore little suspicion, at first, that behind this innocent mask of "resettlement" a scheme was in preparation of a quite different nature – nothing less than the total extermination of the Jews.'[8] Another early historian of the Holocaust, Gerald Reitlinger, also treated these plans as a subterfuge, as did Lucy Dawidowicz some years later.[9] Hillgruber and Jäckel likewise were unable to fit these resettlement schemes into a programmatic view that emphasizes the continuity between Hitler's goals of the 1920s and

Studies Review, II/2 (1979), pp. 263–96. Eberhard Jäckel, Hitler's Weltanschauung: A Blueprint for Power (Middletown, Connecticut, 1972).

[7] One important recent study that has in fact examined the relationship between the Nazi policies of expulsion and mass murder is that of the East German historian Kurt Pätzold, 'Von der Vertreibung zum Genozid. Zu den Ursachen, Treibkräften und Bedingungen der antijüdischen Politik des faschistischen deutschen Imperialismus', Faschismusforschung: Positionen, Probleme, Polemik (Köln, 1980), pp. 181–208.

[8] Philip Friedman, 'The Lublin Reservation and the Madagascar Plan: Two Aspects of Nazi Jewish Policy during the Second World War', YIVO Annual of Jewish Social Studies, VII (1953), pp. 151–77.

[9] Gerald Reitlinger, The Final Solution: The Attempt to Exterminate the Jews of Europe, 1939–1945 (New York: Perpetua Edition, 1961), pp. 77–9; Lucy Dawidowicz, The War Against the Jews (New York, 1975), pp. 154–5.

policies of the 1940s. They therefore dismissed these resettlement schemes as 'half-hearted' policies or 'opportunistic detours' of a cynical and calculating Hitler who awaited the right moment for the realization of his long-held plans.[10] In his most recent book, *Hitler in History*, Jäckel stated emphatically of the Madagascar Plan in particular, 'There is no indication that Hitler had ever intended it seriously'.[11]

On the other hand, functionalists, who maintain that Hitler was envisaging an expulsion of Jews into Russia even as late as the summer or fall of 1941, have taken the seriousness of these resettlement schemes for granted. But they have not examined whether the frustrations and failures of these schemes might not have led the Nazis in general and Hitler in particular to take decisions for mass murder earlier than the military failure of late 1941. Nor have they sought to analyse what the shaping of Nazi Jewish policy in this interim period indicates about the key role of Hitler and the manner in which he made decisions setting the parameters within which the Jewish question was to be solved.

It is my argument that for any reassessment of the resettlement schemes of 1939 and 1940, the historian must avoid the distortion of hindsight and seek to understand Nazi Jewish policy in this period as the Nazi perpetrators themselves did. Seen in this perspective, Nazi Jewish policy was part of a wider demographic project that aimed at a racial restructuring of eastern Europe. But within this wider demographic project, Jewish policy did not *yet* have the priority or centrality in the Nazis' own sense of historical mission that has been argued for on the basis of what happened later. I do not dismiss the significance of Nazi ideology or Hillgruber's and Jäckel's characterization of it as racist and Social Darwinist in nature. But I do argue that such terms as *Lebensraum* and *Endlösung* were not rigidly programmatic, excluding all but one interpretation, and that Jewish policy was not always the undisputed priority or centrepiece of Nazi racial policy. Between 1939 and 1941 the Nazis understood *Lebensraum* and *Endlösung* differently than in the post-Barbarossa period, though not in a way inconsistent with Hitler's racist Social Darwinist outlook.[12] But the Nazis' self-understanding of their historical mission in this period was no less real for being superseded. This was not a 'phony war against the Jews' awaiting

---

[10] The term 'half-hearted' is Hillgruber's. 'Opportunistic detour' is a phrase used by Eberhard Jäckel in a paper 'Hitler und der Mord an den europäischen Juden im Zweiten Weltkrieg' delivered in Warsaw in April 1983.

[11] Eberhard Jäckel, *Hitler in History* (Hanover, New Hampshire, 1984), p. 51.

[12] In this regard I find myself closer to Martin Broszat, who sees Hitler's ideology not as narrowly programmatic, but rather as 'goal-setting' or direction-setting'. However, I would give greater importance than does Broszat to Hitler's individual

the real offensive. Let us trace the outline of Nazi racial and demographic policy from September 1939 to March 1941, taking the Nazis' schemes for population resettlement as seriously as the Nazis did then.

Specific Nazi plans for racial policy and *Lebensraum* in Poland took shape only during September 1939, not before the invasion. Certainly there was a general consensus beforehand on a 'fourth partition' of Poland and a 'neutralization' of anti-German elements through mass arrests and shootings.[13] But it was only on 14 September that Heydrich reported to his division chiefs that 'proposals are being submitted to the Führer by the Reichsführer [Himmler] that only the Führer can decide. . . .'[14] Thus it was in the euphoria of victory over Poland that Hitler approved a specific policy, with the results transmitted to the army commander-in-chief Brauchitsch on 20 September and to Heydrich's division heads and *Einsatzgruppen* commanders on 21 September.[15] The border areas of West Prussia, the Warthegau and East Upper Silesia were to become purely German through the expulsion of all Poles, Jews and Gypsies, and the resettlement there of ethnic Germans or *Volksdeutsche* from eastern Europe. The Poles were to be deported eastward

decisions, in response to changing circumstances, for determining how far in these directions Nazi policies would actually evolve. I would not go so far as Hans Mommsen who evaluates Hitler's statements on the Jews primarily from the 'propagandistic aspect' as 'threats' against the Allied governments presumed to be under Jewish influence. Martin Broszat, 'Soziale Motivation und Führer-Bindung im Nationsozialismus', *VfZ* 18/4 (1970), pp. 392–409. Hans Mommsen, 'Die Realizierung des Utopischen', pp. 390–2.

[13]   National Archives Microfilm, T 175/239/2728499–502 (conference of Heydrich's division heads, 7 September 1939). Zentralstelle der Landesjustizverwaltungen in Ludwigsburg. 'Einsatzgruppen in Polen: Einsatzgruppen der Sicherheitspolizei, Selbstschutz und andere Formationen in der Zeit vom I. September 1939 bis Frühjahr 1940' (hereafter cited as 'EG in Polen'), II, pp. 22–9. Helmut Krausnick and Harold Deutsch, eds, Helmuth Groscurth, *Tagebücher eines Abwehroffiziers 1938–40* (Stuttgart, 1970), p. 362 (Document Nr. 14, Groscurth memorandum over verbal orientation by Major Radke, 22 September 1939). *Nazi Conspiracy and Aggression* (hereafter cited as *NCA*), V, p. 769 (3047-PS: notes by Lahousen from diary of Canaris). For a general overview of the development of Nazi occupation policy in Poland: Martin Broszat, *Nationalsozialistische Polenpolitik* (Stuttgart, 1960); and Waclaw Dlugoborski, 'Die deutsche Besatzungspolitik gegenüber Polen', in Karl Dietrich Bracher, Manfred Funke and Hans-Adolf Jacobsen, eds, *Nationalsozialistische Diktatur 1933–1945* (Bonn, 1983), pp. 572–90.
[14]   National Archives Microfilm, T 175/239/2728513–5 (conference of Heydrich's division heads, 14 September 1939).
[15]   National Archives Microfilm T 175/239/2728524–8 (conference of Heydrich's division heads and Einsatzgruppen leaders, 21 September 1939); *NCA*, VI, pp. 97–101 (3363-PS: Heydrich *Schnellbrief* to Einsatzgruppen leaders, 21 September 1939); Helmuth Groscurth, *Tagebücher*, p. 362. Hans-Adolf Jacobsen, ed., Franz Halder, *Kriegstagebuch* (Stuttgart, 1962), I, pp. 79, 82.

into what became the General Government, and deprived of potential leadership elites through systematic executions (and subsequently through the sifting out of those deemed racially suitable for 're-Germanization'). As for the Jews, they were to be deported to the furthest extremity of the German empire, the Lublin region between the Bug and Vistula rivers, with at least some of them being expelled over the demarcation line into the Soviet zone.[16] The Nazi plan thus envisaged three belts of population – German, Polish and Jewish – from west to east. As Hitler told Rosenberg at the end of September, only time would tell whether – 'after decades' – the German settlement belt would move yet further eastward.[17] The man appointed to be in charge of this vast movement of peoples, both coming and going, was Heinrich Himmler. Within the burgeoning SS, the Reich Commissariat for the Strengthening of Germandom (Reichskommissariat für die Festigung des Deutschen Volkstums – RKFDV) was created to coordinate ethnic German resettlement, while Heydrich's Reich Security Main Office (Reichssicherheitshauptamt – RSHA) handled expulsions eastward.[18] If the Nazis' self-imposed Jewish problem had mushroomed with the conquest of Poland, it is important to remember that in their own minds they now also had a Polish problem and a *volksdeutsch* problem of immense magnitude, and the attempt to solve all three of these simultaneously would often necessitate an ordering of priorities.

The first step in this grandiose program of population transfers was initiated by Gestapo chief Heinrich Müller on 6 October 1939, when he authorized Adolf Eichmann to contact the Gauleiter of East Upper Silesia concerning the deportation of Jews from that region. As Müller told Eichmann, 'This activity shall serve first of all to collect experiences, in order ... to be able to carry out evacuations of much greater numbers'.[19] As the first step. Eichmann was to organize one train of deportees from Kattowitz and one from nearby Mährisch Ostrau in the Protectorate, where many Polish Jews had fled during the recent fighting. Eichmann immediately tried to shift the centre of gravity of this deportation experiment from East Upper Silesia to his old stamping grounds, Austria and the Protectorate, with regular trains from there to

---

[16]   The area east of Cracow and north of the Slovak border was initially carmarked as the *Judenreservat* until Germany unexpectedly found itself with the Lublin region instead of Lithuania by its treaty with the Soviet Union of 28 September 1939.

[17]   Hans-Günther Seraphim, ed., *Das Politische Tagebuch Alfred Rosenbergs* (Göttingen, 1956), p. 81.

[18]   Robert Koehl, *RKFDV: German Resettlement and Population Policy 1939–45* (Cambridge, MA, 1957). This important study deals primarily with the resettlement of the *Volksdeutsche* and only tangentially with the expulsion of Poles and Jews.

[19]   Yad Vashem Archives (hereafter cited as YVA), 0-53/93/283 (Eichmann note, 8 October 1939).

a transit camp in Nisko in the Lublin region. From here the Jews were to be expelled eastward. Moreover, it was Eichmann's openly expressed expectation that within three to four weeks, his deportation programme would encompass the Old Reich as well.[20] But no sooner had the first transport departed from Mährisch Ostrau than on 19 October Berlin ordered an end to Eichmann's increasingly ambitious programme.[21] When the irate Gauleiter of Vienna vented his displeasure on Arthur Seyss-Inquart, Hans Frank's deputy, whom he blamed for preventing the deportation of the Viennese Jews, Himmler intervened and made clear in no uncertain terms that the decision to stop the Nisko transports had been his own – due, he said, to 'technical difficulties'.[22]

Why did the Nisko experiment come to such an abrupt halt? Many unconvincing reasons have been suggested. Protests from Hans Frank or local authorities in Poland against the unwanted influx could not have been decisive, for the Himmler decision was made even as the first of five transports was just arriving. Concern for Russian sensibilities was not crucial, for expulsions over the demarcation line continued into December. Demand for transport was indeed great, but Eichmann found upon inquiry that deportations were not totally excluded for this reason.[23] Nor was Eichmann being disciplined for improvising, given his subsequent appointment as Heydrich's specialist in charge of Jewish affairs and evacuations within the RSHA. In my opinion the decisive factor was the arrival of the first Baltic Germans in Danzig on 15 October.[24] The problem of finding space in West Prussia and the Warthe-

---

[20]  Two recent studies of the Nisko plan are: Seev Goshen, 'Eichmann und die Nisko-Aktion', *VfZ* 27/1 (January 1981), pp. 74–96; and Jonny Moser, 'Nisko: The First Experiment in Deportation', *Simon Wiesenthal Center Annual*, II (1985), pp. 1–30. For the rapid expansion of Eichmann's plans from two experimental transports to a comprehensive deportation programme see: YVA, 0-53/93/258–9 and 284 (Günther notes on conferences of 9 and 10 October 1939), pp. 223–4 (memorandum of 17 October 1939 on Eichmann-Ebner-Becker meeting of 16 October 1939), p. 206 (note for Eichmann of 18 October 1939), p. 289 (Braune to Wagner, 13 October 1939), pp. 299–300 (Eichmann to Nebe, 16 October 1939), pp. 227–9 (Günther-Braune FS-Fernspräch, 18 October 1939); Eichmann Trial Document T-1135 (Löwenherz memorandum, 10 October 1939); Gerhard Botz, *Wohnungspolitik und Judendeportation in Wien 1938 bis 1945: Zur Funktion des Antisemitismus als Ersatz nationalsozialistischer Sozialpolitik* (Wien, 1975), pp. 164–86 (Document VII: Becker memorandum, 11 October 1939).
[21]  YVA, 0-53/93/235–8 (Günther daily report, 19 October 1939), p. 220 (undated Günther telegram), and p. 244 (Günther note, 24 October 1939).
[22]  NCA, VI, 116 (3398-PS: Seyss-Inquart to Himmler, 4 November 1939), and Botz, *Wohnungspolitik und Judendeportation in Wien*. p. 196 (Document X, Himmler to Bürckel, 9 November 1939).
[23]  YVA, 0-53/93/256–7 (Brunner to Eichmann, 28 October 1939).
[24]  Hans Umbreit, *Deutsche Militärverwaltungen 1938/39: Die militärische Besetzung der Tschechoslowakei und Polens* (Stuttgart, 1977), p. 218.

gau for the incoming *Volksdeutsche* now took priority over deporting Jews from East Upper Silesia and especially from Austria and the Protectorate. The deportation of Jews from those regions simply did not provide the lodging and livelihood for incoming *Volksdeutsche* where Himmler needed them. The consolidation of *Lebensraum* in the incorporated territories and solving the Jewish question were turning out to be competing rather than complementary goals, and as we shall see, the latter continually gave way to the former during the next year.

The next major impetus for setting in motion the Nazis' vast resettlement programme was a Himmler order of 30 October 1939. By the end of February 1940, the Reichsführer wanted *all* Jews (estimated at 550,000) removed from the incorporated territories along with *all* so-called 'Congress Poles' from West Prussia, and a sufficient number of anti-German Poles from the other incorporated territories to bring the total to one million.[25] Meanwhile the resettlement of Baltic Germans in West Prussia bogged down, as Gauleiter Albert Forster became increasingly uncooperative. His antipathy to Himmler was no secret; he had been overheard to say of the Reichsführer: 'If I looked like him, I would not speak of race at all.'[26] On 28 November, Heydrich intervened from Berlin, drastically scaling back the deportations ordered by Himmler one month earlier. As a short-range plan he ordered that 80,000 'Poles and Jews' were to be deported from the Warthegau by mid-December so that the incoming Baltic Germans could be lodged there instead of in West Prussia.[27] In a frightening display of brutality, the Warthegau Nazis exceeded this quota, deporting 87,833 people in 80 trainloads by 17 December.[28] In some reports the unfortunate deportees were referred to collectively as 'Poles and Jews', elsewhere only as Poles, and no German records ever distinguished the specific number of Jews involved. The primary thrust of what was to become known as the 'first short-range

[25]  *Faschismus, Getto, Massenmord* [Berlin (East) 1960], pp. 42–3 (NO-5586: Himmler Order of 30 October 1939). *Trials of the War Criminals before the Nürnberg Military Tribunal*, IV, p. 873 (NO-4095: General Orders and Directives of RKFDV, undated, signed by Creutz). YVA, JM 21/1, Frank Tagebuch: Streckenbach report of 31 October 1939.

[26]  Fred Taylor, ed., *The Goebbels Diaries 1939–41* (London, 1982), p. 157 (entry of 30 October 1939); Koehl, *RKFDV*, p. 62; Herbert S. Levine, 'Local Authority and the SS State: The Conflict over Population Policy in Danzig-West Prussia', *Central European History*, II/4 (1969), pp. 331–55; 'EG in Polen', II, p. 117.

[27]  *Biuletyn Głównej Komisji Badania Zbrodni Hitlerowskich W Polsce* (hereafter cited as *Biuletyn*), XII (Warsaw, 1960), pp. 15F–18F (Heydrich to HSSPF Krakau, Breslau, Posen and Danzig, 28 November 1939; and Heydrich to Krüger, Streckenbach, Koppe and Damzog, 28 November 1939).

[28]  Ibid., pp. 22F–31F (Rapp report of 18 December 1939); YVA, JM 3582 (Rapp report of 26 January 1940).

plan' had not been to solve the Jewish question but rather to find space for the Baltic Germans. Many Jews were undoubtedly involved, but that was not what was on the Germans' minds at the moment.

Immediately following the conclusion of the Warthegau deportations of the 'first short-range plan', Adolf Eichmann was appointed Heydrich's 'special adviser' for evacuations and Jewish affairs.[29] Recalling Himmler's 30th October order, Eichmann lost no time in convening a Berlin conference on 4 January 1904, to announce once again the 'urgent' deportation of *all* Jews from the incorporated territories in the coming months.[30]

This was Eichmann's second attempt to get massive Jewish deportations underway, but it fared no better than his Nisko venture. Sobered by the devastating and chaotic influx of Warthegau deportees in December, the Governor General Hans Frank balked at receiving more trainloads of starving, frozen and penniless refugees. In this he was fully supported by the SS leadership of the General Government, a not very frequent concurrence of views. Heydrich thereupon countermanded Eichmann's impending Jewish deportations in order to ensure at least the more urgent deportation of some 160,000 Poles to make space for the incoming Baltic and now Volhynian Germans. Only after the completion of deportations immediately connected with the *volksdeutsch* resettlement would the deportation of *all* Jews from the incorporated territories, along with 30,000 Gypsies from the Old Reich, take place 'as the last mass movement'.[31]

A meeting of Himmler, Frank, the eastern Gauleiters and Göring at the latter's Karinhall estate on 12 February 1940, did little to clarify the issue of deportation priorities. Göring opposed the deportation of any useful manpower, especially agricultural labour, from the incorporated territories. The first priority, he stated unequivocally, was to strengthen the war potential of the Reich by making the new *Gaue* the granary of Germany. As for Jewish deportations, he was not opposed as long as the trains were sent in an orderly manner with prior notification. Frank openly allied himself with Göring's pragmatic stance. Himmler ignored Göring's offer to support Jewish deportations under orderly conditions but immediately emphasized the gravity of the *volksdeutsch* problem. He needed space for 70,000 Baltic Germans and 130,000 Volhynian Germans, and the latter had to be settled on Polish farms in a strip along

---

[29]  YVA, JM 3581, Müller to all Staatspolizeileitstellen, 21 December 1939, and Heydrich to Sipo-SD in Krakau, Breslau, Posen, Danzig and Königsberg, 21 December 1939.

[30]  *Biuletyn*, XII, pp. 37F–39F (Abromeit note of 8 January 1940 on conference of 4 January 1940).

[31]  *Biuletyn*, XII, pp. 44F–45F (NO-5322: conference of 30 January 1940).

the border with the General Government, i.e. precisely the disruption of agriculture that Göring opposed. Himmler volunteered to postpone the return of a further 220,000–270,000 Lithuanian, Bukovinian and Bessarabian Germans, as well as the ethnic Germans of the General Government. But the 30,000 *Volksdeutsche* east of the Vistula in the Lublin region had to be resettled too, because their present homeland was eventually destined to become the *Judenreservat*. He did promise, however, that he and Frank 'would agree upon the procedures of future evacuations'.[32]

Himmler seemed to think that by scaling back the pace of ethnic German resettlement and indefinitely postponing Jewish deportations, he could sufficiently minimize disruption in both the incorporated territories and the General Government so as to continue with his cherished project for resettling *Volksdeutsche* and expelling Poles, despite the misgivings of Frank and Göring. For Himmler the rescue of the *Volksdeutsche* and the consolidation of *Lebensraum* in the incorporated territories clearly had priority over deporting Jews at this time. Frank's understanding of what had transpired at Karinhall was different. He assumed that Göring had given him the power to veto any undesired deportation. Moreover, he boasted,

> the great resettlement ideas have indeed been given up. The idea that one could gradually transport 7½ million Poles to the General Government has been *fully abandoned*. It is now only a question of the transfer of some 100,000–120,000 Poles, some 30,000 Gypsies, and a still to be determined number of Jews from the Reich, because the final goal shall be to make the German Reich free of Jews.

It was 'indescribable' how Berlin still clung to the idea of a Jewish reservation east of the Vistula, Frank noted. However, 'That that shall not occur in a year and especially not under the circumstances of war, Berlin also recognizes'.[33]

In fact, even as Himmler was meeting with Frank and Göring at Karinhall, the SS was unilaterally launching new deportations – 1,000 German Jews from Stettin on 12 February (an exception to Heydrich's own rule against Jewish deportations from the Old Reich at this time) and 40,128 Poles from the Warthegau between 10 February and 15

---

[32] *Trials of the Major War Criminals before the International Military Tribunal* (hereafter cited as *IMT*), vol. 36, pp. 300–6 (EC-305: Karinhall conference of February 12, 1940).

[33] Italics mine. Hans Frank, *Diensttagebuch*, pp. 131 and 146–7 (Sitzung des Reichsverteidigungsausschuß, Warsaw, 2 March 1940, and Dienstversammlung der Kreis- und Stadthauptmänner des Distrikts Lublin, 4 March 1940).

March, in what was known as the 'intermediate plan'.[34] Frank appealed to Göring, who specifically forbade further deportations of Jews without both his permission and proof of Frank's prior agreement.[35] Against the vociferous protest of Gauleiter Greiser, who was most anxious to expel the Jews of Lodz, Himmler agreed with Frank to postpone all Jewish deportations until August, when the Volhynian resettlement action – involving the expulsion of 120,000 Poles in the 'second short-range plan' – was due to be concluded.[36]

Himmler's grandiose design for a sweeping racial reorganization of eastern Europe had been steadily whittled away. In the fall of 1939, he had envisaged the deportation of about one million people (including all Jews) from the incorporated territories into the General Government by the end of February 1940, and eventually the removal of all so-called racially undesirable elements from these lands. By March 1940, however, Frank was boasting that the idea that one could gradually transport 7½ million Poles to the General Government had been 'fully abandoned'. Moreover, the Jewish deportations had been postponed repeatedly – most recently to August – and Göring had invested Frank with a virtual veto power over them. Even the resettlement of ethnic Germans had been scaled back. But if Frank could go over Himmler's head to Göring, Himmler now sought to re-legitimize his threatened dream by going over Göring's head to Hitler.

Since his pronouncements of the previous fall, Hitler had played no visible role in shaping racial policy. In a typical example of the 'institutional Darwinism' of the Third Reich, implementation had been left to a struggle between his subordinates, while the Führer himself turned his attention to loftier matters of grand strategy, in particular preparations for the offensives into Scandinavia, the Low Countries and France. But by spring Hitler seemed to have lost faith in his resettlement plan, at least insofar as it concerned the Jews in Lublin. According to Walther Hewel, Hitler told Colin Ross on 12 March 1940, that:

> the Jewish question really was a space question which was difficult to solve, particularly for him, since he had no space at his disposal. Neither would the establishment of a Jewish state around Lublin ever constitute a solution as even there the Jews lived too close together to be able to

---

[34]    YVA, 0-53/48/650-2 (Umwandererzentrale Abschlußbericht 1940).
[35]    Politisches Archiv des Auswärtigen Amtes (hereafter cited as PA), Inland IIg 173, Göring telegram of 23 March 1940.
[36]    Frank, *Diensttagebuch*, p. 158 (entry of 5 April 1940), and p. 204 (entry of 19 May 1940); *Dokumenty i Materialy Do Dziejow Okupacji Niemieckiej W Polsce*, vol. III, *Getto Lodzkie* (Warsaw, 1946), pp. 168–9 (Regierungspräsident to officials of Bezirk Lodz and Kalisch, 8 May 1940).

attain a somewhat satisfactory standard of living. . . . He, too, would welcome a positive solution to the Jewish question; if only he could indicate a solution; this, however, was not possible under present conditions when he had not even sufficient space for his own people.[37]

The brilliant success of German arms in the first tow weeks of the French campaign, however, gave Himmler the opportunity in late May to seek Hitler's approval for his racial design that stood in stark contrast to the pragmatic arguments of Göring and Frank and included an even more radical resettlement solution for the Jews than the now faltering Lublin Reservation.

Sometime in May 1940 Himmler drafted a memorandum: 'Some Thoughts on the Treatment of Alien Populations in the East.' The 15 million people of the General Government and the 8 million of the incorporated territories – 'ethnic mush' in Himmler's view – were to be splintered into as many ethnic groups as possible for 'screening and sifting'. 'The basis of our considerations must be to fish out of this must the racially valuable, in order to bring them to Germany for assimilation.' The ethnic identity of the leftovers, deprived of their racially valuable stock and dumped together in the General Government along with those from Germany 'of the same racial and human type', would gradually disappear. This non-descript, denationalized population would then serve as a reservoir for migrant labour to Germany.[38]

The Jews were also to disappear but in a different way. 'I hope completely to erase the concept of Jews through the possibility of a great emigration of all Jews to a colony in Africa or elsewhere.' Concerning this systematic eradication of the ethnic composition of eastern Europe, Himmler concluded: 'However cruel and tragic each individual case may be, this method is still the mildest and best, if one rejects the Bolshevik method of physical extermination of a people out of inner conviction as un-German and impossible.'

On 25 May, a week after the German panzers reached the English Channel, Himmler submitted his memorandum to Hitler. Himmler's

---

[37] *Documents on German Foreign Policy*, D, VIII, pp. 912–13 (Hewel memorandum on conversation of Colin Ross and Hitler, 12 March 1940).

[38] Helmut Krausnick, ed., 'Einige Gedanken über die Behandlung der fremd-völkischem im Osten', *VfZ* V/2 (1957), pp. 194–8 (NO-1880). Himmler did not start from scratch in writing this memorandum. A much longer study, 'The Question of the Treatment of the Population of the Former Polish Territories according to a Racial political Viewpoint', developing most of the ideas contained in the Himmler memorandum (with the notable exception of deporting the Jews to an African colony), had been submitted by Erhard Wetzel and Gerhard Hecht of the Racial Political Office on 25 November 1939. *Documenta Occupationis*, V (Poznan, 1949), pp. 2–28 (NO-3732).

timing was impeccable, and he scored a great triumph. 'The Führer read the six pages through and found them very good and correct'. Himmler noted. Moreover, 'The Führer desires that I invite Governor General Frank back to Berlin, in order to show him the memorandum and to say to him that the Führer considers it correct'. Himmler then asked Hitler to authorize its distribution to the eastern Gauleiters and Göring, with the message that the Führer 'had recognized and confirmed' the meorandum as containing authoritative guidelines. Hitler agreed once again.[39]

This episode is of singular importance, in that it is the only first-hand account by a high-ranking participant, i.e. Himmler, of just how a Hitler decision was reached and a *Führerbefehl* was given in the shaping of Nazi racial policy during this period. The initiative came from Himmler. However, he did not present Hitler with a precise plan. It was instead a statement of intent, a set of policy objectives. The details of implementation would be left to Himmler. Hitler indicated not only his enthusiastic agreement but also with whom this information could be shared. Hitler gave no specific orders to the likes of Göring, Frank and the eastern Gauleiters. He simply allowed it to be known what he wanted or approved. Presumably business was often conducted in such a way in the Third Reich.

Himmler's enthusiastic memorandum-writing continued into June, when he encountered the argument that Polish labour would always be necessary in the incorporated territories for economic reasons. Himmler set out as his guiding principle: 'One only possesses a land when even the last inhabitant of this territory belongs to his own people.' Thus the alien population had to be forced off the land into construction work, with seven-eighths of them gradually deported to the east and one-eighth Germanized. 'I am convinced that in the east we can get by without native Polish labour in the long run, and that we cannot and must not leave Poles in the eastern provinces even for economic reasons.'[40]

The beleaguered Hans Frank thus not only faced the influx of Jews scheduled for August, but now also saw resurrected the very plan he thought 'fully abandoned' in March, that is the deportation of more than seven million Poles from the incorporated territories into the General Government as well. Frank became increasingly desperate concerning the 'catastrophic effects' of continued resettlement, when suddenly a surprising order from Himmler stopping the impending expulsion of the Jews into the General Government came to Frank as a

[39]    Ibid., pp. 195–6 (Himmler memorandum, 28 May 1940).
[40]    National Archives Microfilm, T 175/122/2665958ff (Himmler memorandum, 24 June 1940).

veritable deliverance.[41] Himmler had found his colony in Africa for the Jews – the island of Madagascar!

Madagascar had long exercised a fascination among anti-Semites as the ideal dumping ground for the European Jews, but the idea did not take on real form as a concrete proposal among the Nazis until put forward by the Jewish expert of the German Foreign Office, Franz Rademacher, in early June 1940, when Germany's power to redistribute the French empire seemed at hand.[42] The alacrity with which the proposal was seized upon by the Nazi leadership is a measure of the frustration that had built up over the bottlenecks of demographic engineering in eastern Europe over the past nine months. By 18 June Hitler had informed Mussolini of his intention to use Madagascar as a Jewish reservation, and he broached the subject again with Admiral Raeder on 20 June.[43] On 24 June the ever attentive Heydrich asserted his jurisdiction vis-à-vis the Foreign Office over Jewish resettlement there.[44] The news spread quickly eastward. On 1 July, Adam Czerniakow, the lead of the *Judenrat* in Warsaw, learned from an SD official, 'that the war would be over in a month and that we would all leave for Madagascar'.[45] Frank knew by 10 July that he was not only reprieved from the expected deluge of Jews from the Reich but would now be rid of his own Jews as well – a 'colossal relief' he boisterously expounded upon to the *Heiterkeit* or 'amusement' of his assembled court.[46] On Frank's orders ghetto building in the General Government came to an abrupt halt as pointless in view of the 'plan of the Führer' to send the Jews to Madagascar.[47] If

---

[41]   NG-1627 (Frank to Lammers, 25 June 1940). *Biuletyn XII*, 96F-97F (Note on Höppner-IV D 4 discussion, 9 July 1940).

[42]   Leni Yahil, 'Madagascar – Phantom of a Solution for the Jewish Question', in George Mosse and Bela Vago, eds, *Jews and Non-Jews in Eastern Europe* (Jerusalem, 1974), pp. 319–32. Christopher R. Browning, *The Final Solution and the German Foreign Office* (New York, 1978), pp. 35–43.

[43]   Galeazzo Ciano, *The Ciano Diaries 1939–43* (Garden City, New York, 1947), pp. 265–6. Paul Schmidt, *Hitler's Interpreter* (New York, 1951), p. 178. Klaus Hildebrand, *Vom Reich zum Weltreich: Hitler, NSDAP, und koloniale Frage, 1919–1945* (Munich, 1969), pp. 651–2. In August Hitler told the German ambassador to France, Otto Abetz, that he intended to expel all the Jews from Europe at the end of the war. *Akten zur Deutschen Außenpolitik*, D, X, p. 389. Even American diplomats in Bucharest heard rumours of Hitler's mentioning the Madagascar Plan to Rumanian diplomats. *Foreign Relations of the United States*, II, p. 769. I am grateful to Itzhak Mais, director of the Yad Vashem museum, for this last reference.

[44]   PA, Inland IIg 177, Heydrich to Ribbentrop, 24 June 1940.

[45]   Raul Hiberg, Stanislaw Staron and Josef Kermisz, eds, *The Warsaw Diary of Adam Czerniakow* (New York, 1979), 169 (entry of 1 July 1940).

[46]   Frank, *Diensttagebuch*, p. 248 (entry of 10 July 1940), p. 252 (Abteilungsleitersitzung, 12 July 1940) and p. 258 (entry of 25 July 1940).

[47]   *Faschismus-Getto-Massenmord*, p. 96 (report of Kreishauptmann of Minsk Mazowiecki, 11 October 1940) and p. 110 (Schön report of 20 January 1941).

Frank was ecstatic, Greiser in the Warthegau was distraught. The Jewish deportations scheduled for August were cancelled, and he now faced the prospect of having to keep his own Jews for the duration of the war. His attempt in late July to get Frank to take the Warthegau Jews as an interim measure met with a flat refusal.[48]

Realization of the Madagascar Plan required the defeat of not only France but also Great Britain. By mid-September it was clear that this was not imminent, and the plan quickly faded. It was no less real for its brief existence, however. In cancelling the August deportations and halting ghetto construction in the General Government, Nazi leaders were not carrying out an elaborate sham to deceive future historians; they were making decisions based on the Madagascar Plan as the reality of Nazi Jewish policy in the summer of 1940. Despite the constant postponements, the self-imposed 'obligation' to solve the Jewish question still weighed heavily upon the Nazis. The greater the frustration, the lower the threshold to systematic mass murder. Thus the Mada gascar Plan was an important psychological step toward the Final Solution.

Even as Hitler in the last half of 1940 commenced planning for the invasion of Russia, which would fundamentally alter the Nazi perspective on eastern Europe, population transfer policies were not immediately affected. While neither the Lublin Reservation nor Madagascar Plan had been realized by the fall of 1940, old habits, thought patterns and temptations died hard. Through the spring of 1941, the expulsion policy spasmodically revived as local Gauleiters along the borders of the Third Reich – both west and east – successfully prevailed upon Hitler to rid themselves of some of their undesired population through piecemeal deportations into Vichy France and the General Government. Hitler's open encouragement inspired the demographic engineers to produce yet another plan for massive population transfers of both Poles and Jews in early 1941, only once again to encounter insurmountable obstacles and cancellation.

With the defeat of France, Alsace and Lorraine had been reannexed to the Third Reich and joined to the Baden and Saarpfalz *Gaue*. Beginning in July the Germans began deporting Jews, Gypsies, asocials, criminals, mentally ill and ardent French nationalists out of these newly annexed territories into France.[49] By mid-December the Germans had

---

[48]   Frank, *Diensttagebuch*, pp. 261–3 (entry of 31 July 1940.

[49]   That Himmler saw these population expulsions in the same light as the expulsions from the incorporated territories in the east can be seen in his speech to officers of the Waffen-SS in Metz: 'Exactly the same thing took place in Poland at 40 degrees below zero, where we had to ship out thousands and tens of thousands and hundreds of thousands, where we had to have the toughness – this you should hear but

deported over 70,000 people, including 3,300 Jews, from Alsace-Lorraine, and barred the return of an even greater number who had fled.[50]

In this massive upheaval of humanity, it is not surprising that someone perceived the possibility of including the German Jews of Baden and Saarpfalz, thus making those *Gaue judenfrei*. According to Eichmann, it was the Gauleiter of Baden, Robert Wagner, who made the proposal to Himmler, and the latter agreed 'impulsively' without even considering the possible complications.[51] With Hitler's approval 6,504 Geman Jews were expelled into Vichy France on 22–3 October past the unsuspecting French border guards who assumed they were deportees from Alsace-Lorraine.[52] The ensuing diplomatic hassle at the armistice negotiations in Wiesbaden made further such deportations in the west impossible, however.

In the east the momentum behind expulsion policy was also decreasing, as Polish peasants stubbornly evaded roundups by spending their nights in the field or forest. Often only 40 per cent of those earmarked for arrest could actually be seized.[53] No one was more pleased about this than Hans Frank. At a rare meeting of the eastern Gauleiters in Hitler's apartment on 2 October 1940, Frank could not resist boasting to Hitler about his success in the General Government, noting in particular the ghettoization of the Warsaw Jews then underway. Baldur von Schirach, the attentive Gauleiter of Vienna sitting on the other side of Hitler, immediately burst in that he had 50,000 Jews that Frank must take. Koch of East Prussia immediately proffered some Poles and Jews of his own. Hitler made no explicit decision and did not even mention the Jews specifically, but he did indicate his general line of thinking. The population density of the General Government was unimportant, he is alleged to have noted. It was only to be a 'great Polish work camp'.[54]

A month later Hitler, according to Frank, made clear to him his 'urgent wish' that more Poles be taken into the General Government.

then immediately forget – to shoot thousands of leading Poles.' *IMT*, vol. 29, p. 104 (1918-PS: Himmler speech at Metz).

[50]   For Lorraine: *IMT*, vol. 31 pp. 283–94 (2916-PS: overview of evacuations to 15 November 1940, compiled by the Chief of Sipo-SD). For Alsace: Akten der Partei-Kanzlei der NSDAP, 101 23821 (Chef der Zivilverwaltung im Elsass, 22 April 1941, to Bormann, on census of 15 February 1941).

[51]   Eichmann Interrogation, vol. I, pp. 141, 145.

[52]   Bernhard Lösener, 'Als Rassereferent im Reichsministerium des Innern', VfZ IX/3 (1961), p. 295.

[53]   *Documenta Occupationis* (Poznan, 1959), VIII, p. 62 (Lodz Gestapo report, 25 July 1940).

[54]   *IMT*, vol. 39, pp. 426–9 (Bormann note on Hitler discussion of 2 October 1940).

In December Hitler was reported by Frank to have been even more insistent, declaring that 'the Polish resettlement in the General Government was in line with his policy. . . .'[55] The renewed deportations were to include not only Poles but also Jews, as Hitler intervened directly to authorize the expulsion of Viennese Jews to solve the housing shortage in that city.[56]

With Hitler's encouragement expulsion fever among the Germans was clearly on the rise. Eichmann's experts in the east were summoned to Berlin on 17 December for a meeting on the 'third short-range plan' for the resettlement of ethnic Germans from Bessarabia, Bukovina, Dobrudja and Lithuania.[57] To make room for the ethnic Germans, Heydrich intended to deport no less than 831,000 people in the coming year. In addition the army wanted 200,000 people relocated to the General Government to create vast training areas. Thus over one million people were to be moved to the General Government within the framework of the 'third short-range plan'. By its own statistics, that is not including the refugees who fled on their own and 'wild' deportations, the SS had deported a total of 261,517 people to the General Government between December 1939 and January 1941.[58] Thus Heydrich was actually planning to deport four times as many people into the General Government in the coming year as had been deported in the last. In short, the Nazis hoped in 1941 to dwarf the demographic upheavals they had already engineered.

Once again, however, the grandiose schemes of the Nazis reflected their ambitions more than their capacities. The problem was no longer opposition from Frank, who now found Hitler's wishes in this matter all too clear.[59] Instead the transportation situation in the months before Barbarossa made realization of expulsions on the planned scale unattainable. The deportations, begun in late January, uprooted some 25,000 people – including 9,000 Jews – before they were abruptly stopped on 15 March.[60]

---

[55]   Frank, *Diensttagebuch*, p. 302 (entry of 6 November 1940) and p. 327 (entry of 15 January 1941).
[56]   1950-PS (Lammers to Schirach, 3 December 1940).
[57]   YVA, 0-53/66/231 (Eichmann to Höppner, Krumey, Abromeit, Schlegel and Riedel 12 December 1940).
[58]   YVA, JM 3582, Abschlussbericht 1941.
[59]   Frank, *Diensttagebuch*, p. 309 (entry of 2 December 1940), and p. 326 (conference of 15 January 1941).
[60]   YVA, 0-53/68-682-3 (report on Jewish evacuation in Danzig-West Prussia, 19 February 1941). YVA, JM 3582, Abschlussbericht 1941. Herbert Rosenkranz, *Verfolgung und Selbstbehauptung: Die Juden in Österreich 1938–1945* (Munich, 1978), pp. 261–2. *Biuletyn*, XII, 138F–139F (Müller or Königsberg, Gotenhafen, Posen, Lodz, Wien, 15 March 1941).

The repeated failure of German plans for massive population transfers, especially those for solving the Jewish question, frustrated not only the demographic engineers of the SS but Hitler as well. According to an account by Hitler's adjutant, Major Engel, the Führer ruminated openly about the Jewish question before Bormann, Keitel, Speer and Ley in February 1941. Hitler observed that while the war would speed a solution, it also brought forth many more difficulties. Originally he had thought only of breaking the power of the Jews in Germany, but now his goal had to be the exclusion of Jewish influence in the entire Axis sphere. 'If [I] only knew where one could put several million Jews, there were not so many after all', he lamented. When he remarked that he would make France provide Madagascar, Bormann questioned how the Jews could be sent there during the war. Hitler replied that one would have to consider that problem. He would provide the entire German navy for that purpose, except that he would not subject it to the risk of attack. According to Engel, Hitler then revealed that he 'was thinking of many things in a different way, that was not exactly more friendly'.[61]

Indeed, preparations for Barbarossa not only cut short the expulsions of the 'third short-range plan' but opened the way for Hitler and the Nazis to think about many things in a 'different way' by reorienting and transforming the Nazi slogans of *Lebensraum* and *Endlösung*. As articulated and practised between 1939 and 1941, *Lebensraum* meant a long-term process of racial consolidation in the incorporated territories. On several occasions Hitler remarked that his eastern Gauleiters had ten years to tell him that Germanization of their provinces was complete, and he would ask no questions about their methods.[62] Likewise Hitler told Rosenberg in September 1939 that only time would tell if Germanization would – 'after decades' – expand further east. Himmler's argument of June 1940 that a land belonged to the German people only when every last tiller of the soil was German also implied years, even generations, of consolidation. The *Endlösung* in this period meant the expulsion of the Jews to the furthest extremity of the German sphere of influence, first Lublin and then Madagascar. Little was done immediately to implement this version of the Final Solution, however. Of the nearly

[61]  Hildegard von Kotze, ed., *Heeresadjutant bei Hitler 1938–1943: Aufzeichnungen des Majors Engel* (Stuttgart, 1974), pp. 94–5. Though cast in the form of diary notes written at the time, this account was compiled by Engel later. The dating of events has been shown to be unreliable in at least several instances (see the note of the editor on p. 67).
[62]  Groscurth, *Tagebücher*, p. 381 (Document Nr. 24, unsigned memorandum of 18 October 1939). *IMT*, vol. 39, pp. 426–9 (Bormann note of Hitler statement, 2 October 1940), *Hitler's Secret Conversations* (New American Library,1961), p. 48 (entry of 1 August 1941).

half-million Poles and Frenchmen expelled by the Nazi demographic engineers in this period, less than 10 per cent were Jews. Eichmann's frequent attempts to set full-scale Jewish deportations underway in October 1939, January 1940 and again in the summer of 1940 all came to naught, for the Nazis temporarily conceded priority to the need to rescue and resettle endangered ethnic Germans. The Jewish question was just as important though not as urgent as *volksdeutsch* resettlement.

The decision to invade Russia brought about a reversal of these priorities. Driven on by his frustration with the military stalemate in the west, his own fervent anti-Bolshevism, his vision of Russia as a land destined for German expansion, his calculation that through the growth of the US and USSR time worked against Germany, his increasing sense of himself as the man of destiny who must do all in his own lifetime, and the pervasive and ceaseless activism that possessed his own psyche as well as the Nazi movement, Hitler opted for Barbarossa.[63] The ideology of *Lebensraum* as practised between 1939 and 1941 was radical in its methods but relatively conservative in its foreign policy implications. It did not compel an invasion of Russia; on the contrary, it was transformed by that invasion from a doctrine of gradual racial consolidation into one of limitless expansion.

In the process the Nazi view of a final solution to the Jewish Question was radicalized as well. Limitless expansion into Russia meant ever more Jews. A problem that had already proved intractable threatened to reach immense proportions. The whole sequence of thwarted expulsion plans between 1939 and 1941 had both accustomed the Nazis to thinking in terms of an imminent final solution and frustrated them as, like a mirage, this vision of a *judenfrei* German empire continually receded before their advance. The time was ripe to break the vicious circle. Muder was in the air as the Germans prepared for a *Vernichtungskrieg* in Russia, and in these circumstances the Russian Jews could hardly be spared the fate awaiting so many others.

This whole tendency was intensified by the fundamental position of the Jewish-Bolshevik identity in Nazi ideology. When the Nazis invaded

---

[63] For the most recent discussion of Hitler's decision to invade Russia, see the contribution of Jürgen Förster in: *Das Deutsche Reich und der Zweite Weltkrieg*, vol. IV, *Der Angriff auf die Sowjetunion* (Stuttgart, 1983), pp. 3–37. Förster argues that Hitler's anti-Bolshevism and vision of *Lebensraum* in Russia dovetailed with the strategic impasse in which he found himself. 'Das Ausgreifen nach Osten, *das* große außenpolitische Ziel seit den zwanziger Jahren, war für Hitler nun auch zum Mittel geworden, Deutschland aus der Zwangslage zu befreien, in die es durch seine axiomatische Grundvorstellungen, sein politisches Vabanquespiel, die nachgiebige Haltung der britischen Regierung sowie die konsequente globale Politik Roosevelts hineingeraten war' (p. 33).

Poland in September 1939, the fate of the Polish Jews could wait but the fate of the Polish intelligentsia could not. The *Einsatzgruppen* were targeted to carry out the immediate genocidal elimination of all potential carriers of the Polish national identity. As the Nazis prepared to confront Bolshevism in 1941, neither the Russian commissars nor Russian Jews could wait; both would have to be eliminated by the onrushing *Einsatzgruppen*, for ultimately they were one – the political and biological manifestations of the same 'Jewish-Bolshevik conspiracy'.

Once underway the mass-murder of the Jews rapidly intensified. In the summer of 1941, probably in July, Hitler indicated his approval for the preparation of a plan for the mass murder of all European Jews under Nazi control, though just how and when this was communicated to Himmler and Heydrich cannot be established. By October the plan for the Final Solution had emerged in the form of deportation to death camps equipped with poison gas facilities, and steps were being taken (the transfer of euthanasia personnel from Germany to Poland and the beginning of death camp construction at Chelmno and Belzec) that were inconceivable without Hitler's general approval.[64] The physical extermination of all European Jewry had become a top Nazi priority, while other visions of demographic engineering as outlined in the *Generalplan Ost* were for the most part postponed.[65]

Thus the achievement of *Lebensraum* through the invasion of Russia and the Final Solution to the Jewish Question through systematic mass murder were intimately connected and did indeed become the nucleus of Nazi policy, as Hillgruber and Jäckel have so cogently argued. But was this primarily the result of a clever and calculating Hitler awaiting the opportune moment to implement programmatic ideological goals that had crystallized in the 1920s? I would say no. The programmatic view is based primarily upon various statements made by Hitler, such as those in the late 1920s threatening a 'bloody' solution 'through the sword' or his famous January 1939 Reichstag prophecy that the out-break of war would mean the destruction of the Jewish race in Europe.[66] My interpretation does not ignore such evidence or dismiss it as mere rhetoric. I am merely arguing that such statements should be seen in a pre-Auschwitz perspective, remembering that the reality of Auschwitz was literally inconceivable to its contemporaries.

If actually implemented, the Lublin Reservation or Madagascar Plan – with the inevitable decimation of the Jewish population that would

---

[64]  Christopher R. Browning, *Fateful Months: Essays on the Emergence of the Final Solution* (New York, 1985), pp. 8–38.

[65]  Koehl. *RKFDV*, p. 146–62, 226–8. Helmut Heiber, ed., 'Der Generalplan Ost', *VfZ*, VI (1958), pp. 281–325.

[66]  Cited in Jäckel, *Hitler's Weltanschauung*, pp. 60–1.

have been involved – would not have been viewed as falling short of Hitler's pre-war threats of blood and destruction. In this light Hitler's remarks about 'removal' or *Entfernung* of the Jews on the one hand and his threats of destruction on the other should not be seen as duplicity and camouflage juxtaposed with malevolent hints of the Final Solution to come. Rather they referred to one and the same general vision, the destructive expulsion of the Jews (first from Germany and then from a German-dominated Europe) as eventually embodied in the resettlement schemes of 1939–1941. Certainly, Hitler's explicit endorsement of and support for these expulsion schemes do little to sustain the idea that he did not taken them seriously. Nor does the fact that Jewish emigration from Germany was permitted until October 1941 indicate that Hitler already had in mind the ultimate Final Solution, that is the compulsive attempt systematically to murder every last Jewish man, woman and child within the German grasp. Thus the period of 1939–1941 was not a hiatus or detour from Nazi ideology but rather a real attempt to implement *Lebensraum* and the *Endlösung* as they were understood at the time. The transformation of these concepts was brought about in large part by the changing situation and cumulative frustration that the Nazis experienced.

A brief look at chronology would also suggest that the transformation may have been induced as much by Hitler's fluctuating moods as by a fanatically consistent adherence to a fixed programme. In September 1939, in the flush of victory over Poland, Hitler approved the initial plan for a demographic reorganization of eastern Europe along racial lines. In May and June 1940, with the astonishing victory over France, he approved Himmler's memorandum on the treatment of the eastern populations and the Madagascar Plan. In July 1941, after Nazi armies had torn through Russian border defences, encircled huge numbers of Russian troops and raced two-thirds the distance to Moscow, he approved the drawing up of a plan for the mass murder of European Jewry. And in October 1941, with the great encirclement victory of Vyasma and Bryansk and a brief rekindled hope for final triumph before winter, he approved the Final Solution.[67] Nazi racial policy was radicalized in quantum jumps that coincided with the peaks of German military success, as the euphoria of victory emboldened and tempted an elated Hitler to dare ever more drastic policies. It was with the end of military victories that Hitler clung stubbornly and fanatically to the precepts of 1941, investing them with a permanence and ultimacy they did not have until then.

[67]   On Hitler's briefly renewed confidence in quick victory, recalling the atmosphere of July, see Andreas Hillgruber, *Staatsmänner bei Hitler* (Frankfurt, 1967), vol. I, pp. 626–7, 630.

# Index

Lightning Source UK Ltd.
Milton Keynes UK
UKOW06f0107310816

281818UK00001B/93/P